THE SICHUAN FRONTIER AND TIBET

Yingcong Dai

The Sichuan Frontier and Tibet

IMPERIAL STRATEGY IN THE EARLY QING

A China Program Book

UNIVERSITY OF WASHINGTON PRESS

SEATTLE AND LONDON

This book was supported in part by the China Studies Program, a division of the Henry M. Jackson School of International Studies at the University of Washington.

The University of Washington Press gratefully acknowledges the support of the Association for Asian Studies, Inc. (AAS), which provided assistance through its First Book Subvention Program. Support for this book was also provided by the William Paterson University of New Jersey.

Printed in the United States of America
Designed by Pamela Canell
14 13 12 11 10 09 5 4 3 2 1

University of Washington Press
P.O. Box 50096, Seattle, WA 98145, USA
www.washington.edu/uwpress

Library of Congress Cataloging-in-Publication Data
Dai, Yingcong.
The Sichuan frontier and Tibet : imperial strategy in the early Qing / Yingcong Dai.
p. cm. — (A China program book)
Includes bibliographical references and index.
ISBN 978-0-295-98951-8 (hardback : alk. paper)
ISBN 978-0-295-98952-5 (pbk. : alk. paper)
1. Sichuan Sheng (China)—History. 2. Tibet (China)—History.
3. China—History—Qing dynasty, 1644–1912. 4. Imperialism—History. I.Title
DS793.S8D25 2009 951'.3803—dc22 2009019405

The paper used in this publication is acid-free and 90 percent recycled from at least 50 percent post-consumer waste. It meets the minimum requirements of American National Standard for Information Sciences—Permanence of Paper for Printed Library Materials, ANSI Z39.48–1984 ∞ ♻

TO ALL MY TEACHERS

AND TO THE MEMORY OF JACK L. DULL AND JAMES B. PALAIS

CONTENTS

ACKNOWLEDGMENTS

THE FRAMEWORK OF THIS BOOK WAS LARGELY SHAPED DURING MY GRADUATE years at the University of Washington. Thus my thanks go to my adviser, R. Kent Guy, who aroused my interest in the first half of the Qing dynasty and urged me to continue revising the manuscript. Two other teachers from the University of Washington also gave me valuable support and guidance when this project was in its early stages, but they did not live to see its publication. To them, the late Jack L. Dull and James B. Palais, I am forever grateful. I twice received the K. C. Hsiao Fellowship during my research. I express here my deep gratitude for this crucial support as well as for all other financial support I received from the University of Washington.

I would like to thank my current institution, the William Paterson University of New Jersey, for providing me with the financial support to conduct archival research overseas and for the publication of this work. The university shielded me from an onerous teaching load through the Applied Release Time Program, although most of the manuscript writing was done in summers and during my 2004–5 sabbatical leave.

I also received grants for travel to the National Palace Museum in Taipei as well as to libraries throughout the United States from the Small Grant Program of the Association for Asian Studies in 2000 and 2005, from the East Asia Center of the University of Washington in 2002, and from the Harvard-Yenching Library of Harvard University in 2006. I am grateful for all this support.

Access to archives and libraries was indispensable for the completion of this book. I am grateful to the National Palace Museum of Taipei, the Fu Sinian Library of the Institute of History and Philology, Academia Sinica, the Number One Archives of China in Beijing, the Municipal Archives of Chongqing, and the Archives des Missions Etangères de Paris. Thanks are also due to the Gest East Asian Library of Princeton University, the C. V. Starr East Asian Library of Columbia University, the Harvard-Yenching Library of Harvard University, the East Asia Library of the University of Washington, and the David and Lorraine Cheng Library of William Paterson University.

Feedback from colleagues and friends proved to be priceless throughout the long process of research, writing, and rewriting. I am most thankful to Susan Naquin, who read an earlier version of the manuscript in its entirety and made very valuable suggestions. Morris Rossabi, Marie Friquegnon, Jonathan Bone, Gillian Hettinger, and Julie Browne read part or all of the manuscript. I am grateful for their time and input. I thank all of the readers for their critiques and suggestions. Laura Hostetler went extra lengths in closely examining all aspects of the manuscript and providing detailed and insightful suggestions that markedly enhanced the book. Her exemplary work is greatly appreciated. Finally, I thank Lorri Hagman, my sponsoring editor at the University of Washington Press, whose confidence in this work was crucial in my coping with the prolonged process of review and revisions.

To all of my friends with whom I have not been able to spend more time, I feel indebted. The extant Qing archives are of such an enormous quantity that they are very demanding. However, working on these archives is not as dull and tiring as some might think; rather, they are full of serendipities. With the expanding of my research from one frontier to other areas and topics, I will most likely continue to indulge myself in the Qing records for years to come. I could not thank my husband Ming enough for his enduring tolerance and never asking about the business of the Qing.

REIGN DATES OF THE QING DYNASTY, 1636–1911

Chongde (Hung Taiji's reign)	1636–1643
Shunzhi	1644–1661
Kangxi	1662–1722
Yongzheng	1723–1735
Qianlong	1736–1795
Jiaqing	1796–1820
Daoguang	1821–1850
Xianfeng	1851–1861
Tongzhi	1862–1874
Guangxu	1875–1908
Xuantong	1909–1911

THE SICHUAN FRONTIER AND TIBET

INTRODUCTION

The place is surrounded and isolated by many a mountain range, but all kinds of goods under Heaven flow into it. —REVISED GAZETTEER OF CHENGDU COUNTY

IN BUILDING AN EMPIRE THAT ENCOMPASSED CHINA PROPER AND PARTS of Central Asia, the rulers of the Manchu Qing dynasty (1644–1911) had to carefully design and constantly revise their empire-building strategy. After the Manchus had conquered China proper, their further expansion originated in the pressing need to safeguard their northern and northwestern frontiers against the serious challenge posed by the Zunghar Mongols. Hence, they paid paramount attention to those areas in the late seventeenth century. Nevertheless, as the pursuit of security and power could orient the empire in any direction it deemed necessary, the Qing was adept in adjusting its strategy to changed realities. At the end of the seventeenth century the realization that the Tibetan Buddhist establishment was instrumental in pacifying the various Mongol tribes, but was in peril of being subjugated by the Zunghar Mongols, propelled the Qing state into changing its policy toward Tibet. It began to adopt a more interventionist approach to this enigmatic and hard-to-access neighbor.

This strategic shift proved to be a catalyst for the coming into being of a new frontier in the west. As Sichuan's western marches bordered Tibet, it was destined to play a critical role in the Qing strategy with regard to Tibet. A distinctly new perspective emerged in appraising Sichuan's strategic values and administering the new frontier at the turn of the eighteenth century: the Qing expansion began to be directed toward Tibet, and the Qing state endeavored to strengthen Sichuan's capability as a launching pad for its military operations in Tibet. Because of this strategic turn,

Sichuan underwent a fundamental transformation in the course of the eighteenth century, emerging as a key strategic area. This book delineates the dynamics of Sichuan's transformation in relation to the Qing imperial strategy and examines its repercussions on the socioeconomic life of the Sichuan frontier.

Meaning "four rivers," the name Sichuan emerged in Song times (960–1279) and was first adopted by the Mongol rulers to designate the area that constitutes approximately the eastern half of today's Sichuan when they set up eighteen provinces in China during the Yuan dynasty (1264–1368).[1] North of Sichuan was Kokonor (known as Amdo in Tibetan), a vast plateau that had been a domain of the Tibetans since ancient times but came under Mongol control from the mid-seventeenth century.[2] Northeast of Sichuan, perilous trails through the Qinling mountain range connected Sichuan with Shaanxi, the base of the northwestern frontier. South and southwest of Sichuan stood Guizhou and Yunnan. For a long time the boundaries between Sichuan and those neighbors were not defined. The peoples of different ethnic origins who lived astride the borders had strong cultural bonds among themselves, regardless of their different administrative identities. To the east, the Yangzi River connected Sichuan to China's heartland, but the precarious Three Gorges section considerably limited navigation on the waterway. To the west lay Tibet, a giant highland realm. Because of the high altitude and treacherous traveling conditions along the paths from Sichuan to Tibet, most people of Sichuan considered Tibet a remote land, even though commercial exchange on a small scale had existed since ancient times.

In addition to its critical location, Sichuan offered complex yet advantageous natural conditions, which made the unique area an asset for China's rulers. Thanks to the favorable climate, the high degree of humidity, and the long-lasting effects of Dujiangyan, a water project that was constructed in the third century B.C.E., the Chengdu plain in the core of the province was one of the most productive regions in China before the Mongol conquest.[3] Even though Sichuan was difficult to access, it was attractive to merchants from afar, as was noted in a nineteenth-century local gazetteer: "The place is surrounded and isolated by many a mountain range, but all kinds of goods under Heaven flow into it."[4] Two major transportation routes had served as arteries to the heartlands of China since ancient times: the land route in northern Sichuan via the Baoye passage and the water route of the Yangzi River. Built by the Qin state in the fourth century B.C.E., the Baoye passage connected Sichuan to the political center that was located first in the central plain and later in Beijing.[5] In Qing times most officials, military deployments, and all the correspondence between Beijing and Sichuan still went through this long and difficult route in and out of the province, whereas the Yangzi River was more dominated by the private sector for commercial purposes despite the hazardous Three Gorges. Given its impenetrable setting, Sichuan was considered by a statesman of the Tang dynasty (618–907) an ideal retreat place for the rulers in Central China in the event of rebellion and war.[6] This scenario soon occurred when the An Lushan Rebellion erupted in 755, and the Tang imperial court fled to Sichuan for refuge.[7]

Although it is useful to view the core parts of Sichuan as one "upper Yangzi macroregion" for the nineteenth century and beyond, as G. William Skinner defined,[8] this designation requires some modification when applied to the early Qing (from the inception of the dynasty to the end of the eighteenth century—the period examined in this book). Originally referring to the geographic areas that had been enveloped by spontaneous economic activities, the macroregion diagram has often been used to define areas sharing common features. Malleable as the diagram is, it can hardly reflect the extremely dynamic process that Sichuan had gone through before the nineteenth century, in which politics (including its violent form, war) often overrode the boundaries of different regions, and the state had to separate or merge areas in an arbitrary manner. The historical players of the Qing dynasty never allowed regional divisions to stand in their way when it came to the empire's strategic needs; rather, they transgressed the "boundaries" all the time. To make rational use of the resources in each area of the country to achieve its strategic objectives, they never hesitated to reevaluate the significance of a particular area and redirect its resources in building new frontiers. Incidentally, this was done by all the rulers of the Chinese dynasties throughout history.

Despite the unique qualities endowed by its location and natural setting, Sichuan did not merit the status of an important area in the beginning of the Qing dynasty. On the contrary, it received minimal attention from the central authorities, for it had been severely devastated, first in the Ming-Qing transition and then in the eight-year Wu Sangui Rebellion (1673–1681), its population being drastically reduced and its economy ruined. In the first few decades after it was taken into the Manchu empire, Sichuan was tethered to the unimportant "southwest bloc," consisting of four desolate border provinces: Guangxi, Guizhou, Sichuan, and Yunnan. Only when its critical position in the Qing Tibetan strategy became apparent did the state make considerable efforts to transform Sichuan into a key frontier, which proved to be a protracted and complex process. Unlike other frontiers—such as Manchuria, Taiwan, and Chinese Eastern Turkistan, whose frontier features were more evident—Sichuan had arguably gone through the most intricate process of being weighed, defined, and redefined, during which time the state reached sometimes seemingly contradictory dispositions. An important and recurrent theme throughout this book is the search for an ideal structure in administering Sichuan to suit its new position in the Qing empire system. More particularly, the relationship of the Sichuan frontier with its neighbors had fluctuated along the way. At first the Qing state was inclined to attach Sichuan to the northwestern frontier, mainly Shaanxi and Gansu provinces, as the northwest shouldered the task of checking the Zunghar, to which the Tibet question was innately connected. During the Yongzheng period the option to combine the Sichuan frontier again with the southwest was contemplated. The growing importance of the Sichuan frontier eventually earned it its independent position after many twists and turns.

The salient manifestations of an independent Sichuan frontier include the establishment of a banner garrison in Chengdu, the provincial capital (which was primarily aimed at Tibet) and the designation of one governor-general (*zongdu*) to this single province (which was a peculiar and puzzling phenomenon in the political history of the Qing dynasty). For one thing, Sichuan was the only single province besides Zhili province, in which Beijing was located, that had a governor-general exclusively and no provincial governor (*xunfu*) from the mid-eighteenth century to the end of the dynasty. Ranking higher and with more power than a governor, who was by default a civil official, a governor-general was the highest civil and military overseer in a given region that often consisted of two provinces.[9] While the Qing took several steps in building up the banner garrison in Sichuan, the process by which it confirmed the one governor-general structure in administrating Sichuan was long fluctuating, spanning nearly a century. From the beginning of Qing times, the state took pains to try to group Sichuan with another province or two in the module of putting more than one province under one governor-general but eventually determined that this frontier deserved to be ruled as a single military district and by one governor-general.

Another major component in the Qing imperial strategy was to apply different policies in treating the areas that contributed different resources to the empire. In general, two important factors were vital in appraising the value of all the areas: economic importance and strategic importance. In the first half of the twentieth century a historian started to use the phrase "key economic areas," which helped raise recognition of this critical aspect of the imperial statecraft.[10] Ever since the period of Disunion (220–589), the Jiangnan area or the lower Yangzi River valley had functioned as one of the key economic areas for successive dynasties because of its high agricultural productivity and higher level of commercialization of the economy.[11] In Qing times Jiangnan remained a key economic area.

The factor of strategic importance also carried tremendous weight for the empire builders. This author uses the term "key strategic areas" in this book to distinguish the areas that had significant strategic meaning for the central government. If the rationale underscoring the state's policy toward the key economic areas was to augment and maximize revenue collection, the state would not utilize this same rationale toward the key strategic areas. For the latter the state's main concern was to make sure that the areas were sufficiently equipped and supplied to be able to respond to emergencies swiftly and effectively. For those areas, the state put increasing revenues behind ensuring stability and strength; the amount of tax contribution did not affect how much attention and support they would receive from the central government. The key strategic areas merely meant a geographic bloc that bore a common strategic meaning at a given time. It did not necessarily correspond to administrative divisions. Rather, the state could make adjustments to the administrative structure to accommodate the needs of a key strategic area. Strategic values of a certain area could change, either increasing or decreasing, within or beyond a certain historical period. As the state's strategic focus shifted, an area might lose its attraction for and support from the central government. Conversely, an area of no importance could have its position elevated when it became strategically vital. Accordingly, the change of position in either economic or strategic terms would significantly impact the local society in many accounts.

Throughout history Sichuan had experienced much fluctuation in its position regarding imperial strategy. In Tang-Song times, for example, the Sichuan area had been a key economic area, making significant economic contributions to the state comparable to those of Jiangnan.[12] But it lost this status after the devastating Song-Yuan transition in the thirteenth century. Since then, Sichuan had remained as an economically insignificant province until the Ming-Qing transition, during which time it was again leveled to the ground, rendering it one of the least valuable areas, both economically and strategically, to the state in the beginning of the Qing dynasty. Sichuan's rise as a key strategic area in the eighteenth century served as the single most important impetus to the socioeconomic development in Sichuan. This sets to unravel another puzzle regarding Sichuan during this period: the extremely low tax obligations assigned to this province by the Qing state. Sichuan, an area that had been no less productive than Jiangnan throughout history and again from the mid-eighteenth century on, was placed by the Qing in a position even lower than Yunnan and Guizhou, its two economically backward neighbors, in terms of its financial contributions to the state. The existing literature has offered only a partial explanation , which points to the catastrophic devastations Sichuan had sustained during the Ming-Qing transition. But this cannot, however, explain the persistence of the low tax rates *after* the province had regained economic vitality. This book tries to resolve the puzzle by situating the Qing's seemingly irrational choice within the context of its frontier strategy.

The Qing state deemphasized revenue collection from Sichuan for two reasons: (1) in an attempt to retain resources in local society to prepare for urgent military needs and (2) to aid the military buildup in the new frontier and inside Tibet. This policy proved successful, for it allowed the Qing tremendous capacity and flexibility in supplying many sizable and expensive campaigns in and near the area, especially several invasions into Tibet. Shielded by the central government's favorable taxation policy, the area attracted waves of migrants and achieved economic abundance. A frontier economic zone thus took shape, along with the military buildup. Taking advantage of the abundant resources accumulated in Sichuan, especially the surplus of grain, the Qing state encouraged the private sector to ship rice out of Sichuan to relieve serious grain shortages in other areas, including the most productive but heavily taxed Jiangnan area, when there was no military operation in the area. In so doing, the Qing state developed a dual strategy: it was high-handed in exacting heavy taxes in its key economic areas, whereas it was more skillful in manipulating the commercial mechanism to make use of the surplus in Sichuan, turning Sichuan into a major rice exporter from the late Kangxi period (1662–1722) until the end of the eighteenth century. To a degree, the commercial networks that gave the area a distinguished identity that Skinner encapsulates as the "upper Yangzi macroregion" began to be forged within this context in the early Qing period. The favorable taxation policy that outlived the expansion era and its aftereffects—that is, the high-level commercialization of the economy—stimulated the growth of a largely wealth-based gentry class after the military elite phased out with the end of frontier activism in Sichuan.

Yet imperial strategy in directing the frontiers had its side effects. In ruling a vast empire such as China, the central government had to delegate considerable power to its representatives at the provincial level. Being the deputies of the state, those provincial officials also functioned as independent agents to maintain and expand their own power and interests within permissible limits that often needed to be renegotiated with the center. Therefore the competition between the central authorities in the capital and the provincial authorities, including both civil and military leaders, constituted an important theme in the history of imperial China. For the key strategic areas the tension between the central and regional authorities was even more pronounced, for more prerogatives and resources had to be yielded to the area leaders there. In Sichuan its geophysical features gave the provincial leaders another edge in their competition with the center. Barricaded by mountain ranges and the difficult route of the Yangzi River, Sichuan was historically prone to be held by an independent power when the central power was weak.[13] During early Qing times the episode of the Ming renegade and a political strongman Wu Sangui's de facto feudatory in Yunnan and his subsequent rebellion refreshed the fear and concern of the Qing state over its provincial leaders in the remote southwest border regions. Parallel to the growth of the Sichuan frontier in the eighteenth century, the Qing state had kept constant and utmost surveillance over the powerful provincial leaders in the frontier, trying to ward off even the slightest danger of a repeat of Wu Sangui's story (this is a recurring theme throughout this book). As has been convincingly argued elsewhere, one of the important ways for the Qing state to exercise its power was through appointments.[14] The close attention that the Qing state paid to personnel management in Sichuan testifies to this important aspect of imperial statecraft.

Besides chief civil and military officials, the military establishment as a whole also weighed tremendously in both political and socioeconomic terms on the frontier. Thanks to the Qing policy of purposely leaving the military some leeway in pursuing its personal interests, the military elite in Sichuan had turned themselves into a privileged group, enjoying great influence and becoming entrenched in the local society, which contrasted sharply with the small and insignificant literati elite in the province in the first part of the Qing dynasty. But what was more critical to the local economic life was the fact that the military represented a giant consuming corps in both peacetime and wartime, especially during the latter. With a prodigious amount of military funds pouring into the area during most of the frontier wars, and many merchants being attracted to the war zone, the local economy was constantly stimulated. Nevertheless, the state did not lose its grip on the military on this frontier. Other than the generous economic support and concessions, the state managed to make sure that the military was not a tool of any regional power competing with the state. Toward the end of the expansion era, more Manchu generals were sent to this frontier, which undermined the networks of the Chinese generals, proving to be a useful measure in assuring central control.

Although the Qing was largely successful in curbing the powerful frontier leaders and bridling its military on the Sichuan frontier, it was less effective in coping with another side effect of its frontier operations—namely, the social problems that had accumulated along with the unfolding of frontier expansion. Overpopulation, resulting from continuous migration to the province, caused the decline of rice exports and the deterioration of the social order. To make things worse, disarmament left thousands of soldiers and military laborers jobless and potentially rebellious, which fed the White Lotus Rebellion that erupted in 1796. Meanwhile, the affluence of the local society lured area officials into creating ways to tap the wealth from the private sector, which added another hazard that jeopardized social stability. If the successes of the Qing frontier enterprise were at the cost of domestic stability in the short term, the failure of the Qing state to adjust its tax policy toward Sichuan after the frontier era ended would have a more detrimental effect on the dynasty's fate when it struggled for survival at the turn of the twentieth century. Having enjoyed excessively light taxes for a long time, Sichuan was acutely alienated when the state rushed to exact its resources unrelentingly, starting from the mid-nineteenth century to the end of the dynasty in 1911. The strong reaction to the suddenly elevated economic obligations became a hotbed for protest and resistance against the Qing. In this light, the extremely strenuous popular movement opposing the Qing policy of nationalizing the Sichuan-Hubei railroad on the eve of the 1911 Revolution had one of its roots in the early Qing period.

Among all the frontiers of the Qing dynasty, the Sichuan frontier has not been adequately studied. As the Qing expansion was first aimed at wrestling with the Zunghar Mongols, more attention has been directed to the northern and northwestern frontiers; a number of milestone studies have been published recently.[15] Meanwhile, the southwestern and Taiwan frontiers have also been the topics of recent studies, in which the impact of

Qing empire-building on the non-Han communities in those areas, or the interaction between the two, is a focal point.[16] New works on Manchuria—the birthplace of the Manchus that had commanded the close surveillance of the Qing but was ultimately opened to popular migration and exploration—have also been produced recently.[17]

Unlike Qing Eastern Turkistan, Taiwan, and the non-Han communities in the southwest that experienced either conquest, colonization, acculturation, or all of these phenomena, Sichuan's experience was different. Having long been ruled by the Chinese state, the core of Sichuan had been within the quintessential Chinese cultural sphere since ancient times. Its transition to a key frontier was primarily effected by the change of state policy in ruling and treating it, instead of subjugation and imposed cultural transformation. To a degree, the Sichuan frontier was comparable to the Shaanxi-Gansu area relative to Central Asia and Fujian relative to Taiwan. It was their function as base areas in supporting the Qing's outward operations that justified their position as frontiers in the empire system. Hinging on imperial priorities, their strategic significance was often impermanent. Thus Sichuan's quick and quiet phasing out of its status as a key strategic area after the end of the eighteenth century seems to have effectively eclipsed its militarily active past. The leisurely and affluent scenes in the Chengdu plain, the core of Sichuan, that impressed many visitors in the late nineteenth century betrayed no trace of the many wars and massive military operations that had punctuated the entire eighteenth century. Even some historians who study Sichuan's more recent history fail to grasp the fact that the province had once functioned as a key strategic area; rather, they assume that Sichuan had always politically been a "backwater" until the end of the Qing dynasty, when it became a frontrunner in the reform movement.[18]

In previous works on Sichuan in early Qing times, its frontier character has not been articulated in relation to its socioeconomic development.[19] Meanwhile, the studies on the Qing state's intervention and expansion into Tibet over the course of the eighteenth century do not usually give enough attention to the role that Sichuan played.[20] As a result, a connection between Sichuan's experience in the eighteenth century and the Qing Tibetan strategy has been missing in the existing scholarship. This book strives to correlate Qing imperial strategy in relation to Tibet and the socioeconomic transformation of Sichuan and to establish Sichuan's position as one of the key strategic areas in the first half of the Qing dynasty. In so doing, this book will furnish future studies on the area—many important issues in this period deserve specialized study, such as the experience of the annexed Kham area under the Qing—with a long-term perspective. This view pursues the fluctuation of Sichuan's position affected by imperial strategy, but not one that considers its values and identity as static and predetermined by its natural setting. This work takes a similar approach to some of the recent studies of the Qing frontiers by looking into the intersections between political history and socioeconomic history.[21] The book argues that the imperial strategy in building this frontier was pivotal in changing the socioeconomic landscape in Sichuan, even though the consequences for socioeconomic life were not initially intended in the imperial agenda.

In pursing these objectives, this book pays considerable attention to the role played by the central government in the birth and development of the Sichuan frontier. The state was the critical agent in shaping and maintaining its low taxation policy toward the area. So, too, was the state responsible for the influx of funds into the frontier. All these dynamics cannot be thoroughly grasped if the research stays at the local or even provincial level. Hence, this work relies heavily on governmental documents—namely, the correspondence between the central authorities and the provincial and local officials, including both compiled material and original archives. Local gazetteers, private anthologies and accounts compiled or written during the Qing dynasty, and Western missionary accounts have also been consulted. It is now possible to base this book on extensive germane material, thanks to the recent publication of the Qing archives in large quantities by the archives in both mainland China and Taiwan. Also incredibly helpful were the projects initiated by the National Palace Museum and the Academia Sinica, both in Taipei, to digitize hundreds of thousands of Qing archives and to make them accessible through the Internet.[22] The translation and publication of the extant Manchu documents in the Kangxi and Yongzheng periods (1723–1735) also provide a look at the other side of the politics of the Qing ruling elites.[23] While Manchu correspondence did not in general alter the overall picture that could be reconstructed by using the documents in Chinese, it does contain some more detailed and valuable accounts of certain events that were central to this book.

There are seven main chapters in this book. The first five follow a chronological order, tracing Sichuan's change of the position from the Ming-Qing transition to the turn of the nineteenth century. Each of the five chapters focuses on one period: (chapter 1) the era of conquest and consolidation, including the Wu Sangui Rebellion, which was critical in the shaping of the Qing low opinion and corresponding policy toward the area; (chapter 2) the turn of the eighteenth century, when a strategic shift occurred thanks to the rising importance of the Tibet question in the Qing imperial undertakings; (chapter 3) the late Kangxi period—namely, the first two decades of the eighteenth century, in which the Qing sent the first expedition to Tibet and proactively upgraded Sichuan into a major frontier; (chapter 4) the Yongzheng period, during which the state tried to realign the Sichuan frontier in accordance with its new priorities and significantly expanded the territorial scope of Sichuan; and finally (chapter 5) the long and eventful Qianlong period (1736–1795), during which Sichuan experienced many wars, either as a battleground or base area, and achieved its independence in political terms.

The last two chapters, the sixth and seventh ones, treat two important repercussions of Sichuan's becoming a key strategic area. Chapter 6 studies the most important player in the frontier building, the military, by focusing on its privileged position in the local society and its role in invigorating the local economy. Chapter 7 examines the Qing state's unique and creative management of this frontier, which stimulated and fostered the formation and prospering of the Sichuan grain market. The chapter also delineates the state's failure in coping with many a social problem, which ultimately aided the ferment of the White Lotus Rebellion at the turn of the nineteenth century. Finally, an epilogue looks into the Qing's failure to timely adjust its policy toward the once important Sichuan frontier in the remainder of the dynasty, during which Sichuan's strategic significance largely faded. In this light, this author suggests that one of the roots of the political unrest in Sichuan at the end of the Qing dynasty can be found in its earlier period.

1 A HUMBLE BEGINNING, 1644–1696

The four provinces of Guangxi, Sichuan, Guizhou, and Yunnan are all border areas where soil is meager and livelihood difficult. It is different there from the heartland areas where commercial traffic is heavy, and a vast variety of livelihoods are available. —THE KANGXI EMPEROR, 1694

HISTORICALLY, SICHUAN'S ECONOMIC AND STRATEGIC SIGNIFICANCE was noted repeatedly by power contenders in China. During its unification war in the third century B.C.E., the state of Qin chose to conquer two kingdoms in the area, the Ba and the Shu, to tap their rich resources and to secure the Qin backyard.[1] During the Mongol conquest in the thirteenth century, in order to place the Southern Song dynasty (1127–1279) under pincer attack, Kublai Khan first took Yunnan in 1253 and then smashed the Song resistance in Sichuan, thus sealing the Song's defeat in the lower Yangzi valley.[2] Nevertheless, when the area did not contribute either strategically or economically to the new rulers of China, it was put at the bottom of the conqueror's list. Because of the prolonged devastation caused by the Mongol conquest, the population loss in Sichuan was severe and the economy destroyed. Throughout the Yuan dynasty Sichuan had been gradually repopulated, but it never recovered the rich vitality of its economic life. Hence it was no surprise that during the Yuan-Ming transition, the Ming dynasty delayed its conquest of Sichuan until 1371, fifteen years after the Ming was founded in Nanjing in 1356.[3] After the Ming claimed Sichuan, the recovery proved to be sluggish. Accordingly, its tax contribution to the Ming state was low.[4] In a sense Sichuan experienced a loss of status as one of the key economic areas, moving closer to its economically backward neighboring provinces, Yunnan and Guizhou. Interestingly, a similar scenario occurred again in the seventeenth century, when the

Manchus launched their conquest of China, taking advantage of many a crisis that doomed the Ming.

A DELAYED CONQUEST

Sichuan, Yunnan, and Guizhou were the last provinces in mainland China to be claimed by the Manchus, a process not completed until 1662, approximately eighteen years after the Qing dynasty was founded in Beijing in 1644. It was not accidental that the Qing dynasty conquered the southwestern part of the country last; rather, this was a deliberate choice by the conquerors. Facing a vast China and so many resistant forces, including several newly founded Southern Ming regimes, the Manchu conquerors, who only had about a hundred thousand soldiers then and limited financial resources, had to prioritize their conquests.[5] Although the conquerors did not clearly state their war plans in any single document, it was obvious that they had carefully laid down an order of conquest by taking into consideration the varied importance of different areas. After the Qing forces took Beijing, Dorgon, the formidable regent of the young Shunzhi emperor (r. 1644–1662) and the mastermind of the Qing conquest, chose to concentrate on the strategically important Shanxi-Shaanxi area in the northwest, which was regarded as a strategic barrier to the capital against aggressive nomads from the Mongolian steppe. Dorgon sent his two brothers, Ajige and Dodo, to take the Shanxi-Shaanxi area and clear out the remnants of Li Zicheng's forces. Following the area's pacification in late 1644, the Qing court appointed Meng Qiaofang, a Chinese bannerman or "Hanjun," as the governor-general of Shaanxi to govern this strategically important region.[6] While Meng continued clearing the area of banditries, his attempts to infiltrate southward into Sichuan were never successful because of the limited size of his troops.

No sooner had the Shanxi-Shaanxi area been placed under the Manchu flag than Dorgon transferred the valiant Dodo to the financially crucial Jiangnan region in the southeast, which included Jiangnan, Zhejiang, and Jiangxi provinces and part of Anhui province. Although the conquests in Jiangnan were marked by brutal massacres that were chiefly responses to the staunch protests against the notorious hair-shaving orders, this "key economic area" was firmly under Qing control by the summer of 1646.[7] After both the strategically important northwestern and the economically important southeastern regions were taken, the Qing conquerors steadily took provinces in the heartland, such as Henan, Hubei, and Hunan, which also bore the "tribute grain" responsibility.[8] Finally, the Qing cavalry swept through southern China, seizing the southern provinces of Fujian, Guangdong, and Guangxi. By the beginning of the 1650s, most of the country had been conquered by the Qing forces. The areas that had not been claimed—Sichuan, Guizhou, and Yunnan—were considered peripheral to the pressing needs of consolidating the new regime and gaining legitimacy for China's foreign rulers.

Nevertheless, the realities were more complicated. While there seemed to be no sound reason for the conquerors to invest their insufficient resources in Sichuan first, they were apparently concerned with what was unfolding there, as waves of refugees from Sichuan were telling disturbing stories about a force of monsters that had overrun the province, destroying cities and homes and slaughtering thousands of people. The man who led that force was Zhang Xianzhong, a legendary rebel who had competed with Li Zicheng in becoming the Ming dynasty's most fearful enemy.[9] In 1643, Zhang took Wuchang in Hubei and proclaimed himself Xi Wang, or the "King of the West." However, Zhang was soon forced to abandon his holdings in Hubei under joint pressure from both the Ming and Li Zicheng's forces. In early 1644, Zhang intruded into Sichuan at the same time as Li was attacking Beijing. Attempting to make Sichuan his base for his imperial aspirations, Zhang founded his own regime, Daxi, or the "Great West," and enthroned himself as the emperor in Chengdu in late 1644. Although all the rumors depicted him as a cold-blooded monster, some eyewitnesses saw Zhang otherwise. Among these were two Jesuits, Louis Buglio of Sicily and Gabriel de Magalhães of Portugal, who had been captured by the rebels.[10] According to de Magalhães, Zhang had tried hard to build a functional government. He even showed an interest in the Western sciences and promised to uphold Catholicism once he became the ruler of the entire country.[11] Although the cruel side of Zhang's character would soon become manifest, de Magalhães admitted that in the beginning Zhang stirred some sanguine anticipations among the local people.[12]

Unable to verify those rumors telling that the area was engulfed in sheer terror and havoc, the Qing rulers must have taken the message with mixed feelings. On the one hand, the rumors certainly painted Sichuan as a place unworthy of being on top of their conquest agenda. On the other hand, Zhang's regime building in Sichuan was deeply perplexing. For the Manchu conquerors an aimless bandit could be dealt with at a later time, but a competing regime could not be allowed to exist. Therefore, even though

Sichuan itself did not display much strategic or economic significance to the conquerors, it seemed urgent to exterminate Zhang's regime quickly. To this end, Dorgon sent two expeditions to Sichuan in 1646. The first one left the capital in early 1646 and was led by Holohoi, a Manchu general.[13] Holohoi moved slowly, however, caught in fighting with the remnants of Li Zicheng's forces in Shaanxi, and never made his way to Sichuan. The second expedition was sent in March, the chief commander being Haoge, the elder brother of the Shunzhi emperor.[14] Being a loser in a power struggle with Dorgon two years earlier, Haoge remained a thorn in Dorgon's flesh. Sending Haoge to the far Sichuan served Dorgon's purpose to ostracize his rival away from Beijing and more important areas. Haoge was called back from Jiangnan when he was appointed the commander of the Sichuan expedition. Meanwhile, the choice of Haoge also demonstrated the gravity of the concern over Zhang's regime in Sichuan on Dorgon's part. After all, Haoge was one of the leading Qing generals. His expedition would be a sure cure for this nuisance. Sending Haoge to Sichuan was part of Dorgon's strategy of killing two birds with one stone: to banish Haoge and to uproot Zhang's regime.

It is worth noting that Haoge took with him only a relatively small Manchu force that was not proportional to the tasks of conquering Sichuan and clearing the province of all anti-Qing forces.[15] In addition, the central government halted other troops' movement to Sichuan and even suspended their operational funds.[16] It is likely that Haoge himself understood the meaning of this assignment. When he arrived in Shaanxi, he delayed his marching to Sichuan for months.[17] Yet his coming delivered a shockwave to Zhang, who was not prepared for an attack led by such a first-grade Manchu general. In October 1646, when he heard that Haoge and his cohorts were approaching Sichuan from the north, Zhang decided to abandon Sichuan and head toward Shaanxi. An obviously unwise decision, Zhang's moving this direction would make his confrontation with Haoge inevitable. Before Zhang withdrew from Sichuan, however, he made an arrangement that would have a long-lasting impact on Sichuan and the two southwestern provinces after Zhang himself was dead: he divided his forces into four divisions led, respectively, by his four key generals and instructed them to operate independently if anything happened to himself. Zhang ultimately turned sinister toward the people of Sichuan, where he had failed to take root, and ordered massacres before his departure from Chengdu.

On February 1, 1647, Zhang encountered Haoge head-on in Xichong, central Sichuan, and was killed in battle; details about his death varied widely from one story to another.[18] With Zhang's death his regime collapsed, and Sichuan lay open to Haoge's conquest. Haoge soon took Chengdu, only to find that the previously splendid provincial capital had been sacked by Yang Zhan, a former Ming official, in the interval between Zhang's leaving and Haoge's arrival.[19] The countryside was no better: years of war and destruction had caused serious food shortages everywhere. Haoge let loose his soldiers in their food hunting; they fought each other, looted, and even killed residents who failed to surrender their food.[20] The worst occurred in Xuyong, southern Sichuan, where a detachment of Haoge's had to eat weeds and kill all their horses and mules for food, finally resorting to cannibalism on every enemy they caught, as reported by the commander of the detachment.[21] To make things worse, an epidemic erupted that killed many and drove others to flee.[22] It is plausible that more people left their homes at this time to escape Haoge's troops and the plague than during Zhang's brief rule.

Having lost many of his soldiers in battle and to famine and diseases during his several-month stay in Sichuan, Haoge did not see any reason to linger longer in this inhospitable land. He retreated to Baoning, northern Sichuan, leaving behind Li Guoying, the newly appointed governor of Sichuan, and several thousands of Green Standard soldiers, who had been brought to Sichuan by Haoge. To prove that he had already conquered the province, Haoge hastily appointed a host of officials to administrative posts at various levels. But many of those appointees turned out later to be completely incompetent.[23] In the fall of 1647, Haoge reported to the central government that he had claimed Sichuan.[24] The Qing throne held a celebration upon receiving Haoge's report and ordered him to return to Beijing shortly afterward. What was waiting for Haoge in Beijing was not awards, however. Instead, he was arrested and died in prison later that year. Although there is no question that Haoge's demise was wrought by Dorgon, there is one thing that Dorgon got right: Haoge's claim that Sichuan was pacified was premature.[25] Sichuan was not fully controlled by the Qing authorities for another dozen years after his leaving. What Haoge and his subordinates witnessed and experienced in Sichuan—the extent of famine and the severity of destruction were far more serious than the Manchu conquerors had expected—would reconfirm the disinterest of the new regime in occupying Sichuan at this crucial early stage.[26] Justifiably, they paid more attention to the other areas following Haoge's withdrawal from Sichuan.

Similar to his own obscure status in Qing history, Haoge's expedition to Sichuan has been overshadowed by the more popular stories about Zhang Xianzhong's alleged massacres, by which nearly the entire population in Sichuan had been killed by Zhang's men. To a degree, Zhang's massacres in Sichuan became one of the most well-known folklores from the Ming-Qing transition. As is the case with many myths, this one is certainly an exaggeration while containing some historical truth—namely, that Zhang was capable of committing cold-blooded atrocities. Nevertheless, many historians question the scale and impact of Zhang's massacres.[27] Among the most important questions raised, there are two critical points worth noting. First, Zhang's short regime in Sichuan had never firmly controlled the area beyond the Chengdu plain.[28] Even at the height of Zhang's reign, pro-Ming forces still occupied some strategic places in the province. For instance, Chongqing, the second largest city in Sichuan, was recaptured by a Ming official, Zeng Ying, in the spring of 1645. The city of Zunyi remained in the hands of Ming officials throughout Zhang's regime.[29] Therefore, the areas affected by Zhang's cruel decision were limited to Chengdu and its surrounding counties, as well as the places he passed through when he marched toward Shaaxi in late 1646.

Second, Zhang did not start his massacres until Haoge was approaching Chengdu, and he decided to give away Sichuan, according to the two Jesuits who stayed with Zhang's headquarters. Four months later, however, Zhang was killed by Haoge and his followers scattered. It was simply impossible for him to have killed millions of people in Sichuan within a few months. When Haoge took Chengdu, he had great difficulties in obtaining supplies but did not complain about the lack of population. As has been pointed out, many records that were allegedly written by witnesses and contemporaries but published decades or a century later and most extant local gazetteers that were compiled during or after the eighteenth century were colored by political inclination.[30] While all of these records exaggerated Zhang's killings, they neglected the important fact that there was a hiatus of more than a dozen years between Zhang's death in 1647 and the complete Qing conquest in the early 1660s. The delay of the Qing conquest gave rise to an optimum environment for the outgrowth of bandits and warlords who would render further and more serious devastation in Sichuan. In this sense Zhang's massacres were only a prelude to many years of anarchy to come.

After Haoge left, Li Guoying, the newly appointed governor of Sichuan, was ordered to take charge of clearing bandits and rebuilding Sichuan. At this point Qing troops numbering in the thousands controlled Chengdu and several pockets of territories in Sichuan amidst flocks of rebels, former Ming forces and bandits, and against excruciating food shortages and lethal epidemic diseases.[31] Li's repeated and desperate pleas to the central government for reinforcements and funds fell only on deaf ears. Unable to sustain the occupation, Li abandoned Chengdu and withdrew to Baoning at the end of 1647, by which time most of Sichuan had likely once again fallen into the hands of the enemies of the Qing dynasty.[32] Li and others began digging in on the borders between Shaanxi and Sichuan and turned Baoning into the temporary provincial capital, from which Li administered the limited Qing territories in northern Sichuan.

As revealed in their reports in 1647 and 1648, it becomes apparent that the central government did not attempt any follow-up to Haoge's Sichuan campaign, their paramount concern still being to safeguard Shaanxi province. Although the Qing troops from Shaanxi had been sent to reinforce Li's Sichuan regiment, they were few in number and many deserted along the way before they reached their rendezvous. When the long-expected funds finally arrived, they were only for the Shaanxi soldiers. Luo Xiujing, the governor-general of Sichuan and Huguang (later becoming Hubei and Hunan provinces) during those years, had only discussed affairs in Huguang in his reports to the throne, never concerning himself with the affairs in Sichuan.[33] Feeling neglected and helpless, Li submitted his resignation request time and again, but it had no effect on Beijing's attitude.[34]

After Li Guoying's withdrawal from Chengdu, a power vacuum was created in Sichuan. In fact, the elimination of Zhang Xianzhong's regime cleared the ground for many power contenders, most of whom were rebels-turned-bandits and Ming-officials-turned-warlords, and kept some kind of connection with the Southern Ming regime based in Guilin, Guangxi province.[35] As Claudine Lombard-Salmon has pointed out, the lack of genuine commitment to the cause of the Southern Ming, combined with self-interest, meant that the many rebel forces could go no further than warlordism as it unfolded in Sichuan and the two southwestern provinces.[36] Meanwhile, the Southern Ming court in Guilin also took advantage of the competition among the warlords to extend its own influence. Although the anti-Qing movement in the southwestern areas had remarkable longevity, it lacked the intensity and commitment of the short-lived resistance in Jiangnan. To a great degree, it was the deliberate delay of the Qing dynasty in taking this region that prolonged the decentralized and impotent anti-Qing movements in the area. As a result, Sichuan,

Yunnan, Guizhou, and Guangxi were turned into a shambles by the warlords, generating major emigrations during this hiatus. Those left in their homes had to risk constant killing, starvation, and diseases. Cannibalism occurred in some worst cases.[37]

The stalemate in the Qing conquest of the mainland's last parts was broken in 1652, when Sun Kewang, one of four leading generals of Zhang Xianzhong and the chief warlords of this time, submitted himself to the Guilin regime.[38] Sun's throwing in his support greatly strengthened the tottering Guilin regime so that it was able to claim Guangxi, southern Hunan, and most parts of Sichuan, which hugely alarmed the Manchu conquerors. With most of the country under its control, the Qing could now turn its attention to the southwestern areas, five years after Haoge's expedition had failed. In 1652 the Qing court sent Nikan, a grandson of Nurhaci, to head the campaign. After Nikan was killed in Hunan shortly after his appointment, the Qing appointed the retired Hong Chengchou to be the chief coordinator of the campaign.[39] Despite the Qing determination, the campaign to conquer the entire region lingered on for another decade or so. After having cleared Huguang, Guangdong, and Guangxi of the Southern Ming forces, Hong decided to hold his invasions to Sichuan, Yunnan, and Guizhou, as the difficulty in keeping the armies supplied in the mountainous and desolate provinces seemed to be insurmountable.[40] On the Sichuan front, Wu Sangui, who since 1648 had dug himself in around Hanzhong, a strategic point in southern Shaanxi, was urged to attack Sichuan from the north. In 1652 he and others made incursions into Sichuan and occupied Chengdu, Chongqing, and Xuzhou, but they withdrew from those places a while later when assaulted by the remnants of Zhang Xianzhong's forces. Although Hong was frequently criticized by some officials, Chinese and Manchu alike, for his slow moves, the throne backed his plan not to wage the showdown until the right moment.[41]

That moment finally came when a new round of infighting erupted in 1657 between Sun Kewang and Li Dingguo, another chief general under Zhang Xianzhong who had submitted himself to the Guilin regime before Sun. Upon being defeated, Sun made the dramatic choice of surrendering to the Qing, thus bringing about a turn in the Qing's southwestward campaign. Almost five years after his taking the commandership, Hong Chengchou launched offensives on the three provinces. This same year Wu Sangui was also ordered to push into Sichuan from Shaanxi. In 1658 the Qing forces captured two important cities in Sichuan (Chongqing and Zunyi) and entered Guizhou from three directions. In early 1659, Wu Sangui and his cohorts seized Kunming, the capital of Yunnan, driving Zhu Youlang, the emperor of the Southern Ming court, into Myanmar to seek refuge.[42] Meanwhile, a reinforced offensive was launched to recover the entire Sichuan province from the warlords and bandits; Li Guoying was able to move from Baoning to Chengdu later that year.[43] Although most of Sichuan was conquered by the Qing by 1659, the fighting did not completely end in eastern Sichuan until 1664, when Li Laiheng, the last bandit chief, killed himself under tremendous pressure from the Qing forces.

A LAGGARD RECOVERY

When Guizhou, Yunnan, and Sichuan ultimately came under Qing control, the conquerors found themselves facing an utterly devastated country. Although the protracted Ming-Qing transition created havoc and carnage everywhere in China, reducing the entire population drastically, nowhere was the situation as disheartening as in these last provinces to be conquered, among which Sichuan was hit hardest.[44] In 1661 only 16,096 adult males were registered in Sichuan, which put the province even behind Yunnan.[45] Completely devoid of human existence, some areas were turned into reserves for such wild animals as tigers, boars, and deer. Chengdu, the provincial capital used to enjoying the fame of splendor, became a virtual ghost town also frequented by tigers.[46] In some worst cases only several dozens of households were left in an entire county, in which the scenes were depicted as "bleak and deserted, like the original stage of the human world."[47] In 1661 the amount of the registered land in Sichuan was almost negligible, being only about 3,400 *qing* (1 *qing* equals approximately 6 hectares), even less than one tenth of that of Guangxi.

Nationwide, recovery from the catastrophic transition proceeded slowly at first but started gaining momentum in the 1660s, the beginning of the Kangxi reign. Like the situation during the conquest era, the areas that proved to be more important, either strategically or economically, received more attention and assistance from the state and thus fared better. After the long-delayed pacification, Sichuan did not demonstrate to the Qing state any reason that justified extra attention and support. Rather, the crude realities in that province further reinforced the presumption of a peripheral and valueless Sichuan that had been held by the Qing ruling elite throughout the conquest era. In the early years after the conquest, Sichuan was often grouped together by the Qing central authorities with the three less-developed border provinces, Yunnan, Guizhou, and Guangxi. In this book the geopolitical bloc consisting of these four provinces is referred to as the southwest bloc. Although this was mainly a perception on the state's part, there was not any sign at a societal level at this time that suggested otherwise. In other words the socioeconomic initiatives in society, such as commercial networks, local elite activism, and cultural development, were invariably minimal in these four provinces.

TABLE 1.1. TAXABLE LAND IN 1661

Province	*Land* (qing) (1 qing = 6 hectares)
Jiangnan	978,140
Shandong	746,840
Huguang	657,800
Shaanxi	505,580
Zhili	493,990
Zhejiang	481,300
Jiangxi	449,680
Henan	445,790
Shanxi	423,750
Guangdong	336,500
Fujian	145,580
Guangxi	53,450
Sichuan	3,440

SOURCE: *Qingdai dang'an shiliao congbian* (A collection of the archives of the Qing dynasty), vol. 4, 7.

As a result of Sichuan's placement on the Qing's priority list, the recovery in Sichuan was mainly left to the provincial officials, who were not able to do much with their limited resources. The extremely serious population losses affected the restoration of the administrative system in the province. Some administrative units were either cancelled or merged. Officials, including high-ranking provincial officials, were reluctant to serve in this war-torn province, often making their services in the area a springboard for better appointments elsewhere. Thus many posts were filled with people without examination degrees or even any education at all.[48] It was also commonplace for the surrendered warlords to be appointed to various posts, especially military ones. Although some court officials had recognized the danger of putting so many ex-rebels in official positions and suggested transferring some of them to other provinces, Sichuan was in urgent need of bureaucratic personnel and could not afford to be more selective.[49] Meanwhile, many of the rank-and-filers of the former rebel forces were co-opted into the Green Standard Army, who also settled their families in the province.[50] Although a large proportion of a small civilian population in Sichuan consisted of the former rebels, bandits, and their dependents, a disproportionately large military presence—likely numbering one hundred thousand Green Standard troops—had been left in Sichuan in the wake of the conquest.[51] Having resorted to living off the land during the conquest, the military continued harassing the surviving residents when the war ended by exacting supplies and imposing military *corvée* (forced services such as transporting matériel and building facilities), causing many to flee from their homes. Although the provincial officials tried to cut down the size of the military and build up military agricultural colonies near Chengdu to alleviate the burden on society, neither push seems to have had much success.[52]

It became clear to the provincial officials that the key to Sichuan's reconstruction was to reverse the direction of migration—that is, to lure the emigrants to return and encourage new settlers to come. In late 1668, Liu Zhaoqi, a short-time governor-general of Sichuan, proposed after he had been transferred elsewhere to adopt more flexible methods in attracting settlers to Sichuan. Liu's strategy was to reinstate the policy of rewarding local officials for calling back emigrants, which had been a general policy for the entire country in the beginning of the conquest but had been terminated.[53] Liu's suggestion was accepted. His successor, Zhang Dedi, expanded Liu's initiative, again requesting to give local officials more incentives. He proposed to attract paupers and drifters to Sichuan with the prospects of becoming property owners, since unclaimed land was abundant in the province.[54] Perhaps in response to Zhang's request, the Qing state laid down a new policy for Sichuan about this time that allowed anybody to register as a resident (*ruji*) in the province if he brought his wife to the province and reclaimed deserted land.[55]

In light of the unwillingness of high officials to serve in Sichuan, the Qing merged the post of the governorship-general of Sichuan with that of

Huguang in 1670. Another consideration might be that given that many Sichuanese had fled to Huguang during the war years, a joint position might work to call those people back to their native land. Cai Yurong, a Chinese bannerman, was appointed to this position straddling both Sichuan and Huguang. He was first stationed in Jingzhou, Hubei, a city closer to the border between Hubei and Sichuan.[56] Wishing to be more vigorous in speeding up the repopulation in Sichuan, Cai sent a lengthy and renowned memorial in 1671, in which he suggested lowering benchmarks in rewarding officials in reclamation and repopulation but prolonging the tax-free period for newly reclaimed land. He also proposed more specific methods to "broaden the way to call people [to the province]," which included measures to reward any officials, expectant officials, commoners, and even former rebel chiefs with either promotion or official positions as long as they brought in a certain number of people to Sichuan.[57] In 1672, Cai petitioned to allow the offspring of the former soldiers who had settled in his jurisdiction to take part in the examinations, which would also encourage the demobilized soldiers to settle in Sichuan.[58]

Thanks to the Liu-Cai initiatives, more directed repopulation in Sichuan eventually started around 1670 and 1671, which altered a state of inaction owing to the lack of impetus for either organizers or migrants during the first decade after the conquest. To be sure, the central government was still not an active agent in promoting repopulation other than endorsing what had been proposed by the provincial officials. As Robert Entenmann has pointed out: "Much of the effort to attract settlers to Sichuan evidently came from local and provincial officials."[59] Among the people who moved back to Sichuan at this time was the ancestor of an important twentieth-century Chinese leader, Deng Xiaoping. The Deng family moved back to Sichuan in 1671 in response to the call to repopulate the province from Guangdong, where the family had lived since the Ming dynasty, when an earlier ancestor had taken office in the province.[60] While the Liu-Cai initiatives gave some incentives to officials, they did not give enough to migrants, which accounts for the fact that migrations were often orchestrated and coerced by local officials eager for promotions and rewards. It is difficult to estimate the scope of forced migration, but records suggest that it did occur.[61] In Sichuanese folklore it is believed that a local slang word, *jieshou* (literally meaning "untying one's hands" but hinting at "relieving oneself"), originated from the forced migration, for the people who were escorted to Sichuan by soldiers had their hands tied up, and they were only untied when they had to relieve themselves.[62] Although this slang had also been used in other areas of the country, it can still serve as a reference to the forced migration to Sichuan.

Not only did Sichuan not compare to many other provinces in the recovery period, the province even lagged behind its two close neighbors that had always been more backward than itself in economic development: Yunnan and Guizhou. The key to the relatively swift recovery in these two provinces lies in the establishment of Wu Sangui's feudatory in Yunnan and part of Guizhou. Near the end of the southwestward campaign in 1659, the Shunzhi emperor granted three newly conquered peripheral provinces (Yunnan, Guangdong, and Sichuan) to three Chinese generals (Wu Sangui, Shang Kexi, and Geng Jimao) who were allegedly instrumental in the Manchu conquest of China.[63] In the following years, however, Geng Jimao was moved from Sichuan first to Guangxi, then to Fujian. Although no reason was recorded for his leaving Sichuan, it might be plausible that it was due to the extremely barren conditions in the province. As Frederic Wakeman Jr. has argued, the compromises that the Manchu rulers made to the few Chinese generals—what the three Chinese generals received were even more advantageous than the Qing state had granted to Manchu generals, to whom it tried not to give such luxuries—were an inevitable consequence of the drawn-out conquest but not a desirable arrangement for the Qing.[64] Meanwhile, it should also be pointed out that the Qing state did not view Yunnan as a strategically important area in those early years. Neither did they value much, at this point, the other two provinces where generals Wu Sangui and Shang Kexi set up their feudatories. Furthermore, unaccustomed to the climate in the south, the Manchu bannermen would not consider living in those provinces an alluring prospect.

Nevertheless, the financial costs of maintaining those feudatories were staggering. Of the three generals, Wu received the most money from the Qing state.[65] Using the excuse of pacifying the non-Han communities in the southwestern region of the country, Wu squeezed enormous financial support and permission to possess an oversized army. Then he was able to subjugate the non-Han peoples to his rule, seizing their land and exacting their wealth.[66] With huge financial input and Wu's deliberate management, Yunnan and part of Guizhou, which were previously far more backward in all aspects than Sichuan, were relatively faster in recovering from the war devastation. As Wu had more money to spend in subsidizing migrants and merchants, sometimes appropriating military funds,[67] repopulation and reclamation in both Yunnan and Guizhou surpassed that in Sichuan, which lacked the leverage to press for funding. While both Yunnan and Guizhou started reporting progress in reclaiming land from the early 1660s, there was no such report from Sichuan in the same period. In another account military examinations were resumed in 1666 for the first time in the two southwestern provinces but failed, however, to be held in Sichuan because too few candidates had registered.[68]

POLITICAL VIGILANCE TAKES PRIORITY

The late-in-coming recovery in Sichuan was soon interrupted in December 1673, when Wu Sangui rebelled against the Qing, dragging the country into a large-scale civil war.[69] In early 1674 several chief provincial officials in Sichuan joined the rebellion, thus turning the whole province under Wu's banner. Although the rebellion had posed a severe challenge to the Qing, which suffered from territory losses and military fiascos in the early stage of the war, the Qing eventually prevailed against the rebels, who failed to rally popular support. After Wu died in late 1678, his grandson, Wu Shifan, retreated from Hunan to the southwest. However, it took another three years for the exhausted Qing forces to reconquer the southwest, where rugged terrains hindered the movement of the armies as well as supplies. Although Sichuan was recovered by the Qing in 1679, the peace was disturbed when a surrendered rebel chief revolted against the Qing again in late 1680. Not until the end of 1681 was the Qing able to fully reclaim the three provinces of Guizhou, Sichuan, and Yunnan. The eight-year civil war left many parts of the country marred and scarred, but these three provinces endured the most devastation. All reconstruction efforts before the rebellion were wasted; large-scale emigrations took place both during the civil war and in its wake. Entenmann has estimated for Sichuan that approximately two-thirds or three-fourths of the population was lost, after about forty years of continuous warfare.[70] In 1685 the number of registered adult males in Sichuan was 18,509, which only represented a 2,000-person increase from 1661. Meanwhile, Yunnan and Guizhou did not do much better, numbering 15,857 and 13,697, respectively.[71]

There is no question that the rebellion prompted the Qing state to reevaluate the southwest bloc—namely, Sichuan, Yunnan, Guizhou, and Guangxi provinces. It continued to be regarded as economically insignificant and strategically peripheral. Nevertheless, taking a lesson from the rebellion, the Qing authorities could no longer maintain that the bloc was negligible in terms of the dynasty's political stability. In the decade after the civil war a new rationale emerged in the ruling of the southwest bloc: to avoid nourishing another feudatory or powerful satrap. This precaution did not lead to the exclusion of the Chinese from taking the principal posts in these provinces. Instead, both Manchu and Chinese officials were subject to close surveillance. This over-nervousness led to the central authorities' excessive reaction to even marginally harmful initiatives from these provinces and made serving the area a dangerous job for high officials.[72]

The first person who fell victim to this postrebellion syndrome was Cai Yurong, the governor-general of Sichuan and Huguang when the rebellion erupted. He was made one of the chief commanders of the campaign to suppress the rebellion. Being a Chinese bannerman, Cai had to face suspicion and distrust. However, the Kangxi emperor had never waived his trust of Cai throughout the war and appointed him the first governor-general of Yunnan and Guizhou at the end of the war, making Cai the highest official in the former feudatory of Wu Sangui. Nevertheless, Cai's contribution in the campaign could not immunize him from being scrutinized in the postbellum era. His misfortune all started with his hawkish stance in dealing with the non-Han peoples in Yunnan and Guizhou. From the beginning, the Qing dynasty had favored appeasement over high-handedness in pacifying and ruling the non-Han peoples in the southwest. Therefore, Kangxi's regents turned down Wu Sangui's proposal in 1666 to replace the traditional local chieftains with Qing officials.[73] Using a variety of pretexts, however, Wu Sangui launched military operations against the non-Han peoples for both territories and wealth, and then used his campaigns as an excuse to exact large amounts of funds from the central government. Since Wu's story was too well-known, Kangxi was particularly on the alert against any similar initiatives in this regard. He continued his adherence to an appeasement policy during the postbellum period, discouraging provincial officials from wielding the stick on the ethnic aboriginals in the southwest.[74]

Unfortunately for him, Cai Yurong seemed not to be aware of this imperial mind-set. He carefully studied local conditions and problems before he submitted a detailed memorial on the governance of the non-Han peoples and the economic recovery and further development in the two provinces. In one of his ten proposals raised in this memorial, *Zhi turen shu* (the proposal regarding control of the native peoples), Cai outlined several measures, some of which were forceful. In his opinion Wu Sangui had played the card of the non-Han peoples in his contention with the central government by giving native chieftains military ranks and titles and allowing them more authority in their local communities. Therefore, Cai proposed to repeal those military ranks and titles given to them by Wu, while allowing them to maintain their titles as hereditary local chieftains. He also suggested letting the offspring of native chieftains take part in the civil service examinations, as he reasoned that the opening up of the Qing bureaucracy to the non-Han degree holders would lead to a weakening of the native chieftain system, when birth status was no longer the only path to power in their communities. But more important, Cai betrayed his hawkish position by suggesting using force to put down any armed feuds among the native communities whenever such incidents occurred.[75]

Later, Cai went further in imposing tighter control on the natives: he proposed forbidding them to possess any arms and forbidding the Han Chinese from trading with them the materials for making gunpowder, such as lead, niter, and sulfur.[76] But Kangxi turned down this proposal. Meanwhile, in a discussion regarding the restoration of the local chieftain system in the Shuixi area, Kangxi made it clear that the native chieftain system was the most desirable way of harnessing the non-Han peoples of the southwest.[77] It seemed that Cai was not in accord with the throne in this matter. In the spring of 1683 the emperor sent a commissioner to Yunnan and Guizhou especially to investigate the affairs of the non-Han peoples. Subsequently, the commissioner and Cai Yurong submitted a joint report and insisted that it was not necessary to restore the local chieftain system in Shuixi, for it had been many years since Wu had installed regular officials in the area in 1665. The central government approved their request, although this was not what Kangxi intended.[78]

Three years later, in early 1686, Cai requested a military campaign to suppress the Miao people in Guizhou because their feud disturbed the local order. This time Kangxi was particularly irritated, as he suspected that Cai was following the old tactic of Wu Sangui in the attempt to extract the wealth of the local chieftains and then attacking them if they failed to comply.[79] Shortly after he rejected Cai's petition, Kangxi issued two edicts to criticize provincial officials' hawkish position in the affairs of non-Han peoples. In the first one he bluntly accused Cai and his cohorts of attempting to seize the Miao chieftains' wealth and gain awards and promotion. In the second edict that followed the first one in one week, Kangxi reiterated his appeasement policy toward the non-Han peoples in the southwest and other places and warned provincial officials not to upset the status quo in those frontier provinces.[80]

Three months after this incident, in the spring of 1686, Cai was removed from his position and demoted to a not-too-important post in the capital. Obviously, the throne had withdrawn its trust from Cai, whose ordeal was to come. In 1687, Cai was arrested and charged with illegally appropriating Wu Sangui's wealth and taking Wu's granddaughter as his own concubine. Cai was subsequently sentenced to death. With the emperor's intervention his punishment was reduced to life exile in Heilongjiang, following months of imprisonment and torture. The accusations against Cai were suspicious and might not have been the true cause of his downfall.[81] In his later years Cai lamented at the end of a memoir of the campaign against the Wu Sangui Rebellion that it was difficult for a meritorious official to fare once the peace was restored, for it was a commonplace that the throne would turn suspicious of the general when he was no longer useful.[82]

Coincidentally, when Cai was trying to persuade the throne to take a harder line against the local chieftains, Xifo, the governor-general of Sichuan and Shaanxi, also lobbied to ban selling arms to the non-Han peoples in Sichuan.[83] Although the Board of War approved his petition, he was soon transferred to the capital and became a vice minister of the Board of Punishment in the fall of 1686, only three months after Cai was recalled from the southwest. Serving in his new position, Xifo had his first case with Cai's trial. Immediately after Cai's case was closed, Xifo was accused of trying to shield Cai in the trial. Jailed and beaten, he was also exiled to Heilongjiang by the emperor's order. Several other officials in the Board of Punishment were also punished on the same charge.[84] The existing documents do not reveal all aspects of Xifo's case, but it is quite possible that his downfall was related to his militant stance in dealing with the non-Han peoples in Sichuan, which seemed to be an oversensitive issue for the Kangxi emperor.

Seven years later the third provincial official from the area was condemned. This victim was Wei Jiqi, the governor of Guizhou. Being a pretentious bureaucrat, Wei once compared himself to Junchen and Zhaobo, two outstanding rulers in China's antiquity, in a memorial to the emperor.[85] Kangxi was so impressed with his self-aggrandizement that he still remembered this memorial when Wei was found guilty two years after. Shortly after he was appointed the governor of Guizhou in 1691, Wei launched a military campaign against the Miao people in the Liping prefecture as he was misled by phony information supplied by his subordinates. Then he reported the false result, provided again by his subordinates, that the Qing troops had killed more than a thousand Miao people.

Although Wei quickly corrected this, it was enough to shake the imperial trust in him. He was arrested and put on trial in 1692. Meanwhile, Kangxi harshly criticized his belligerent conduct. Like Cai, Wei was first sentenced to death but this was changed by the emperor himself into exile to Heilongjiang.[86]

These three cases were not accidental and unrelated. They mirrored the Qing state's profound concern over the stability in the southwest bloc in the postrebellion period. The different backgrounds of the three officials who were punished—Cai being a Chinese bannerman, Xifo a Manchu, and Wei a Chinese—show that the vigilance of the Qing state was not targeted to a single group among the ruling elite. Instead, the central authorities wanted to send a message to all who served in the area that Wu's story would not be allowed to be repeated. Thus the penalties the three officials received had more of a symbolic meaning. In fact, none of the three remained in exile for long before they were pardoned.

While being strict with the viceroys who were inclined to go off the track, the throne tried to send reliable ones to this peripheral but potentially perilous area. In 1685, Yao Diyu, an official who had previously served in Sichuan in 1658 and earned himself a good reputation there, was appointed the governor of Sichuan. Yao also won the emperor's trust while later serving in the capital for his candid criticisms of the politics and his advocating for the emperor to listen to unpleasing opinions.[87] To Yunnan and Guizhou, Kangxi sent Fan Chengxun, from a prominent Chinese bannerman's family, to succeed Cai Yurong as the governor-general.[88] Fan seemed to understand Kangxi's low-key inclination in ruling this peripheral area—he never tried to resort to force in handling the non-Han peoples' affairs during his eight-year tenure, an unusually long one. Instead, he tended to be tactful and keep clear of escalation when any incident involving the non-Han peoples occurred. Apparently, Kangxi was pleased with Fan's governing style. He later praised Fan as "firm and smooth," which reveals what kind of person the emperor preferred for the area.[89]

At the time when Fan Chengxun left his post in 1694, the Qing state was, by and large, satisfied with the political situation in the southwest bloc. The vigilance toward the provincial officials had finally relaxed. Nevertheless, political stability was at the expense of economic recovery. Neither repopulation nor reclamation of land was on a par with that in the other areas of China. Although registered adult males in Sichuan increased to 197,965 in 1692, which was the level of the prerebellion era, the registered arable land remained low.[90] Hence Sichuan's tax contributions to the state remained at the bottom among all provinces, even significantly lower than those of the other members of the southwest bloc, Guangxi, Guizhou, and Yunnan. Because of the low rate of taxation in those four provinces, provincial officials did not even bother to report poor harvests in the case of bad weather to get further reductions.[91] The startlingly low figures of population and arable land in Sichuan are dubious, however. They may well be due to the combination of slow recovery and bureaucratic neglect—the administration below the provincial level was incapable of monitoring and reporting the progress of the restoration in society.

TABLE 1.2 LAND TAXES IN 1685

Province	*Land tax in-kind* (shi) (1 shi = 100 liters)	*Land tax in cash* (tael)
Jiangsu	365,570	3,680,192
Shandong	506,965	2,818,019
Zhejiang	1,345,772	2,618,416
Henan	—	2,606,004
Guangdong	30,643	2,027,793
Jiangxi	925,423	1,743,245
Anhui	166,427	1,441,325
Shaanxi	170,922	1,315,012
Hubei	138,197	923,288
Hunan	65,366	517,092
Guangxi	221,718	293,604
Yunnan	203,360	99,182
Guizhou	59,482	53,512
Sichuan	1,215	32,211

—. No information available.

SOURCE: Liang, *Zhongguo lidai hukou, tiandi, tianfu tongji* (Statistics of households, land, and taxation in Chinese history), 392.

Similar to the situation in the wake of the conquest era, officials who were appointed to the southwest bloc were reluctant to come, leaving many posts unfilled. The common strategy was to delay their arrival in order to be dismissed and thus be reappointed to better places. Even some military officers joined the trend to ask for transfers to more prosperous places.[92] To reverse the trend, the state tried a number of things. As early as 1681, when it was suggested that those officials who could recruit settlers to their jurisdiction be rewarded, Kangxi ruled that this policy could only be applied in Guizhou, Sichuan, and Yunnan.[93] In 1683, in response to Kangxi's call for a solution to the problem that bureaucrats appointed to Sichuan and Guangxi always delayed their arrival, the Board of Personnel proposed changing the official stipends in the two provinces from the category of inland standard (*fufeng*) to that of border standard (*bianfeng*), as the latter was at a higher rate than the former.[94]

What became especially alarming to the provincial authorities was the draining away of the elite class. Some officials used bureaucratic service as a stepping-stone to move to more affluent areas. In Sichuan this phenomenon was most conspicuous. After the gentry families had settled in other provinces, some sent their offspring back to Sichuan to take the examinations, as the chances of passing were better, given so few candidates there. But no one planned to return to Sichuan once he got the degrees and appointments. In the summer of 1686, Governor Yao Diyu suggested to the central government that those emigrated elite families (*guanhu xiangshen*) be forced to return, as commoners would follow their example. He reasoned: "If one gentry family comes back in response to the government's call, it would be equal to several households of commoners coming back." He also reported that he had located more than a hundred such families that had moved to other provinces and requested cooperation from the concerned local officials in those places.[95]

Although it is difficult to estimate the effect of Yao's initiative, it certainly became harder for the gentry class to move out of Sichuan through bureaucratic service, for a rule was set up later by the central government to oblige the officials from Sichuan and some other provinces to return to their original home areas when they retired. This rule remained in place for Sichuan at least to 1716.[96] As one of the results of the expatriation of the literati families, revival in education and classical scholarship in Sichuan proceeded at a slow pace.[97] To cultivate a new elite stratum among the settlers in Sichuan, Gesitai, the governor-general of Sichuan and Shaanxi, petitioned in 1690 to allow the offspring of migrants to take part in the civil service examinations regardless of their parents' domiciles.[98] But this measure would take years to show effects. During the sixty-one-year Kangxi reign Sichuan produced only a small number of successful candidates in the civil service examinations.[99]

Although some efforts to repopulate the area were initiated by the provincial authorities, reviving Sichuan had never been a priority for the state. After the rebellion the throne sent special commissioners from the capital to oversee the repopulation and restoration of the economy in some provinces that had been ruined by the war, such as Fujian, Guangdong, Jiangnan, and Zhejiang, but there was no such commissioner sent to Sichuan and other members of the southwest bloc.[100] Nationwide, the Qing had extricated itself from economic difficulties inflicted by the civil war in 1685, by which time the depleted central treasury was full again. Since then, the state had been able to invest in some major water projects, to give tax relief to the provinces that had been tightly squeezed for supporting the war, including Jiangnan, the key economic area. What the state did for the southwest bloc was no more than granting tax reductions and exemptions.

In the 1680s, following the suggestions of such provincial officials as Yao Diyu, the state further exempted Sichuan from contributing the *nanmu* logs to the capital, a traditional tribute from the Emei Mountain area in Sichuan and ideal construction material for palaces.[101] In addition, Kangxi did pay lip service to the reconstruction in the southwest bloc. Each time a viceroy was appointed to the area, he would tell him to take care of the matter.[102] Nevertheless, he never allocated any substantial amount of funds for the area's reconstruction, which was in contrast to his generous spending in the water projects in Jiangnan during the same period. The extant records show that the provincial officials from the southwest bloc made no request for monetary support, either. Apparently, there was a tacit understanding among those provincial officials to avoid raising this question.[103] With the fresh memories of Wu Sangui's story and the harsh disciplinary actions of the state toward those viceroys who were more proactive, the lesson learned was that it would be safe to be low-key and cautious.

In 1693, when the Kangxi emperor once again granted all four provinces in the southwest bloc a total exemption from capitation for the following year, he lamented over the lack of abundance in those provinces: "The four provinces of Guangxi, Sichuan, Guizhou and Yunnan are all border areas where soil is meager and livelihood difficult. It is different there from the heartland areas where commercial traffic is heavy, and a vast variety of livelihoods are available."[104] Although he probably knew that Sichuan had enjoyed economic abundance in the past and had more favorable natural conditions than the other three provinces, the emperor had no difficulty at this time in ranking Sichuan as one of the "meager" provinces. What is conveyed in this remark is that it would take tremendous efforts to revive the southwest bloc, but it was not a priority for the Qing state at this point. The essential policy of the central government was still laissez-faire in nature. Lacking even the faintest hint of the dense population, bustling marketing towns, and "a higher appreciation of art" it came to possess two hundred years later, Sichuan had a humble beginning in the first few decades of the Qing dynasty.[105]

2 A STRATEGIC TURN FROM THE STEPPE TO TIBET, 1696–1701

The key to Mongol affairs lies in the right approach, not in the distance between them and us.—THE KANGXI EMPEROR, 1697

WHILE SICHUAN AND ITS NEIGHBORS IN THE SOUTHWEST BLOC REMAINED in the shadows after the Wu Sangui Rebellion, the Qing state turned to a critical matter on its northern frontier: checking the aggression of the Zunghar Mongols. No longer present in the Central Asian theater today, the Zunghar Mongols were in the seventeenth century a real power on the vast steppe between the Qing empire and a rapidly expanding Russian empire. The Qing considered them an intolerable threat. In the beginning, the focal point was the steppe, not Tibet. Although the Qing state started even before its conquest of China to patronize Tibetan Buddhism, the nature of this remote and mysterious realm had not been fully revealed to the Manchus, and the Qing relationship with Tibet had not been interventionist. Being bordered by Tibet had not benefited Sichuan when its strategic significance was assessed by the Qing state, but the situation was to change by the end of the seventeenth century; Sichuan's importance was about to rise. During the Zunghar crisis the Qing state discovered the close ties between the Zunghar and the Tibetan Buddhist establishment and began to realize that the key to the resolution of the Zunghar problem lay in the control of Lhasa. The Tibet question came to the center of the Qing frontier strategy and had an immediate and profound impact on Sichuan: it stood as the onset of Qing frontier activism in Sichuan, as its geographical location would make it an ideal launching pad in the event of military operations in Tibet.

Despite being a close neighbor to China, Tibet had not been a familiar realm to the people of the central kingdom before the seventh century.[1] However, when Tibet rose to power in a sudden and mysterious manner in that century, it came to compete with the Tang dynasty (618–907) in China both diplomatically and militarily.[2] Not always as triumphant as it was on other frontiers when dealing with the Tibetans, the Tang dynasty made earnest efforts to woo the friendship of the Nanzhao kingdom, which included part of Sichuan and Guizhou and most of Yunnan, to forestall the disastrous scenario of Nanzhao allying itself with Tibet.[3] This dynamic became the major motive for Tang aggression in the empire's southwestern corner. Nevertheless, the Tibetan empire fell apart in the mid-ninth century, several decades before the Tang collapsed. Unlike in China, where a new centralized power reemerged after a period of disunity, the disintegration of the Tibetan empire doomed the land to political fragmentation—no centralized power ever developed in Tibet in the centuries to come, which left the local aristocrats to compete with each other for supremacy.

Perhaps the most enduring legacy of the Tibetan empire in medieval times was its embrace of Buddhism, which largely supplanted the native and animist Bon religion. Introduced to Tibet in the seventh century during the reign of the legendary king Songtsen Gampo and fostered by royal patronage, Buddhism gained astounding momentum in its propagation. However, its rapid success was interrupted by a major religious persecution in the ninth century, allegedly championed by the king Lang Darma. Not until the tenth century did Buddhism recover from this devastation and undergo a renaissance. During the following centuries, a cluster of different sects of Tibetan Buddhism emerged, among which conflicts were frequent, as was common for other religions. The fact that there lacked a centralized political structure in Tibet unwittingly aided the multicenter state of the religion, prompting the competing sects to ally themselves with local powers. Turning to outside powers for patronage became a real option for weaker sects, which constituted the backdrop of the close relationship between the Tibetan religious establishment and the Mongol warriors of various groups starting from the thirteenth century.[4]

When the Mongols founded the Yuan dynasty in China in 1264, they chose to bestow their support upon one of the Buddhist sects in Tibet, the Sakya sect. This gave the Sakya sect tremendous political power at home, although its supremacy had never been fully accepted by all Buddhist orders in Tibet.[5] When the Yuan fell, the Sakya sect also lost its superior position. Once again, division and contention prevailed in the Tibetan Buddhist world until the rise of yet another sect, Gelugpa, meaning "model of virtue." Gelugpa was and still is also referred to as the Yellow Sect or Yellow Hat, since its monks were clad in yellow. Founded by the great religious reformer Tsongkhapa in the late fourteenth century, the Yellow Sect took on the mission of rectifying the religion, advocating rigorous moral reforms. At its inception the Yellow Sect was the weakest sect and therefore often opposed and oppressed by stronger ones. Nevertheless, it survived and grew against all odds. After Tsongkhapa died, his disciple Gedun Truppa continued to expand the new order. When Gedun Truppa died, a newborn baby was selected as his successor, thus starting the tradition of reincarnating a deceased leader, which had been an established tradition for some other sects.

At that time the Ming dynasty in China did not pursue an active policy of intervening in the internal affairs of Tibet, let alone placing any political control over Tibet. Instead, the Ming adopted a policy of sponsoring all Buddhist sects in Tibet in an attempt to keep the Tibetan Buddhist world divided, which would serve the Ming interests best. The Ming nonactivist position left the Mongols as the single power player in the Tibetan theater. In 1578 a historical event occurred: Altan Khan of the Tumed Mongols invited Sonam Gyatso, the fourth leader of the Yellow Sect, to Mongolia.[6] Following a passionate sermon on Tibetan Buddhism, the thirty-five-year-old Sonam converted Altan Khan to the Yellow Sect. This event has since been cited as the restoring of the close bond between the Mongols and Tibetans and the starting point of the propagation of the Yellow Sect to the Mongols.[7]

At their meeting the two exchanged title-granting. What Altan Khan gave to Sonam Gyatso was the title Dalai Lama.[8] Later, Sonam's two predecessors were named posthumously as the First and the Second Dalai Lama, which placed Sonam as the Third Dalai Lama. Following Altan Khan's conversion, Mongol military assistance helped the Yellow Sect consolidate its holdings in Tibet proper and spread its influence to Kokonor and Mongolia. After Sonam Gyatso died, a great-grandson of Altan Khan, Yonten Gyatso, was chosen as Sonam's reincarnation and became the Fourth Dalai Lama. Although it was an apparent manipulation of the

Tumed Mongols, the Yellow Sect clergy acquiesced. Just as the Catholic Church in early medieval Europe courted Charlemagne's military support, the Yellow Sect resorted to the Mongols to fight against its enemies both inside and outside Tibet. Again, as the relationship between the Catholic Church and Charlemagne was reciprocal, the Mongols also benefited from their close bonds with the Yellow Sect—it was ever helpful for warriors to have the backing of a religious establishment. In the decades to come, the different branches of the Mongols would compete to become the patrons of the Yellow Sect.

In 1622 the Fifth Dalai Lama, Lozang Gyatso, the most important personage of the Yellow Sect since Tsongkhapa, was inaugurated. Among other things he has often been credited with reestablishing unity in Tibet following centuries of political unrest. He was, in the first place, responsible for solidifying the holding of power of the Yellow Sect, however. At the time of his inauguration the Yellow Sect was facing serious challenges from other sects, especially Karmapa, and other hostile forces in Tibet and Kokonor. But the Tumed Mongols no longer had power at this time; Lindhan Khan's demise in 1634 sealed their downfall.[9] Under pressure the Yellow Sect turned to another Mongol group, the Khoshot Mongols, for help. The Khoshot Mongols were part of the Oirat (or Oyirad) Mongols, a non-Chinggisid Mongol branch originating from the area north of the Altai Mountains. Having dominated the steppe and threatened the Ming dynasty during the fifteenth century, the Oirat retreated to Eastern Turkistan.[10] In the early seventeenth century the disintegrating Oirat, who also became known as the Eleuth from this time on, split into four major groups: the Choros, the Dorbet, the Khoshot, and the Torghut, among which the strongest was the Khoshot. It was Gushri Khan, the leader of the Khoshot Mongols, who expressed his willingness to offer the Tibetans his help.[11]

Following an extremely bloody battle between Gushri Khan and the Khalkha Mongols in Kokonor, in which the latter was defeated, Gushri Khan became the overlord of Kokonor.[12] At the invitation of the Fifth Dalai Lama, Gushri Khan came to Lhasa in 1638 and accepted a title conferred by the Fifth Dalai Lama, which upheld him as the "religious king who maintains the teachings." After Gushri Khan defeated the other sects and those who had not yet converted to the Yellow Sect, the Yellow Sect gained domination in Tibet and tremendous influence on the territories of Mongol tribes. In 1642, Gushri Khan conferred upon the Fifth Dalai Lama supreme authority over Tibet at a ceremony in Shigatse, the second largest city in Tibet.[13] Meanwhile, Gushri Khan established himself as the overlord in Tibet. Not only did he station the Mongol armies in Tibet, he also rebuilt the Tibetan governmental system and legal system. For the next seventy-five years (1642–1717), the Khoshot Mongols were the de facto rulers of Tibet. Insofar as this changed the Tibetan political landscape, the late Ming dynasty even considered Tibet part of the Mongol territories.[14]

Gushri Khan was a farsighted power player in the Mongol-Tibetan world. He sent envoys to Shengjing, the early capital of the Manchus, as early as 1636, when the Manchus had just founded their dynasty there. He also urged the Fifth Dalai Lama to follow suit by sending a goodwill mission to Manchuria. In 1642 a Tibetan mission arrived in Shengjing that was very favorably treated by the first emperor of the Qing dynasty Hung Taiji (r. 1636–1643) for eight months. As a people rising on the Chinese frontier themselves, the Manchus were sensitive to the magnitude of various peoples on China's borderlands, which had been well-demonstrated in their management of some Mongol tribes before and after they conquered China proper.[15] As for the Tibetans, the Manchus paid particular attention to them because most Mongol tribes were followers of Tibetan Buddhism. Since 1637, Hung Taiji had sent his own envoys to Lhasa on several occasions. He also invited Tibetan monks to come to his kingdom and provide religious services for the Manchus.[16]

After the Manchus took Beijing in 1644, they renewed their efforts in cementing their relationship with the Yellow Sect. Lamas were sent from Beijing to Lhasa to deliver the emperor's greetings to the Fifth Dalai Lama and offer *manja* ceremonies in leading monasteries in Tibet.[17] In 1645 Gushri Khan sent one of his sons to Beijing with a letter to the Shunzhi emperor expressing his loyalty to the new Qing regime. Following this, he and the Dalai Lama sent missions to Beijing almost yearly. Among those early contacts the most significant and dramatic event was the Fifth Dalai Lama's visit to Beijing in 1652 at the repeated invitations of the Qing dynasty.[18] Gushri Khan also played a role in urging the Dalai Lama to take this extraordinary trip. After a long journey the Dalai Lama arrived in Beijing and was warmly received. But the Qing failed to keep the holy man indefinitely in its capital, in which a lamasery had been built to accommodate him; the Dalai Lama insisted on returning to Tibet, using the excuse of not being acclimated to Beijing. Before his departure the Qing throne bestowed on the Dalai Lama a gold cachet and a gold seal with the inscription of a long title, which could be translated as "the Dalai Lama who has the knowledge of Vajra Dhara, is the great benevolent Buddha of the western territory and is the leader of Buddhism." In return, the Dalai Lama presented to the emperor a gold plate on which the inscription praised the emperor as the great master, superior one, god of the sky, and bodhisattva.[19] The Qing throne also recognized Gushri Khan's overlordship over Tibet; he was upheld to be "the emperor's assistant and take control of the territories [of Tibet]" (*Zuozhenpingfu, ji'naifengqi*).[20] But only three years later, Gushri Khan died at the age of seventy-four in 1656.[21]

As Johan Elverskog has pointed out, the Fifth Dalai Lama's visit greatly enhanced his own authority in the Tibetan Buddhist world, as the Qing support of him was to the exclusion of other Tibetan Buddhist sects. In doing so, the Qing parted with its earlier policy that did not favor any particular sect and began to forge the so-called "one priest" and "one patron" relationship with the Yellow Sect.[22] Despite the fact that the Qing clearly demonstrated this new intent through the Dalai Lama's visit, its diplomacy toward Tibet was still at an early stage in the mid-seventeenth century. It was a far cry from the Qing state in its early years that was too preoccupied with conquest, consolidation, and restoration to try to interfere in a more direct manner into affairs in Tibet. Nor did the Qing desire to tighten economic and cultural bonds with the snow kingdom. Therefore, there was no other substantial step taken in the Qing-Tibetan relationship following the Dalai Lama's visit. During the regent period of the Kangxi era (1661–1669), Qing interest in Tibet was minimal.[23] This inaction on the Qing side left room for Tibet's other neighbors. By a commercial treaty with Tibet in the mid-seventeenth century, Nepal's Malla dynasty (thirteenth century through 1769) not only shared the control of two Tibetan border towns, Kuti and Kerung, but was also given the right to mint coins for Tibet. From this time on the Tibetans used only the coins minted in Nepal with the names of the Nepalese kings cast on them, for which the Tibetans paid with silver.[24] Interestingly, this fact escaped the attention of the Qing state until it had two wars with Nepal at the end of the eighteenth century.

On a personal level the early Qing rulers were not as keen on the Tibetan Buddhist doctrines as their successors were in the eighteenth century.[25] Hung Taiji once criticized the Mongols pointedly for their indulgence in the Yellow Sect, blaming it for the decline of their kingdoms.[26] The young Kangxi emperor inherited this attitude. He commented in 1673: "When I was ten years old [in 1664], a lama came to the court to receive an audience. When he mentioned the Buddhism in the west land, I repudiated it as being wrong, making him speechless. I have ever disliked this kind of thing."[27] This disbelief in Tibetan Buddhism on the part of the early Qing rulers was also spotted by the Zunghar. A notable Zunghar Yellow Sect lama once said: "That khan [the Shunzhi emperor] doesn't believe in it [Tibetan Buddhism]."[28] Arguably, it was the pure strategic concerns and needs that were behind the Qing efforts in maintaining the relationship with the Yellow Sect and the Dalai Lama at this time.[29]

The early relationship between the Qing and Tibet was cracked by the Wu Sangui Rebellion. Throughout the years of building his power base in the southwest, Wu Sangui had tried to befriend Lhasa. In so doing, he had made concessions to the Tibetans in territories and border trade. When Wu rebelled in 1673, he kept making efforts to ally with the Tibetans, sending envoys and gifts, time and again, to the Fifth Dalai Lama, who took an ambiguous position in the conflict. On the one hand, the Dalai Lama kept correspondence and gift exchange with Wu and Wu's grandson. On the other hand, he repeatedly assured Beijing of his not siding with the rebels. Nevertheless, the Dalai Lama declined to comply with the Qing request of sending his troops to join the war against Wu.[30]

In the midst of the rebellion the Dalai Lama proposed to the Qing a truce by dividing the country between the two sides of the civil war. Having flatly rejected the Dalai's proposal, Kangxi was, however, alarmed by the suspicious relationship between Wu and the Tibetans.[31] While maintaining the normal policy toward Lhasa, he tried to find out more about Wu's ties with Lhasa. In 1680, when the Qing armies were about to push into Yunnan and Guizhou, Kangxi ordered a search for any correspondence between the Dalai Lama and Wu Sangui, having them sent to Beijing once found.[32] Meanwhile, he sent a commissioner to conduct reconnaissance along the border marches between Sichuan and Tibet.[33] The next year he ordered the sending of former rebels who had inside information on the connections between the Wu family and the Dalai Lama to the capital for interrogation.[34] In the postrebellion era Kangxi had placed a high degree of surveillance on the provincial officials in the southwest bloc, as discussed in the previous chapter. Besides the concern about another powerful satrap rising from the border region, the potential alliance between his officials and Lhasa was also at stake.

Not long after the Wu Sangui Rebellion the Fifth Dalai Lama passed away in 1682. His death tilted the political equilibrium in Tibet and gave rise to the drama of hiding his death for fourteen years, in which the central figure was Sangye Gyatso, the governor of Tibet, or *desi* in Tibetan, meaning "regent" (*diba* in Chinese transliteration). The position of governor was created early in the rule of the Khoshot Mongols to remedy the fact that the Mongol overlord lived in Tibet only part of a year but spent the rest of his time in Kokonor.[35] Usually, it was the Dalai Lama who had the right to appoint. In 1679 the Fifth Dalai Lama appointed his protégé, Sangye Gyatso, as *desi* in the hope that the able and shrewd Sangye could help counteract the Mongol influence in Tibet. The Fifth Dalai Lama had unusually close bonds with Sangye Gyatso.[36] He summoned eight-year-old Sangye to the Potala Palace to receive religious and literary education in 1661 and closely supervised Sangye's studies. The Dalai Lama had long wanted Sangye to become the governor. Having turned down the Dalai Lama's first offer to be the new governor in 1675 by using the excuse that he was too young, Sangye accepted the position in 1679, when the Dalai Lama appointed him for the second time and wrote a proclamation expounding Sangye's virtues.[37]

Compared with Sangye Gyatso, Gushri Khan's son Dalai Khan, who inherited his father's position in Tibet, was a man of mediocre competence. Yet Dalai Khan had the final say over the selection of a new Dalai Lama, which would cause uncertainties for Sangye. To maintain his own position and power, Sangye decided not to release news of the Dalai Lama's death to both Dalai Khan and the Qing. He created the impression to the outside world that the Fifth Dalai Lama was still alive by having a human decoy preside over ceremonies and forging all correspondence with the Qing court in the name of the Fifth Dalai Lama. Meanwhile, Sangye continued the policy of the deceased Dalai Lama of maintaining a close relationship with another Mongol in Eastern Turkistan: Galdan, the formidable leader of the Zunghar Mongols. It was this relationship between Sangye and Galdan, especially the entangling of Sangye's concealing the Dalai Lama's death and Galdan's aggression in the northern frontier of the Qing empire, that eventually led to the direct and intense Qing involvement in Tibet, which in turn affected the strategic position of Sichuan.

THE GALDAN STORM

Galdan's clan belonged to the Choros group, the most likely rival to the Khoshot after the Oirat split into four groups in the early seventeenth century.[38] The first leader of the Choros was Khara-Khula, Galdan's grandfather. In striving to surpass the Khoshot, Khara-Khula even accepted the status of vassalage to the Muscovite state, which, however, did not yield much fruit.[39] After Khara-Khula died in 1634, his son and Galdan's father, Ba'atur, led the Choros into a renaissance. Ba'atur organized a confederation in the 1630s, naming it "Zunghar," meaning "left wing," because the Choros was located on the left among the four Oirat groups. Thus the Choros Mongols started to be known as the Zunghar. While expanding Zunghar territories, Ba'atur turned to the Yellow Sect for support. The Fifth Dalai Lama bestowed upon Ba'atur the title of "Erdeni," which means "treasure" in Mongolian, and upheld him as the overlord of all the Oirat, even though this was not recognized by the other Oirat groups.[40]

In 1640, Ba'atur summoned a pan-Mongol confederation in Zungharia. All the Mongol tribes, except those in southern Mongolia, who had been under the control of the Manchus, attended the confederation. A new code for all Mongol tribes was promulgated, and Yellow Sect Buddhism was adopted as the official religion of the Mongols. To strengthen the bonds with Lhasa, Ba'atur sent his third son, Galdan, to Lhasa to be a lama. This turned out to be a critical opportunity for Galdan, as he developed a close relationship with the Dalai Lama and other Tibetan dignitaries during this sojourn. After Gushri Khan of the Khoshot failed in the bitter power struggle with the Zunghar in Eastern Turkistan, Ba'atur encouraged him to move to Kokonor and then backed his invasion of Tibet in 1642. When the Qing dynasty was proclaimed in Beijing in 1644, Ba'atur adopted a defiant attitude toward the new sovereign of China and renewed relations with the Russians.[41]

The ascendancy of the Zunghar was temporarily interrupted by Ba'atur's death in 1653. As Ba'atur's arrangement of dividing his territories among his ten sons favored Sengge, his second son, infighting ensued, plaguing Sengge's entire reign. In early 1671, Galdan returned from Lhasa to Zungharia, after Sengge was killed by two of his younger brothers, and enthroned himself as the leader of Zungharia following more bloodshed. Aspiring to build another Mongol empire in the steppe, Galdan subjugated the Khoshot Mongols and then annexed the Muslim oases in Eastern Turkistan, putting the transportation route between China and the Mediterranean under his control. In 1679 the Fifth Dalai Lama coronated Galdan "Boshoktu Khan," which, like the title he gave to Ba'atur, confirmed his support of Galdan and endorsed him as the supreme leader of all the Mongols.[42] Galdan reversed Sengge's aggressive policy toward the Russians, trying to secure the northern frontiers of his empire, so that he could concentrate on his contention with the Manchus to the east.[43] Having harbored a desire to one day replace the Khoshot as the overlord of Tibet, Galdan struck a partnership with Sangye Gyatso after the Fifth Dalai Lama passed away: he backed the latter's efforts in swinging away from the Dalai Khan's control and maintaining a distance from the Qing, while Galdan obtained Sangye's support in his aggression against the Khalkha Mongols in northern Mongolia.

Being part of the Eastern Mongols, the Khalkha had three khanates in northern Mongolia during the Ming-Qing period. While the Qing had co-opted the Mongol tribes in southern Mongolia before they took power in China, the Khalkha Mongols had maintained their independence, even though they regularly sent tributes to the Qing court in Beijing. Weakened by the long-term internal strife, the Khalkha tribes were easy prey for the aggressive Zunghar.[44] During the Wu Sangui Rebellion the Zunghar took the opportunity to attack the Khalkha, driving many of them into southern Mongolia to seek refuge. Preoccupied with the crisis in China, Kangxi resorted to appeasement before he was able to deal with the Zunghar with force: he allowed an on-and-off trade relationship with the Zunghar and appealed to the Dalai Lama to reconcile the conflicts among the Khalkha, which had served as an enticement for Zunghar attacks.[45] In 1687 and 1688 the Zunghar launched two offensives against the Khalkha Mongols. Defeated the first time, Galdan came to control northern Mongolia and reached the Kerulen River in his second attack, when he massed a bigger army, again driving massive crowds of Khalkha refugees to southern Mongolia. By allowing the Khalkha to enter its domain for safety, the Qing deprived the Khalkha Mongols of their independence, turning them into Qing subjects thereafter.[46] Meanwhile, the Qing took the Zunghar aggression against the Khalkha Mongols as an unmistakable challenge to itself, for the Zunghar conquest of northern Mongolia would gravely undermine stability in southern Mongolia, which the Qing had fought for decades to achieve. Therefore the Qing came to view Galdan as the most dangerous enemy, whose existence on its northwestern frontier could no longer be tolerated.

After the Wu Sangui Rebellion the Qing was finally able to cope with the problems on its frontiers. It first took the island of Taiwan in 1683. Released from costly coastal defense maneuvers, the Qing could concentrate on the Manchurian frontier and tried to check Russian expansion in the Amur valley, which jeopardized the security of the Manchu birthplace.[47] In 1685 and 1686 the Qing was engaged with the Russians in its northeastern frontier. With an array of largely superior military forces, the Qing was able to establish a better footing for its subsequent negotiations with the Russians. With the Treaty of Nerchinsk concluded in 1689, which regulated the boundary between Russia and the Qing dynasty along the Argun and the Amur rivers, the tension in the northeastern periphery was thus mitigated. As many scholars have noted, the settlement also thwarted the likelihood of a Russo-Zunghar alliance, which seemed not to be a remote possibility on the Qing side. In fact, Galdan was very anxious to find out, during the Qing-Russian crisis in the Amur valley, whether the Zunghar and the Russians could form a kind of military alliance against the Manchus.[48] With the Treaty of Nerchinsk largely removing this concern, the Qing was then able to concentrate on the Zunghar problem in the northwest.

In the 1690s the Qing was fully prepared to wage wars with Galdan.[49] The first war erupted in 1690 in southern Mongolia, when Galdan marched toward Beijing, claiming he came to mend the relationship with the Qing. Galdan gained the upper hand in the initial exchange, but Kangxi amassed heavy Qing forces and eventually forced Galdan to withdraw from Mongolia when the battleground moved to Ulaan Butung in southern Mongolia, about two hundred miles north of Beijing. Expecting that Galdan would be more obedient after this showdown, the Qing stopped short of pursuing him but placed economic blockades instead, banning all commercial exchanges with the Zunghar. In the summer of 1695, Galdan again invaded northern Mongolia, attempting to attack southern Mongolia thereafter. Alarmed and outraged, Kangxi became determined to eradicate this peril, although only a few of his courtiers supported his war decision.

In the spring of 1696, Kangxi organized a massive expedition of more than 140,000 troops and marched to the Gobi area in several directions. Aided by intelligence provided by Galdan's nephew, Tsewang Rabdan, who had a personal grudge against Galdan, coupled with an epidemic that claimed many Zunghar lives, the Qing troops dealt Galdan a fatal blow in Zunmod (south of today's Ulaanbaatar).[50] Most of the Zunghar armies were either killed in battle or succumbed to the plague, including Galdan's wife, but Galdan escaped with a small group of his men. Late in 1696, Kangxi led another expedition into the Gobi area to hunt for Galdan. When the expedition reached Ningxia, Galdan sent an envoy to Kangxi and expressed his willingness to surrender. Kangxi gave him seventy days to surrender and then returned. In the spring of 1697, having failed to receive Galdan's surrender, Kangxi launched another expedition aimed at Galdan's home region. The Qing armies returned before they encountered any Zunghar army because of logistical problems. It turned out later that Galdan had died of the plague himself.[51]

Particularly important for this book is an accidental discovery made during Kangxi's expedition in the spring of 1696: the Zunghar captives revealed to their captors the well-kept secret that the Fifth Dalai Lama had been dead for many years and that Sangye Gyatso had concealed it, forging all the Dalai Lama's correspondence to the Qing court ever since the latter's death.[52] Meanwhile, they also reported that Sangye, in the name of the Dalai Lama, had encouraged Galdan in his attack of the Khalkha in 1695.[53] Even after Galdan's defeat Sangye still tried to aid Galdan by keeping Tsewang Rabdan neutral and enlisting the Mongols in Kokonor to help Galdan. But all his envoys as well as Galdan's were captured by the Qing troops.[54] Although the captured correspondence between Galdan and Sangye had begun to arouse Kangxi's suspicions before this disclosure—he ordered the sending of all correspondence between the Tibetans and Galdan to his headquarters immediately and confidentially once they were found[55]—Kangxi was still seized by a strong sense of betrayal when he learned of Sangye's conspiracy: "Our dynasty is the protector of the Dalai Lama's religion and has treated him favorably for sixty years. *Desi* [Sangye] should have reported to us when he passed away. But he hid it, and what is more, he even seduced Galdan to wage the war [against us]. The *desi*'s crime is indeed great!"[56] He also recalled that during the 1690 campaign in Ulaan Butung, Sangye (again in the name of the deceased Dalai Lama) had sent a high lama to Galdan, who prayed and chose the date of combat for the Zunghar. When the Zunghar were routed, Sangye had pleaded with the Qing to pardon Galdan.[57]

Piecing together all these facts, Kangxi was convinced that Lhasa had played a bigger role in the Zunghar problem than he had ever thought and that Sangye was the primary culprit behind Galdan.[58] Before this incident Kangxi had mainly been concerned with a scenario in which Galdan sought to ally with the Russians. In fact, Galdan had frequently contracted with the Russians for firearms and military collaboration in the early 1690s. No longer willing to upset the peace with the Qing after the Treaty of Nerchinsk, the Russians either ignored or turned down Galdan's repeated pleas.[59] What the Qing authorities did not have good knowledge of, however, was the exact mechanism of the close relationship between Galdan and Sangye. In 1694, two years before Sangye's scheme was revealed, the Qing conferred on Sangye a golden seal upon his request, which was tantamount to acknowledging him as the "king of Tibet" (*tubote guowang*), as Kangxi read it.[60] It shows that the Qing had no doubt about Sangye's loyalty then. It also proves that Sangye was a man of extraordinary political wisdom. Twelve years into his boldly machinated and adroitly acted plot of concealing the Dalai Lama's death, Sangye ventured to take a more aggressive step—requesting a higher title for himself from the Qing by using the excuse that the Dalai Lama was aging.[61] Following the shock upon the disclosure of the Dalai Lama's death, was a dramatic change in Kangxi's perspective on the Qing frontier strategy. He realized that he had to give more attention to Tibet, a land that had not occupied a pivotal position in the Qing grand frontier strategy, although the Qing dynasty had maintained a loosely defined position of patronizing the Yellow Sect since its founding era.

THE FOCUS TURNS TO LHASA

Immediately after Kangxi returned to Beijing in the fall of 1696, he set to work on a momentous diplomatic campaign to bring Sangye to subjugation.[62] He sent an envoy, Booju, a secretary from the Court of Border Affairs (Lifanyuan), to Tibet to relate his harsh reprimand of Sangye and to place an explicit military threat on Lhasa. Being an experienced envoy in frontier affairs, Booju was once locked up by Galdan for several months during a mission to Zungharia. His mission to Lhasa this time was no less risky, as it was meant as a virtual mission of ultimatum. Before Booju set out, Kangxi discussed with him the details and probable hurdles during his stay in Lhasa and gave him minute instructions, as Kangxi knew that "this mission matters a great deal" (*cixing shiguan zhongda*).[63]Among other things, Kangxi stressed two issues. First, he directed that Booju insist on a meeting with the Dalai Lama if he was still alive. Kangxi would be willing to pardon the Tibetans only if the Dalai Lama met with Booju and exhorted Galdan to bend to the Qing. If Sangye continued cheating on the Qing envoy, or preventing the envoy from meeting with the Dalai Lama, Kangxi would "not let it go easily."[64] On the eve of Booju's departure Kangxi reiterated that in the event that Sangye refused to cooperate, "you get evidence, and return immediately [as a gesture of severing the relationship]."[65]

Second, Kangxi expressed a strong inclination of upholding the fifth Panchen Lama, another important figure in the Yellow Sect hierarchy, as the highest leader of Tibetan Buddhism, if the Dalai Lama had indeed passed away.[66] Kangxi had been pushing for the Panchen Lama to visit Beijing, but he suspected that Sangye had hindered him from going. Thus Kangxi set it as one of the goals for the Booju mission to press permission from Sangye for the Panchen Lama to visit. Given that Kangxi knew clearly that the Dalai Lama had been deceased, his insistence on a meeting with the Dalai was only aimed at testing Sangye's trustworthiness. He was keener, between the two things, to make the Panchen Lama the new helmsman of the Yellow Sect. This intention of designedly elevating the Panchen's position would be closely followed by the Qing in the eighteenth century and is extremely consequential in today's Sino-Tibetan relationship.

To back Booju's mission to Lhasa on September 12, 1696, Kangxi wrote a group of long letters to the Dalai Lama, the Panchen Lama, the Dalai Khan, Sangye Gyatso, and Tsewang Rabdan, the new Zunghar leader following Galdan's death. In these letters Kangxi reaffirmed his support of the Yellow Sect and recalled the harmonious relationship between the Manchus and the Fifth Dalai Lama. He then put his finger on Sangye Gyatso's instigating Galdan to attack southern Mongolia. Finally, Kangxi boasted of his recent victory over Galdan with an overtone of his willingness to use force wherever it was necessary. To prove Galdan's defeat, Kangxi enclosed to the Dalai Lama a dagger captured in his Zunghar campaign that had supposedly belonged to Galdan as well as a small Buddha statue and a charm that had been carried by Galdan's wife, who was killed in the battle. In his letter to the Panchen Lama, Kangxi overtly expressed his intent to let the Panchen Lama replace the Dalai Lama as the leading figure of the Yellow Sect: "The Dalai Lama is now old, and the religious attainments of Khutukutu [the Panchen Lama] are the same [as the Dalai Lama's], yet you keep studying diligently, chanting sutras and doing all the charities, so I sent an envoy to invite you [to Beijing]. What I desired was to work with you in guiding the vicious onto the right track, so that the religious principles inside and outside the country would be the same."[67]

Kangxi's letter to Sangye Gyatso is most significant. Besides repeating what he said in the other letters, Kangxi clearly stated to Sangye that he had learned from the captives that the Dalai Lama had been dead for many years. Kangxi dwelt on possible military action against Tibet in an unusually harsh tone. He demanded that Sangye comply with the following four matters: (1) to report truthfully the death of the Fifth Dalai Lama; (2) to uphold the Panchen as the leader of the Yellow Sect and allow him to go to Beijing; (3) to surrender to the Qing Rjedrung Khutuktu, the lama who had prayed and selected the date of Galdan's fight in 1690; and (4) to escort Galdan's daughter, who was married to Gushri Khan's offspring in Kokonor, to Beijing. Kangxi warned Sangye that if he failed to comply with only one of the above: "I would send troops of Yunnan, Sichuan, and Shaanxi to Tibet, and as in the case of defeating Galdan, I would either lead the expedition myself or send one of my princes to attack you."[68] Apparently boosted by his recent victory over Galdan, Kangxi was strongly leaning toward a military solution to the Tibetan problem. It is worth noting that Kangxi indicated that he would use troops from Yunnan, Sichuan, and Shaanxi if a war on Tibet became necessary. No matter how casually he listed these provinces—he probably knew it was a long shot for Yunnan and Sichuan to be ready for any engagement in Tibet—it is evident that Sichuan, along with its neighbor Yunnan, registered for the first time with the central authorities for its strategic potential.

While Booju was on his mission to Lhasa, Kangxi mounted another expedition to the Gobi area in late 1696 to hunt down Galdan. En route to the front Kangxi stopped at Guihuacheng (today's Hohhot), when both the Dalai Lama's envoy and Sangye's envoy arrived. Kangxi met only with the former, giving a grand banquet for him, but declined an audience to Sangye's envoy, even though both men might have been sent by Sangye.[69] Purported in Kangxi's gestures was his determination to be resolute in dealing with the refractory Sangye. Under tremendous pressure from the Qing, Sangye did not easily give in. One by one he rebutted all four demands Booju had brought to his attention when the Qing envoy arrived in Lhasa in the beginning of 1697. Sangye insisted that the Dalai Lama had retreated into a private meditation that would only end in the following year, so that he could not meet with anybody. He also defended the Panchen Lama's decision not to go to Beijing as a personal choice that had nothing to do with Galdan or his own interference. Sangye then refused to turn in the lama who prayed for Galdan by claiming that he had already been sent to the remote Kham area and that he could not be arrested because he was the reincarnation of a high lama. Finally, Sangye declined to send Galdan's daughter in, as she was only a helpless woman who had her husband and family to care for.[70] Although Sangye acknowledged that the Qing war against Galdan was just, as a staunch friend of Galdan, he did not throw too much dirt on the fugitive now running for his life. Given the high possibility of a war on Tibet at this moment, Sangye's uncompromising attitude was remarkable. He might have counted on the geographic advantages of Tibet—its sheer distance and unfriendly conditions to most outsiders. After all, no previous regime in Chinese history had ever attempted an invasion of Tibet.

Upon receiving Booju's report on the meeting and Sangye's letter to Kangxi, which repeated the positions he had expressed to Booju personally, Kangxi initially left them to his courtiers for discussion; it is likely that he wanted to fathom what his top advisers thought on these matters. Considering Kangxi's unbending attitude at the time he had sent the envoy out and Sangye's confrontational responses, the courtiers felt hesitant to make any suggestions. They replied that they did not have an opinion, as everything seemed open-ended. Kangxi said: "But my opinion differs from yours." He declared that he had decided to forgive Sangye and give up the option of a military solution, which instantly prompted all his courtiers to leap to praise the emperor's generosity. Kangxi reasoned that Sangye had shown his awe to the Qing military might and his regrets for his crimes, so that a war was not necessary, as a war should only serve as the last resort when all other means had been exhausted. He further explained that Sangye had promised to send a secret envoy to Beijing, who would, Kangxi expected, report in person the death of the Dalai Lama then.[71]

In the spring of 1697, Sangye's secret envoy arrived in Beijing and confessed to Kangxi privately that the Fifth Dalai Lama had been dead for sixteen years and that his reincarnation—namely, the Sixth Dalai Lama—was already fifteen years old.[72] Nevertheless, Sangye asked Kangxi to keep this secret for a while longer and to continue telling others that the Dalai Lama was in a private seclusion until the Sixth Dalai Lama was formally inaugurated later in the year. Kangxi assented to Sangye's request and was satisfied that he told the truth this time.[73] To confirm his approval of Sangye's good will embassy, Kangxi sent Booju to Lhasa again, along with the Tibetan envoy. This time Kangxi instructed Booju to be softer in language and let Sangye know that "the emperor had led a huge army and reached Ningxia, but he halted his expedition [to Tibet] because he was greatly delighted with your promises to comply with his four demands."[74] In a letter to Sangye, Kangxi also stressed his intention to maintain peace; he did not want to overrun the other's country. Nevertheless, the premise for peace was that Sangye abided by his orders from then on, as indicated in the letter.[75]

Another twist occurred one day after Booju and Sangye's envoy had left Beijing for Lhasa. Having just returned from his mission to Zungharia, Yinggui, a Qing envoy, brought back alarming news: that Sangye had informed Tsewang Rabdan of the Fifth Dalai Lama's death and that Sangye's envoy had stopped Tsewang from joining the Qing armies to hunt for Galdan in late 1696. Meanwhile, it was also reported that Sangye had summoned an unusual gathering of the Mongol tribes. Convinced that Sangye was "still associated himself with Galdan and continued cheating on us," Kangxi and his courtiers decided to catch Booju and Sangye's envoys, who were already on their way, and give Booju some new instructions.[76] When the two envoys were brought back, Kangxi declared that he no longer had any obligation to keep secret the Dalai Lama's death, since Sangye had already made it known to everybody. But he did not alter his other messages to Sangye. Instead of relating his anger to Sangye, Kangxi ordered the interrogation and punishment of the Tibetan lamas who lived in Tibetan Buddhist monasteries in Beijing, as they had failed to detect and report the death of the Fifth Dalai Lama after they were sent to Lhasa in the previous years.[77] After sending Booju off to Lhasa again, Kangxi led another expedition to hunt for Galdan on the steppe. It was on his return trip that Kangxi learned that Galdan was dead.

Although Sangye had put up a remarkable resistance in the face of the Qing browbeating, Galdan's demise must have effected a reassessment of Tibet's position in the triangular relationship between the Qing, Zungharia, and Tibet. Without close ties with Tsewang Rabdan, the new Zunghar leader, Sangye had to adjust his policy toward the Qing. After having met with Booju for the second time, Sangye mollified considerably his intransigent position and began seeking compromise. He agreed to release two people Kangxi demanded—Rjedrung Khutukutu and Galdan's daughter, Zhongqihai—to the Qing and promised to talk to the Panchen Lama about his visit to Beijing.[78] With Galdan gone, Kangxi was more inclined to embrace Sangye's conciliating stance. In late 1697 the new Sixth Dalai Lama, Tsangyang Gyatso, was inaugurated. Although the selection of the new dalai had been completely under Sangye's auspices, Kangxi chose to acquiesce in his choice and sent a respected high lama from Beijing, lCangskya Khutuktu Blobzang Chosbrten, to attend the ceremony.[79] Apparently upon Kangxi's insistence, Sangye let the Panchen Lama tonsure the new Dalai Lama.[80] Ultimately, a much tangled crisis was settled.

The unfolding of the intriguing interaction between the Qing and Tibet in 1696 and 1697 is of seminal significance in the Tibet-Qing relationship. Initially tilted to resorting to forceful means in subjugating Sangye, Kangxi veered sharply from this earlier and more antagonistic scheme to that of appeasement, even before Sangye finally softened his position upon Booju's second Lhasa mission. Being a skilled player in this multilateral relationship, Kangxi knew that the Qing had to be cautious and patient with any attempt to unseat Sangye, who had a solid power base in Tibet. Moreover, a war on Tibet would disturb the Mongols, particularly when the Qing relationship with Tsewang Rabdan, Galdan's successor, was still tentative and fragile. The worst nightmare for the Qing, in the event of a war on Tibet, might be that it gave Tsewang opportunity to extend his influence to Lhasa. Having learned a lesson from Galdan's partnership with Sangye, the Qing would do anything to prevent a new liaison between the Zunghar and the Tibetans. Perhaps out of this concern, when Tsewang suggested, not without a sinister overtone, a punitive war on Sangye in early 1698, Kangxi bluntly turned his proposal down and insisted that he preferred peace.[81] Kangxi did not completely rule out the option of war, however. He tolerated Sangye Gyatso as the Tibetan leader at the end of the crisis, but the premise had changed; the status quo was contingent on Sangye's manifest loyalty. If Sangye did not conform himself to the role of a puppet acting only on commands from Beijing, Kangxi would not forgive him again.

In any case the 1696–97 period stands as a turning point in the Qing frontier strategy. The magnitude of the Tibet question was tremendously elevated. Treated as a subjugated partner in the Qing grand strategy, Tibet had never been within the purview of Qing frontier operations before the crisis. But now the Qing clearly realized the importance of Tibet in its struggle with the Zunghar as well as the other Mongol tribes. This shift coincided with a reappraisal of the effectiveness of the long-distance campaign into the habitat of the nomads. Indeed, Kangxi took great pride in his Gobi expeditions, recalling them proudly in his later years. Nevertheless, he also remembered how difficult it was to keep the massive troops supplied in the immense steppe. Although this frustration was not often discussed, the emperor did betray it on several occasions. In early spring 1697, en route in his last expedition to the Gobi area trying to capture Galdan, Kangxi said: "I have marched with armies and know very well the conditions in the Gobi area. The place is, as people have believed since ancient times, too difficult to conduct wars in. In the places of the desert, transportation of provisions is extremely hard, while it is also difficult to find firewood in times of rain. Without careful planning, how can one undertake an expedition lightly?"[82]

It turned out that the Qing expedition had to turn back early this time because of logistical difficulties before it encountered any enemy. Shortly after, Kangxi made the following comments: "There had been much discussion about recovering the Loop Area of the Yellow River valley [from the Mongols] during the Ming time. The Ming officials Xia Yan and Zeng Xian were even executed for their opinions concerning the matter. In my opinion this place itself is not important. If the Mongols are harnessed properly, how could they make trouble even though they have the place? If they are not properly controlled, they could make trouble anywhere. The Mongols are nomads. There is no way to prevent every possible trouble made by them. It was of no benefit to concentrate only on retaking the Loop Area."[83] These afterthoughts convey Kangxi's doubts about direct military engagement with the Zunghar and conquest of their territories. He did not make this an articulate policy; in fact, he waged more war on the Zunghar in the last few years of his life, but he did pass on his concerns to his son, the future Yongzheng emperor. More than three decades later, when Yongzheng was about to conclude his fruitless campaign against the Zunghar, he justified his decision by claiming that Kangxi once gave him a secret edict that warned him to avoid penetrating into the Gobi area, the home base of the Zunghar.[84]

Later in 1697, when the issue was brought to Kangxi as to whether some Mongol tribes should be moved away from the borders, closer to the heartland of China, for security purposes, Kangxi ruled negatively: "The key to Mongol affairs lies in the right approach, not in the distance between them and us."[85] It seems that Kangxi, after having marched to the steppe himself several times, had set foot in a search for some more effective approach in coping with the nomads. What was the "right approach," then? At the moment the "right approach" could well mean to tighten the yoke on the Tibetan religious establishment in Lhasa, for it possessed the spiritual power to command the Mongol warriors. On the eve of the eighteenth century, Tibet loomed larger and larger on the Qing frontier map. As Kangxi had chosen a wait-and-see policy regarding Sangye Gyatso, what became urgent was to start transforming the hitherto insignificant Sichuan into a strategically operative area capable of supporting future military actions in Tibet.

YUE SHENGLONG COMES TO SICHUAN

As Kangxi stated in his letter to Sangye in September 1696, the Qing would use their armies in Yunnan, Sichuan, and Shaanxi to mount a punitive expedition to Tibet if Sangye failed to comply with the Qing requests. The words were strong and resolute. Nevertheless, Kangxi knew clearly that the troops in both Sichuan and Yunnan were far from being ready for such an invasion. After the Wu Sangui Rebellion there had been no military action in the two provinces, and the Green Standard armies there had not been under close surveillance by the central authorities. In other words it was doubtful that they could be counted on for any major frontier action without some shake-up. In this context one should not take as routine the appointment that Kangxi made during a short interval between his two expeditions to the steppe to engage Galdan in 1696. On August 11, Kangxi appointed one of his protégés, Yue Shenglong, as provincial military commander of Sichuan (Sichuan *tidu*), the highest military position in the province.[86]

Yue had been an upstart in the Green Standard hierarchy. From Gansu, a frontier region in the northwest and abundant in the production of good soldiers in the early Qing period, he started his career as a rank-and-filer in the Green Standard Army. Having caught imperial attention because of his outstanding contributions in the campaign against Wu Sangui, he was promoted quickly. In the early 1690s Yue was appointed to the noteworthy position of regional commander of Tianjin (Tianjin *zongbing*), of which the appointee took charge of the security of the areas close to the capital and often accompanied the emperor on his hunting trips and other excursions. This position served, in turn, as a stepping-stone for further promotion. Yue participated in the Zunghar campaign in the spring of 1696. He was first assigned to escorting the corps of provisions but was transferred to combat force when the engagements began.[87] Marching and living together with his armies in the wilderness of the steppe, the Kangxi emperor stopped by Yue's camp time and again during the four-month expedition.[88] Although only a few Chinese generals joined the campaign, Kangxi paid personal attention to and had high opinion of them: "Yue Shenglong, Ma Jinliang, Bai Bing and others are generals of great strength and talents. They were all hand-picked by me."[89] Apparently, Yue's participation in this expedition was crucial in his favored relationship with the emperor.

After the triumph, when the deployed generals were sent back to their respective garrisons, Kangxi singled Yue out to head to the capital instead of returning to Tianjin.[90] At the imperial court Kangxi endowed Yue with an honorable rank, "commandant of fleet-as-clouds cavalry" (*yunqiwei*), a rare honor for a Chinese general of the Green Standard Army.[91] Then he appointed Yue to the highest military position in Sichuan. Kangxi also gave him the privilege of submitting secret memorials directly to him. At this time only a small number of officials, including Kangxi's bondsmen, Cao Yin and Li Xu, were allowed to use this method to communicate with the throne.[92] Yue's new appointment was not routine for either himself or the province. For Yue he was now at the highest post of the Green Standard ranks, and his relocation would usher in his family's dominance in Sichuan and beyond for more than half a century.

Sending an imperial protégé to Sichuan marked the beginning of a position change for the province. Bordering Tibet, Sichuan would become critical in implementing the Qing's new frontier strategy: shifting focus from the northwest to Tibet and from fighting directly with nomadic warriors in the steppe to exercising influence on the spiritual leader in Lhasa, who commanded respect and submission from those warriors. Sichuan's low revenue contribution would not matter if its strategic potential warranted a prominent position in the empire's political map. In hindsight, one earlier anecdote tells clearly the change in Kangxi's attitude toward Sichuan. In 1685 he transferred He Fu, Sichuan's provincial military commander, to the same position in Shaanxi for the reason that Shaanxi, being a critical frontier, needed a competent general such as He Fu, who had served as Tianjin's regional commander.[93] If Kangxi did not think that Sichuan deserved a capable general who had been regional commander of Tianjin then, he certainly thought so when he appointed Yue Shenglong, Tianjing's regional commander eleven years later, as he deemed that "the western borderlands are extremely important" (*xichui jinyao*).[94]

When Yue Shenglong first arrived in Sichuan in late 1696, he was faced with a peripheral province that for years had not been given adequate attention by the central authorities. As Kangxi told him, the military in the province had been in poor shape.[95] Yue spent his first years familiarizing himself with the province, especially its border areas, and tried to realign the Green Standard garrisons and put tighter control over the ethnic minorities in the peripheries of the province. A primary issue became defining the border between Sichuan and Tibet, which had not been on the agenda of any previous provincial official. The possession of Dartsedo (it was called Dajianlu in Chinese), a Tibetan town located on the border between Sichuan and Tibet and about 140 miles southwest of Chengdu, took the central attention of the new commandant.[96] Although very sparsely populated by the Tibetans and Tibetan-speaking peoples, Dartsedo was an important border market town in the Kham area, serving as a hub for staple transactions between Tibetan and Chinese merchants.[97]

Regarded as the westernmost point of the Chinese empire and the easternmost tip of Tibet, Dartsedo had been traditionally ruled by Tibetan local chieftains.[98] After the Yellow Sect gained dominance in Lhasa, it extended its control over the Dartsedo area. The Fifth Dalai Lama had his officials sent there to oversee trade and levy taxes.[99] Until the mid-seventeenth century there had not been a Qing administrative presence in the area except a Green Standard outpost in Hualinping (the garrison was thus referred as the Hualin garrison), southeast of Dartsedo, which was first set up in 1663 and had only two hundred troops.[100] The only known Qing effort was a mission sent by the central government to survey the border between Sichuan and Tibet during the Wu Sangui Rebellion, as mentioned earlier. But it did not result in any reinforcement of Qing control over the area. A couple of years before his Zunghar campaign in the spring of 1696, Kangxi bluntly dismissed the idea of stationing a garrison in Dartsedo itself.[101]

Dartsedo's evolution into an important border town was clearly related to the so-called tea-horse trade (*chama maoyi*) begun during the Song dynasty, in which the Chinese traded tea for horses with the Tibetans. Although tea was the most needed commodity purchased from the Chinese by the Tibetans, horses were a chief military necessity for the Song. Nurtured by the tea-horse trade, Sichuan became one of the major tea-production areas in the Song times.[102] Nevertheless, the tea-horse trade greatly declined during the Ming dynasty because of more restrictions placed by the Ming government in an attempt to use the trade as an instrument to control the Tibetans. This caused tea production in Sichuan to drop to two-thirds of the level in the Song times.[103] Under the Qing the tea-horse trade on the Sichuan-Tibetan border had never boomed, given that the Qing had not paid sufficient attention to Sichuan until Yue's appointment.[104] Nevertheless, the Tibetan demands for tea and other commodities (such as rice, cloth, tobacco, and so on) continued to stimulate trading activities in Dartsedo in the early Qing period. The closure of the border trade in Yunnan, upon Cai Yurong's request after the Wu Sangui Rebellion, left Dartsedo the only important marketing town in Sino-Tibetan border trade.[105]

For the Tibetan secular and monastic elites, the border trade in Dartsedo was a great source of luxury commodities and wealth. Taking advantage of the Ming-Qing transition, the Tibetans consolidated their hold on Dartsedo by stationing their officials and troops there. By 1696 the Tibetan influence had become the strongest. Largely ignorant of the border trade in Dartsedo, the Qing did not set up customs to levy transactions. This, however, provided the local Qing officials with opportunities to cash in on the border trade. Yu Yangzhi, the governor of Sichuan from 1693, had reportedly been bribed by the Tibetan officials in Dartsedo and the merchants on both sides. With the Tibetans he had a tacit agreement: he would not try to challenge Tibetan control of the Dartsedo area. At the same time Yu lined his pocket with taxes he levied on all tea packs sold by Chinese merchants to the Tibetans (more than eight hundred thousand packs each year).[106]

Two months after Kangxi appointed Yue Shenglong, the emperor also ordered Governor Yu, together with the Tibetan officials, to survey the boundary between Sichuan and Tibet. Only then did Yu report that Dartsedo used to be ruled by the "inner native chieftains" (*nei tusi*) in the Ming dynasty, but it was occupied and ruled by the Tibetans at the time.[107] He tried to persuade the throne to maintain the status quo by pointing to the fact that the Qing had granted the Dalai Lama permission to trade in the border areas. As a result, Kangxi allowed the Tibetans, as noblesse oblige, to continue their businesses in Dartsedo. But he chose to be vague on the "sovereignty" over the area. On the one hand, Kangxi ordered the inclusion of the Dartsedo area into *Yitongzhi* (the imperial gazetteers of the unified country). On the other hand, he did not explicitly seek to challenge the Tibetan occupation of the area; rather, he ordered to let the local chieftains continue their rule.[108] As the local chieftains had been at the mercy of the Tibetan officials, Kangxi's ruling amounted to acquiescing in the status quo.

It was General Yue Shenglong who pressed for the capturing of Dartsedo, as he argued that it was in a strategic position on the highway between Chengdu and Lhasa. He reported that the Tibetans occupied, in addition to Dartsedo, thousands of *li* (1 *li* equals approximately one sixth mile) of the native chieftains' territories and controlled tens of thousands of households in the area. Yue turned Muya, a town west of Dartsedo, into a stock house for weapons and supplies. To counterbalance the Tibetan influence, in 1698 Yue transferred 375 soldiers along with an assistant regional commander (*canjiang*), 2 company commanders (*qianzong*), and 3 squad leaders (*bazong*) from the Liangshan-Wanxian garrison in eastern Sichuan to the Hualin garrison.[109] This aggressive step apparently annoyed the Tibetans in Dartsedo, and tension began to build up. A year later, in late summer 1699, the chief Tibetan official in the area, Changcejilie, sent several thousands of soldiers and took several strategic points along the route between Yazhou and Dartsedo. Yue responded to the move promptly and decisively. While he banned trading activities, prohibiting Chinese merchants from going to Dartsedo, he ordered the reinforcing of the Hualin garrison with five hundred more troops. Upon being informed by General Yue of these moves, Governor Yu immediately sent a subordinate to shuttle between

Yue Shenglong and Changcejilie to mediate the conflict. Yu stopped the Qing armies from moving to Hualinping on Yue's order.[110]

Although Governor Yu managed to prevent a clash between the two sides in 1699, General Yue's hawkish stance in dealing with the Tibetans had completely altered the harmonious landscape in the border marches that Yu had nurtured for some time. Deeply distressed, Yu decided to challenge this imperial protégé by accusing him of agitating the Tibetans and of disturbing the normalcy among the merchants and the local residents.[111] Having no intention of bending to Governor Yu, who did not seem to have any backing in the central government, Yue Shenglong adamantly fought back, blaming Yu for exchanging gifts with the Tibetans, surrendering the emperor's territories to the latter without authorization, and exploiting the merchants in the border trade for his own enrichment.[112] This bitter bickering between the two provincial officials exposed a deplorable situation in this neglected border area: it seemed that both men had been involved in some illicit businesses to enhance their own fortunes.[113]

Things had gone so far that the emperor had to give his favored general, Yue Shenglong, some punishment to show his impartiality. He suspended both officials from their posts and sent two court officials to Sichuan to investigate the case.[114] After a lingering process of investigation and prosecution, both Yue and Yu were found guilty and were dismissed from their posts in early 1700.[115] Although Kangxi endorsed this decision, he ordered a review of the case later that year, which was to be conducted by Xierda, the governor-general of Sichuan and Shaanxi. The result of Xierda's review was, as one might expect, that Yu Yangzhi was to receive a far more severe punishment while the penalty for Yue remained the same as in the initial investigation and prosecution. Yu was given the death penalty and was escorted to the capital to await execution.[116] Kangxi also ordered demotion by three ranks for the two court commissioners who had presided over the first investigation, for they had failed to produce a fair judgment.[117] Kangxi might have felt they had not taken into consideration that General Yue was an imperial protégé, who ought to be treated differently. Xierda's amendment thus left room for the throne to pardon Yue Shenglong at a later date.

The drawn-out investigation in the Yu-Yue case did not slow down the Qing's moves against the Tibetans in the Dartsedo area. In fact, Yue's aggressive policies continued even after he was cashiered. To fill the vacancies in leadership, Kangxi appointed Nengtai, a Manchu, as the new governor of Sichuan, and Tang Xishun, a subordinate of Yue's, as the

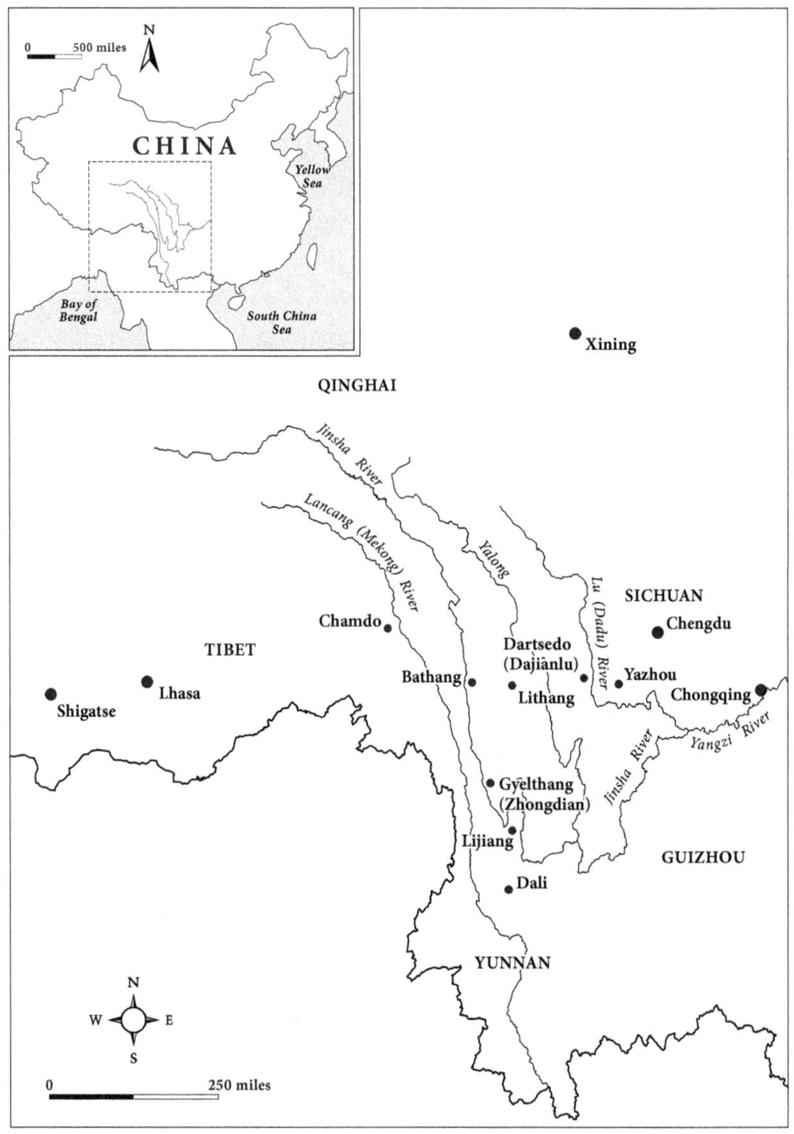

MAP 2.1 *The border marches between Sichuan and Tibet*

new provincial military commander. He put Xierda in charge of all military operations in Sichuan. On August 14, 1700, Xierda petitioned Kangxi to pressure Sangye Gyatso to have Changcejilie, the chief Tibetan official in Dartsedo, arrested, for he had killed a local chieftain. Xierda also requested that the Qing Hualin garrison be moved to Dartsedo. Kangxi gave his support to Xierda's motions, which marks the beginning of the Qing's military actions in Dartsedo.[118] The emperor also issued an edict to Sangye Gyatso. In a strikingly different tone than before, Kangxi claimed that Dartsedo *belonged* to the Qing and that the Tibetans had committed acts of aggression by occupying the area and killing the local chieftain. He explicitly pointed to Sangye as bearing responsibility for all the "crimes" and exhorted him to return the occupied territories and yield the Tibetan who had killed the local chieftain to the Qing authorities.[119]

This edict of the Kangxi emperor was tantamount to an ultimatum to Sangye, escalating the tense standoff. Having no intention of giving up Dartsedo, the Tibetans killed Qing soldiers who were paving a road when they marched to Dartsedo from the Hualin garrison at the end of 1700. They pulled down bridges to stop the advance of the Qing armies. At this point the Qing officials still wished to press Sangye in restraining his soldiers.[120] However, the Tibetans pushed things further by taking another place in the area, Pengba, intending to intercept the Qing Hualin garrison from behind. Irritated by the hostile actions on the Tibetans' part, the Qing officers were eager for a fight. Li Lin, the assistant regional commander of the Hualin garrison, submitted his tactics for taking Dartsedo. Tang Xishun, the new provincial military commander of Sichuan, had moved his headquarters to the Hualin garrison to maneuver the armies. Through a secret memorial Xierda also lay down his plan of a major campaign to take Dartsedo. Finally, Kangxi made the decision to go to war. Two thousand Manchu troops were dispatched from the banner garrison in Jingzhou, western Hubei. Meanwhile, Manpi, a court official, was sent to western Sichuan to oversee the operations.[121]

On January 28, 1701, the Qing troops attacked Dartsedo from three directions. The Tibetan resistance soon collapsed in the face of a large Qing force. More than five thousand Tibetan men were allegedly killed in the battle. The Tibetan officials in Dartsedo, including Changcejilie himself, were all killed.[122] After the battle the Qing armies inflicted massive slaughter on the town. Consequently, almost all male Tibetans were killed; most surviving Tibetans were women.[123] On February 20, Tang Xishun arrived in Dartsedo and proclaimed the Qing rulership to approximately twelve thousand households of Tibetans and other non-Chinese peoples in the town and adjacent areas.[124] The Manchu forces dispatched from Jingzhou stayed in the area until fall 1702. Manpi, the imperial commissioner, also stayed to supervise the establishment of the Qing administration.[125] In early 1702, Beijing sent a Yellow Sect lama and two court officials to Dartsedo to investigate the border trade, which was the first time that the central government had looked into trade affairs in the area.[126] They were more concerned with Qing political control than trade per se, however. In 1707 the Hualin garrison was upgraded to a major garrison under the leadership of a regional vice commander (*fujiang*), and a thousand troops were transferred to reinforce it.[127]

In 1706 an iron chain suspension bridge was built in Anle over the Lu River (today's Dadu River), a tributary of the Yangzi River, which runs from north to south, east of Dartsedo, at the request of the governor of Sichuan, Nengtai. Kangxi named the bridge Luding, meaning "the Lu River pacified," and composed an essay to mark its completion.[128] Before this bridge was built, the locals had to crawl over an iron chain to cross the river, as the current was too torrential and rapid to navigate. With the new bridge, river crossing surely became much easier. But first and foremost the bridge was meant to facilitate the movements of the Qing troops in the Hualin garrison to go to and from Dartsedo, as Hualinping was located at the eastern bend of the Dadu River. More than two centuries later the communist Red Army soldiers allegedly crossed the bridge during the Long March when exposed to enemy fire from the other shore (this event has been celebrated as a communist legend). Overshadowed by this well-propagandized episode, the birth of this suspension bridge is actually associated with the Qing rediscovery of its Sichuan frontier in the beginning of the eighteenth century.

Although it has not received much attention in the existing studies of the Qing frontiers, the battle of Dartsedo of 1701 is a critical event. The display of the Qing's military power in this operation delivered an explicit message to Sangye Gyatso that the relations between the two sides were, after all, power based. It therefore marked the end of the Qing's laissez-faire policy and the commencement of its aggressive expansion in the Kham area (as well as the whole of Tibet), presaging a violent eighteenth century in which more military operations would occur. In the coming decades, Dartsedo became a stronghold in the Qing military alignment from Sichuan to Lhasa. What has formerly escaped the lens of all historians is the correlation between Yue Shenglong's appointment to Sichuan and the onset of frontier activism in the Sichuan frontier. Although Yue had been dismissed from his post before the battle of Dartsedo, he was the one who first urged taking possession of the strategic town and pioneered the Qing aggression into the area. In fact, Yue had never left Sichuan after his dismissal, and it was believed that Kangxi let him join the battle of Dartsedo.[129]

Later in 1701, Kangxi decided to put Yue back into his former position of provincial military commander—the needs in this new frontier overrode the legal procedures—reasoning that "Sichuan is an important area" and that Tang Xishun was not able to serve the position due to his "illness."[130] Thus Yue Shenglong returned to the post after only a brief hiatus of about a year and a half. Since then, he stayed in the position until 1711, when he retired. As personnel administration was often an important instrument for policy implementation, General Yue's story is a strong testament to the Qing's attitude change concerning the Sichuan frontier. For some unclear reasons Yue Shenglong did not receive the attention he deserved in the historiography compiled during the Qing dynasty. It might be the case that he was overshadowed by his son, Yue Zhongqi, who climbed to a higher position than his father and became a national military star of his time. But Yue Zhongqi also suffered disgrace for a time (this story is told in chapter 4). Whatever the case, in the Qing's westward expansion Yue Shenglong's role should not be underestimated.

3 THE FORMATIVE ERA, 1701–1722

As for the places that are far away and at high altitudes, and enshrouded with sickening miasmas, to which it is difficult to transport provisions, we would give them away without trying [to conquer]. Nevertheless, for the sake of the Yellow Sect, I am determined and resolute to act. How can it be deemed easy?

—THE KANGXI EMPEROR, 1718

PARALLEL TO A TURN IN SICHUAN'S STRATEGIC POSITION AT THE OUTset of the eighteenth century, the Qing state began conceiving a new economic policy, the gist of which was to deemphasize revenue collection to prepare for coping with emergencies and supporting military operations within the province and beyond. As Sichuan had not contributed in any significant way to the state treasury up to this point, it is difficult at first glance to discern the shift. Nevertheless, the underlying rationale had changed. If the low revenue rate had been imposed by crude reality before, it soon became a deliberate choice, for the Qing central government purposely maintained a low rate of taxation even when the economy had largely recovered in Sichuan. A common difficulty for many historians examining the Qing period is often to trace the clear evolution and formal inauguration of a policy or scheme, for the eighteenth-century Qing state preferred a much less articulated manner in launching a new policy than would a modern state. This is certainly the case regarding the formation of the economic policy toward the Sichuan frontier. Nevertheless, by assembling scattered data and digging deep into unarticulated but relevant documents, it is possible to recognize the emergence of a new strategy. Before the end of the Kangxi reign this policy was tested for the first time on its validity when an invasion by a Zunghar dispatch threw Tibet into uncertainty and prompted the Qing to send expeditions to Tibet to expel the Zunghar invaders. This incident became a critical juncture in the Qing strategy in both Tibet and the Sichuan frontier.

THE MAKING OF A SPECIAL ECONOMIC POLICY

It is often believed that the imperial states in Chinese history had always been revenue-thirsty, trying to exact as much revenue as possible, either in kind or in cash, from a given area. But realities were often more complicated than this general assertion. It is true that the state at different periods preferred to focus on the key economic areas, as Chi Ch'ao-ting has pointed out. Ever since its incipiency, the Qing dynasty had given the utmost attention to safeguarding the revenue income from key economic areas, of which the most prominent one was the Jiangnan area—namely, the lower Yangzi valley, or the southeast. As a popular saying suggested, half the wealth of the country was from the southeast (*tianxia caifu, banchu dongnan*). Although the Manchu rulers reiterated their intention of altering the Ming dynasty's harsh taxation policies, they had never loosened their tight grip on this area. In fact, they readily inherited the Ming fiscal strategy, which was to place a heavy tax load on Jiangnan.[1] As early as in June 1645, only two weeks after Yangzhou fell and one week before Nanjing was taken, a court official urged the immediate transportation of "tribute grain" from Jiangnan to the north, to relieve the hike of grain prices in the capital and other northern areas.[2] Shortly thereafter, Hong Chengchou, one of the highest Ming officials who had surrendered to the Qing before the Manchu invasion, was appointed as the governor-general of Jiangnan. One of his responsibilities was to collect revenues and ship them to Beijing.[3]

In the Qing dynasty's first three decades, although it was a commonplace for the state to exempt the war-worn areas from regular taxes and arrears, Jiangnan was never allowed to escape from paying off arrears and never exempted from submitting the so-called tribute grain, even in times of natural disasters.[4] In the Qing's early years, of all the taxes levied from the country, more than 50 percent of grain taxes and 25 percent of monetary taxes came from Jiangnan alone.[5] Unsurprisingly, the high-handed exaction left both local officials and the taxpayers in Jiangnan extremely bitter, which led to a well-known tax protest in 1661 in Jiangnan, when tens of thousands of gentry members joined the action. Under the harsh order of the young Kangxi emperor's regent Oboi, the protest was brutally put down, with hundreds beheaded.[6] Although one objective of the crackdown was to destroy the gentry monopoly of communal affairs, as Jerry Dennerline has suggested, the economic concern was nevertheless at the center.[7] It was meant to set up a precedent to forestall any future resistance against the Qing tapping this key economic area. After all, the political leverage of the gentry class had already been largely limited when the Jiangnan loyalist movement was crushed in 1647.

Having secured its control over this key economic area, the Qing was then able to show considerable leniency to other areas and support a costly conquest of the rest of China. As an important way to foster acceptance of the Manchu rule among the conquered Chinese, the new regime had often accentuated the idea that the Qing would forever restrain itself from exploiting the people for any purpose. In October 1644 the regent Dorgon issued a milestone edict in the name of the young Shunzhi emperor to the Board of Revenue, which would serve as a yardstick for Qing overall taxation policy. In the edict the cause of the fall of the Ming dynasty was first discussed: "In the beginning of the Ming dynasty, there were some regulations with regard to taxing people, which allowed people to relax and to reproduce. In the Wanli [1573–1620] period the country was rich and all families and people were adequately fed. During the Tianqi [1621–27] and Chongzhen [1628–44] periods taxes were added due to the wars, and surcharges were rampant. Greedy officials and clerks took their advantage to do malicious things. People could not bear this suffering. Then the fate of the dynasty was doomed. This lesson well deserves to be our warning."[8]

What was intoned in this self-righteous condemnation of the Ming was a profound concern for the image and legitimacy of the Qing, which vowed to cleanse all the evils of the deceased Ming. Later in this edict it was ordered that the Qing's tax rate be the same as that of the Wanli reign of the Ming dynasty, and that all taxes added during the Tianqi and Chongzhen periods be abolished.[9] The same message and rhetoric was repeated time and again throughout the dynasty's first century. China's new sovereigns were eager to implement their avowed resolutions; it was not mere lip service. In August 1644, two months after the Qing state was proclaimed in Beijing and two months before Dorgon's edict, the Qing had already abolished the infamous "three surcharges of military rations" (*sanxiang jiapai*), which had been believed to be one of the reasons why so many uprisings had risen against the Ming.[10] In addition, the central government routinely granted tax deductions or even exemptions to newly conquered areas, with the exception of the Jiangnan area. At the same time it had not been parsimonious in supporting the ongoing war of conquest, either. As another yardstick to distinguish itself from the Ming, the Qing made it clear that the burden of military campaigns would never be transferred to the populace; rather, all military expenditures would be allocated from the state coffers. Sometimes it was difficult for the Qing to live with this commitment, however. There are numerous records in the archives showing the chronic and serious shortage of military funds from the conquest era.[11]

The conquest era left important legacies in Qing economic statecraft. Relying on the key economic areas turned out not just to be a wartime expedient but a perpetual strategy for two centuries, until it was challenged during the Taiping Rebellion in the mid-nineteenth century. Enduring peace and prosperity enabled the state to render some adjustments in this set policy, however. While Jiangnan continued contributing the lion's share of revenues to the state treasuries, it began to receive enormous investments from the state to ensure long-term productiveness in the latter part of the Kangxi reign. As Kangxi said: "The southeast is the important financial area; I often give my thoughts to it" (*Dongnan wei caifu zhongdi, zhen shijia zhennian*).[12] For one thing, the state spent approximately three million taels of silver each year on water projects in the Huai River and other water systems in the southeast, which Kangxi thought was justifiable.[13] When the central government granted generous tax deductions and exemptions to all areas during this period, Jiangnan was also on the list. Such key strategic areas as Manchuria and Mongolia had received prodigious subsidies ever since the beginning of the dynasty, although neither contributed much to the Qing central treasuries.[14]

For the provinces and areas that were neither key economic areas nor key strategic areas, the treatment was tangibly different. Theoretically, they could not count on significant investments and subsidies from the central government. But the other side of the coin was that the state did not expect more than standard revenue income from these provinces, either. At the bottom of the list of nonstrategically or noneconomically important areas were the four southwestern provinces: Guangxi, Guizhou, Sichuan, and Yunnan (termed the southwest bloc in this book). Nevertheless, there was a pronounced change in the Qing state's perception of Sichuan in the last two decades of the Kangxi reign. With Yue Shenglong's appointment to Sichuan the new frontier began to receive increasing attention with the unfolding of such border operations as the battle of Dartsedo. It is possible that Kangxi began to look more closely at the social and economic situation there. Likely embarrassed by the degree of desolation in Sichuan—not only did about half of the arable land still lie deserted, but population recovery also lagged far behind the other areas—it is understandable that he would want to find a scapegoat for it.

Even though Kangxi had acknowledged before that there were other rebels and bandits in Sichuan during the Ming-Qing transition, he tended, particularly in the later years of his reign, to fix Zhang Xianzhong alone to the stake when it came to the serious depopulation and devastations in Sichuan.[15] When Kangxi appointed Yue Shenglong to Sichuan in 1696, he started to blame Zhang Xianzhong for the fact that 90 percent of the population in the province had been lost.[16] In the early summer of 1701, when an official reported that Shaanxi's Hanzhong area that bordered with Sichuan had become completely deserted during the Wu Sangui Rebellion, Kangxi was outraged. Repudiating it as an "absurdity," he pointed to Zhang Xianzhong as being responsible: "There have not yet been many years since then; how could the people get back and the place become populated?"[17]

A dozen years later, in 1713, in a conversation with Zhang Penghe, the head of the Board of Revenue and a Sichuan native, Kangxi mentioned again that Zhang Xianzhong had massacred innumerable people in Sichuan but acknowledged that not many details had been known. He asked Zhang about the records written by the Sichuanese on the massacres. When Zhang replied that no one recorded the massacres because all the people were killed, Kangxi wanted Zhang Penghe to check the facts with his father, who had experienced the Ming-Qing transition in Sichuan.[18] It is not clear what Zhang Penghe's father told his son about Zhang's massacres and what Zhang in turn told the emperor. However, when the official history of the Ming dynasty, *Mingshi*, was completed in 1739, it gave a ridiculous account of Zhang's massacres in his biography—he allegedly killed six hundred million people, much more than the total population of the entire country in the late Ming.[19] Following this sanctioned version in the official Ming history, more literature was produced depicting the atrocious slaughters and the severe devastation by the villain in Sichuan.[20] The firm conviction that Zhang Xianzhong was responsible for all the population losses in Sichuan thus emerged over the rest of the eighteenth century.[21] Although it cannot be proven that Kangxi initiated the myth that made Zhang the scapegoat for the slow economic recovery in Sichuan, it would have been a convenient way to exonerate the Qing of responsibility for the deplorable situation in the province up to the beginning of the eighteenth century.

Regardless of how the central government perceived the causes of the backwardness in Sichuan, the more urgent thing was to reorient its policy toward the province, as Sichuan now had a new strategic meaning for the empire. At this point the basic principle was to cultivate economic vitality by deemphasizing revenue collection from the area. Although the Qing did not give systematic financial subsidies to the area, it focused on further relieving the province from tax obligation and maintaining a low tax rate without regard to the growth of productivity in the area.[22] Following the battle of Dartsedo in 1701, Kangxi exempted all taxes, one more time, for the year 1703 in Guangxi, Guizhou, Sichuan, and Yunnan.[23] To be sure, this was the last time that the throne treated all four provinces in unison with regard to a favor in taxation, as this bloc was going to dissolve. Because of its superior natural conditions, Sichuan was soon to distance itself from the other three peripheral provinces in economic development. Toward the end of Kangxi's reign, it was no longer tax reduction or exemption that was the main method in administering Sichuan financially. Instead, the main issue was to resist tax increases. Kangxi rejected suggestions, time and again in his last years, for conducting a land survey and household registration in Sichuan for the purpose of a tax increase. Many times he warned the official appointees to the province not to upset the status quo.

In 1709, Kangxi appointed Nian Gengyao, a Chinese bannerman, as the governor of Sichuan. Nian replaced Nengtai, who did not have many distinguished achievements in his five-year tenure. Nian had briefly served as provincial examiner in Sichuan, but this time he was to stay in the province for the next fifteen years. To a certain degree, Nian's appointment also signaled Kangxi's waning confidence in Yue Shenglong. Although Yue, who had been in Sichuan for thirteen years, was extremely knowledgeable and aggressive in border affairs, he was not a competent frontier builder with vision, planning, and strong interpersonal skills. Worse than that, Yue was not as vigorous in setting up a solid framework for the province's expanding frontier responsibilities as in building his own family's fortune and networks. At the end of the first decade of the eighteenth century, Yue was aging, suffering from illness and ultimately blindness.[24] Almost all of his extant memorials after 1705 are only routine greetings to the emperor, not mentioning any substantial affairs. Given the increasing importance of the Sichuan frontier, it became necessary to send another energetic and instrumental overseer there. At the time of Nian's appointment to Sichuan, his banner, the Chinese Bordered Yellow banner, became subordinated to Yinzhen, Kangxi's fourth son and the future Yongzheng emperor. Plus, one of Nian's sisters was also taken as Yinzhen's concubine. Because of these ties, Nian began to develop personal bonds with the future emperor, even though he was far away in Sichuan.

During the audience with the emperor before Nian's departure, Kangxi warned him emphatically not to upset the stability in Sichuan by attempting to raise taxes: "Many people from Huguang have gone to Sichuan to farm and live in recent years. The place is getting productive and rich. As the new governor, if you try to examine the reclaimed land, and to increase taxes upon your arrival, you will lose popularity. The land survey in Hunan resulted in troubles and unrest. Years ago, the governor of Sichuan, Gaertu, proposed carrying out a survey. But he failed to achieve his goal. It is all right [for you] to take care of the issue of taxation later. But you must keep the people undisturbed. This is the most important matter in Sichuan."[25]

Although Kangxi had reliable knowledge that a considerable amount of newly reclaimed land had not been reported to the local authorities, hence escaping taxation, he seemed not to be concerned. Instead, he worried more about the numerous brawls among natives and newcomers scrambling for land, which disturbed stability in the local society.[26] As an ambitious new governor, however, Nian Gengyao would not be satisfied with just maintaining the status quo. Only a few months after he arrived in Chengdu, he submitted a five-point proposal to the throne in which he outlined several things he deemed urgent in redressing the province's "many drawbacks." These suggested measures were mainly aimed at strengthening political control and weeding out corruption, which was rampant within the officialdom in the province.[27] In one year Nian sent another seven-point plan, attempting to further overhaul the administrative and financial systems, which in his words had been "reduced to basics," ever since the end of the Wu Sangui Rebellion. He was concerned that in the face of population growth and ongoing land clearance, the government was unable to reap the fruits of those progresses by increasing taxes and setting up granaries. Therefore, among the seven things he suggested, four were financial matters—namely, to boost land registration, to set up granaries, to mint coins, and to legalize mining. Given that illegal levies by the local officials stood for the main obstacle to discourage farmers from registering their land, Nian suggested using promotion as an incentive to lure the local officials away from blackmailing the farmers.[28]

It seems that it was a far cry for Nian's suggestions to be fully put into practice, given that the emperor persisted in his laissez-faire attitude toward the taxation issue in Sichuan. In 1713, Kangxi clearly declared, again, that he had not attempted to collect tax from the newly reclaimed land in Sichuan, even though he knew that the loss resulting from this leniency would amount to 300,000 taels of silver a year.[29] In addition, the tax-free period for newly reclaimed land remained seven years in Sichuan, the same in Yunnan and Guizhou, but it had been reduced to three to five years in other provinces. Although Sichuan periodically reported on the progress in repopulation and reclamation, in general both were prodigiously underreported, since there was no real pressure from the state to ascertain accurate figures.[30] Historians have commonly complained about the erroneous and deceptive data of the population and the arable land from this period in Sichuan, which renders it impossible to reconstruct a true picture of the economic development.[31] Although the local officials should be blamed for creating the confusion, the central authorities' deliberate generosity and tolerance also bore some responsibility. Drastically contrasting with its iron-fisted exaction of Jiangnan for revenues, the state's easy-going position toward Sichuan exemplifies its different treatment of a key strategic area. As such, the Sichuan frontier had to be guaranteed resources and also stability. But a land survey would, as proved elsewhere, arouse resistance and upset social order and stability. In particular, a considerable amount of unreported land in Sichuan was probably under military control.

Kangxi's laissez-faire position was also embodied in his policy regarding taxing the border trade in western Sichuan. Beginning to put the border trade on its agenda after the capture of Dartsedo in 1701, the Qing state sent a lama and two court officials from Beijing to Dartsedo, in 1702, to oversee trade affairs. But Kangxi stressed that taxing the border trade was not an important issue: "The Tibetans are most greedy. Yet they can be pleased with any small benefit. The transaction tax will not be levied upon them, only upon the merchants of our country. Don't take levying the transaction tax as a serious matter. If you are determined to make profits, merchants will not come. Then what is different from banning the trade at all? The sum of income from this is not significant; do not care too much. You must foster good reputations [for the dynasty]. They [the Tibetans] would praise us even though they only get a modicum of benefit."[32] It is clear that Kangxi was concerned more with Tibetan relations than with revenue from the border trade. This edict set the tone for Qing management of the border trade in Dartsedo for decades to come. Strategic considerations overrode the desire for the maximizing of financial gains. Upon his arrival in 1709, Nian Gengyao found out that tea merchants who went to Dartsedo were bothered more by the illegal exactions of tax officials than by official levies, as the latter "was not much at all."[33]

Despite a slow and bumpy start, the state's consistently lax taxation policy would ultimately bring economic vitality back to the province. For one thing it attracted more and more migrants from neighboring provinces—the turn of the eighteenth century witnessed the first big wave of migration into Sichuan.[34] Among all the provinces from which migrants came, Hunan and Hubei, the two provinces bordering Sichuan to its east and jointly known as "Huguang," supplied most migrants, so that there emerged a popular saying: "Sichuan was refilled by the people from Huguang" (*Huguang tian Sichuan*). Take one county in Hunan, Lingling, as an example: from 1697 to 1713 more than a hundred thousand people from this single county migrated to Sichuan.[35] To be sure, population pressure had started having an impact nationwide around this time. Although a logical consequence of overpopulation would prompt migrations to the more sparsely populated areas, the major impetus for migrating into Sichuan at the turn of the eighteenth century was not overpopulation but overtaxation. In fact, unclaimed land was widely available in some of the places from which migrants came, at least in the early eighteenth century.[36]

But heavier tax obligations as well as unbearable burdens of surcharges, such as *huohao* (meltage fees), drove farmers to look for opportunities beyond their home provinces. When huge numbers of farmers moved to Sichuan, they left large amounts of land deserted in their home areas. Alarmed by the farmers' tacit protest against heavy exactions in the Huguang region, the central government began to pay attention and intervene. In 1703, Kangxi issued an edict to the newly appointed governor of Hunan, Zhao Shenqiao, to alert him to this problem.[37] As a result, provincial authorities in both Hubei and Hunan imposed a ban on emigration to Sichuan. Each year thousands of migrants to Sichuan were caught and escorted back to their home villages. Thus many had lost their properties and savings due to forced return. In 1713 a county magistrate from Hunan appealed to Kangxi to lift the ban.[38] But it is not clear whether it had been followed through.

No matter what the government did, migrants continued flowing into Sichuan, legally and illegally, since the opportunities there looked too seductive to be ignored. This constitutes a stark contrast to the reluctant and even forced migration to Sichuan after the Qing conquest in the early 1660s. In some specialized studies on the migrations to Sichuan in the first half of the Qing dynasty, what has been emphasized is the active policy of the Qing state to encourage migration to Sichuan.[39] Although it is true that the Qing state adopted some encouraging measures in the early times after the conquest, including extending the tax-free period to newly reclaimed land and loaning farmers seeds and oxen, the irony is that the sizable migration to the province did not materialize under the auspices of the state; the heights of spontaneous migration, instead, came only when the local governments became more restrictive toward the migration to Sichuan.

Therefore it was not such undependable state subsidies as free oxen and seeds that convinced migrants to make the critical decision in their lives to leave their own hometowns and move to Sichuan.[40] Rather, it was the prospect of escaping from the heavy taxes and surcharges and possessing some land at a low cost that prompted them to go. It was widely believed that the life was easier, the land abundant, and taxes low in Sichuan. Although the picture could become even rosier when words traveled, it did have some truth in it. Nian Gengyao admitted in 1715 that "Sichuan is indeed a paradise, in which people have no difficulty in paying off the taxes [since they are so low]."[41] Records in some local gazetteers also reveal a relatively affluent local society in Sichuan during the eighteenth and early nineteenth centuries.[42] Unlike other provinces, where depopulation was not as thorough as in Sichuan, the gentry class in Sichuan was largely uprooted and slow in coming back. This left society free from the dominance and exaction of the rural elite class, which proved to be an optimum environment for small landowners. Therefore no ban could really work in stopping the population movement to what many saw as a dreamland.

To fully take advantage of the favorable conditions in Sichuan, new migrants pursued different strategies. One was to become "commuting farmers," who only stayed in their new settlements for the tax-free period, then returned to their home places in Hunan or Hubei once the tax-free period was over. Although it is impossible to assess how many people followed such a strategy, its social consequences were tangible. One of them was the increase of land disputes in the home areas of the commuting farmers, as they usually sold their land and houses before they left for Sichuan but tried to recover the sold properties when they returned.[43] Meanwhile, the high mobility of these people invariably caused confusion in population and land registration in both their home provinces and

Sichuan. Another strategy was the so-called bouncing migration, in which many migrants did not settle down in the first place they reached but often moved from place to place to choose a better living environment and to maximize their gains given the vast availability of ownerless land. Most likely they left the land they had reclaimed for a new place when the tax-free privilege expired. This also contributed to the underreporting of the taxable land in Sichuan. After the core area was filled, the new settlers gradually radiated to the peripheries of the province and lastly to Yunnan and Guizhou, where unclaimed land was also available in large quantities.[44] Finally, many migrants adeptly availed themselves of the lax regulations in land registration to evade tax. One account that was written in the early twentieth century claims: "As long as they [new settlers] paid tax on several *mu* of land, they could possess several dozen *mu* of land."[45] This might have been a widespread phenomenon in the late Kangxi period.

With a steady flow of migrants pouring into Sichuan, the province, especially its core area—namely, the Chengdu plain—had been considerably repopulated by the end of the Kangxi reign. The official figure for people who paid capitation in Sichuan in 1724 was 409,310. If the people who were not obliged to pay capitation were four times this figure, the total population would have been approximately 1.6 million.[46] Given the degree of the official data's incompletion, the real figures should be considerably higher.[47] With more people in the area, some counties that had been abolished and merged into other counties in the early Qing were restored, and more official posts were added in 1721.[48] Although the population density in Sichuan could not yet be compared to that in some more developed regions, such as Jiangnan, it is safe to say that by the end of the Kangxi period the province as a whole had stepped out of the shadow of the war devastation.

Apparently, the central authorities did not feel it imperative to stop the population movements to Sichuan—they could be slowed or stopped if the taxation situation in Sichuan was no longer favorable for the migrants, which would not be too difficult to do on the Qing part. Nevertheless, the high priority for the Qing empire in the province was not to increase revenues but to foster the growth of a new frontier. What underscored its seemingly excessive leniency in treating Sichuan was that the throne wanted to retain a certain quantity of resources in the region to prepare for any frontier emergency. In as early as 1709, Kangxi had expounded his idea regarding allowing provinces to retain some of their grain taxes to prepare for an unexpected situation.[49] In 1712, Kangxi specifically urged

Guangxi, Guizhou, Sichuan, and Yunnan (all border provinces) to store grain.[50] For such frontier areas as Sichuan that bordered Tibet, the most unpredictable factor in Qing frontier affairs, it might be even more critical to store some resources locally. For it would be inefficient and slow to transport the grain and other supplies from outside in the event of a frontier emergency. As Nian Gengyao pointed out in his seven-point plan in 1711, given Sichuan's location in the upper valley of the Yangzi River, it was easy to ship grain down to the lower valleys but almost impossible to ship it the other way. If there was a poor harvest in Sichuan, the soldiers there would be short of grain supplies.[51]

Although Nian suggested setting up granaries and storing grain in several key locations, a tacit understanding was that it was most desirable to let the local market be constantly in good supply, so that the military could purchase grain at any time from the market. As Sichuan's revenues were too small to cover its military expenses, the province always received the funds allocated from other provinces to support Sichuan's Green Standard garrisons; the amount of the funds tended to increase after Sichuan's strategic importance became apparent at the turn of the eighteenth century.[52] Therefore the provincial authorities were not in any way motivated to try to increase taxes in Sichuan. Rather, they would be more than happy to allow the populace a bigger share of the surplus, as a richer society would be ideal when it came to arbitrary exactions. The slogan of "preserving the wealth among the people" was turned into a convenient excuse for the local authorities to fend off any pressure from the central government for tax increases. Having stayed in Sichuan for a few years, Nian Gengyao himself also turned mute when it came to the issue of straightening out the land registrations, which was an interesting contrast to his initial position in arguing for a more rigorous effort in land registration. Suffice it to say, by the end of the Kangxi period the land registrations in Sichuan were far less than adequate with so much arable land not registered. But the situation remained so with royal acquiescence.

Ever since the Wu Sangui Rebellion, the Qing central government had been careful to avoid another strong satrap from emerging in the southwest bloc by not providing generous financial support. For two decades it was a risky business for provincial officials to request a raise in monetary support from the state. This became passé with the advent of the eighteenth century, however. The persistent vigilance against the rise to power of a local strongman was outweighed by the escalating importance of the Sichuan frontier in the Qing's effort to subjugate Tibet. In the coming decades, not only did Sichuan continue to contribute little revenue to the central treasury, it also received and consumed military funds in great quantity in the times of frontier wars.

By studying the economic development in Yunnan and Guizhou of the late imperial period, James Z. Lee has noticed that it was not the core of the empire that extracted resources from the peripheries; instead, it was the peripheries that received the financial support from the core, which constitutes a contrast to the realities in other empires in world history.[53] It was true that almost all the peripheral areas under the Qing were on the receiving end of the financial support before the mid-nineteenth century but did not make any weighty financial contributions to the state. Nevertheless, there was one significant difference between the case of Sichuan and its neighbors in the southwest. While Yunnan and Guizhou kept receiving support from the state because they did not achieve economic abundance, Sichuan, given its superior natural conditions, could have been capable of matching the key economic areas in productivity and revenue contribution once economic restoration had been largely achieved. The continuously low revenue obligations assigned to Sichuan, even lower than those of Yunnan and Guizhou, can only be understood as a deliberate choice of the state to satisfy its strategic needs in this new frontier.

THE FIRST INVASION INTO TIBET

Kangxi's lenient economic policy toward the Sichuan frontier would prove farsighted, as a real crisis occurred in the late 1710s that would test the preparedness of the new frontier in coping with emergencies. As predicted by Kangxi, this crisis was again precipitated by the Zunghar, but the location was in Tibet rather than the steppe. Its mastermind was Tsewang Rabdan, successor to Galdan, the formidable leader of the Zunghar Mongols. After the debilitating defeats in the 1690s, the Zunghar empire under Tsewang underwent a resurrection, reaching its apogee by subjugating most of the Khoshot and Dorbet tribes that were still in Zungharia, largely expanding the Zunghar territories, and extending its influence into the sphere of the Torghut Mongols in the Volga valley. In Tsewang's prime there might have been forty thousand to fifty thousand soldiers under his command, according to a German traveler and scholar who visited the surviving Zunghar Mongols in southern Russia in the late eighteenth century.[54] Like his uncle, Tsewang also envisioned using Tibetan religious influence in his bid for power in the Central Asian theater. Between the Tibetan leader

Sangye Gyatso and Lajang Khan, Gushri Khan's grandson, Tsewang supported Sangye, as he had been steadfastly pro-Zunghar. For Sangye the Zunghar power could back his struggle to ward off the Qing influence and oust the Gushri family. It was rumored that Sangye had fatally poisoned the Dalai Khan, Lajang's father, and also attempted to poison Lajang, who had taken the position as Tibet's overlord in 1703 from his own brother.[55] Meanwhile, the Qing chose to tacitly support Lajang Khan, as he would serve as the best tool for the Qing to fell Sangye. In fact, the contention between the Zunghar Mongols and the Qing was mirrored in the power struggle between Sangye and Lajang, although it was also interlaced with many personal factors.

In the first decade of the eighteenth century the political situation in Tibet took an unfavorable turn for the Zunghar: Sangye Gyatso met his demise.[56] The fuse was the Sixth Dalai Lama, Tsangyang Gyatso, who was enthroned by Sangye Gyatso in 1697. To Sangye's advantage as well as disadvantage, Tsangyang was hardly a devoted Buddhist but instead a talented romantic poet and a womanizer. Abandoning himself to composing poems and pursuing amours, the young Sixth Dalai Lama outwardly disregarded the sacred role he was obliged to play. Having frequently reported to the Qing court on Tsangyang's deeds, Lajang Khan used it as a pretext to overtly challenge Sangye Gyatso. In 1703 at a religious gathering on Tibetan New Year's day, Lajang Khan caught and killed several confidants of Sangye. But Sangye immediately drove Lajang out of Lhasa by force. Lajang retreated to the north and then mounted an expedition on Lhasa. With the mediation of high lamas, Sangye agreed to retire but on the condition that his son become the new governor. Peace resumed following Sangye's stepping down but did not last long. In early 1705 the fighting started again between Lajang and Sangye. Although a truce was reached briefly when the high lamas intervened again, both men were determined to fight to the end. Lajang launched a sizable expedition consisting of crack Mongol cavalry from Kokonor in two directions and routed Sangye's force, which had been scrambled from recruits from militia households. In early September 1705, Sangye was caught by Lajang Khan's wife and subsequently killed by her. As believed among the Tibetans, she had been in love with Sangye before she was married to Lajang but was declined by Sangye.

Sangye's death left Lajang Khan in full control. For the Qing it was a mixed blessing. On the one hand, the dynasty was relieved of the constant apprehension that Sangye would openly ally himself with the Zunghar and resist the Qing. On the other hand, Lajang Khan's coming to power aroused ill feeling on the part of the Tibetan elite, thus presaging more unrest ahead. For the moment, however, the Qing had no choice other than to endorse Lajang's rulership. To show its support for Lajang, the Qing declared Tsangyang Gyatso the "phony" Dalai Lama, although it had previously approved his enthronement. Afraid that the Zunghar might try to get the denounced Sixth Dalai Lama, Kangxi ordered Tsangyang Gyatso, as well as Sangye's wife, to Beijing. Indeed interested in having Tsangyang in his possession, Tsewang sent his envoys to fetch the deposed Dalai Lama. But his envoys found out, only upon their arrival in Lhasa, that Tsangyang was already en route to Beijing.[57] In 1707, Lajang Khan named another Sixth Dalai Lama who was generally believed to be Lajang's own son. Outraged, the Tibetan upper clergy strongly opposed Lajang's choice. After the Qing approved the new Sixth Dalai Lama in 1710, the high lamas from the leading Yellow Sect monasteries declared that they had found the true reincarnation of the Fifth Dalai Lama and placed this "soul boy" in a monastery in Lithang, west of Dartsedo, the boy's birth place, for the time being.[58]

Looking over toward Tibet from Zungharia, Tsewang Rabdan must have been dismayed by Sangye Gyatso's death, which meant a great setback in his competition with Gushri Khan's clan in controlling the Yellow Sect. He had to bend to the changed reality in Tibet. In the following years, Tsewang tried cultivating a rapport with Lajang through marital ties. He first married the elder sister of Lajang Khan himself. Then he married one of Lajang's sons to his own daughter but turned this son-in-law into his hostage in Ili.[59] Having kept a watchful eye on all the developments in Tibet, Kangxi once voiced his worries about Lajang, who did not have much support from the Tibetans, and about the Qing capacity to cope with any emergency in Tibet due to the sheer geographic disadvantage.[60]

To prepare for unexpected situations, Kangxi adopted a series of preventative measures after Sangye's death. In 1709 he appointed the able Nian Gengyao as the governor of Sichuan. In 1713, to assuage the anger of the Tibetan high clergy over Lajang's choice of the new Sixth Dalai Lama, Kangxi entitled the Fifth Panchen Lama "Erdeni" and granted him a cachet like the one the Qing throne had given to the Fifth Dalai Lama.[61] This formally elevated Panchen Lama's position to the near equivalence of the Dalai Lama, thus creating a balance to the tremendous influence of the Dalai Lama. In the decades to come, sponsoring both Dalai and Panchen Lamas became an important component in the Qing policy toward Tibet, ultimately leading to strife between the two foremost figures of the Yellow Sect. In the spring of 1715, Kangxi ordered to move the so-called soul boy, who was claimed to be the true reincarnation of the Fifth Dalai Lama by the Tibetan clergy, from Lithang to Kumbum (Ta'ersi), a renowned Yellow Sect monastery in Xining, Kokonor, which was not far away from the Qing garrisons in Gansu.[62] This move gave the Qing leverage in the controversy, as it had taken on the persona of patron to the soul boy, who could be used, when the time came, to replace the unpopular second Sixth Dalai Lama installed by Lajang.

Kangxi's circumspection proved to be judicious. In 1715, Tsewang Rabdan attacked Hami, the easternmost Qing stronghold in Eastern Turkistan. Although the Qing garrison army near Hami quickly foiled this attack, Kangxi was so alarmed that he launched another campaign against the Zunghar. However, the prairie along the long road to Hami was not lush enough to provide adequate forage for a large number of livestock (camels and horses) that carried the provisions. The circumstance forced the Qing to adopt a new tactic: to set up a number of permanent military colonies in Eastern Turkistan and to connect them to the heartland with a string of outposts.[63] Expanding the horizon of the Qing frontier operations, this tactic would aid the Qing decisively in the long run, and it greatly pressured Tsewang Rabdan, as he felt the urgent need to deter the Qing from digging-in in his sphere of influence. Tsewang had two options: to either raid Kokonor or invade Tibet. Having foreseen both probabilities, the Qing was inclined to believe that Kokonor was the more possible target. So it had focused on safeguarding the defense of Kokonor by sending heavy reinforcements to be stationed in Xining and sealing all passes leading to Kokonor in 1716 through 1717.[64]

Tsewang Rabdan did not act as the Qing had predicted: he decided on an invasion of Tibet. At the end of 1716, encouraged by a positive signal from the Tibetan elite who resented Lajang Khan, Tsewang sent his brother, Tsering Dondup, to lead an army of six thousand men to invade Tibet. To take its enemy by surprise, the expedition chose a difficult route to Tibet; it took them more than a year to reach their destination.[65] In the summer of 1717 the Qing court was informed by captured Zunghar soldiers that Tsering Donbup had led an army to Tibet. Worrying that Lajang would ally with the Zunghar, Kangxi sent a letter to Lajang to warn him not to collaborate with them. But, shortly after, Lajang's plea for help reached Beijing, as he was in immediate danger of being attacked by the Zunghar.[66] Lajang's resistance to the Zunghar invaders lasted only two months. In the beginning of December 1717, Tsering Dondup seized Lhasa, killed Lajang Khan, and deposed the second Sixth Dalai Lama.[67] Following the fall of Lhasa, Tsewang killed Lajang's elder son, who had become a useless hostage. Nevertheless, the Zunghar Mongols soon lost the favor of the Tibetans, since they had failed to enthrone a new and legitimate Dalai Lama (they merely proclaimed the soul boy in Kumbum as the new Dalai Lama). Furthermore, the Zunghar army's banditlike behaviors in Lhasa—they killed lamas and looted some monasteries—aroused strenuous resistance against the invaders.

When the news of the fall of Lhasa reached Beijing, Kangxi was shocked. Despite ailing since earlier that year, he was determined to mount an expedition to Tibet to expel the Zunghar.[68] This bold decision, however, encountered passionate opposition from his courtiers, who considered it too risky. Fully aware of the magnitude of this action, Kangxi pressed his will through. For the first time in Chinese history an invasion into Tibet was ordered. Nevertheless, the lack of preparedness for such an unprecedented campaign significantly crippled the Qing operations. In 1717 and 1718 the Qing engaged in extensive maneuvers of military forces and launched two expeditions to Tibet via Kokonor. Because of inadequate preparations, both expeditions failed. Unfamiliar with the conditions in the Tibetan Plateau, the Qing expeditions—consisting mainly of the Manchu troops from Xi'an, Xining, and Gansu, which had fewer than four thousand men each—suffered from inclement weather, illness, and food shortages. Without firewood to boil water, the troops had to sometimes eat fried flour, the only food they carried, with icy water.[69] In the expedition of 1718, which was led by Erentei, a Manchu general, more than three thousand Qing troops encountered the Zunghar on their way to Lhasa in mid-August. Having run out of their provisions after two months of fighting, during which the Qing logistical corps was raided, Erentei decided to withdraw on November 20. They were caught up, however, by the Zunghar and Tibetans in large numbers the following day. Most of the Qing troops were either killed or captured. Erentei himself was killed in battle.[70]

After this devastating defeat, Kangxi halted the plan to launch another invasion in 1719. While spreading rumors of an imminent invasion, Kangxi called for a new round of mobilization.[71] More bannermen were sent to the frontlines; Sichuan, Yunnan, and Guizhou were called to arms; an embargo on Tibet was also ordered, no goods being permitted to go beyond the borders to Tibet. To check the Zunghar from sending reinforcements to Tibet, Kangxi deployed elite Manchu regiments from

Manchuria to engage Tsewang Rabdan in the northwest.[72] At the beginning of 1719, Kangxi appointed Yinti, his fourteenth son, to be the new commander-in-chief of the Tibetan campaign.[73] The most significant tactical change for the new invasion was that an invading force would be sent into Tibet via Sichuan simultaneously as another expedition thrust into Tibet from Kokonor. This adventurous plan was proposed by Nian Gengyao, who had in fact conducted active reconnaissance of Tibet ever since the crisis started. He interrogated Tibetan and Chinese merchants and Buddhist students from Tibet and sent into Tibet spies disguised as merchants. Nian particularly paid attention to the conditions of the roads from Dartsedo to Lhasa that had only been used by merchants and monks in the past.[74] Apparently convinced of the feasibility of an invasion from Sichuan, thanks to Nian's intelligence, Kangxi endorsed the plan of two invasions simultaneously from Kokonor and Sichuan.

In the fall of 1719, Kangxi entitled the soul boy at Kumbum the new Sixth Dalai Lama and granted him a cachet that signified the Qing endorsement. Kangxi also declared that the Qing armies would invade Tibet in the following spring and enthrone the new Dalai Lama in Lhasa.[75] In so doing, Kangxi took full advantage of the Qing possession of the soul boy to both delegitimize the Zunghar occupation of Tibet and to justify the coming Qing invasion. The invasion started in the spring of 1720. The Kokonor route was led by Yansin, the grandson of Haoge, and consisted of more than twelve thousand troops, including Manchu and Green Standard armies currently stationed in Songpan, northern Sichuan. The Sichuan route was led by another Manchu general, Galbi, and had three thousand troops (a thousand Manchu troops and two thousand Green Standard troops from Sichuan).[76]

While Nian Gengyao was ordered to stay behind, taking charge of logistics, Yue Zhongqi, the second son of Yue Shenglong and a regional vice commander (*fujiang*) in Sichuan, was named the leader of the six hundred advance guards selected from Sichuan garrisons. En route to Tibet, the Sichuan route of the expedition was joined, in Chamdo, by two thousand Manchu troops stationed in Gyelthang, a Tibetan town close to northwestern Yunnan. They had been sent from the Jiangning banner garrison and the Hangzhou banner garrison a year earlier. Five hundred Green Standard soldiers from Yunnan also joined the expedition.[77] As Nian Gengyao insisted, the reinforcements from northwestern Yunnan would give the Sichuan route a great boost.[78] During their march toward Lhasa through steep snow-covered mountains and desolate areas, Galbi once hesitated and intended to halt the advance and wait for reinforcements. At this point it was Yue Zhongqi who persuaded Galbi to keep marching to Lhasa, for the troops had only brought with them provisions enough for two months, and any delay would put them in a dangerous situation.[79]

In September 1720, after a grueling four-month journey, the Sichuan route reached the outskirts of Lhasa before those on the Kokonor route. Instead of waiting for Yansin's expedition, Galbi and his staff made a decision to raid Maizhokunggar, east of Lhasa. Encouraged by a relatively easy success in taking Maizhokunggar, the Sichuan route proceeded to Lhasa. Apparently not anticipating an expedition from Sichuan, since the road between Dartsedo and Lhasa was more treacherous and had never been used by military force, Tsering Dondup had only concentrated on intercepting the Qing armies from Kokonor. On September 24 the soldiers of the Sichuan route took Lhasa after fierce fighting. Yue Zhongqi allegedly made the first entry into the city.[80] On October 10 the Qing armies from Kokonor also made their way to Lhasa after smashing the heavier Zunghar resistance. Along with them was the newly proclaimed Sixth Dalai Lama. Tsering Dondup, who had occupied Tibet for three years, and a thousand Zunghar troops escaped and returned to Zungharia.[81] In Lhasa the new Sixth Dalai Lama, who later became known as the Seventh Dalai Lama, was formally inaugurated in the presence of the Qing armies.[82] When the invasion into Tibet was launched, the Qing started another campaign in Chinese Turkistan to check the Zunghar from sending more troops to Tibet. It was also successful; the Qing armies captured Hami as well as the oasis of Turfan about 175 miles west of Hami.[83]

Kangxi's decision to invade Tibet to expel the Zunghar proved to be a milestone in the grand strategy of Qing empire-building. His endorsement of the soul boy selected by the Tibetan clergy won the Qing dynasty immense popularity among the Tibetans and the Mongols in Tibet and Kokonor who resented Lajang Khan. Hence the Qing gained considerable leverage in furthering its influence in Tibetan domestic affairs. With the military presence in Lhasa the Qing commanders reformed the Tibetan government. They abolished the office of *desi* and set up a council consisting of four *kaloon* (councilors), two of them being clergymen and two others laymen, as the new governing body in Tibet. Meanwhile, Kangxi ordered to station in Tibet three thousand Qing troops, of whom twelve hundred were from Sichuan.[84] A little later, the garrison was reinforced by a thousand men, five hundred being Manchus and five hundred being Green Standard troops. All those developments were drastic, marking the beginning of a process of turning Tibet into a Qing protectorate, as Luciano Petech has pointed out.[85]

Ippolito Desideri, a Jesuit who was in Lhasa at this time, insightfully sensed that the fate of Tibet was to be changed because of the presence of those Qing people in Lhasa.[86] Noticeably, the clan of Gushri Khan was completely stripped of its power over Tibet. Although Gushri Khan's offspring in Kokonor envisaged that they could take over Lajang Khan's position in the wake of the expelling of the Zunghar, the Qing bluntly closed this door to them. In so doing, the Qing dynasty commenced imposing the isolation of Tibet from the outside world, especially from the Mongols. As noted by many, the close relationship between the Tibetans and Mongols—which had been maintained in a natural, free, and unrestricted manner for generations—came to an end in 1720. The new superpower in Central Asia, the Qing dynasty, thereafter monitored and regulated all the contacts between the Tibetans and the Mongols.[87]

THE SICHUAN FRONTIER IS TRANSFORMED

The three-year military operations indisputably confirmed what the Qing had begun to realize since the turn of the eighteenth century: Sichuan, an ideal launching pad for military actions in Tibet, was of great strategic value. Conversely, an underprepared Sichuan would be detrimental. During the time when Erentei mounted his invasion to Tibet in 1718, Kangxi experienced utter helplessness in directing a campaign so far away from the capital: "After having received his report, I've been feeling anxious and concerned. Although I gave orders, they would by no means reach [the front] given the many snow mountains and big rivers on their way. So I didn't send out my orders. Besides praying for good news to come, there is nothing I can do."[88] But the emperor's prayers were not answered. What came next to the throne was the news of Erentei's fiasco. Dismayed and outraged, the Qing central authorities had to face reality, trying to remedy what had not been done properly. Among other things, to strengthen the Sichuan frontier so that it could become a fully functional launching pad seemed an urgent task. In fact, parallel to the unfolding of the 1717–20 Tibetan campaign, a number of developments were already under way in the new frontier.

A banner garrison in Chengdu was established in 1718. This was the first permanent banner garrison in the entire southwestern part of China. Although the bannermen had been deployed to the southwest during the

Qing conquest and then again in the war to suppress the Wu Sangui Rebellion, they were withdrawn once military operations were over. Following the civil war against Wu Sangui, the Qing set up three banner garrisons in Guangzhou, Fuzhou, and Jingzhou, but it seemed that there was no need for such a garrison in either Yunnan or Sichuan, from whence the rebellion erupted.[89] With no bannermen present in this part of China, it was the nearest banner garrisons in Xi'an of Shaanxi province and Jingzhou of Hubei province, both hundreds of miles away from Chengdu, that had to respond to the emergency in and near the Sichuan frontier.

Upon hearing of the Tibetan crisis in the fall of 1717, the throne immediately ordered the dispatch of two thousand soldiers from the Jingzhou garrison to Chengdu.[90] Meanwhile, some of the Green Standard troops in Sichuan were also mobilized for the expedition to Tibet. Nevertheless, about twelve hundred Green Standard soldiers rioted in the midst of the war preparations, claiming that they were seriously underpaid.[91] Although the rioting soldiers were soon calmed down after they were promised adequate compensation by their superiors, this mutiny might have reinforced Kangxi's conviction that the absence of the bannermen at the Sichuan frontier could cripple the Qing efforts in responding swiftly to any emergency in Tibet, as he believed that only the elite banner forces were dependable in the event of a frontier crisis. But he felt relieved since two thousand Manchu soldiers had been on their way from the Jingzhou garrison to Chengdu by his order. One year later he directed the additional dispatch of a thousand soldiers from Jingzhou to Sichuan.[92] The war mobilization might have prompted the Qing top tier of the ruling elite to a consensus that a banner garrison in Chengdu, the provincial capital nearest to Tibet, was now indispensable.

In 1718, Nian Gengyao first put forward a banner garrison in Chengdu to the throne, and he suggested staffing it by retaining a thousand Manchu troops of the Jingzhou garrison. Annoyed by the disappointing performance of the Green Standard troops in Sichuan, Nian, a civil official with no affiliation to the military thus far, justified his motion by pointing to Sichuan's critical position—it bordered Tibet and Kokonor—and the poor quality of the soldiers in the province, who were not entirely reliable.[93] For Nian a permanent station of some elite Manchu bannermen would be a timely remedy. Later in the year Kangxi gave his approval to Nian's proposal but increased the number of soldiers in the garrison to sixteen hundred and appointed a vice banner military commander (*fudutong*) to head the new garrison.[94] Being the seventh banner garrison outside Beijing and Shengjing, the Chengdu garrison stayed in place from 1718 until 1911. The timing of the establishment of the Chengdu garrison exemplifies the correlation between Tibetan affairs and the growth of the Sichuan frontier. However, given that most existing banner garrisons were headed by a general (*jiangjun*), the highest banner position outside of the capital, the designation of a vice banner military commander indicates that the Chengdu garrison had not yet attained the same importance as the other ones for the time being, being only a second tier banner garrison from the state's perspective. When Nian Gengyao started building the garrison west of Chengdu in early 1719, however, he seemed to have anticipated the inevitable upgrading of this new garrison in the future. He planned a compound of considerable scale, consisting of 5,632 rooms.[95] It turned out that Nian was farsighted, however. As the eighteenth century progressed, the Chengdu garrison further expanded and eventually obtained the same status as other banner garrisons by having a general appointed as its head.

The Qing also focused on building a frontier outpost system in the border marches between China proper and Tibet, which affected both Sichuan and Yunnan. No sooner had the Tibetan crisis been touched off by the Zunghar invasion than the Qing central government sent high-ranking officials to both the Dartsedo area and northwestern Yunnan to inspect the military lineup.[96] After the 1701 battle of Dartsedo the Qing forces had not yet pushed further beyond Dartsedo, as there had been no immediate need for doing so in this area with extremely harsh natural conditions. With the onset of the Tibetan crisis, however, further westward expansion became imperative, which would facilitate the invasion of Tibet from Sichuan. Two major Tibetan towns west of Dartsedo, Lithang and Bathang, both on the passage connecting Dartsedo with Lhasa, became the major targets in this round of expansion. The main residents in the two towns were Tibetans and Mongols who were the offspring of Gushri Khan and under the leadership of Lobdzan Dandzin, Lajang Khan's cousin, in Kokonor. Unlike many places in the Kham area whose residents were not followers of the Yellow Sect, both of these towns were staunchly pro-Yellow Sect. As early as 1580, Sonam Gyatso, the Third Dalai Lama of the Yellow Sect, had traveled to Lithang and founded a monastery there.[97] Before the Zunghar invasion the Tibetan lamas who had been opposed to Lajang Khan found in Lithang the allegedly true soul boy, who had been kept there until his moving to Xining by Kangxi's order in 1715.

In early 1718 five hundred Manchu soldiers of the Jingzhou garrison were sent from Chengdu to Dartsedo to reinforce the Qing military presence.[98] In the summer of 1718, upon hearing that the Zunghar Mongols from Lhasa were persuading the Tibetan officials in Kham to submit to Tsering Dondup, Fala, the Manchu general who had led these five hundred troops, requested to move forward to Lithang. After it was endorsed, however, he did not act for some reason within 1718. The following spring, Fala once again requested to launch an offensive and capture Lithang and Bathang.[99] Having again received approval, Fala sent Yue Zhongqi to move west and to take the two places. In Lithang the Tibetan officials refused to submit themselves to the Qing. Resorting to his superior force, Yue Zhongqi took the town after having allegedly killed several thousands of Tibetan soldiers. By the order of Fala, seven of the Tibetan officials of Lithang were executed. Yue then advanced toward Bathang, which was further west. This time the Tibetan chieftain surrendered the town to him without a fight.[100] By the fall of 1719 a vast area of Kham west of Dartsedo, including other such towns as Chaya, Chamdo, and Chawa, all came under Qing control; twenty-seven hundred Qing troops were stationed in the area. In Lithang, Bathang, and Chamdo logistical stations were immediately set up to store provisions.[101]

Control of the Kham area west of Dartsedo provided the Qing invading forces with a new passage other than Kokonor to reach into the center of Tibet. As it unfolded, the Qing expedition from Sichuan and via Kham reached Lhasa ahead of the Kokonor route, the traditional corridor connecting Tibet and China. Kangxi was apparently impressed by the effectiveness of the Sichuan-Lhasa route. When the main Qing armies were to withdraw from Tibet, he purposely instructed all the armies to take the route via Kham to Chengdu, from which they returned to their respective garrisons.[102] It had become clear by then that the Qing expansion into Kham was irreversible. In the wake of the first invasion of Tibet, the Qing set up sixty-six outposts, each of which was staffed by thirty Qing and native soldiers of the local chieftains, along the route from Dartsedo to Lari, a town about 140 miles northeast of Lhasa.[103] In so doing, most of Kham fell under Qing military occupation, even though the formal annexation of the eastern part of Kham into the jurisdiction of Sichuan province did not materialize until a few years later during the Yongzheng period.[104]

Meanwhile, the Qing military buildup in northwestern Yunnan, another corridor to Tibet, was also in progress. As early as in the late 1690s, after Yue Shenglong was appointed to Sichuan, the Qing state began paying attention to the northwestern tip of the province that also bordered Tibet. In late 1698 the Qing upgraded Beisheng zhou subprefecture of Yunnan, which was adjacent to Kham, to Yongbei prefecture.[105] In early 1699 a Manchu official, Baxi, was appointed as the governor-general of Yunnan and Guizhou, the first Manchu appointed to this position after the Wu Sangui Rebellion.[106] In 1709 the Qing troops were stationed in Gyelthang, which was an overdue implementation of an order from the Qing state following the Wu Sangui Rebellion, thus terminating Lhasa's control over this Tibetan town.[107] In the early 1710s some administrative positions in several border areas of the province (such as Heqing, Shunning, Yongchang, and Yongbei) became the positions of "special appointments" (*tejian*), which means that the emperor handpicked appointees himself instead of following bureaucratic procedures.[108]

The Zunghar invasion of Tibet surely gave the Qing more impetus to further integrate northwestern Yunnan into the Qing frontier strategy. In 1718 half a dozen high-ranking Manchu officers were sent there to inspect and supervise military training and war preparations.[109] In 1719, amidst the new round of mobilization for the invasion of Tibet, a thousand Manchu troops from the Jiangning garrison of Jiangnan province and another thousand from the Hangzhou garrison of Zhejiang province were deployed to Yunnan, and stationed in Gyelthang, later joining the Sichuan route to invade Tibet. In the early winter of 1719, another Manchu general, Wuge, was sent to Yunnan to oversee all those troops and military affairs. These moves marked the beginning of the sizable Manchu military station in Yunnan, even though no banner garrison had ever been founded in the province. Meanwhile, relay horse stations began to be built in western Yunnan to facilitate military operations.[110] By the 1720s the developments in northwestern Yunnan suggested a possible merger of this part of the province or the whole province of Yunnan into the Sichuan frontier in view of their common responsibility of supporting the Qing garrisons and operations inside Tibet. However, this did not mature into reality because of new strategic designs for the southwest during the Yongzheng era. Although Guizhou did not send an army to join the invasion, it was obliged to contribute horses. In addition, the garrisons in Guizhou had to be on the alert, because the emperor had mentioned time and again, for the purposes of propaganda, that all those provinces nearby would send expeditions to Tibet.

The Qing dynasty made some adjustments to the bureaucratic system in the Sichuan frontier to give the local officials more power and leeway in coordinating military matters. In October 1718, Nian Gengyao requested the emperor to name him governor-general of Sichuan temporarily so that he could supervise the Green Standard Army in Sichuan, which he had no right to command in his capacity as the governor of Sichuan, despite the fact that he had already been shouldering many military tasks ever since the start of the Tibetan crisis.[111] Kangxi agreed, however, and changed Nian's title from *governor* of Sichuan to that of *governor-general* of Sichuan. Meanwhile, the post of the governor-general of Shaanxi and Sichuan was split into two posts—namely, governor-general of Shaanxi and that of Sichuan.[112] According to Qing practice, the governor was not typically responsible for directing military forces, although he was often ordered to assist in logistical matters; but the governor-general was more frequently involved in military operations. More often than not, a governor-general would be appointed one of the chief commanders in a campaign. In addition, the rank of governor-general was one rank higher than that of governor because a governor-general usually oversaw more than one province. The 1718 arrangement of an independent governor-general of Sichuan was surely a strong indication of the surging military responsibilities of the province due to the Tibetan crisis.

To be sure, this change was merely one link in the long chain of evolution in Sichuan's provincial administration, the most complex case among all provinces in the Qing times. The first provincial post, that of governor of Sichuan, was established in 1644, long before the province was fully conquered. For a long time the governor had to reside in Baoning, in northern Sichuan, because most of the province was not yet controlled by Qing forces. In 1654 the province began to be under the supervision of the governor-general of Sichuan and Shaanxi, and the position was called *Chuan-Shaan sanbian zongdu* (governor-general of three frontiers in Sichuan and Shaanxi). But soon a new post, that of governor-general of Sichuan and Huguang, was created to lump Sichuan and Huguang together. The post of governor-general of Sichuan was first instituted in 1661 when the province was conquered by Qing forces. Then in 1670 the governor-general of Sichuan and Huguang was reinstated. During the Wu Sangui Rebellion a separate governor-general of Sichuan was appointed in 1674 to give him more power and discretion in directing the war. After the rebellion that position was merged in 1680 with that of governor-general of Shaanxi as the governor-general of Shaanxi and Sichuan. The 1718 installation of a governor-general of Sichuan was the third time when such a post was set up exclusively for Sichuan.

But again this disposition did not last long. After the Tibetan campaign ended, Kangxi let Nian Gengyao hold concurrently the post of the governor-general of Shaanxi in the summer of 1721, when the former governor-general of Shaanxi, Ehai, was transferred to the Eastern Turkistan front. Therefore the post of the governor of Sichuan was again restored, and a Manchu was appointed the acting governor of Sichuan during Nian's absence.[113] All these administrative changes reflected the fact that the Qing state had been trying to assess the magnitude of the Sichuan frontier and to find a proper position for it on the political map. The 1718 installation of the governor-general of Sichuan represents a prelude to the ultimate separation of the governorship-general of Sichuan from other military districts due to its own importance in the subsequent Yongzheng and the Qianlong periods. More changes would occur in the decades to come.

Another important personnel move was the appointment of Yue Zhongqi as the provincial military commander of Sichuan in 1721.[114] Being Yue Shenglong's son, Zhongqi came of age in Sichuan and was conversant with the geographic and human conditions in the border marches of the province. In 1711, at the age of twenty-five, Yue Zhongqi went to Beijing for an audience with the emperor, likely a favor granted to the Yue family on the occasion of Yue Shenglong's retirement. During the audience Kangxi appointed him a brigade commander in Songpan (*Songpan zhen zhongjun youji*) of northwestern Sichuan, thus starting his military career.[115] In 1718, during the Tibetan crisis, Yue was promoted to a position in Shanxi province. Before he left Sichuan, however, Kangxi changed Yue's appointment to a higher position in Sichuan: regional vice commander in Yongning (*Yongning fujiang*). Therefore Yue stayed in Sichuan and took advantage of the first invasion of Tibet to make his debut as a promising frontier military leader. The fame he gained in turn served as a stepping-stone for his rapid promotions afterward. However, Yue Zhongqi's 1721 promotion to the post of provincial military commander of Sichuan, the same position that his father had occupied for many years, violated the law of avoidance as he was already a resident of Chengdu—his father had requested the change of the family's domicile to Chengdu before his death in 1713. Nevertheless, given the rising strategic importance of Sichuan, the state could not afford to lose this talented general to another locale.

The Qing state had been assured that the lenient tax requirements in the Sichuan frontier were not only justifiable but indispensable, for it had been demonstrated that an unprepared Sichuan frontier without sufficient resources would be extremely detrimental to the military operations. Now that a banner garrison was established in Chengdu, the province was on a better footing in terms of military strength. What became an obvious necessity next was to guarantee that the military stationed in both Sichuan and Tibet was adequately supplied and that any future military operation in this area was well supported. In view of the fact that the economy had been recovering in Sichuan, Kangxi found further justifications for his lax taxation policy toward the Sichuan frontier following the Tibetan campaign. In Chengdu laborers were recruited to build the banner garrison. Along the highway that connected Sichuan with Lhasa, military outposts were set up, and the traffic of the troops in and out of Tibet became an excuse for the provincial authorities in Sichuan to ask for more subsidies. Nian Gengyao had requested to store grain in the border areas to prepare for emergencies. He also demanded to retain some land tax in kind to be used as military provisions, which meant that the actual revenue contributions of Sichuan to Beijing were even smaller than the tax quotas assigned to the province.

After the first invasion of Tibet the frequent reports to the throne by the provincial officials about the difficulties of provisions in the Sichuan-Tibet outpost system served only to remind the central government of the fact that Sichuan province was now undertaking an onerous and expensive task in supporting the Tibetan strategy, so that the province should be rewarded in one way or another. It seemed that the most convenient way for the state to do this was not to upset the status quo of the light tax responsibilities of this province, leaving the provincial authorities larger leeway in deposing the surplus resources in society. For the people in Sichuan the Tibetan campaign was a mixed blessing: on the one hand, they were mobilized to support the military operation; on the other hand, they were shielded by the ongoing military buildup in the new frontier against being subject to a tax increase. In the long run the advantages would surely outweigh the disadvantages; the light taxation obligation would eventually foster prosperity in the local society and attract more migrants to Sichuan. Meanwhile, an affluent Sichuan would reverse the practice for bureaucrats to avoid serving in the province, since a wealthy constituency would make extra-taxation exaction by local officials facile. In fact, the local officials in Sichuan had already started relentlessly levying surcharges on the taxpayers to line their own pockets.[116]

4 REALIGNMENT IN THE YONGZHENG PERIOD, 1723–1735

I am considering either grouping Yunnan and Guangxi together under one governor-general, and placing Sichuan and Guizhou under another governor-general, or grouping Yunnan and Sichuan together under one governor-general, and Guizhou and Guangxi together under another one. Please carefully consider and plan for me on how to divide [the four provinces] in administrative terms.

—THE YONGZHENG EMPEROR, 1730

THE TWO PREVIOUS CHAPTERS SPANNED THE LAST THREE DECADES OF the Kangxi period, which was bracketed by two major frontier wars: the Zunghar campaigns of the 1690s and the first Qing invasion into Tibet in 1718 through 1720. With the Zunghar Mongols remaining the most perilous enemy, Tibet's entering onto the central stage indicates a fundamental transition in the Qing overall frontier strategy—it became essential for the Qing state to keep an active and interventionist policy in Tibet. Meanwhile, a fundamental transition also befell Sichuan. By the time of the first invasion of Tibet, it was no longer practical for the Qing to treat Sichuan as a member of the meager and unimportant southwest bloc. Indisputably, Sichuan was a rising key strategic area whose continuous growth would be in the best interests of the Qing empire. The next question that confronted the Qing state was how to administer this new frontier. In the last few years of the Kangxi era, the merger of the positions of governor-general of Sichuan with that of Shaanxi indicated that the emperor wished to group this new frontier with the traditional key strategic area, the northwest (the Shaanxi-Gansu area), which had been the launching-pad area for the operations in the steppe. Nevertheless, he passed away shortly before fully developing or altering his plan.

During the Yongzheng period the Sichuan frontier experienced a degree of uncertainty—the Yongzheng emperor took pains to try to give it a new orientation. He first took over his father's scheme of attaching Sichuan to the northwest strategic area, and then he tried to remerge Sichuan with the southwest, which was on the rise under the auspices of Ortai, one of Yongzheng's most trusted satraps as well as his adviser. Finally, Yongzheng was convinced that the best way to administer this frontier was to make it independent—namely, separating it from both the northwest and southwest administratively. Although the completion of an independent Sichuan frontier would be wrought by the Qianlong emperor, Yongzheng's brief yet dynamic reign was a significant passage to that destination. Another important legacy of the Yongzheng era concerned the changes in the territory of Sichuan, which on the one hand was dramatically enlarged due to the expansion to Tibet, and on the other lost several prefectures in the southwestern part of the province to Yunnan and Guizhou, as the result of its rivalry with the southwest.

PERSEVERING IN FRONTIER ACTIVISM

Kangxi's successful Tibetan invasion thwarted Tsewang Rabdan's attempt to kidnap the Tibetan Yellow Sect to aid his empire-building in Central Asia. But the Zunghar threat did not evaporate with Tsering Dondup's withdrawal from Lhasa. After the Tibetan campaign Kangxi seriously looked for an ultimate solution to the Zunghar problem. He kept his fourteenth son, Yinti, along with a massive force, based in the northwest. Stationed first in Gansu, then in Turfan, Yinti actively prepared for another operation against the Zunghar Mongols. Nevertheless, time ran out for Kangxi—he passed away in December 1722, after a long sixty-one-year reign. His fourth son, Yinzhen, succeeded to the throne, becoming the new Yongzheng emperor. For many, especially some of his brothers, Yongzheng was a usurper, partially because Kangxi had never publicly declared Yinzhen as his successor.[1] Although not a concern of this book, the succession controversy of 1722 caused a temporary interruption of the frontier strategy that had been set in motion by Kangxi.

An obviously more capable one among a group of contenders for the throne, Yinti seemed to be the most likely challenger to Yongzheng. Given the loud rumors in the capital, Yongzheng would not allow this potential rival to command a large army at the northwestern front, although being away from the political center at the time of Kangxi's death allowed Yinti virtually no chance even for a doomed fight. Immediately after he took the throne, Yongzheng called Yinti back to the capital and suspended the war preparations. Then he began seeking peace with the Zunghar Mongols and reduced the Qing forces on the northwestern frontier.[2] Meanwhile, Yongzheng ordered a withdrawal of all Qing troops from Lhasa under the pretext that it was simply too expensive to support the military garrison there, despite the expressed concerns of some Tibetan political leaders.[3] Yongzheng's peace initiatives had dual purposes. On the one hand, he adroitly deprived Yinti of his military power. On the other hand, withdrawal from Kangxi's active frontier agenda would aid his crusade of rectifying the financial administration, as frontier undertakings were one of the chief causes for the near depletion of the state exchequer, a legacy Yongzheng had inherited from his father.

Yongzheng would soon regret his actions, however. His appeasement policy weakened the Qing control at several frontiers, providing the foes of the Qing empire with a good opportunity for action. Shortly after the Qing armies withdrew from the northwestern frontier, Lobdzan Dandzin, the leader of the Khoshot Mongols in Kokonor, led a revolt against the Qing, precipitating the entire northwestern frontier into uncertainty. Although the revolt started in the summer of 1723, it was an overdue reaction to the Qing Tibetan policy following the war that had expelled Tsering Dondup in 1720.[4] After Gushri Khan took over Kokonor from the Khalkha Mongols in 1637, his family had ruled Kokonor. In the 1680s and 1690s, Galdan overran Kokonor when he waged war against the Khalkha Mongols. After Galdan was defeated by Kangxi, the tenth and only surviving son of Gushri Khan, Dasi Batur, submitted himself to the Qing in 1698, which brought Kokonor into the Qing sphere of influence.[5] Dasi Batur's son, Lobdzan Dandzin, succeeded his father in 1714, and he had been closely watching the developments in Tibet. Seeing that Lajang Khan, his cousin, was losing popularity among the Tibetans, Lobdzan was tempted to replace Lajang to become the overlord of Tibet. He thus chose to sponsor the "soul boy," who was allegedly the reincarnation of the Fifth Dalai Lama and whom the Tibetan high clergy found in Lithang. When the Qing armies escorted the soul boy to Lhasa in 1720, Lobdzan, along with many Tibetan and Mongol dignitaries from Kokonor, joined the expedition, envisioning that he would be appointed to the position that Lajang Khan had held when the Zunghar Mongols were ousted.

The Qing dynasty did not act on Lobdzan's wish, however. It abolished the Mongol overlordship, ending the rule of the Gushri Khan family in Tibet. At the new Dalai Lama's inauguration, only the Qing officials and generals were seated in prominent positions; the notables from Kokonor were left out in the cold. The Qing officials also declined Lobdzan's request to forgive Tagtsepa, the Tibetan governor under the Zunghar occupation, who was executed in late 1720 for his collaboration with the Zunghar. Feeling that his long-standing patronage of the new Dalai Lama had not paid off, Lobdzan was utterly dismayed.[6] Returning from his Tibetan trip, he no longer concealed his frustration and ambition to become one day the ruler of Tibet. Shortly before the revolt, Nian Gengyao had reported in a secret memorial Lobdzan's interest in ruling Tibet, but Nian downplayed the possibility for him to actually act, pointing to Lobdzan's turbulent relationship with other Mongol leaders in Kokonor.[7] However, the withdrawal of the main Qing forces from the northwestern frontier encouraged him. In July 1723, Lobdzan Dandzin started a revolt against the Qing, which soon drew many Mongol and Tibetan tribe leaders and Buddhist clerics in Kokonor to his side, including the prestigious Yellow Sect abbot at Kumbum. The Tibetans in Gyelthang, which had been under Khoshot Mongol control, rebelled too. Lobdzan also contacted Tsewang Rabdan to form an anti-Qing coalition, but the latter was not willing to get involved.[8]

Yongzheng had to confront this crisis in the midst of his uphill battle to guard his legitimacy. Resorting to diplomacy first, he sent a peace envoy to Kokonor in an attempt to persuade Lobdzan Dandzin to lay down arms. But Lobdzan had the envoy imprisoned. Then Yongzheng had no choice but to use force. He appointed Nian Gengyao the chief commander and Yue Zhongqi and a couple of others as Nian's staff members in October 1723.[9] Meanwhile, Yongzheng quickly ordered Zhou Ying, the regional commander of Songpan, Sichuan, to lead a thousand troops to go to Lhasa and to ensure to the Tibetan leaders the support of the Qing dynasty.[10] This step was obviously a remedy for Yongzheng's earlier decision to withdraw all Qing troops from Lhasa. In a few years Yongzheng would have to formally restore the military station in Tibet.

Having sealed all possible routes and passes from Kokonor to the heartland of China and Tibet, Nian Gengyao launched offensives to Kokonor in the early spring of 1724. Yue Zhongqi stormed Lobdzan's strongholds near Xining. After fierce fighting, the Qing forces captured the Xining area, leaving thousands of their enemies slaughtered. Lobdzan Dandzin retreated to the Tsaidam River valley. At this point Yue Zhongqi proposed launching a surprise attack on Tsaidam before the grass began sprouting. Impressed by Yue's courage, for it would be dangerous to march such a long distance without having sufficient grass to feed horses, Yongzheng endorsed his motion and granted Yue an ad hoc title as the chief commander. Yue led five thousand troops of crème de la crème caliber to pierce the Tsaidam River valley and annihilated the main force of Lobdzan within only two weeks. Lobdzan Dandzin, along with his wife, fled to Zungharia.[11] Having triumphed in this legendary expedition, Yue immediately engaged in a merciless crackdown on minor resistances by various Tibetan tribes in eastern Kokonor.[12] By the summer of 1724, Kokonor was firmly under Qing control, although the area had suffered extensive damage from the Qing military conquest.[13]

At the suggestion of Nian Gengyao, the Qing took advantage of its military victory to expand its jurisdiction into the region.[14] It reorganized the Mongol tribes in Kokonor into *zuoling* (company; "*niru*" in Manchu) and banner, following the models in southern Mongolia. All the Mongol dignitaries were required to go to Beijing every three years to pay tribute. To separate the Tibetans from the Mongols, the Qing ordered that the Tibetans only live south of the Yellow River. It also restored the system of local chieftains among the Tibetan tribes to further ensure the severing of their submission to the Khoshot Mongols. Later in 1725 the Qing established the Xining Bureau as Beijing's representative to rule the Kokonor area. Thereafter, Kokonor, which consisted of more than 278,000 square miles, was officially taken into the jurisdiction of the Qing dynasty, becoming known as Qinghai.[15] The Qing also took over the control of some Kham territories that had been under the Khoshot Mongols. Gyelthang, known in Chinese as Zhongdian, was thus placed under the jurisdiction of Yunnan province.[16]

Yongzheng was visibly lifted from his pessimistic mood by the swift and total victory in Qinghai. Not only did he feel confident about his hold on the throne—his survival of this severe challenge proved his competence—he was also convinced of the validity of Kangxi's active frontier strategy. It became clear to Yongzheng that the Qing empire could only rely on a military-backed diplomacy in dealing with its challengers at all the frontiers. Regretting his mistake in withdrawing troops from the northwestern frontier and Tibet, Yongzheng went to the length of forging the records to maintain his image as a hawk. In the officially published collection of Yongzheng's edicts, *Yongzheng zhupi yuzhi*, he replaced his original comments on a memorial by Cai Ting, the governor of Sichuan, in

1722, with a different passage. Although the original comments endorsed the withdrawal of garrison troops from Lhasa, the fabricated comments showcased a firm determination to continue Kangxi's frontier activism.[17] Most likely for the same purpose, a conversation between Kangxi and Yongzheng, then known as Heshi Prince, in 1715 was included in *Shengzu shilu*, or the "Veritable records of the Kangxi Emperor," which was compiled under Yongzheng's auspices. Unusual as it was to include a conversation between the emperor and his son in the "Veritable records," in this conversation Yongzheng expressed his firm support of Kangxi's plan to launch a military campaign against the Zunghar Mongols in Eastern Turkistan. This was but another example of Yongzheng's relish for a nonconformist persona in frontier politics.[18]

Only a couple of years after the dust in Qinghai had settled, a new emergency occurred in Tibet. For quite a while the four *kaloon* (councilors) who had been appointed in the wake of Kangxi's Tibetan invasion had been at odds. The three *kaloon* from the U area (Ngabo, Lumpa, and Jaranas) were in a bitter conflict with Khangchennas, who was from the Tsang area and was the leading *kaloon* among the four. Resenting the haughty Khangchennas, the three *kaloon* from the U area became a clique and had a closer relationship with the Zunghar Mongols and marital connections with Lobdzan Dandzin; they also made the father of the Seventh Dalai Lama their ally. In the beginning of 1727, Oci, the Qing envoy to Tibet, had already sensed danger and suggested the dismissal of two members of the U clique. But Yongzheng did not heed his words. Rather, he exhorted the four *kaloon* and the Dalai Lama to be harmonious to each other and sent two officials, Sengge and Mala, to Lhasa to bridle the two parties.[19]

In late 1725, Yue Zhongqi—who had just became the governor-general of Sichuan and Shaanxi and was more aggressive than his father, Yue Shenglong, when it came to territorial expansion—made a motion to the throne that would have serious repercussions in the Qing-Tibetan relationship: to formally annex the Kham territories west of Dartsedo into Sichuan province and the southwest part of Kham into Yunnan province, even though those places had been under the Qing military control since the first invasion of Tibet. Yongzheng endorsed Yue's proposal and notified the Dalai Lama of his decision to take those territories; at the same time Yongzheng "granted" the territories west of Chamdo to the Dalai Lama. In the following year, Oci, Bandi, and Zhou Ying were sent to survey and decide the border lines between Tibet and Sichuan as well as between Tibet and Yunnan. As a result, the size of Sichuan province was greatly enlarged. Being pushed about two hundred miles west, the new border line between Sichuan and Tibet thus lay between Bathang and Chamdo; the gateway from Sichuan to Tibet was thus moved from Dartsedo to Jiangka.[20] Dartsedo, thence better known by its Chinese name, Dajianlu, became a town in the middle of Sichuan province.[21]

Shortly after the annexation of Kham into Sichuan, which would give the Qing military a great edge in future operations in Tibet, Yue Zhongqi further urged the throne to endorse his plan of sending troops to Lhasa so that the Qing could have a firm hold of the Dalai Lama in the event of another Zunghar invasion. But Yongzheng did not think that it was necessary at that time.[22] The crisis occurred sooner than Yongzheng anticipated, however. On August 5, 1727 the U clique assassinated Khangchennas, precipitating Tibet into uncertainty again.[23] Yongzheng immediately ordered that the Qing armies in Shaanxi, Sichuan, and Yunnan be placed on alert and sent a Chinese general of Sichuan, Yan Qingru, to accompany the two court officials, Mala and Sengge, who had only reached Sichuan, to go to Lhasa and to monitor the situation there.[24] Yongzheng also let Yue Zhongqi go to Xi'an to prepare an expedition and then rush to Beijing for "some instructions in person" from the emperor.[25] Nevertheless, afraid that a Qing invasion would compel the three *kaloon* to flee to Zungharia and take the Dalai Lama with them, Yongzheng withheld the invasion to wait and see.[26] At this point the situation in Tibet took a dramatic turn. Another *kaloon* of Tsang, Pholhanas, launched an expedition from Shigatse against the three *kaloon* of U. After months of seesaw battles between the two sides, Pholhanas approached Lhasa.[27]

Although pleased by Pholhanas's moves—he had been considered pro-Qing among the Tibetan leaders—Yongzheng still came up with a decision of another invasion into Tibet, as he saw it as a good chance to reinforce the Qing influence in Lhasa that had been weakened with the withdrawal of the Qing armies from Tibet in 1723. Meanwhile, Yongzheng gave instructions to pass a message to Pholhanas, informing him that the Qing supported him.[28] In the early summer of 1728 the Qing armies set out for Lhasa under Jalangga, the plenipotentiary of Tibetan affairs, from three directions: Qinghai, Sichuan, and Yunnan. The armies on the Qinghai route consisted of more than eight thousand troops who had been deployed from Shaanxi, while the Sichuan route had four thousand and the Yunnan route three thousand. This time, only the Qinghai route had Manchu troops, and both the Sichuan and Yunnan routes consisted only of the Green Standard troops.[29] In late summer about sixty-five hundred

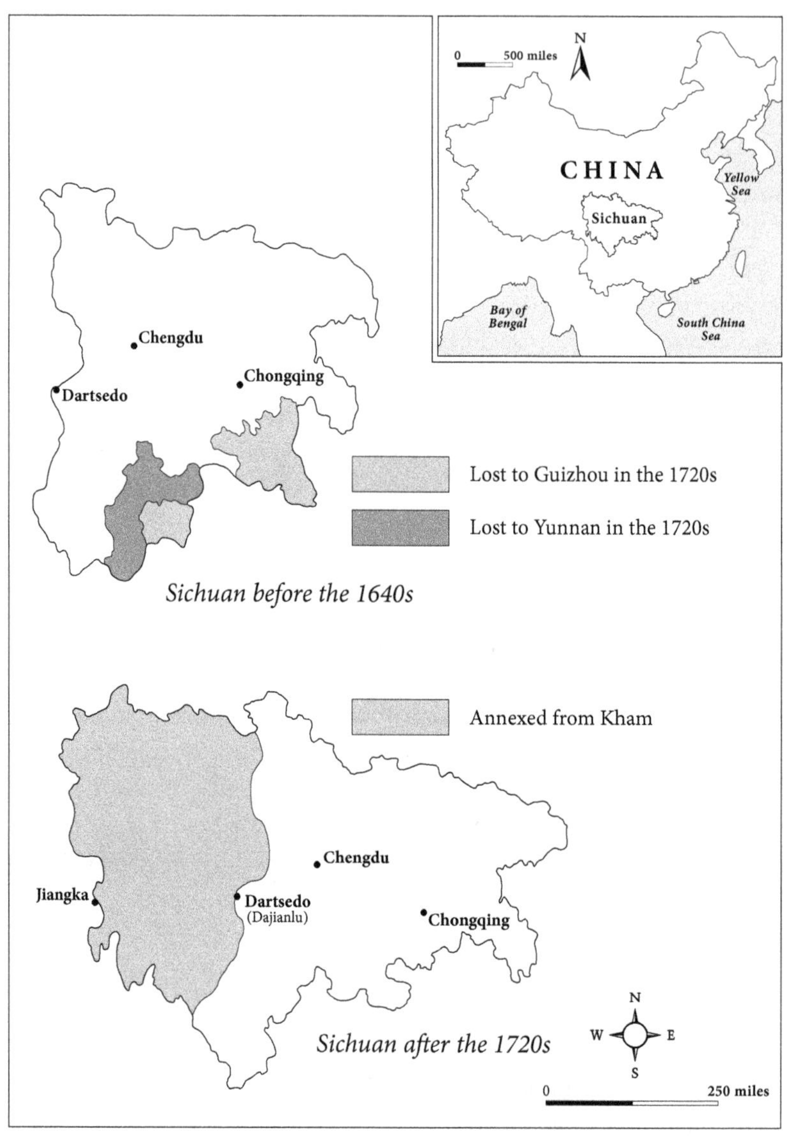

MAP 4.1. Sichuan before and after the 1720s

soldiers from all three routes arrived in Lhasa (the rest were left at strategic points along the routes to Lhasa). Shortly before the arrival of the Qing expedition, Pholhanas seized Lhasa and had the U clique arrested.[30]

In Lhasa the Qing military presided at the execution in public of the members of the U clique and their relatives and key followers. Yongzheng did not let the opportunity of revamping the Tibet political system slip through his fingers. He authorized to abolish the *kaloon* system and made Pholhanas the chief political leader in Tibet by entitling him "prince" (*beile* in Manchu).[31] To remedy his earlier mistake of withdrawing the Qing garrison, Yongzheng ordered the stationing of two grand minister residents of Tibet (*zhuZangdachen*) or *amban* (meaning "official" in Manchu) known to the Tibetans, as well as two thousand troops in Lhasa.[32] While Pholhanas had shown his loyalty to the Qing dynasty, Yongzheng still thought it was necessary to curb his power. He placed Tsang under the separate control of the Panchen Lama, which sowed the seeds of chronic grudges between the Dalai Lama and the Panchen Lama.[33]

Another significant outcome of Yongzheng's invasion of Tibet was the exile of the Seventh Dalai Lama. When Yongzheng first received the news of the riot in Lhasa, he suspected the Zunghar Mongols were behind this incident.[34] It turned out, however, that the Zunghar had not played any part. Yongzheng became concerned that the Dalai Lama would be an enticement for another Zunghar invasion. Thus he began entertaining the idea of moving the Dalai Lama out of Tibet. Initially he thought of Xining, deeming that "Tibet will be in peace forever if the Dalai Lama is moved to Xining."[35] This option was dropped, however. Yongzheng then invited the Dalai Lama to Beijing, which had been desired by both Kangxi and Yongzheng, since the Shunzhi emperor had met the Fifth Dalai Lama in Beijing in 1652. When Yongzheng extended his invitation, the Dalai Lama, declined it with the excuse that he was not immune to smallpox, a fatal disease that was rampant in the area.[36] It was finally decided to place the Dalai Lama in Lithang, his birthplace in Kham but now within the jurisdiction of Sichuan, for the time being, despite Pholhanas's strong plea not to take him away from Lhasa. The Seventh Dalai Lama was escorted to Lithang when the major Qing forces withdrew from Tibet at the end of 1728.[37] For the next six years he became a de facto hostage of the Qing dynasty. To safeguard the Dalai Lama's security, the Qing sent Ren Guorong, the regional commander of Chongqing, and two thousand soldiers to Lithang to guard his residence. Naige, the chief commander of the

Chengdu garrison, was also sent to Lithang to supervise the accommodation of the Dalai Lama and his equipage.[38]

For Yongzheng the results of the second invasion into Tibet, which put the pro-Qing Pholhanas in power, were encouraging. Also in June 1728 the Qing and Russia concluded another treaty, the Treaty of Kiakhta, which settled the protracted disputes between the two empires over trade, the borders (more specifically, the border between northern Mongolia and Russia), and other matters. Like Kangxi, who felt assured of Russian neutrality by the Treaty of Nerchinsk, Yongzheng was also relieved from the concern of possible Russian meddling in the Qing-Zunghar conflict.[39] He became less cautious in waging another war against the Zunghar than he was at the beginning of his reign. Meanwhile, there were some new and critical developments on the side of the Zunghar. In 1727, Tsewang Rabdan was murdered as the result of infighting.[40] A war scrambling for power ensued among his offspring until Galdan Tsereng, Tsewang's eldest son, crowned himself as the new leader of the Zunghar empire. No less fierce and strong-willed than his predecessors, Galdan Tsereng continued defying the Qing request to turn over the fugitive Lobdzan Dandzin, the perpetrator of the Qinghai revolt, rejected a peace proposal from Yongzheng, and initiated harassments against the Khalkha Mongols.

What was most alarming to Beijing was that Galdan Tsereng also had the ambition to control Tibet, making noises about going to Tibet for the *mangja* ceremony and sending two of Lajang Khan's sons back to Tibet. Despite the lukewarm support of his courtiers, Yongzheng raised a new war against the Zunghar in the spring of 1729, stressing that it was necessary for stability in Khalkha Mongolia, Tibet, and Qinghai. In his capacity as the governor-general of Sichuan and Shaanxi, Yue Zhongqi was made one of the chief commanders of this campaign. Contrary to the emperor's expectation, however, this war that lingered until his sudden death in 1735 was not successful. The Qing forces suffered great debacles and were not able to achieve much in the way of results.[41] As some historians have pointed out, the Yongzheng emperor's self-opinionated personality and his overreaching manner in monitoring military operations contributed much to the failure of his Zunghar campaign.[42] Although this war was waged in the far northwestern frontier, it impacted the Sichuan frontier and its neighbors in the southwest bloc, serving as a catalyst for some new perceptions and policies regarding the Sichuan frontier and the southwestern frontier.

A new development during the Yongzheng period was the ascending of the southwestern frontier, which mainly consisted of Yunnan and Guizhou provinces. What contributed to the southwest's rise was not the increase of its traditional economic contribution to the state—that is, land taxes, which remained low throughout the eighteenth century. Instead, it was the rich copper ores in Yunnan that gave the Qing state impetus to explore this remote area, as the country was faced with increasingly serious copper shortages.[43] At the same time Yongzheng's going back to frontier activism after the Qinghai campaign necessitated a more secured southwest. After all, part of the region was directly connected to Tibet.[44] Fragmented and isolated as they were, the ethnic communities in the far southwestern frontier still posed a threat to the Qing empire in the scenario that they would empower themselves by courting support from the Tibetans. This was not merely an unproved hypothesis. Historically, the Nanzhao kingdom in Yunnan had given the Tang dynasty much distress by allying itself with Tibet in its contention with the Tang.[45] Hence, it was imperative for Yongzheng to work on the southwestern frontier both for copper procurement and achieving stability. Reminiscent of Kangxi's sending his protégé Yue Shenglong to Sichuan twenty some years earlier, Yongzheng sent his protégé Ortai to the southwest early in his reign.

From the Manchu Bordered Blue Banner, Ortai did not fare well in his official career during the Kangxi period, only serving a minor position in the Imperial Household Department after he obtained a *juren* (a degree that was conferred upon one's passing the second level's [provincial] civil service examinations) degree. However, being Yongzheng's confidant helped him to climb up quickly on the bureaucratic ladder after the Yongzheng was enthroned. Ortai was first sent to Yunnan as deputy examination commissioner in 1723. But he did not stay long this time. In 1725 he was appointed the governor of Yunnan and was promoted the following year to the governor-general of Yunnan and Guizhou. Throughout his almost six-year stay in the southwestern frontier, Ortai kept functioning as a key adviser to Yongzheng through their more than frequent correspondence, and as a propagandist by bringing to Yongzheng's attention the so-called "auspicious omens" that appeared in his jurisdiction.[46] Noted by many historians, the intimate manner in which the two related to each other suggests an unusual relationship between them.[47] Sending Ortai to the southwestern frontier indubitably demonstrates Yongzheng's keen attention to this hitherto unimportant area. Soon after he took his post as the chief viceroy in the southwest, Ortai identified the most urgent issue in the area that needed to be dealt with: the autonomous local chieftains of ethnic peoples obstructing the Qing rule in the southwest, which confirmed Yongzheng's impression that the local chieftains in the southern provinces were still outside the Qing's political control.[48] Ortai convinced Yongzheng to embark on a sweeping *gaitu guiliu* (integrating local chieftains into the regular administrative system) campaign in the southwest, as well as parts of Sichuan, Guangxi, and Hunan, where native ethnic peoples lived.[49] Not necessarily more interested in assimilating ethnic peoples than the Kangxi emperor, Yongzheng was certainly more daring in taking action if it was deemed necessary.[50] Meanwhile, Ortai's burning desire for extraordinary achievements—not a surprise for a political upstart—also played a role in engineering this radical departure from Kangxi's laissez-faire policy toward the non-Han peoples in the southwestern frontier.[51]

For a few years Ortai orchestrated an unprecedented reform backed by military force to uproot many local chieftains' holds on their communities. The areas that were most affected were central Guizhou, where the Zhongjia people lived, and the border marches between southern Sichuan and northeastern Yunnan, where the Lolo people were dominant. The results of the campaign were mixed. On the one hand, the Qing empire greatly extended its administrative domain in the southwest. In the newly claimed areas, local chieftains were either removed or absorbed into the Qing bureaucracy, dozens of new official posts were added, thousands of soldiers were sent to new garrisons, granaries were installed, water projects launched, and schools set up. On the other hand, the landscape of the local communities was savagely sabotaged, and tens of thousands of ethnic peoples were slaughtered when they rose to resist the intrusion of the Qing imperial order. In response to the strenuous defiance of the native peoples, Ortai and his subordinates resorted to ferocious means. The atrocities committed by the Qing troops at this time were not even common during the Qing conquest of China a century earlier. Following the military campaigns, the ethnic communities' arable land became deserted, and food prices were hiked. To fill the vacuum left by the natives, the provincial government recruited farmers to reclaim the land, most of whom were presumably Han Chinese, and families of the Qing troops. A few years after Ortai's leaving in 1731, mounting tension in southeastern Guizhou culminated in a sizable revolt against the Qing. Feeling guilty,

Ortai requested to be demoted. He was only given some symbolic punishment, however. It did not help anything in Guizhou; the rebellion continued until the Qianlong era.[52]

In examining Ortai's rule, what has not attracted enough attention is that Ortai, taking advantage of his commandership of the *gaitu guiliu* campaign, tried to extend his authority into Sichuan, a province that was beyond his official jurisdiction. Without doubt, he had acquired royal sanction to function as a plenipotentiary to supervise a pan-southwestern region—namely, the four provinces in the southwest bloc, Guizhou, Guangxi, Sichuan, and Yunnan. In fact, Yongzheng added Guangxi to Ortai's jurisdiction by making him the governor-general of Yunnan, Guizhou, and Guangxi in 1728.[53] Uncommon as it was, Yongzheng apparently intended that Ortai wield his wand in this peripheral province that was also plagued with the problems of untamed ethnic peoples and the impotence of the provincial authorities. Upon receiving the mandate, Ortai did endeavor to strengthen the military buildup and tighten the control over the ethnic peoples in Guangxi. Yet for Sichuan, Yongzheng chose not to give Ortai any official title but encouraged him to intervene whenever it became necessary. Given that Yue Zhongqi was the ruler of the Sichuan frontier at this time—he was the newly appointed governor-general of Sichuan and Shaanxi—Ortai's coming to the southwestern frontier posed a challenge to Yue.

Yue's rise to prominence in the Sichuan frontier and beyond paralleled the downfall of Nian Gengyao in the wake of the Qinghai campaign. As Yongzheng's trusted consultant who had kept frequent and secret correspondence, mostly in Manchu, with Yongzheng ever since his appointment to Sichuan in 1709, Nian reached the pinnacle in his fame and influence after the triumphant Qinghai campaign.[54] Nevertheless, Nian apparently misunderstood his relationship with Yongzheng, not realizing that he should have changed his attitude after the latter became the emperor. Instead, Nian acted arrogantly toward his colleagues and excessively informally toward the emperor.[55] Beginning in early 1725, Yongzheng started undermining Nian's flamboyant position by criticizing his trivial mistakes. Within a year Nian was stripped of all power and banished to Hangzhou. He soon was ordered to commit suicide under the accusation of ninety-two crimes.[56] Nian's case shows clearly that Yongzheng would not allow anybody to take his own authority lightly, especially when this one was a powerful satrap governing two critical frontier areas.

Nian Gengyao's fall did not necessarily cause any policy change on either the northwestern or the Sichuan frontier. Rather, many measures that had been installed by Nian continued working long after his demise. To maintain a stable situation in the border areas and fill the vacuum left by Nian, Yongzheng turned to Yue Zhongqi, whose fame also surged due to his stunning bravery in the Qinghai campaign. For this reason Yue was not implicated in Nian's case, despite his long-term association with Nian. Instead, Yue was instrumental in purging Nian's clique in both Sichuan and the northwest. More important, every step by which Nian walked closer to his demise was accompanied by Yue Zhongqi's promotion: he was first appointed as the governor of Gansu, then to acting governor-general of Sichuan and Shaanxi at the same time when Nian was ordered to leave for Hangzhou. Three months later Yue's appointment became formal. Meanwhile, he was also showered with many honors.[57] By appointing Yue, whose domicile was then in Sichuan, as governor-general of Sichuan and Shaanxi, Yongzheng, like the Kangxi emperor, breached the law of avoidance too. It was the first case, perhaps the only case, in the entire history of the Qing dynasty, that a person was appointed governor-general in his own home province. Furthermore, the post of the governor-general of Sichuan and Shaanxi had been exclusively reserved for either a Manchu or Chinese bannerman starting in 1668 because of its strategic importance.[58] As a nonbannerman Chinese, Yue's appointment was exceptional.

Although Yongzheng maintained a facade of utmost trust in Yue after Nian's fall, the personnel arrangement in the southwest indicates that Yongzheng's wariness about Yue had long been present. One of the aims in Yongzheng's sending Ortai to the southwestern frontier was likely to counterbalance Yue's towering power. During the *gaitu guiliu* movement Ortai and Yue Zhongqi had cooperated in a few battles against the indigenous people who resisted such changes in the border areas between Sichuan, Yunnan, and Guizhou. Although their cooperation had been effective in military terms, there had been hints of discord between the two.[59] From time to time Ortai transgressed into Yue's jurisdiction, either sending troops into Sichuan fighting against the local chieftains or taking affairs in Sichuan to his own disposition. The most important development in this not-too-covert rivalry between Ortai and Yue Zhongqi was the transferring of the three prefectures in southeastern Sichuan to Yunnan and several other prefectures in the same area to Guizhou in 1726 and 1727.

The three prefectures Zhenxiong, Wumeng, and Dongchuan were located in the southeastern corner of Sichuan province and had been home to a number of non-Han peoples, among whom the Lolo people were most dominant. Its location at the conjunction of the three provinces, Sichuan, Yunnan, and Guizhou, made its administrative identity ever ambiguous. For many years after the Qing conquest, this area had only nominally belonged to Sichuan, but its de facto rulers were the local chieftains. Dongchuan, the southernmost one of the three prefectures did not come under Sichuan until 1699, when Yu Yangzhi, the governor of Sichuan, set up *junminfu*, meaning "office for soldiers and civilians" or "tribal office," in Dongchuan and installed a prefect and a thousand soldiers to the prefecture. It is worth noting that the thousand soldiers were transferred from garrisons nearby in all three provinces.[60] Because of their relative proximity to Kunming, the provincial capital of Yunnan, there had been discussion about placing these three prefectures in Yunnan instead of Sichuan, before Ortai's coming to the southwestern frontier.[61] At the time of Ortai's tenure there was a more pressing reason for Ortai to take grip of Dongchuan: it was extremely rich in copper ore. In 1726, Ortai pushed Yongzheng to endorse the transferring of Dongchuan prefecture from Sichuan to Yunnan. Yue Zhongqi was political enough not to voice his legitimate grudges against this decision.[62] Immediately after the annexation of Dongchuan, Ortai launched copper mining there. By the mid-eighteenth century, Dongchuan was the biggest copper producer in Yunnan, contributing 75 percent of the province's annual copper output.[63]

Soon after Yongzheng endorsed Yunnan's annexation of Dongchuan, Ortai turned his attention to Sichuan's Wumeng and Zhenxiong prefectures, which were located north of Dongchu, in the eastern bend of the Jinsha River.[64] From Ortai's perspective, taking Wumeng and Zhenxiong would give Yunnan an access to Yangzi River (the Jinsha River, of which most parts were not navigable at that time, became the Yangzi River at the northern border of Wumeng), which made great sense since the Yangzi waterway could take the Yunnan copper to other parts of the country. Without consulting Yue Zhongqi first, Ortai started to reform the local chieftain system in these two places. After having deprived the Lolo chieftain of Wumeng of his title, Ortai demanded that Yue send Sichuan officials to Wumeng to discuss the reform there. Nevertheless, before the officials arrived, Ortai had mounted a campaign to seize both Wumeng and Zhenxiong, taking the excuse that the Lolo people had a conflict with his troops.

When Yue Zhongqi arrived, after both prefectures had been occupied by Ortai's men, Ortai's subordinates blamed Yue for his delay in arriving and not helping in the action. Yongzheng did not criticize Ortai for his overt stepping into Yue's territories, although he had previously advised the latter to cooperate with Yue.[65] Instead, he praised Ortai's resolute action and quick victory. Realizing that he was not in a position to compete with Ortai, Yue proposed to give both Wumeng and Zhenxiong prefectures to Yunnan, which was readily accepted by Yongzheng and Ortai.[66] To mend the marred relationship between these two frontier strongmen and rivals, Yongzheng played a role of conciliator later that year, albeit in a manner clearly favorable for Ortai over Yue.[67] In 1728, Ortai acquired five counties and a subprefecture, including Zunyi, Tongzi, and Huairen (the future home of the Maotai liquor) in southeastern Sichuan to be transferred to Guizhou province.[68]

In the following years, Ortai drastically transformed the local government in Yunnan's three new prefectures, setting up new official positions and opening schools. To tap more revenues for the local government, he also promoted mining and agriculture. Nevertheless, the Lolo there had put up strenuous defiance against Qing imperialism. A large revolt erupted in the fall of 1730, involving not only the Lolo in the three prefectures, but also those across the entire intersecting area of Yunnan, Sichuan, and Guizhou. To suppress this big rebellion, Ortai summoned armies from all three provinces and mounted draconic attacks on the Lolo strongholds.[69] In the campaign the Qing troops inflicted indiscriminate slaughters and atrocities against the natives. According to numerous records in Ortai's memorials from this time, tens of thousands of people were slaughtered, including captives, women, and children; and thousands more were given to Qing soldiers as slaves. To leave a permanent warning to the local tribes, Ortai ordered that some captives' hands be cut off before they were released.[70] One time, at least, Ortai felt uncomfortable for the senseless massacres of the prisoners of war, women, and children, calling it "excessive" and saying that he felt "deeply sorry."[71]

The degree of intensity in suppressing the Lolo insurrection in 1730 and 1731 showcased that this campaign was a critical link in Ortai's vision of a frontier that embraced the region's three provinces. In this campaign, when the Qing troops captured Daguan—a strategic point located on the borders astride Sichuan, Yunnan, and Guizhou—Ortai emphatically pointed out that "now that Daguan was conquered, the artery that connects to the three provinces is running its course."[72] Clearly, he considered it an important matter to build physical connections between the provinces. There is little doubt that Ortai's governance in the southwest had posted a threat to the Sichuan frontier in political terms, since Sichuan was left no powerful figure to compete with Ortai after Yue Zhongqi had been sent to the northwestern front to lead the Zunghar campaign in 1729. By the end of 1730 it seemed that Ortai had assumed a pretension that he would eventually take over the Sichuan frontier, becoming an overlord in the pan-southwestern area.

Nevertheless, Yongzheng would soon need Ortai back at the capital. In the early summer of 1730, Yongzheng was stricken with a personal loss: Yinxiang, his brother and right-hand man, died of illness. Yongzheng himself suffered from health problems for a period of time following Yinxiang's death. Leaning more on Ortai, the lonely emperor considered calling Ortai back from the southwest sooner. He discussed the arrangement for the southwestern frontier and Sichuan with Ortai right after Yinxiang's death: "You may bestir yourself in managing the affairs in the three provinces for another couple of years. If there is nobody among all officials, both Manchu and Chinese, civil and military, who is competent enough to replace you as the governor-general of the three provinces—perhaps only Gao Qizhuo is good-natured [enough for that position], but he is short in ability, plus I intend to use him in nearby provinces, I'm considering either grouping Yunnan and Guangxi together under one governor-general, and placing Sichuan and Guizhou under another governor-general, or grouping Yunnan and Sichuan together under one governor-general, and Guizhou and Guangxi together under another one. Please carefully consider and plan for me on how to divide [the four provinces] in administrative terms."[73] This was an important documentation of Yongzheng's strategic planning for these four provinces. Evidently, for Yongzheng the four provinces stood as one strategic bloc over which Ortai was the de facto supreme authority. In fact, the two options Yongzheng envisaged for the area—either to group Sichuan with Yunnan or with Guizhou—further substantiate the assertion that Yongzheng had the intention of stripping Yue Zhongqi of his jurisdiction and power base, Sichuan province, which also underlined his decision to separate the governorship-general of the northwestern frontier and that of Sichuan, which is discussed further below.

It seems that Ortai was not enthusiastic about the idea of regrouping the four provinces, however. Instead, he made suggestions in the direction of reshuffling the personnel at the provincial level. There was extensive discussion on the matter between the emperor and Ortai after Yongzheng's instruction. As a result, a number of promising Manchu civil officials and Chinese bannermen, quite a few of whom had a special relationship with

Ortai, were promoted in or appointed to the southwestern frontier. Meanwhile, Ortai had hand-picked officials to staff all levels of bureaucracies in Yunnan and Guizhou.[74] In fact, Ortai had long paid attention to the personnel matter in the southwest, recommending his protégés to the key positions in the two provinces, among whom were Zhang Guangsi (the governor of Guizhou), Ha Yuansheng (the provincial military commander of Guizhou), and Zhang Yunsui (the governor of Yunnan). When Ortai left the southwest in late 1731, his successor was Gao Qizhuo, an established Chinese viceroy who had served in Yunnan before and was in the important position of governor-general of Jiangnan at the time of his appointment. But in only two years Gao was replaced by Yinjishan, a Manchu upstart who was only in his thirties and was married to one of Ortai's nieces.[75] It might be the case that Gao, a quintessential man of letters, was not quite at home directing the military campaign against the Miao revolt in Guizhou. Overall, Yongzheng must have been satisfied with the personnel buildup in the southwest, even without Ortai's presence. Nevertheless, nobody in the southwest after Ortai had either the pretension or the emperor's trust to extend his influence into the Sichuan frontier. Yongzheng had to plan differently for Sichuan.

THE DEMARCATION OF THE SICHUAN AND NORTHWESTERN FRONTIERS

Given that Yongzheng never went back to his fleeting inclination of regrouping Sichuan, Yunnan, Guizhou, and Guangxi into two governors-general's areas, it could be assumed that he soon changed his mind, with or without Ortai's input. Although Ortai had boosted the position of the southwest and created a pressing situation to overtake Sichuan, his leaving marked the end of the experiment of merging Sichuan into the southwestern sphere. With the war against the Zunghar Mongols in the far northwestern frontier not going well, Yongzheng was more concerned with Sichuan, the key strategic area whose responsibility to secure the stability in Tibet outweighed all other considerations. In the spring of 1731, shortly before he called Ortai back from the southwest, Yongzheng made a seminal decision to split the position of governor-general of Sichuan and Shaanxi into two positions, which was tantamount to a demarcation of the Sichuan frontier and the northwestern frontier. The northwest refers to Shaanxi and Gansu provinces, including Ningxia (Ningxia was part of Gansu province during the Qing), an area that traditionally had served both as a buffer to protect Beijing and as a base area for expeditions to China's northern and northwestern borderlands. From the time of the founding of the Qing dynasty, the northwestern frontier had been a key strategic area par excellence. Shaanxi province was among the first to be conquered and consolidated in the prolonged Manchu conquest. After the Wu Sangui Rebellion started, the Qing state was again most concerned with the security of Shaanxi and tried to keep a firm hold of it at all costs. Compared with the northwestern front, Sichuan had never obtained such a position in history. Instead, it was sometimes treated as an appendage to the northwest. During the Yuan dynasty, for example, there were a number of times when Shaanxi and Sichuan were combined into one province and then separated.[76]

With the onset of the Tibet question at the end of the seventeenth century, Sichuan began undergoing a radical transition in its strategic position. Between Yue Shenglong's coming to Sichuan in 1696 and the Zunghar invasion of Tibet in 1717, tangible endeavors were made to strengthen political control over this new frontier and to increase the military buildup there so that it could back up the Qing diplomacy with Tibet. The Zunghar invasion of Tibet prompted the Qing to the realization that it was not sufficient only to array military forces along the Tibetan border, but it was also necessary to be able to render direct military intervention into Tibet proper, given the ever-present Zunghar ambition over the Yellow Sect church. The most significant move in this direction was the establishment of the banner garrison in Chengdu in 1718. Meanwhile, there was a short-lived separation of the position of governor-general of Sichuan and that of Shaanxi in 1718 to give Nian Gengyao more power in helping direct the invasion into Tibet. But this separation ended with the conclusion of the Tibetan campaign in 1720, and Nian became governor-general of Sichuan and Shaanxi in 1721. From the Qing perspective it was apparent that Sichuan was not yet a full-fledged frontier, unable to undertake frontier responsibilities independently without military and financial assistance from Shaanxi.

More important, the Qing central authorities had been convinced that the Zunghar and Tibetan affairs were intricately intertwined. Yongzheng clearly stated this point along with its gravity: "The Tibetan and the Zunghar affairs, which cannot be reduced to a parallel to the affairs concerning the remote countries such as Vietnam and Russia, were closely watched by all the Mongol tribes, including the forty-eight Mongol banners, the Mongols in the Qinghai area, and the Khalkha Mongols. As long as the

Zunghar problem is not resolved, the arrangements for Tibet can not be settled; if there is no appropriate disposition made for Tibet, the Mongol tribes would have mistrust and doubts. The two problems, that of Zunghar and that of Tibet, are real threats to our country. The destiny of our imperial house and our people is tied to them."[77] Thus the two affairs needed to be handled in a concerted manner, given their comparable importance and innate interrelationship. This understanding would have been a pivotal justification for the continuing placing of Shaanxi and Sichuan, the two strategic areas that bore the responsibilities of Zunghar and Tibetan affairs, under one governor-general, besides practical considerations.

In 1726, Yongzheng briefly separated the position into two—that of Sichuan and that of Shaanxi—and let Yue Zhongqi take the position of governor-general of Sichuan. But he changed it back shortly within the year. So Yue Zhongqi retook the post of governor-general of Sichuan and Shaanxi. Moreover, Yongzheng ordered Yue to act as the governor of Xi'an a couple of months later.[78] This kind of whimsical disposition was not uncommon for Yongzheng. Given that this happened in the immediate wake of Nian Gengyao's death, it might be a reflection of Yongzheng's weighing the pros and cons of letting Yue Zhongqi fill Nian's gap, rather than as a result of his recognition of the necessity of separating the two strategic areas. The situation changed once Yongzheng's war against the Zunghar Mongols started. The entire province of Sichuan was under pressure to heighten security; secret agents were sent to the border areas, such as Songpan, to spy on the non-Han peoples for possible connections with the Zunghar. In addition, the provincial officials asked time and time again to expand the size of the Green Standard Army.[79] In the beginning of the war, Sichuan provided both military forces and matériel to the Qing field armies in Eastern Turkistan. Meanwhile, it shouldered the heavy duties of supporting the Qing garrisons in Tibet and the newly annexed Kham area in western Sichuan. More particularly, the Dalai Lama's exile in western Sichuan considerably compounded Sichuan's responsibilities. Not only did the Dalai Lama's residency in Lithang strain Sichuan's military capacity, it also exhausted the province financially because of the prodigious expenses of the religious and diplomatic rituals that the Dalai Lama performed.

The Dalai Lama could have returned to Lhasa in 1729, for the pro-Qing Pholhanas had solidified his power in Lhasa and maintained a reasonably smooth relationship with the Qing. Meanwhile, the Qing state exercised more influence over Tibet through the *amban* and sizable troops stationed in Lhasa. Nevertheless, the advent of the war in Zungharia shattered the brief peace in Lhasa. In the fall of 1731, Galdan Tsereng, after a successful attack on the Qing northern route army, claimed that he was to send five thousand Zunghar soldiers to escort Surya, Lajang Khan's son who had been captured when Tsering Dondup invaded Tibet in 1717, to Tibet and to enthrone him as the king of Tibet. No matter whether this was a real plan or merely political blackmail, both Pholhanas and Yongzheng were alarmed at the reminiscences of Tsewang Rabdan's claim in 1717 that he would send another of Lajang Khan's sons, the son-in-law of Tsewang, back to Tibet, which presaged Tsering Dondup's invasion of Tibet. Having firmly refuted the Zunghar challenge, Yongzheng immediately ordered the Qing troops in Tibet to be on guard and hurried a thousand soldiers stationed in Chamdo to Lhasa.[80] Later in the year, at Pholhanas's request, the Qing granted Pholhanas a seal that read: "*Duoluo beile* who administers the affairs of the *kaloon* in Nearer Tibet and Further Tibet."[81] Amounting to the entitlement of Pholhanas as the king of Tibet, this measure was intended to foil the Zunghar scheme to place Lajang's son as the new king of Tibet.

This interlude prolonged the Dalai Lama's exile in Sichuan. More precisely, it gave the Qing a good pretext to keep him. At this time a new monastery named Huiyuan by Yongzheng, which means "to benefit the remoteness," had been completed in Kata (Gada in Chinese transliteration), west of Dartsedo. Having cost the Qing hundreds of thousands of taels of silver, the stately new monastery was an emulation of a famous Yellow Sect monastery in Tibet. In late 1731 the Seventh Dalai Lama was moved to this new monastery, upon which Yongzheng changed the place name from Kata to Taining, meaning "peace and tranquility," attempting to keep the Dalai Lama there permanently.[82] The Huiyuan monastery was allegedly grand in scale; the main building had more than a thousand rooms and the annex had four hundred single-storied rooms. But the Dalai Lama complained during his stay that it was poorly constructed, the facilities being simple and supplies being scant and many rooms leaking, which should be taken as another proof to the long-standing tradition in Sichuan for local officials to misappropriate funds earmarked for frontier affairs.[83] What the Dalai Lama did not lack at the monastery, however, was the assurance of his security, as he had five hundred Qing soldiers living with him in Taining. Presumably some of those single-storied rooms were used as barracks for those troops. Outside of Taining, several checkpoints were set up and staffed by more troops. Altogether, eighteen hundred troops were arranged in the Taining area. In addition, a number of new officer's positions were created to head those checkpoints.[84]

Although Yongzheng still adhered to the conviction that the Tibet question was central to the Zunghar problem and stability in Mongolia, the prospect of the Zunghar campaign turning into a protracted one and the multiplication of the Tibetan responsibilities forced him to consider freeing the northwestern frontier from the tasks related to Tibet and designating Sichuan to take on Tibetan affairs exclusively. In March 1731, Yongzheng ruled that Shaanxi's military forces no longer had the responsibility to send soldiers to Tibet, and that Sichuan alone would supply and rotate two thousand troops to the garrison in Lhasa. Meanwhile, Sichuan was also discharged from the duty of supplying personnel to the Zunghar campaign.[85] After the Qing forces suffered a fiasco at Khobdo in the Zunghar campaign in the summer of 1731, Yongzheng ordered two thousand troops from the Songpan garrison in northern Sichuan to be sent to Xining to reinforce the defense in Qinghai.[86] Other than that, the military in Sichuan became exclusively focused on Tibet.

The separation of the military responsibilities for Shaanxi and Sichuan paved the way for an administrative demarcation between the traditionally important northwestern frontier and the new Sichuan frontier. On April 5, 1731, Yongzheng ordered the formal separation of the governorship-general of Shaanxi and Sichuan into two positions: "The territory of Sichuan and Shaanxi extends thousands of *li*, really an enormous region. Now there are the logistical affairs [for the war] in the west. It was difficult for one governor-general to handle [both provinces]. There had been a governor-general of Sichuan installed before. Now [I order to] add again a governor-general of Sichuan."[87] In the same edict Yongzheng appointed Huang Tinggui, a Chinese bannerman who was holding the position of provincial military commander of Sichuan, as the new governor-general of Sichuan. Yongzheng also appointed Ji Chengbin as the provincial military commander. But Huang was ordered to continue taking charge of the duties of the military commander, as Ji was retained at the Zunghar front for the time being. Yue Zhongqi, who had been the governor-general of Sichuan and Shaanxi since Nian Gengyao's removal, became only the governor-general of Shaanxi. Meanwhile, the post of governor of Sichuan, the highest civil position in Sichuan, was kept. About half a year after the edict was issued, Yongzheng restated his reason for separating Shaanxi and Sichuan on another occasion: "Considering that the territory of Sichuan is so enormous, and the military and civilians are mixed-up with the Tibetans and the Miaos, in particular, there being military affairs going on in the western border areas [of Sichuan], one governor-general of Shaanxi [would find it] difficult to control. Therefore, the governor-general of Sichuan was installed for these reasons."[88]

It is important to tally these two edicts to get a complete picture of the demarcation. In the first one Yongzheng stressed the ongoing Zunghar war in Eastern Turkistan. But in the second one he gave more weight to the Tibetan affairs that fell mainly on Sichuan, while repeating the fact of territorial size. The "military affairs going on in the western border areas" must refer to the installation of military outposts in the newly annexed Kham area and allude to the residence of the Dalai Lama in Lithang (even though he did not mention it directly) and the campaign in the Wumeng area to suppress the Lolo revolt. Although Sichuan did not play a major role in that operation, it gave the provincial officials enough excuse to cry for more funds, given that it had military operations in several fronts at the same time.[89] The fact that Yongzheng stated his reasoning twice within a few months in a complementary manner indicates that he had given careful consideration to this decision and come to a realization of the eventuality of the separation in administrative terms of the Zunghar and Tibetan affairs. Indeed, the 1731 decision differed from the previous brief separations of the governors-general of Shaanxi and Sichuan, when it had been temporary in nature. As in the cases of the campaign against Wu Sangui and the first Tibetan invasion in the late Kangxi period, the chief consideration for the separation of the two governors-general was to give one of them more latitude in directing military operations. Once the military actions ended, however, the grounds for the separation dissolved. Although the Zunghar campaign was still a temporary factor, the mounting tasks of the Tibetan garrison and the protection of the Dalai Lama seemed to Yongzheng, in 1731, more permanent issues. Therefore, this separation was meant as a strategic decision, tantamount to another milestone in the building of the Sichuan frontier.

There was yet another factor that underlay Yongzheng's decision: his changed attitude toward Yue Zhongqi. By the end of the 1720s Yue had risen to a status comparable to that possessed by Nian Gengyao shortly before his fall. Not coincidentally, some of Yue's kin had also been granted imperial favors during these years. In 1727, Yue Zhongqi's eldest son, Yue Jun, was appointed the governor of Shandong, becoming the youngest governor in the entire country. In 1728, Yue Chaolong, Yue Shenglong's elder brother and Zhongqi's uncle, was named acting provincial military commander of Huguang.[90] Two years later, Yue Zhonghuang, Chaolong's son and Zhongqi's cousin, was appointed junior guardsman (*lanling shiwei*) and was given the honor of accompanying the crown prince, the future Qianlong emperor, in his studies of Confucian classics and martial skills.[91] Thus the Yue family had exercised influence in a number of provinces in addition to Sichuan.

In 1728, Zeng Jing, an anti-Qing scholar, chose Yue Zhongqi as the agent for his anti-Qing cause, but Yue immediately reported Zeng's plot to the throne, thus precipitating one of the most serious political persecution cases in Qing times, in which many were either killed or imprisoned.[92] Unlike other political persecutions, which typically only involved literary expressions, this case was complicated by an attempt to instigate an insurrection and court a Qing provincial leader to side with the plotters. The choice of Yue Zhongqi by Zeng Jing was not without a reason; Yue was considered the most powerful Chinese regional leader after Wu Sangui. Meanwhile, a rumor circulating in society at that time made Yue even more attractive to those Chinese nationalists: Yue was the descendant of Yue Fei, a Chinese hero who had fought relentlessly against the Jurchens, the ancestors of the Manchus, in the twelfth century. Although Yongzheng assured Yue after this incident that he did not have any doubt about Yue's loyalty to the Qing, Yue met his own downfall a few years later during the Zunghar campaign, of which he was one of the chief commanders.

Before the war Yue was one of few high officials who supported this risky war.[93] His optimism had apparently pleased Yongzheng in the initial stages of the war. However, after the Qing forces suffered a setback in the summer of 1730, in which the Qing expedition lost most livestock, the emperor became increasingly bitter and suspicious toward Yue. Meanwhile, Yue became more conservative in his tactics and more cautious in his behavior. In the spring of 1731, Yue proposed a sixteen-point plan of setting up a garrison and military colony in the area of Turfan, but it was dismissed by Yongzheng as "none of them [were considered] valuable."[94] Meanwhile a Manchu general, Yilibu, was appointed the deputy commander-in-chief of the western route, whose main task was to oversee Yue's actions.[95] Knowing that he was no longer trusted, Yue Zhongqi was not in a position to take any active initiative. He had retreated to a defensive strategy and was more concerned with proving his loyalty. His last suggestion was to build a garrison and military colony in Mulei, a place about ninety miles to the east of Urumqi. Yue insisted that the digging-in at Mulei was the only way to check the Zunghar eastward expansion.[96] Although Yongzheng approved Yue's Mulei plan reluctantly, he was determined to remove Yue from the commandership. In 1732, Yongzheng sent Zhang Guangsi, the governor of Guizhou, to be Yue's deputy. A few months later he sent Ortai to the northwestern front to oversee the campaign and ordered Yue Zhongqi back to the capital with his commandership removed. Yue was shortly arrested under many accusations—most of them related to his personality and character.[97] After a trial Yue was sentenced to death, which was later changed to "imprisonment awaiting execution." For Yongzheng, a Chinese general reminiscent of Wu Sangui could not be allowed to hold his powerful position for too long.

The separation of the governorships-general of Sichuan and Shaanxi in 1731 came shortly after Yue's sixteen-point proposal was rebutted, which suggests the link between this administrative change and Yue's fate: it would serve as a forceful step to undermine Yue Zhongqi's influence as it deprived Yue of his governorship over Sichuan, his own domicile and power base. Huang Tinggui's taking the governorship-general of Sichuan also shows that Yongzheng no longer wished to join Sichuan with either province of the southwest: no southwestern provincial official after Ortai merited the hefty responsibility of taking Sichuan, especially since neither Gao Qizhuo nor Yinjishan was more experienced than Huang Tinggui in the affairs of Sichuan. Before Huang was appointed Sichuan's provincial military commander in 1727, there had been five turnovers in the position within a three-year period. But Huang stayed. He also won Yongzheng's praise for his tough position in suppressing non-Han peoples.[98] Not only did Huang become the paramount administrative authority in Sichuan, he continued holding the position of the provincial military commander, as the two successive appointees, both of whom were Yue Zhongqi's protégés, did not come back from the Zunghar campaign to take the position.[99]

Yue Zhongqi lost imperial favor in the middle of 1731, although there was no tangible purge of his family members and his protégés. Yongzheng signaled his intention of revamping the personnel buildup in Sichuan, calling for Sichuan's neighboring provinces to select able military officials and send them to Huang Tinggui for appointments, as there was a dearth of talented generals in Sichuan, according to Yongzheng.[100] This was an obvious fallacy, as it was no secret that many of Yue's subordinates were experienced officers. It is difficult to ascertain how many military officials had been recommended to Sichuan by other provinces. But there are indeed records in the archives that indicate that Ortai responded to the emperor's call and sent some officers from his jurisdiction to Sichuan, who were understandably promoted quickly in Sichuan.[101]

In early 1733, Yongzheng named Ortai's nephew, Echang, as the governor of Sichuan. But Echang proved a disappointment and was dismissed only one year later.[102] Suffice it to say that with Ortai's leaving the southwestern frontier in 1731, no one was capable of ruling both the southwest and Sichuan. Ortai's overlordship in the pan-southwestern region proved to be ephemeral. At last, Yongzheng had to accept the realities in the northwestern, Sichuan, and southwestern frontiers (Guangxi had been placed under the jurisdiction of the governor-general of Guangdong after Ortai left); namely, they became independent and were ruled by different viceroys, none of whom had the prerogative to supersede the other's jurisdiction. It made sense for a monarch who was always on the alert against the expansion of power of his viceroys, as smaller jurisdictions for those regional leaders would serve the central government better.

5 THE SHAPING OF INDEPENDENCE IN THE QIANLONG PERIOD, 1736–1795

Tibet is the place that my grandfather and father had repeatedly used force to pacify. There is no way [for us] to abandon it because of the harassment of those petty devils [the Gurkhas]. If we give away Tibet without a fight, where do we place the Dalai Lama, the Panchen Erdeni, and their people? [This option] is senseless. —THE QIANLONG EMPEROR, 1791

ON 8 OCTOBER 1735 THE YONGZHENG EMPEROR DIED SUDDENLY AT the age of fifty-six. His fourth son, Hongli, was enthroned as had been arranged by Yongzheng, adopting Qianlong as his reign name. The Qianlong emperor inherited from his father an enlarged empire and two ongoing wars: a northwestern war against the Zunghar people and a southwestern one suppressing a fierce Miao uprising in Guizhou. Although negotiations with the Zunghar had started in 1734, the Miao uprising was in full swing when Yongzheng died. Just as Yongzheng had come to power with his own agendas, the Qianlong emperor also envisaged recasting the course of the Qing empire.[1]

Among other things, he had to make a choice about whether to continue his father's set course or make a turn to assume a low-key stance in frontier affairs. What he chose at the start of his reign was the latter. He abolished in December 1735 the Grand Council, the very legacy of Yongzheng frontier activism.[2] While urging the commanders in charge of suppressing the Miao in Guizhou to speed up the operation, he set to work to conclude the fruitless Zunghar campaign. In only two years he had settled both wars. The Miao uprising was put down in 1736 after the able Zhang Guangsi was appointed chief commander.

Meanwhile, the sweeping reform to incorporate the local chieftains' territories into the Qing empire was slowed down, as the new emperor held a more conservative position on the matter.[3] In 1737 negotiations with the Zunghar Mongols were satisfactorily concluded, and the Zunghar again conformed with the terms of being a tributary to the Qing. Along the corridor of the Yellow River hundreds of thousands of Qing troops were returning home from the seven-year-long exhausting campaign. In a word, the atmosphere in the beginning of Qianlong's reign pointed to peace. Apparently, he wanted to focus on some increasingly urgent domestic issues, such as the mounting grain prices, which had not been possible with the protracted Zunghar war and the *gaitu guiliu* campaign draining the empire's resources. Nevertheless, the peace orientation did not last long. Starting from the second decade of his reign, Qianlong returned to frontier activism that both the Kangxi and Yongzheng emperors championed. Waging more frontier wars than his predecessors, Qianlong made his reign the most violent one in the Qing period to date, although he also hoped to be remembered as a grand patron for cultural life.

A PEACEFUL INTERLUDE, 1735–1745

Although Qianlong showed a strong inclination to tone down frontier activism, he was prudent when it came to the delicate issue of the military station in Tibet. When his father, Yongzheng, had first became emperor, he withdrew the Qing garrison in Lhasa, restoring it after the Tibetan civil war of 1727 and1728. Once his war on the Zunghar started, Yongzheng sent a few more *amban* to Lhasa. However, in 1733, at Pholhanas's request, the Qing withdrew fifteen hundred soldiers from Lhasa, leaving there only five hundred troops.[4] In the fall of 1734, Yongzheng decided to send the Seventh Dalai Lama back to Lhasa, as the tension on the Zunghar front was abating. Yinli, Yongzheng's younger brother, went to Taining and escorted the Dalai Lama back after his six-year exile. At the same time the Qing outposts along the route from Dartsedo to Lhasa were taken over by the native soldiers of the local chieftains; the Qing soldiers were sent back to their original garrisons.[5]

By any measure, the end of the Yongzheng reign witnessed a tangible alleviation of the Qing's concerns about the Zunghar threat toward Tibet. The new Qianlong administration was thus faced with a reassessment of its Tibetan policy. In April 1736 the members of the Deliberative Council, a consultant body to the emperor to which the power was restored upon the abolition of the Grand Council, proposed the withdrawal of the Qing plenipotentiaries who had been sent during the Zunghar war to such strategic locations as Guihua, Hami, Lhasa, and Xining. In the case of Lhasa, they held that the *amban* and the Qing military station in Lhasa had been temporary in nature and that it was no longer necessary to continue them, given that the Dalai Lama had returned. But they tried to be cautious; they suggested waiting for a report from Hangyilu, a Qing envoy who was heading to Tibet to assess the situation.[6]

In late 1736, Hangyilu sent in his report. As was expected, he recommended withdrawing all thirteen hundred or so Qing troops from Lhasa and other places in Tibet. He suggested sending Mongol envoys to Tibet as liaison to the Tibetans. But Qianlong disagreed with this recommendation. He argued that it was the Tibetan leaders, such as Pholhanas, who considered the continuous Qing military presence in Tibet "beneficial" and that the economic burden on the Tibetans should not be a problem, since the garrison only had several hundred troops. Hence he decided to wait a couple of years to see whether a final withdrawal was necessary.[7] It was simply not true that the Tibetans were not burdened by the Qing military station in Lhasa. Even the staunchly pro-Qing Pholhanas thought it was better for the Qing troops to leave, according to Pholhanas's biographer and a close follower of his.[8] Obviously, Qianlong clearly knew how crucial stability in Tibet was for the success of the Qing overall frontier strategy. It would be too risky to completely release the hold on Tibet for which the previous Qing emperors, Kangxi and Yongzheng, had paid so dear a price. Therefore, even in the appeasement climate of the early Qianlong reign, the essential part of the Tibetan policy set by previous emperors was kept intact. Instead, Qianlong reduced the size of the military stationed in Tibet and reduced the number of *amban* in Lhasa to one person.[9] A couple of years later, Qianlong granted Pholhanas the title of prince (*junwang*), higher than the title granted by Yongzheng—*beile*, which confirmed Pholhanas's position as the ruler of Tibet and served again to discourage the Zunghar in attempting to claim Tibet.[10]

Qianlong did not hesitate to redefine other aspects of the Yongzheng legacy, however. In early 1736 he abolished the post of the governorship-general of Sichuan one more time and restored the governorship-general of Sichuan and Shaanxi. According to the convention, he reasoned, there had been only one governor-general for the two provinces of Sichuan and Shaanxi. A separate governor-general of Sichuan had been installed because military operations were carried out on the western frontier then, and there were logistical affairs to be dealt with. Now that the expedition had been withdrawn, and the military affairs were to be completed, Qianlong pushed to follow the conventional system by reinstating the governorship-general of Sichuan and Shaanxi and abolishing the post of the governor-general of Sichuan.[11]

As Qianlong saw it, the two governors-general were merely a wartime expedient. Since the war on the Zunghar had been brought to an end, it was no longer necessary to keep two positions for the three provinces (Sichuan, Shaanxi, and Gansu), even though their total size was the biggest among all governors-general's jurisdictions in the empire. The territory of Sichuan had been greatly enlarged as a result of the annexation of Tibet's Kham in the 1720s. Arguably, this disposition downplayed the strategic role of the Sichuan frontier in checking Tibet. Residing in Xi'an, the governor-general was far from Tibet and thus incapable of reacting swiftly to emergencies there. If the separation of the governorship-general of Sichuan and that of Shaanxi in the Yongzheng period exemplified the escalating magnitude of Tibetan affairs, the inexperienced Qianlong readily dismissed the issue as a temporary measure when he was so preoccupied with the new orientation of peace.

As Qianlong might have foreseen, the remerging of the two positions would create troubled times. Having readily enjoyed, since 1731, much independence from the northwestern frontier in addition to the prerogatives usually associated with the locality of a governor-general, provincial officials in Sichuan obviously resented being subordinated again to the reinstated governor-general of Sichuan and Shaanxi. Chengdu's losing its status of being the residence city of a governor-general hinted at a degree of marginalization of Sichuan province, as many might have read. Plus, there were personal grudges. Being demoted to Sichuan's provincial military commander by the same edict that abolished his post of governor-general of Sichuan, Huang Tinggui must have found his demotion hard to take and was thus at odds with both Jalangga, the new governor-general of Sichuan and Shaanxi, and Yang Bi, the governor of Sichuan who was formerly under Huang. Before long Qianlong transferred Huang to the capital and gave him a ceremonial post there.[12] Huang's leaving did not solve the problem, however. Between then and 1743, Qianlong found himself in a situation of serving as a mediator between the governor-general in Xi'an and the governor of Sichuan in Chengdu. When the conflict between them could not be solved, more personnel changes had to be made. Within a few years Qianlong changed the governor-general of Sichuan and Shaanxi three times and the governor of Sichuan four times. Most of them stayed in their position no longer than three years. During this period achieving a good working relationship between the two viceroys was one of their tasks.[13]

TABLE 5.1 PROVINCE RULERS 1736–1749

Governor-general of Sichuan and Shaanxi	*Governor of Sichuan*
Jalangga (1736–1738)	Yang Bi (1736–1737)
Emida (1738–1740)	Shuose (1736–1739)
Yinjishan (1740–1743)	Fang Xian (1739–1740)
Qingfu (1743–1747)	Shuose (1740–1743)
	Jishan (1743–1749)

In 1743, Qianlong replaced both positions with new appointees: he sent Qingfu as the governor-general of Sichuan and Shaanxi, and Jishan as the governor of Sichuan. Following their arrivals, the strained relationship between Xi'an and Chengdu began to be improved after years of imperial maneuvers. Qingfu could finally exercise his jurisdiction in Sichuan in his capacity as the governor-general. Looking back, the high rate of turnovers for both these positions in the first decade of the Qianlong reign was unusual. As R. Kent Guy has pointed out in his recent study on the governorship of the Qing dynasty, frequent turnover usually occurred in moments of crisis, of which the early Qianlong period was one.[14] Compared with the relative longevity of the viceroys' tenures before and after this period in Sichuan, it is apparent that the frequent turnovers in Shaanxi and Sichuan were resonating to the disturbances caused by Qianlong's remerging of the two strategic areas (that is, the northwestern and the Sichuan frontiers).

Two trends became pronounced in the appointments to these two positions. First, all but one appointee (Fang Xian) were Manchus, which shows Qianlong's propensity to use more Manchus in frontier positions, a different attitude from his grandfather and father. Second, most of the appointees had previous experience in frontier affairs. Jalangga had been the chief commander of the Tibet invasion in 1728 and one of the chief commanders of the Zunghar war in the Yongzheng period. Qingfu had acted as the commander-in-chief of the northern route army during the Zunghar campaign in 1735 and served as the governor-general of Yunnan.[15] Jishan's father, Erentei, had been the chief commander of the Qing expedition to Tibet in 1718; he was killed when his expedition was routed by the Zunghar. Jishan himself had led the Qing garrison in Lhasa.[16] These were not coincidences. As Guy has argued, starting from the middle of the Qing dynasty, expertise mattered more in the selection of officials to particular posts that required higher credentials and more experience.[17] The influx of the frontier-oriented officials into these two areas showcases a more mature stage in the Qing administration of its frontiers, although the emperor preferred keeping the status quo to action at this moment for the frontiers.

At the same time as the central government was painstakingly wrestling with the aftermath of reintegrating Sichuan into the northwest, it engaged itself in doing away with yet another legacy of the Yongzheng era—that is, a sizable military apparatus in the northwestern, Sichuan, and southwestern frontiers. This was relatively simple for the northwest. After the truce most field armies returned to their original garrisons. Some were demobilized locally. Others were retained in the Hami area to accelerate military colonization, since many were convinced that the fortification of Hami was the key in curbing the Zunghar expansion.[18] Although demobilized soldiers turned out to be a source of unrest in the Hami area, it was in general smooth.[19]

On the Sichuan frontier and in the southwest, however, it was a different story. Starting from the first invasion into Tibet at the end of the Kangxi period, the military buildup in Sichuan had been gaining momentum. In 1723, Nian Gengyao suggested further reinforcing the Qing garrisons at Dartsedo and its surrounding areas in a thirteen-point proposal after the Qinghai campaign.[20] Although Nian was purged a year later, many of his initiatives remained in place. Then military operations in the Yongzheng era continued augmenting the size of the military in the province. Unlike in Eastern Turkistan the oversized military in Sichuan and the southwest had more or less become entrenched in society as they were all localized Green Standard armies, instead of the Manchu troops deployed from the outside. In some territories newly claimed from the non-Han local chieftains, where a civil administration had not been installed, the military outposts were the only representation of the Qing authorities. Soldiers there had to undertake the duties of civil officials such as tax collecting. As James Z. Lee has pointed out, the military played a pioneering role in migration to the peripheries.[21] Along with the soldiers came their families and relatives, as well as such people with special skills as blacksmiths, carpenters, bow-makers, tailors, doctors, veterinarians, leather makers, and cooks, who often found employment with the garrisons. Qianlong once noted that half the population in these areas was military-related.[22] Even in the core areas of Sichuan, the military played a critical role in socioeconomic life by absorbing superfluous hands and being a reliable and generous consumer of local products, especially foodstuffs. Above all, more troops meant more funds from the state. Thus it was bound to be difficult to cut its size, even in peacetime.

In fact, disarmament had begun in the final year of the Yongzheng reign. When the Dalai Lama returned to Lhasa, the issue surfaced of disbanding the three brigades that had been recruited particularly for guarding him in Taining. Aware of the difficulty in making those several thousands of troops jobless instantly, Huang Tinggui, then governor-general of Sichuan, proposed that most of the officers and soldiers be transferred to garrisons nearby.[23] This passive resistance to disarmament was heeded by Yunnan and Guizhou, where oversized military was also a reality.[24] Although Qianlong had reiterated his determination of liquidating all "extra" military forces that had been recruited during the Yongzheng period, and constantly placed pressure on the provinces involved, the provincial authorities in Sichuan were not enthusiastic about it at all. The seesaw battle to downsize the military buildup did not accomplish much. An oversized military remained in place after the first decade of the Qianlong period. In 1744, Liang Shizheng, a vice minister of the Board of Revenue and an outspoken proponent for curtailing state expenditures in military and construction projects, proposed a new motion to cut the soldiers who had been recruited in Sichuan during the Yongzheng reign.[25] This proposal was doomed to be unwelcome. Qingfu, the governor-general of Sichuan and Shaanxi, rebutted it by insisting that the ten thousand soldiers who had been recruited in 1730 had been demobilized. He argued further that many garrisons in Sichuan were strategically important, so that it was not appropriate to reduce their size.[26] As in previous times, Liang's inititive went nowhere.

THE HEIGHT OF FRONTIER WARS, 1745–1793

The gingerly maintained peace in the early Qianlong era was shattered by new frontier exigencies when the Qianlong period entered its second decade. Like his father, the Yongzheng emperor, Qianlong adeptly turned back to activism in frontier affairs when he was confronted with those exigencies. Not coincidentally, the Sichuan frontier became most involved in Qianlong's frontier undertakings, experiencing more frontier wars than all other regions of the empire in the second half of the eighteenth century.

The Zhandui Incident, 1745–1746

The first trouble occurred in Zhandui of the Kham area, the Tibetan territory that had been annexed by the Qing dynasty in the Yongzheng era. [27] For centuries most parts of the Kham area had been ruled by autonomous local chieftains, who were only symbolically subjugated to the political authorities in Lhasa and at times to the Chinese authorities, when the Chinese empire was expanding. Even after Kham had been annexed by the Qing, Qing political control remained nominal—civil officials shunned taking the posts there—except in a few strategic points such as Dartsedo, Lithang, and Bathang. Taking advantage of their convenient position—to the west of Darsondo and on both shores of the Yalong River, which cut through the Sichuan-Lhasa highway—the people of Zhandui made a reputation for their Robinhood-like behavior—that is, pillaging passing official equipages and merchant caravans starting from the Yongzheng period. Despite several attempts by the Qing local authorities to root out the problem in the Yongzheng period, the highway pillage persisted.[28] After the Qing outposts from Dartsedo to Lhasa were yielded to the native soldiers in 1734, the cases of pillage of the Qing troops and missions dramatically increased.[29]

At the end of 1744 and in early 1745 the Qing troops going to and returning from Tibet were repeatedly ambushed and looted. In the spring of 1745, Qingfu, the governor-general of Sichuan and Shaanxi, proposed using military force to clear the highway of assaults by the Zhandui people. Although he was reluctant to diverge from his peace agenda and wary of being dragged into a meaningless frontier conflict by the local officials, who had their own vested interests in having such a war, Qianlong endorsed the action. For him, what weighed more was the safety of the artery connecting Sichuan and Lhasa: "The armies are now stationed in Tibet. How can it be allowed to be harassed by those ugly villains? It really reaches the point that we have to resort to military action."[30] With the imperial endorsement the Qing armies in Sichuan began raiding villages in Zhandui in mid-1745.

When the war first started, what was in the air was a speedy triumph as both the throne and local officials talked about a "once and for all" (*yilaoyongyi*) solution. The Qing state sent mostly the native soldiers who had been recruited from the other local chieftains' tribes in the area. A couple of thousand Tibetan soldiers were also deployed with Pholhanas's consent. Nevertheless, it soon turned out that it was a difficult and costly campaign. Not only did more and more money pour into it at the request of the Sichuan officials, but also the scale of war kept escalating. The native soldiers were replaced by regular Qing armies; the neighboring provinces, Yunnan and Guizhou, were also mobilized to provide military forces and supplies. In the fall of 1745, Qingfu himself headed to Chengdu from Xi'an to command the campaign. He was then tied down in Sichuan without being able to oversee affairs in Shaanxi and Gansu. Hiding in and shooting from many stone ramparts and blockhouses that were built on cliffs, passes, and mountaintops, the Zhandui soldiers deprived the sizable Qing armies of all their advantages. Moreover, the distance and rugged terrain of Zhandui made supplies for the troops a serious problem. By the spring of 1746, seven months after the campaign started, 1 million taels of silver had been used but with no sign of a victory on the horizon. Already at the end of his patience, the emperor urged Qingfu to conclude the operation as soon as possible.

Under pressure, Qingfu had to find a way out for himself. He enlisted a personal rival of Bangun, the Zhandui leader, and sent him to Zhandui to undermine the resistance from inside. Meanwhile, Qingfu and other commanders planned a scheme to bring this futile campaign to an end. On July 19, 1746, Qing soldiers piled straw in some dozens of abandoned blockhouses and burned them. Then Qingfu and his colleagues reported that Bangun, the person who had caused so much trouble to the Qing, had been burned to ashes and the war was therefore concluded successfully. Satisfied, Qianlong readily accepted the fabricated triumph, but he found out later that Bangun had not died—he had escaped to another village when those blockhouses were set aflame.[31] Worse than that, this incident set a precedent in which the local officials and commanders would influence the central authorities in starting and escalating a frontier war. The Kangxi emperor had been extremely wary of this scenario, but it was to be a déjà vu repeatedly haunting the rest of the Qianlong period. This incident prompted the Qing to reconsider the disposition of leaving the outposts in the Kham area to native soldiers; it started talking about restaffing them with the Green Standard troops.[32]

The First Jinchuan Campaign

No sooner had the fire in Zhandui been completely extinguished than a new crisis in the Jinchuan area started.[33] About 120 miles northwest of Chengdu, the Jinchuan area, in which two rivers, Jinchuan and Small Jinchuan, intersected layers of mountains, was a hermit domain of some Gyalrong tribes. Among them Rardan (Cujin in Chinese) of the Jinchuan valley and Tsanla (Zanla in Chinese) of the Small Jinchuan valley were the most powerful tribes. The tribal people called themselves Gyalrongwa and spoke Gyalrong, a different language from Tibetan.[34] Without unifying authority in the area separated by mountains, the tribes identified themselves by their chieftains; feuds among them were not a rare occurrence. Due to the limited output from their crops, mainly barley and buckwheat, on small pieces of arable land, the Jinchuan people went to the nearby Songpan subprefecture and the Chengdu plain and hired themselves out as agricultural laborers for half a year. This hiring out was referred to by the locals as *xiaba* ("go down to the plain").[35] The tribesmen in the Jinchuan area were believers in Bon, or Bonpo, an animistic religion that had been predominant in Tibet before Buddhism was introduced. Refusing to relinquish their traditional belief system, Jinchuan tribes had not been in a subordinate relation with the Yellow Sect. The Jinchuan area had never been within the regular pale of the Chinese authorities, although nominal administrative offices had been set up by the Chinese state several times in history.[36] After the Manchu conquest of Sichuan, however, both the chieftains of Jinchuan and Small Jinchuan had the title *tusi* (local chieftain) conferred on them from the Qing, as many other local chieftains did to back up their positions in their local communities.[37]

The chieftain of the Rardan tribe in Jinchuan was a recognized strongman in the area.[38] During the Qing first invasion into Tibet the chieftain and his men were recruited by Yue Zhongqi and joined the Qing expedition. In the early Yongzheng period he was given the title *anfushi* (pacification commissioner) by the Qing. To expand his influence, he began attacking other neighboring tribes in early 1747. In responding to the disturbance in Jinchuan, Jishan, the governor of Sichuan, sent troops down and tried to restore order. Meanwhile, he and other provincial officials began to clamor for a war; the familiar argument "to resolve the problem once and for all" was again brought to the emperor's attention. Although he had great doubts about the validity of another war in western Sichuan, Qianlong bent to pressure from the Sichuan officials and endorsed a campaign against Jinchuan in late spring. He appointed Zhang Guangsi the governor-general of Sichuan and Shaanxi and let him command the campaign, as Qianlong was so impressed with Zhang's speedy victory in suppressing the Miao uprising in Guizhou a decade earlier. Led by the misperception that the Jinchuan problem was similar to that in the Miao area in Guizhou, Qianlong encouraged Zhang to apply whatever means he used against the Miao people in Jinchuan.[39]

A year into the war, however, Zhang had not made any substantial progress. He was facing a similar situation as the Qing forces had in Zhandui: steep mountains and hard-to-destroy stone blockhouses. With his confidence in Zhang fading away, Qianlong made two personnel decisions in the spring of 1748. First, he reinstated Yue Zhongqi, who had been living at home without any official title in Chengdu after he was released from jail in 1737.[40] Yue was appointed as a regional commander and soon promoted to provincial military commander of Sichuan, the same position he had held two decades earlier. As Qianlong acknowledged, Yue's expertise in Sichuan border affairs was peerless among all the Qing officials. Then Qianlong sent Necin, his chief adviser and leading member of the Grand Council, to Sichuan as a royal commissioner to oversee the war.[41] Necin's coming to Sichuan marked the escalation of the war. Initially reluctant to endorse this war, Qianlong became more resolute as the war progressed. Especially after the conspiracy by the Sichuan officials to forge the victory in Zhandui was exposed by Zhang Guangsi, Qianlong was convinced that his provincial officials' impotent disposition of the Zhandui incident had encouraged more rebellious incidents in western Sichuan. He was thus determined to carry this current war to a complete victory. Qianlong turned down a proposal to accept the Jinchuan chieftain's offer of a surrender and sent in more troops from other provinces.

Nevertheless, Necin was not able to turn back the clock—he had made no progress, either, several months after he had arrived on the front. The war spending kept rising at a startling rate, which prompted Qianlong to suspect that he might have been misled again. In late 1748, Qianlong called Necin and Zhang Guangsi back to the capital to report on the campaign in person.[42] Meanwhile, he appointed another member of the Grand Council, Fuheng, as the new commissioner to replace Necin. Only in his twenties and being the younger brother of Qianlong's beloved first empress who had died earlier that year, Fuheng had been trusted by the emperor after he joined the Grand Council in 1745. Fuheng's appointment occurred at another shift in Qianlong's attitude toward the war—he had realized that the war was a mistake and was geared to bringing it to an end; sending Fuheng to Sichuan was meant to smooth the way for the emperor to call off the war, even though it was not clearly laid out by the emperor to Fuheng. After Fuheng's appointment Necin and Zhang Guangsi were both put on trial. They were given the death penalty for their botched handling of the war.[43] Being the only death penalty given to a chief grand councilor who had been in good terms with the emperor throughout the Qianlong reign, Necin's death testified to Qianlong's outrage over this fruitless, yet costly, war.

To Qianlong's disappointment, Fuheng seemed not to have comprehended his real mission. Being a young and hawkish Manchu aristocrat, he did not want to get out of this war with empty hands. Although he reported on the grave difficulties that the Qing forces encountered in Jinchuan, which had been concealed by both Zhang and Necin, Fuheng was also adamant in overcoming those disadvantages and bringing the Jinchuan chieftain to subjugation. Perplexed by Fuheng's obstinate inclination, Qianlong had to articulate his intention. Over the following two weeks after Qianlong received Fuheng's first reports, he issued lengthy edicts on an almost daily basis to Fuheng, urging him to end the war. In these edicts Qianlong reiterated that the war had been too costly, and that it was not worth the enormous expense to take full control of this piece of barren land.

Despite the imperial orders that deluged him, Fuheng was still firm in sticking to his own plan. He bet on two advantages: First, the people of Jinchuan had been exhausted by the two-year war; they had begun talking about a truce with the Qing forces. Second, Yue Zhongqi had apparently become more active and constructive in cooperating with Fuheng after Zhang Guangsi was removed. Obviously still harboring the ill feelings against Zhang, who was instrumental in Yue's dismissal and arrest back in 1732 during the Zunghar campaign, Yue did not contribute much when Zhang was still in Sichuan. But in early 1749, Yue suggested to Fuheng that he lead a small dispatch and go to the Jinchuan chieftain's headquarters via a byway and persuade the latter to surrender. Fuheng agreed to Yue's bold plan and ordered the attacking of the Jinchuan forces on the front to divert their attention. When Yue and a dozen or so Qing soldiers suddenly appeared in front of the chieftain's blockhouse, the already demoralized chieftain was completely taken by surprise and awe. That night, Yue Zhongqi was treated by the chieftain as if he were still the latter's superior as during the invasion into Tibet in 1720. The following morning, the chieftain followed Yue to the Qing headquarters and surrendered.[44]

Greatly relieved by this unexpected happy ending, Qianlong granted both Fuheng and Yue Zhongqi many honors as well as hereditary ranks. As an inexperienced grand councilor, Fuheng proved his competence and replaced Necin to become the leading member of the Grand Council. For Yue his legendary deed in ending the first Jinchuan war was another turning point in his career. He returned to power and fame, although he would stay in the position of provincial military commander and was not promoted further until his death in 1754. Despite the pompous celebrations, however, the first Jinchuan campaign failed to root out the problem of the borderland strongmen who tended to challenge the Qing's authority. In this sense the result of the first Jinchuan war was not unlike that of the Zhandui campaign. In both cases Qianlong had been misinformed and misguided by the provincial officials and was manipulated by his field commanders once the war started. To a great degree, the war was fought according to their timetable, but not the emperor's.[45] Fiscally, this war was not cost effective, either. More than 7 million taels of silver had been spent on the two-year campaign, a great portion of which had been spent on hiring military laborers to transport grain and other supplies to the Jinchuan front.[46]

The Lhasa Riot of 1750 and Qianlong's Tibetan Expedition

In the late 1740s the Qing dynasty was concerned about not only Sichuan's western borderland but also Tibet's stability. In February 1747, Pholhanas passed away, leaving Tibetan domestic politics on the verge of tilting. Having been an able leader of Tibet, Pholhanas had made his reign a relatively tranquil period since the Fifth Dalai Lama.[47] However, reports about the discord between him and the Seventh Dalai Lama began reaching Beijing after 1745. The Qing *amban* stationed in Lhasa had to, from time to time, mediate their conflicts. In 1746 the Dalai Lama secretly sent an envoy to

Beijing to complain about Pholhanas's allegedly unfair treatment of him.[48] As the result of this secret visit, Qianlong issued an edict to Pholhanas in January 1747, shortly before Pholhanas's death, to try to mend their relationship.[49] After Pholhanas's death, his second son, Gyumey Namgyal, succeeded to his position.

The new prince had more trouble getting along with the Dalai Lama. He even rejected the Dalai Lama's offer to chant sutras at the mourning ceremony for his father. Only through the mediation of Fucing, the Qing *amban*, did the young prince allow the Dalai Lama to pray for the deceased.[50] As portrayed by both Tibetans and Qing officials, Gyumey Namgyal was haughty and imperious. During the three years he ruled Tibet from 1747 to 1750, the strained relations between him and the Dalai Lama became exacerbated. The Qing believed that the young ruler made military arrangements aiming to prevent Qing intervention and to isolate the Dalai Lama from his following. He had also killed his own elder brother, Gyumey Tseten, who was more pro-Qing and the chief official in Ngari, the area bordering Zungharia. Then he reportedly sent his deputy to the Zunghar seeking support.[51] Since the beginning of 1750, Sichuan had been on alert; the provincial officials had entertained a preemptive expedition before the young prince made any major move.[52]

As Gyumey Namgyal's scheme became increasingly open, the two Qing *amban* in Lhasa, Fucing and Labdon, acted first. On November 11, 1750, they managed to trap and kill the young prince. Then the two *amban* asked Doring Pandita, a Tibetan noble with the title of duke granted by the Qing, to act as head of the Tibetan government. At this point, however, a follower of Gyumey Namgyal scrambled together a mob of more than a thousand and stormed the *amban* residence in Lhasa (which used to be Lajang Khan's residence). Fucing and Labdon were both killed in the melee, along with more than a hundred Manchus and Chinese, both soldiers and civilians, who died either by suicide or at the hands of the mob. The mob dispersed after the slaughter and pillage. The Dalai Lama and Doring Pandita stepped in to restore order in Lhasa.[53]

Outraged by the deaths of the two Qing *amban* and others in Lhasa, Qianlong ordered another expedition to Tibet. Initially, five thousand troops from Sichuan and eight thousand from Shaanxi were deployed for this expedition, which was led by Cereng and Yue Zhongqi, while Yinjishan, the governor-general of Shaanxi and Gansu, went to Sichuan to supervise the logistical affairs.[54] Nevertheless, before the joined expedition of Sichuan and Shaanxi left Sichuan, Qianlong changed his mind. Since order had been restored in Lhasa with many perpetrators being arrested by Pandita and the Dalai Lama, there was no need to send a sizable army. Therefore, the emperor let only Cereng lead an expedition of eight hundred soldiers from Sichuan to Lhasa. Yue Zhongqi was ordered to stay at Dartsedo and secure the borderlands.[55] When Cereng was still on his way to Lhasa, Bandi, the Qing plenipotentiary, arrived in Lhasa on January 18, 1751. Pandita warmly greeted him and handed the people he had arrested to Bandi.[56] As in previous times, the Qing dynasty took the opportunity to reorganize the Tibetan government. Once Cereng arrived, he and Bandi abolished the position of prince, thus ending the Pholha family's rule in Tibet that had begun in 1728. They set up a new Tibetan government, known since as Kashag, which consisted of four *kaloon* (councilors) of equal position; and they made it a rule that all *kaloon* had to obey the Dalai Lama, Panchen Lama, and the Qing *amban*. In the following year, Cereng and his cohorts submitted a thirteen-point proposal to solidify the political reform and the *amban* system in Tibet.[57] Because both the Dalai Lama and Panchen Lama were again allowed to take the reins of government, it is commonly held that the combination of church and state started in Tibet in 1751. The Qing military station in Tibet was also reinforced. From this time on, fifteen hundred Green Standard soldiers were regularly stationed in Tibet.

The Zunghar threat toward Tibet remained a grave concern for the Qing after the 1750 incident. Although Qianlong had been cautious in launching a new war, he would not let slip a perfect chance to do away with this long-time enemy. After Galdan Tsering died in 1745, the Zunghar empire was plagued with another succession crisis. By the mid-1750s the Zunghar home region had been in chaos because of years of civil war. Seeing the crisis with the Zunghar as a great opportunity for the Qing, Qianlong called for a full-scale war against them in 1755.[58] Although he did not intend to wipe out the Zunghar empire at the onset of the war, he quickly shifted his tone in 1756, starting to use rhetoric such as "annihilation" (*yongjue genchu*) instead of just trying to subjugate his enemies. While the Qing armies indiscriminately slaughtered hundreds of thousands of Zunghar people, an epidemic of smallpox in 1757 killed many others. As a result, the once thriving nomadic empire met its tragic termination and only a small number of the Zunghar people survived. The Qing therefore obtained its biggest prize in its territorial expansion: Eastern Turkistan, which began to be known as Xinjiang, meaning "new dominion."

The collapse of the Zunghar empire in 1757 stands as a turning point in the frontier enterprise of the Qing dynasty. With the Zunghar threat no longer on the horizon, stability in the vast Mongol steppe could be secured. More pertinent to this book, the Qing no longer needed to worry about the Zunghar competition for Tibet; the Qing became the sole powerful patron and protector of the Yellow Sect. It was a few years after the Qing conquest of the Zunghar homeland that a replica of the Potala palace in Lhasa started to be built in the imperial summer palace in Chengde.[59] Yet there was another important ramification of the triumph over the Zunghar people: Qianlong's confidence in the military might of the Qing empire was greatly inflated, and his ambition for further expansion was whetted. He relinquished his preference for peaceful diplomacy, which had been his mind-set when he first came to the throne in 1735, and came to embrace a hawkish stance in frontier politics.

Vehemently defending his brutal decision of "annihilating" the Zunghar people, Qianlong argued that it was vital for Qing security. He could hardly hide his joy in watching his territory expanding, and his pride in surpassing previous Chinese monarchs in so doing. Repeatedly pointing to the increased wealth in the country, Qianlong was content in seeing and boasting that his frontier wars did not impair his people's welfare. Thus he would be willing to fight more wars if he desired to do so, as indicated in many edicts he issued after his success in Eastern Turkistan. In the immediate wake of his Zunghar campaign, Qianlong launched another war in 1758 against the Muslim tribes in the border marches of his "new dominion" and claimed victory the following year.[60] A few years later, from 1765 to 1769, he allowed himself to slip into an unnecessary war in the southwestern borders with Myanmar, but this turned out to be a sheer disaster.[61] With a power-based and aggressive frontier policy in command, the Sichuan frontier would experience more wars in the remainder of the eighteenth century.

The Second Jinchuan Campaign, 1770–1776

After the first Jinchuan campaign the Jinchuan area never ceased to make trouble for the Qing; feuds among the local chieftains over various issues were reported now and then.[62] For some years the Qing state favored a tactic of "attacking the barbarians with the barbarians" (*yiman gongman*), by which the successive Qing officials in Sichuan acquiesced in or even encouraged other local chieftains to attack the Rardan tribe of the Jinchuan valley, the perpetrator of the first Jinchuan war and the most recalcitrant tribe in this area.[63] However, in 1770 it was the Tsanla tribe of the Small Jinchuan valley, instead of the Jinchuan tribe, that caused new trouble. Tsengasang, the chieftain of that tribe in Small Jinchuan, made a series of attacks on his neighbors. The Qing forces that had been sent to stop the conflict became involved in the fight with Small Jinchuans themselves. Still lamenting the Qing defeats in the Myanmar war, however, Qianlong saw in the Jinchuan unrest a chance to reclaim his lost pretension as a victorious warrior. He called off the preparedness on the Yunnan front for a new campaign with Myanmar and deployed massive troops to western Sichuan for a major war against the Tsanla tribe. Unlike the first Jinchuan war in which Qianlong was a passive being pushed into war by his provincial officials, here he himself was the mastermind, urging the commanders to relentlessly beat down the rebellious Tsengasang. So determined was Qianlong to achieve a complete victory that he reiterated that he would not accept Tsengasang's surrender as he had that of the Jinchuan chieftain in the first Jinchuan war.

Although Qianlong thought that the terrain in Small Jinchuan was not as challenging as in Jinchuan, the war did not proceed smoothly in its initial stage. Outraged by the provincial authorities' slowness in moving against Small Jinchuan, the emperor issued many edicts condemning Aertai, the governor-general of Sichuan, for his reluctance to launch a major operation.[64] In the fall of 1771, Wenfu and Guilin, both from aristocratic Manchu families and both serving on the Grand Council, were appointed as the new commanders-in-chief. Their coming to Sichuan marked the first escalation of the war. Meanwhile, a complication unfolded on the Jinchuan front: the Qing forces found in early 1772 that Suonuomu, the chieftain of Jinchuan at the time, had sent his soldiers to help Small Jinchuan. A year later, when the Qing forces crushed Tsengasang's headquarters, Tsengasang had fled to Jinchuan and sought refuge. Since Suonuomu refused to surrender Tsengasang to the Qing forces, the war was extended to Jinchuan as well. More Qing troops were deployed from other provinces, including the Manchu regiments from the capital and Manchuria. This borderland war thus became a major engagement of the empire.

Facing an enemy that had advantages in size and resources, the Jinchuan people persisted in their resistance. In the summer of 1773, in a surprise attack on the Qing camp in Muguomu, the Jinchuan armies killed the Qing troops by the thousands, including many officers and one of the commanders-in-chief, Wenfu, and recovered Small Jinchuan from Qing control. In the wake of the Muguomu fiasco, Qianlong reshuffled the campaign's commandership one more time. He appointed Agūi as the new chief commander. Baptized in the first Jinchuan campaign, Agūi had since participated in more wars, emerging as a rising star in frontier affairs. When he was transferred from Yunnan to Sichuan in 1770, however, he was at a low ebb in his career—he had come under severe criticism from the emperor for his role in the unsuccessful invasion into Myanmar, of which he was a deputy commander.[65] His new appointment in 1773 turned his fortune around, as it did the fate of the second Jinchuan war.

Under Agūi's direction the Qing forces began to gain the upper hand. They soon reconquered Small Jinchuan in the fall of 1773. Yet it took another two years before the Qing forces managed to destroy blockhouses in Lewuwei, the headquarters of Jinchuan. Suonuomu and his brother fled to Galayi, their last stronghold. Several months later, in March 1776, Galayi yielded to the Qing forces. The Suonuomu brothers surrendered (Tsengasang, the chieftain of Small Jinchuan, had died of illness a year earlier).[66] After nearly six years of long and difficult fighting, the second Jinchuan campaign was brought to its conclusion with extremely heavy casualties on both sides and a staggering financial cost of 61 million taels of silver on the Qing part.

While the final stage of the war was approaching, Qianlong authorized a radical reform of the area. He decided to establish a regular administrative system in the Jinchuan area to replace the local chieftains and set up military colonies as had been done in the Miao area in southern Guizhou. This was a sheer departure from his past policy of maintaining the status quo. At the emperor's order the major chieftains of the two Jinchuan tribes were escorted to Beijing and executed in an extremely brutal manner following the ceremony of submitting the captives to the throne; more than a thousand lesser chieftains were relocated to other parts of China. In addition, the remaining local chieftains in the area were required to go to the capital and pay homage to the emperor in rotation.[67]

Qianlong also ordered a religious proselytism: he forced the people to give up their traditional Bon belief and adopt Yellow Sect Buddhism. To facilitate the conversion, he sent several Yellow Sect lamas from Beijing to Jinchuan, while refusing the Dalai Lama's request of sending lamas from Lhasa.[68] With the traditional system largely dismantled, the Qing state set up two subprefectures (*ting*) in this "new dominion" (*xinjiang*, the same name that was used earlier to refer to the conquered Eastern Turkistan), Meinuo ting in Small Jinchuan, and Aergu ting in Jinchuan.[69] Military colonies were set up in the area, in which six thousand Green Standard soldiers were initially stationed, although the number declined to twenty-six hundred by the end of the Qianlong reign largely because of concerns over expenses.[70] At the call of the Qing local authorities, Han Chinese immigrants began to move into the area, which forced some Jinchuan natives over time to emigrate to avoid being enslaved by the Han Chinese.[71] Meanwhile, the Qing state made good use of the Jinchuan native soldiers by sending them to fight in several wars in the remainder of the Qianlong period, which was considered, among other thing, one of the ways to strengthen the ties between the Qing state and the newly conquered area.[72]

Two Gurkha Campaigns and the Settlement of the Tibet Question

Ever since the watershed of the elimination of the Zunghar empire in the late 1750s, the Tibetan domestic situation had been more stable than in the first half of the eighteenth century.[73] In Qianlong's view Tibet was already the secured backyard of the Qing empire, free from challenge posed by outsiders.[74] Entering the 1770s, however, one of Tibet's neighbors, Nepal, began to rise to power after a new dynasty was founded by the Gurkhas in 1769.[75] Since then, some disputes over the cross-border trade between Nepal and Tibet, an essential part of the economic life of the Gurkha dynasty, had accumulated. The Gurkhas' chief grievance was that the Tibetans had banned the importation of coins minted in Nepal because of their declining quality.[76] Other problems included duties being increased on Nepali commodities and the salt imported from Tibet being always mixed with sand.

The situation became more complicated, thanks to the British involvement in the region. Ever since the British had set their feet on India in the early eighteenth century, they had shown interest to India's neighbors. In 1767 the East India Company sent a military expedition led by G. Kinloch to Nepal, but it never reached its core part.[77] In 1774, Warren Hastings, the newly appointed governor-general of British India, sent George Bogle as his envoy to Tibet. During his meeting with the Sixth Panchen Lama, Bogle suggested that British India and Tibet join hands to check the expansion of the Gurkha dynasty, as the latter had increased influence on the Indian-Tibetan trade. But the Panchen Lama only agreed to report his message to the Qing court.[78] In 1783, Hastings sent Captain Samuel Turner to Tibet to negotiate a trade agreement between British India and Tibet. Turner managed to reach an agreement with the Tibetans in the spring of 1784. However, this agreement did not significantly enhance the relationship between the two.[79] While little progress was achieved in the opening of Tibet, the British turned to Nepal as a go-between for Indian-Tibetan trade. The British efforts bore fruit in 1788, when the Gurkha dynasty changed its attitude toward the British from being hostile and began to negotiate with the British on trade matters. The improvement in Gurkha-British relations became one of the factors in the Gurhka decision to raid Tibet in 1788, as they were ensured that the British would not attack them while they were engaged in a war with Tibet.[80]

While the tension in the Tibetan-Nepali relationship had long mounted, the catalyst of the war was a feud over the inheritance of the deceased Sixth Panchen Lama between his two brothers. When the sixth Panchen Lama died during his visit to Beijing in November 1780, one of his brothers, Hutuktu Chungpa, the regent of Tashilhunpo monastery near Shigatse, which was customarily the residency of the Panchen Lama, took all the treasures in the monastery into his own possession.[81] Another brother of the deceased Panchen Lama, Samarpa, who was believed to be an incarnated lama of the Red Sect, did not get anything. Outraged with his brother, Samarpa went to Nepal in 1786 and instigated the Gurkhas to invade Tibet. The convergence of the trade disputes and the fight over the Panchen Lama's inheritance thus prompted the Gurkhas to go to war with Tibet.

In the spring of 1788 the Gurkha forces crossed the border and took Nyelam, Kerong, and Jungka across the Tibetan-Nepali border. Upon receiving an appeal for help from Lhasa, the Qianlong emperor immediately ordered an expedition to Tibet that consisted of five hundred bannermen from the Chengdu garrison, thirteen hundred Green Standard troops, and thirteen hundred ethnic native soldiers from Sichuan. Ehui, the Chengdu general, was summoned to the emperor's summer palace in Rehe for an emergency audience before he headed to Tibet. Meanwhile, Qianlong also sent Bazhong, a former *amban* who knew Tibetan, to Lhasa to assist in settling the incident. In May 1789, before the Qing forces from Sichuan engaged the Gurkha invaders, the Tibetan authorities, with the backing of Bazhong, had arranged a peace agreement with the Gurkhas.[82] Subsequently, Bazhong reported to the emperor that the Gurkhas had withdrawn and sent tributes to the Qing forces in Tibet, but he concealed the fact that the agreement stipulated that the Tibetans pay 9,600 taels of silver to the Gurkhas annually.[83] Qianlong was satisfied to hear that the enemy was beaten back and the lost territories were recovered.

Two years later, in 1791, the Gurkhas invaded Tibet again under the excuse of seeking the payment promised by the Tibetans in the 1789 agreement. The Gurkha troops broke up the Tibetan resistance and again took Nyelam, Kerong, and Jungka. They also looted the Tashilhunpo monastery that housed the Panchen Lama's treasures. Upon hearing the news of the Gurkha invasion, Bazhong committed suicide, knowing that he could not escape from taking the responsibility for having cheated the throne. To safeguard Tibet from Gurkha aggression, Qianlong decided on another punitive expedition to first expel the Gurkhas from Tibet and then to chase them to Nepal, which would be the most far-flung and difficult frontier campaign, given the distance of Nepal from China proper and the extremely treacherous conditions across the Tibetan plateau and into mountainous Nepal. In several edicts he issued in defense of his staging this war, Qianlong was even more adamant and assertive than he had been on the occasions of the wars in Myanmar and Vietnam.[84] In one of those edicts he stated: "Tibet is the place that my grandfather and father had repeatedly used force to pacify. There is no way [for us] to abandon it because of the harassment of those petty devils [the Gurkhas]. If we give away Tibet without a fight, where do we place the Dalai Lama, the Panchen Erdeni, and their people? . . . I have never been afraid of difficult situations in coping with critical matters in so many years ever since my enthronement. This has been well-known to all. Now I am eighty-one years old and have been reigning for fifty-six years. How can we open our door and let enemies in only because of the threat from those petty devils?"[85]

It was clear that the aging monarch would not shun another long-distance expedition when Tibet's security was at stake. Determined and seasoned by his years of handling frontier exigencies, Qianlong set out for another war mobilization. He first ordered Ehui, who was in the position of the governor-general of Sichuan at that time, and Chengde, the Chengdu general, to lead more than seven thousand troops from Sichuan to go to Tibet. More than half of these troops were ethnic soldiers recruited from western Sichuan. Meanwhile, he sent eleven hundred bannermen from the capital and Mongolia to Tibet and appointed the decorated Manchu generals, Fukang'an, Hailancha, and Kuilin, as the chief-commander and deputy chief-commanders to lead the campaign. In early 1792 the eleven hundred bannermen arrived in Tibet via Qinghai. Feeling that the size of the Qing forces was not big enough for the risky task of invading Nepal, the commanders requested an additional three thousand troops from Sichuan to enforce the expedition.[86]

In early summer the reinforced Qing expedition headed to the Tibetan-Nepali border area. After having recovered the occupied places inside

Tibet, the Qing expedition of more than seven thousand invaded Nepal on July 3, 1792. Although the Gurkha forces routed the Qing expedition by assembling massive troops and attacking the Qing invaders from three directions in late July, the approaching of the Qing expedition to Kathmandu, the capital of the Gurkha dynasty, was threatening. The Gurkha king sought a settlement. On the Qing side there were also good reasons to conclude the invasion as soon as possible. Not only did the Qing invading forces suffer heavy casualties by marching and fighting in a foreign and inhospitable environment, but it had proved extremely expensive and difficult to support such a long-distance campaign beyond the regular calibers of its logistical functions. In addition, the approaching of winter in mountainous Nepal was not to the advantage of the exhausted Qing expedition. With Qianlong's endorsement Fukang'an accepted the terms the Gurkha king offered in September and withdrew from Nepal on October 6. In the wake of the invasion, the Gurkha dynasty sent its mission to Beijing and formally entered a tributary relationship with the Qing dynasty. The Gurkhas were deprived of the right of minting coins for the Tibetans and other trade privileges.[87]

THE INDEPENDENCE OF THE SICHUAN FRONTIER

The many wars in the Qianlong period dramatically elevated the importance of the Sichuan frontier. It became the most militarized area in the country in the latter part of the eighteenth century—it had remained militarily active long after the Pax Manjurica (Manchu peace) was established in Eastern Turkistan and the Mongol steppe upon the collapse of the Zunghar empire in the late 1750s. Many first-class generals of the Qing empire either fought in the battlefields or served in key positions on the Sichuan frontier. Some top officials and generals paid a high price, even their lives, for their unsatisfactory performance in the wars in the area. At the beginning of his reign, the new emperor was inclined to downplay Sichuan's importance, for he was geared to steer clear of his father's proactive frontier strategy. Chiefly, among other things, he remerged the governors-general of Sichuan and Shaanxi into one position, attaching Sichuan again to the Shaanxi-Gansu frontier. Although he never openly admitted that this was a misstep, Qianlong would readily correct it once the circumstances proved it a necessary step to take.

During the first Jinchuan war Qianlong went back to what had been laid down by Yongzheng and separated the two frontiers, the Shaanxi-Gansu area and Sichuan, in administrative terms, one more time. Upon the start of the Jinchuan war in early 1747, Qianlong's appointing of Zhang Guangsi to the post of the governor-general of Sichuan and Shaanxi triggered a chain of changes in the provincial administration in the southwestern frontier and then in Sichuan. Shortly after Zhang left his original post, the governor-general of Guizhou, and headed to Sichuan, Qianlong ordered the posts of governor-general of Yunnan and that of Guizhou merged into one, which had been separated into the two positions in 1736 when Zhang Guangsi swiftly and brutally put down the revolt by the Miao people in southeastern Guizhou.[88] Probably out of his wariness of Zhang, who had gained too big a reputation in this campaign, Qianlong only promoted him to the position of governor-general of Guizhou, instead of the traditional position that oversaw the two southwestern provinces, governor-general of Yunnan and Guizhou, but appointed another governor-general for Yunnan. When Zhang left the southwest, this precaution was no longer justified.

Not long after his arrival at his new post in Sichuan, Zhang Guangsi felt that he was not able to take charge of the affairs of Shaanxi and Gansu that his position had entitled him to while he was stationed in western Sichuan to direct the Jinchuan war. In November 1747 he requested the throne to appoint another governor-general to Shaanxi-Gansu so that Zhang himself could concentrate on Sichuan. But Qianlong did not seem to concur with him: "What you see may be correct. But there is no important business in Shaanxi and Gansu right now. It is just right for you to stay in Sichuan to carefully manage the settlement of the Jinchuan affairs. Why should we bother to have the system changed?"[89] There might have been another reason for Qianlong to have kept the status quo—the vigilance against the Zunghar—but it was not revealed to Zhang. Since the truce between the Qing and Galdan Tsering at the end of the Yongzheng reign, the fragile peace between the two sides in the far northwestern frontier had been interrupted by numerous alarms. More particularly, the Zunghar people still held an aggressive stance toward Tibet.

Galdan Tsering asked repeatedly for the Qing throne's permission to go to Tibet for the *mangja* ceremony. They ultimately made the trip to Lhasa in 1743. But the Tibetan leader, Pholhanas, did not give them a warm reception. In addition, the Tibetans refused the Zunghar request to have Tibetan lamas sent to Zungharia. These developments did not escape the Qing surveillance.[90] In 1747 a team of Zunghar people who had been sent to Tibet for the *mangja* ceremony abruptly halted their journey en route, which aroused the Qing suspicion that they might be getting ready for an attack on Qinghai. To prepare for a possible emergency, Qianlong directed Qingfu, the dismissed governor-general of Sichuan and Shaanxi, to stay in Shaanxi for the time being and help make necessary arrangements. In the meantime Qianlong ruled that every action be kept secret from the Zunghar people. Therefore, it was not a good time to overhaul the provincial administration in Shaanxi, the base of the northwestern frontier, although the emperor was indeed concerned with the fact that there was no leading provincial official in Xi'an at this delicate moment.[91]

Nevertheless, the escalation of the Jinchuan campaign would soon convince Qianlong that Zhang's suggestion was the only solution for both securing the northwest and having a high-ranking official to lead the Jinchuan war. Yet Qianlong took several steps to divide the position of governor-general of Sichuan and Shaanxi into two. In the beginning of 1748, Qianlong ordered Huang Tinggui, the governor of Gansu at that time, to take charge of the affairs in both Gansu and Shaanxi.[92] Soon after that, Huang was given the right to take over routine affairs in Sichuan, when Zhang Guangsi was no longer favored by the emperor. After Zhang was removed, Qianlong sent Fuheng as the new imperial plenipotentiary to Sichuan. It is likely that Fuheng helped convince Qianlong that it had become imperative to separate the position of governorship-general of Sichuan and that of Shaanxi, as there was discussion between Fuheng and the emperor on the selection of candidates for the new positions for both Sichuan and Shaanxi.[93] On January 18, 1749, Qianlong issued an edict to formalize the separation. He reasoned: "The governor-general of Sichuan and Shaanxi presides over Sichuan, Shaanxi, and Gansu, which is a vast area. In times of no emergency, it is yet too immense for him to take good control. Now the campaign in Jinchuan is not finished; there are all kinds of local and logistical affairs [in Sichuan]. If the governor-general is stationed in Xi'an, it would be difficult for him to take care of [all these affairs] from such a distance. Even after the campaign is called off, it is necessary to have somebody to take charge of the area [meaning Sichuan]."[94]

Qianlong cited the same reason that Zhang Guangsi presented in 1747 for his returning to Yongzheng's disposition of 1731. It is worth noting that in both 1731 and 1749 it was a war circumstance that prompted the split of the position. At the time of Qianlong's decision, the Jinchuan war was about to end, however. In this light this change was not just a temporary wartime disposition but also reflected Qianlong's reconfirmation of Sichuan's strategic importance: it could be explosive if it was not under a reliable and strong leadership. To the positions of the new governors-general for the two strategic areas, Qianlong appointed only Manchus. Cereng became the governor-general of Sichuan, albeit the fact that he was the elder brother of Necin, who was also on the slate to be penalized for his procrastination in directing the first Jinchuan war. Yinjishan, who had been the governor-general of Sichuan and Shaanxi between 1740 and 1743, was picked as the governor-general of Shaanxi and Gansu. The position of governor of Sichuan was abolished soon after.[95] To a degree, Qianlong's restoration of Yongzheng's scheme of keeping Sichuan and the Shaanxi-Gansu region under two separated governors-general became the most important legacy of the first Jinchuan war for the Sichuan frontier.

After Cereng became the new governor-general of Sichuan, his first main task was to lead the Qing expedition into Tibet in 1750 and 1751 in the wake of the riot in Lhasa in which two Qing *amban* and hundreds of Qing troops and civilians were killed. This event might have confirmed again Sichuan's strategic value to the emperor. A few years later, when Cereng took a leave in mourning for his parent in 1753, Qianlong filled his position with Huang Tinggui, who had served in this position since 1731, when Yongzheng had placed Sichuan and Shaanxi under two governors-general, but who was demoted to the post of provincial military commander when Qianlong combined them into one position in 1735. At a personal level Huang's coming back to this same position in Sichuan that he had left about eighteen years previously must have stirred emotions; he revealed his sentiments over these career fluctuations in a subtle manner in a stele inscription for the repairs of a dam in Sichuan.[96]But the change also exemplifies the fluctuation in Qianlong's vision regarding the Sichuan frontier. After Huang was transferred to the northwest in 1755 to direct logistical affairs when the Qing started to engage the Zunghar Mongols in Eastern Turkistan, Qianlong sent Kaitai, a Manchu who had a *jinshi* degree (a degree conferred on the one who passed the highest level's civil service examinations), as Huang's successor. This inaugurated a practice that more Manchus were to be appointed to the critical position of governor-general of Sichuan in the coming decades. Ever since the mid-eighteenth century, the Qianlong emperor had told officials who were appointed to Sichuan that their positions were not "remote" ones but "important" ones (*cifeidiaoyuan, gaidiaoyaoye*).[97]

During the interlocked wars in Eastern Turkistan in the latter part of the 1750s, first with the Zunghar people and then with the Muslim tribes, Sichuan was mobilized to send the front grain, horses, and other matériel. This situation probably prompted some officials in the northwest who directed the war logistics to consider bringing Sichuan into the region again administratively. On September 20, 1759, Yang Yingju, the governor-general of Shaanxi and Gansu, proposed restoring the governorship-general of Sichuan and Shaanxi and setting up a new post of governor-general of Gansu. Yang argued that Gansu was an extensive area, and it managed many affairs in the Qing territories in Eastern Turkistan since no formal Qing administration had been established there during the duration of those wars, so that a separate governor-general for Gansu seemed necessary. Qianlong's response to Yang's suggestion was unusual. He changed the title of the current governor-general of Sichuan to the "governor-general of Sichuan and Shaanxi," but he let this governor-general continue to be stationed in Sichuan and only administer civil affairs in the two provinces. Meanwhile, he appointed Yang as the governor-general of Gansu and gave him the power to direct the military forces in both Shaanxi and Gansu provinces.[98] By so doing, the throne split the provincial authority of Shaanxi between two governors-general—one in Sichuan and one in Gansu. Apparently this was a wartime expedient, which only lasted for fewer than three months.

With the Zunghar defeated and Eastern Turkistan pacified, it was predictable that there would be less possibility in the future for the northwestern frontier to take in Sichuan in its jurisdiction to facilitate wartime logistical undertakings. Meanwhile, a general of Ili was appointed to oversee the recently conquered Eastern Turkistan; Gansu was no longer in a position to take care of the business over there. On January 21, 1760, Qianlong ruled on the abolition of the governor-general of Gansu and the restoration of both the governor-general of Shaanxi and Gansu and the governor-general of Sichuan.[99] To be sure, this was the last time in which the Qing state made adjustment to the position of governor-general of Sichuan. After this incident an exclusive governor-general for Sichuan became the permanent structure until the end of the Qing dynasty. It remained in place even during the war against the White Lotus Rebellion, when coordination between Sichuan and Shaanxi was imperative.

During the second Jinchuan war of 1770 through 1776, another important step was taken to upgrade the Sichuan frontier: a banner general (*jiangjun*) in Sichuan was installed. In the fall of 1775, when the war reached its final phase, Qianlong transferred a thousand soldiers from the banner garrison in Chengdu to Dartsedo, for it was "indeed a strategically critical point."[100] Then in 1776 he appointed Mingliang, the banner general in the

Guangzhou garrison, as the new Chengdu general and sent him to head the banner regiment at Dartsedo. This was the first time a banner general, the highest banner official outside of the capital, was appointed to the Sichuan frontier. When the Chengdu garrison was first established in 1718 during the first invasion of Tibet, the Kangxi emperor assigned a vice commander-in-chief (*fudutong*), which was the next highest banner position outside of the capital, to head the new banner garrison in Chengdu. It signified Kangxi's perception of the area's position at the time: Sichuan was becoming strategically important, yet it was not as critical as other areas to which a banner general was assigned. Kangxi's arrangement for the Sichuan frontier remained unchanged until this upgrade in the second Jinchuan campaign, from which time on two leading banner officials, a general and a vice commander-in-chief, were regularly stationed in Sichuan.

A few years after the second Jinchuan war, the Qing state adjusted the formula of the banner station in Sichuan. It was decided then that the vice commander-in-chief of the Chengdu garrison replace the Chengdu general to be stationed at Dartsedo, and that the latter was assigned to be stationed at the Chengdu garrison. While the permanent stationing of a Manchu vice commander-in-chief at Dartsedo culminated decades of Qing expansion into the Kham area, the stationing of the Manchu general in Chengdu marked the elevation of the position of the Chengdu garrison. Unlike the Manchu generals in most of the other major garrisons in the country who only had authority over the Manchu troops, but were not given the responsibility to take charge of the Green Standard garrisons, the Chengdu general was mandated to command both the Manchu troops in Sichuan and all Qing outposts on the main road from western Sichuan to Lhasa, which were staffed mainly with the Green Standard troops and ethnic soldiers.[101]

In addition, the Chengdu general oversaw both civil and military affairs in Tibet and the non-Han areas in Sichuan in association with the governor-general of Sichuan. But he was a higher authority in both civil and military affairs than the governor-general of Sichuan, even though the latter was also obliged to take full charge of Tibetan affairs and to be responsible for any military actions in Tibet, as stipulated in Qianlong's edict to define the responsibilities of the Chengdu general.[102] Both the *yamen* of the governor-general of Sichuan and the Chengdu general hired secretaries who specialized in Tibetan language and learning to process documents concerning Tibetan affairs. In the case of military action, usually the governor-general of Sichuan took care of the logistics, while the Chengdu general was the commander-in-chief leading military actions. The Chengdu general maintained his special prerogatives to the end of the Qing dynasty. Because of this, he was regarded as more prestigious than other Manchu generals. Over the eighteenth and nineteenth centuries the garrison's compound, which was located in western Chengdu, came to become a sizable city within the city, about 1.6 miles in circumference, housing tens of thousands of Manchus and Mongols, including bannermen and their families.[103]

Ever since the second Jinchuan war, Qianlong was inclined to appoint only Manchus or Chinese bannermen to the key positions of the Sichuan frontier. From 1772 to the early nineteenth century, almost no Chinese were appointed to the position of provincial military commander of Sichuan, which contrasts starkly with the previous century in which there was not a single Manchu in the position.[104] Meanwhile, the position of the governor-general of Sichuan was also filled mostly by Manchus in the last several decades of the eighteenth century, with only two exceptions—Li Shijie and Sun Shiyi. Li was a Guizhou native and was governor-general of Sichuan twice in the 1780s. But in 1788, during the first Gurkha campaign, the Qianlong emperor overtly expressed his doubts about Li, because of the fact that "he is Han Chinese," among other things.[105] Sun Shiyi was appointed to this position in 1789 and again during the second Gurkha war. He was probably the only quintessential Chinese who had been trusted by Qianlong in frontier affairs in his late reign.

By the late eighteenth century it became common for a number of Manchu generals to be rotated among the four top positions on the Sichuan frontier: the governor-general, the Chengdu general, the provincial military commander, and the *amban* in Lhasa. More specifically, the provincial military commander was often promoted to either the Chengdu general or the governor-general or *amban* in Lhasa, and it was also common for an *amban* to be transferred to Sichuan as either the Chengdu general or governor-general, or vice versa.[106] Interestingly, among those Manchu appointees a number of them had one or more relatives who had been either famous or infamous in the Sichuan frontier. For instance, Mingliang was Fuheng and Fucing's nephew, Fukang'an was Fuheng's eldest son, Techeng'e was Cereng's son, and Lebao was the son of Wenfu, the chief commander who had been killed in the Muguomu fiasco during the second Jinchuan war. It is not an exaggeration that almost all the prominent military leaders in the late eighteenth century had served in the Sichuan frontier in one or more of those positions. With those positions being made banner positions, it is evident that the Sichuan frontier had been comparable in importance to the northwestern frontier on which exclusive Manchu appointments were a yardstick. However, it had been a long way for Sichuan to reach this point from the time in which it had to count on the banner troops in either the Xi'an garrison or Jingzhou garrison in times of emergency.

The Gurkha invasion of Tibet in 1788 raised again the question of Tibet's security to the Qing dynasty, but it was a question of different nature and gravity from the Zunghar threat that had been considered a matter of life and death. Although Qianlong was firm in resorting to force to settle this crisis, he saw a long-term solution for Tibet's security in the line of enhancing the self-defense capabilities of the Tibetans.[107] As a result, in 1789, Ehui and his cohorts drafted a nineteen-point proposal regarding the reinforcement of the defense system in Tibet, which was subsequently ratified by the Qing century government.[108] Among other things, they suggested the stationing of 150 Qing troops in the Tsang area, which bordered Nepal (the former Qing military station had only been in Central Tibet), and setting up outposts there and staffing them with Tibetan troops. It also stipulated that the Tibetan soldiers undergo military training. In addition, this document cleared up a gray area concerning *amban* and the Sichuan provincial government: the proposal gave the Chengdu general and the Sichuan provincial government full authority to rule the annexed Kham area west of Dartsedo, which had hitherto been within the jurisdiction of the Qing *amban* in Lhasa.[109]

When the Gurkhas invaded Tibet for the second time in 1791, Qianlong was more inclined to believe that the troubles in Tibet lay in that his *amban* in Lhasa had not been conscientious in doing their jobs, but only counted the days for transferring back to the capital.[110] Hence Qianlong ordered to have their responsibilities redefined. He instructed the officials who were drafting new rules to use the Qing administrative system in Eastern Turkistan as a model for the Qing *amban* in Tibet. In other words, he wanted the *amban* to be more involved in the affairs of the Tibetan government but not to function as merely observers and liaisons to Beijing.[111] In the spring of 1793, a twenty-nine-point proposal—the so-called "Twenty-Nine Article Ordinance of Government"—was produced by the Qing.[112] Although this document has long been regarded as a hallmark of the full-scale Manchu/Chinese control of Tibet—it placed the Tibetan political and religious hierarchies under the stricter supervision of the Qing *amban*—it should be pointed out that many of its articles were aimed at strengthening the Tibetan authorities, so that they could effectively rule their land and no longer needed to turn to the Qing frequently for intervention, especially for military assistance. As was stipulated in the document, Tibet was obliged to set up its own standing army but do away with the practice of temporarily recruited militiamen.[113] Needless to say, this was the key for Tibet to become militarily independent in the long run. Compared with the nineteen-point proposal of 1789, the twenty-nine-point proposal of 1793 went much further in trying to revamp the Tibetan political and military systems. Nevertheless, the Qing did not seem to have the determination nor the means to implement all those reforms in the years to come.

What is apparent from reading many edicts that Qianlong issued during the second Gurkha crisis is that the Qing state was no longer willing to safeguard Tibet at all costs—Qianlong was bitter and angry, at times, about the costly responsibility of sending another expedition to Tibet.[114] The emperor tried, for the first time, to let the Tibetans share the war costs and was stringent whenever it came to money.[115] Although the Qing succeeded in stopping the Gurkha aggression toward Tibet, it became evident to both the emperor and his military elite that the Qing empire had reached its limit of expansion, both temporally and spatially. Therefore, the war on the Gurkhas also marked the end of the frontier activism that the Qing dynasty had been assuming since the late seventeenth century. This change of attitude on the part of the Qing state explains partially why the inclusion of Nepal in the Qing tributary system did not stimulate further Qing interest in the Himalayan region.[116] For the Sichuan frontier, the two wars with the Gurkhas represented the last pitch of the military lineup and general mobilization. With Tibet secured again and the Qing oriented to fostering a self-reliant Tibetan government, there would not be any major military operation in and out of Tibet after 1792. Consequently, the Sichuan frontier gradually and quietly lost its significance as a key strategic area when the nineteenth century descended.

6 THE MILITARY PRESENCE IN SOCIETY AND ECONOMY

On the frontiers it is best to put the military ahead of the civil bureaucracy, which is secondary. —THE YONGZHENG EMPEROR, 1734

THE EIGHTEENTH-CENTURY FRONTIER CRISES AND MILITARY OPERATIONS had a great impact on the socioeconomic life of the Sichuan frontier. One of the most notable developments was the ascendancy of the military. Unlike most other areas, where the literati class was the bellwether in local society, in Sichuan this class was small and nearly invisible. By contrast, as a critical player in the Qing frontier enterprise, the military received much special treatment from the state, enjoying a privileged position in both political and economic terms. By the middle of the Qianlong period the military establishment in Sichuan had reached its zenith. With huge amounts of state funds flowing to the area to support the military buildup and the surrounding frontier campaigns, the military had numerous opportunities to augment its interests. Meanwhile, the local economy was constantly stimulated by the extensive demands of the armies and the frontier wars. The Qing state and the private sector had, between roughly 1700 and 1800, developed an intricate partnership in supporting the frontier wars. In the end the economic landscape in Sichuan had been largely revamped, thanks to the constant military operations.

A PRIVILEGED EXISTENCE

After the traumatic Wu Sangui Rebellion the Kangxi emperor had paid much attention to checking the power of the provincial viceroys and military leaders in the southwestern frontier, including Sichuan. Although he had given some leeway in appointing military officials in those provinces before and during the rebellion, he obviously became more restrictive after. The rising importance of Tibetan affairs reversed the trend, however. Following Kangxi's footprint, both Yongzheng and Qianlong yielded concessions to the military on the Sichuan frontier. As a result, the military personnel, especially the military leaders, enjoyed many prerogatives and formed a special interest group on this frontier.

The Kangxi Period

With Yue Shenglong's appointment to Sichuan in 1696, and with the battle of Dartsedo in 1701, Kangxi was ready to brush his precautions aside, as well as many bureaucratic rules and conventions.[1] The new yardsticks in treating the officials in the Sichuan frontier were pragmatism and flexibility. During the battle of Dartsedo, Kangxi gave the provincial authorities prerogatives in selecting qualified officers: he allowed officers in Sichuan to be promoted within the province, which was against the rule that prohibited officers from being promoted within the same province; he also allowed the provincial authorities to appoint officers, bypassing routine bureaucratic procedures. He reasoned: "Sichuan is an important place, so the positions of military officials cannot be vacant for too long."[2]

In 1708, Kangxi endorsed a motion by which all border and coastal areas would use the method of *tibu* in military appointments. Meaning "appointment by recommendation," the *tibu* method allowed provincial officials to recommend lower officers to the higher openings within their provinces, whereas the regular procedures required the Board of War to prepare the slate from a pool of candidates who were often from other provinces.[3] In 1718, Kangxi even agreed that in practicing the *tibu* system, the post of regional commanders (*zongbing*), a high military post, could be filled by lower officers in nearby areas.[4] The *tibu* practice enabled all the vacancies to be filled quickly but compromised the law of avoidance for the military ranks on the frontiers. In his last year of life Kangxi came to the realization that the *tibu* system had been abused to a certain degree, but he did not retreat from it.[5]

In his later years Kangxi also allowed experienced military officials to stay in their positions for unusually long periods, especially in strategically important areas, which contrasted with his earlier precaution against such a practice.[6] His justification was that to be familiar with their local environments was a special asset, so that it was not wise to frequently transfer them around for the sake of bureaucratic routines. While turnovers of civil officials were commonplace, it seems that military officials, once the emperor felt the appointed officials were the right persons for the posts, would stay in their posts until they retired or until illness made them unable to perform their duties. In Sichuan the tenure of the chief military officials was often much longer than that of the civil officials. The most illuminating case was that of Yue Shenglong, who was the highest military commander in Sichuan between 1696 and 1711, with only a short hiatus when he was impeached in 1700. A longtime stay in one place would prompt those military officials to seek to settle permanently in the places of their appointments, since many had purchased properties there, even though they were forbidden to do so. Having pointedly criticized this practice among the military officials in 1711, calling it "not a beautiful thing," Kangxi compromised his position only two years later.[7] In 1713, shortly before Yue Shenglong died of illness, he requested that his family be allowed to change its official domicile to Chengdu, the capital city of Sichuan, saying that his over ninety-year-old mother was unable to make the move back to their hometown in barren Gansu province. Kangxi gave his consent to Yue's request without question, even though he emphasized that this could not be cited as precedent for others.[8]

In fact, long before Yue Shenglong officially requested the throne to allow his family's taking root in Sichuan, he had made efforts for years to expand the family's interests in the province. He placed more than a hundred of his family members and servants in the local garrisons, and recommended his elder brother, Yue Chaolong, also a military professional, to a high military position in Sichuan.[9] To get around the law of avoidance, which forbade serving under one's relative, Chaolong changed his name, both his family name and given name, to Liu Jie. When this scheme was exposed, Kangxi blamed neither of the Yue brothers. Instead, he let Yue Chaolong change his name back to the original and promoted him to the position of a brigade commander in Dongchuan, southwestern Sichuan.[10] It seems that Yue Chaolong also changed his domicile to Chengdu, following his younger brother's suit.[11]

Kangxi also openly extended his favor to Yue Shenglong's second son, Yue Zhongqi. Like many official families, Yue Shenglong purchased a petty civil official post for his son—that of a subprefectural magistrate in Sichuan.[12] When Yue Shenglong retired in 1711, Kangxi summoned Yue Zhongqi to the capital for an audience. Apparently impressed by Yue

Zhongqi's military potential, Kangxi changed his career by appointing him the brigade commander of Songpan, northwestern Sichuan. Then in 1721, due to his outstanding act of taking Lhasa during the first invasion into Tibet, Kangxi promoted Yue Zhongqi to the position of Sichuan's provincial military commander, the same position that his father had occupied for many years, which was tantamount to a royal sanction of the establishing of this family dynasty in Sichuan.

Besides Yue Shenglong, several other military leaders obtained imperial permission to change their domiciles and settle in Sichuan. Among them was Tang Xishun, who replaced Yue Shenglong as the provincial military commander when Yue was accused by Governor Yu Yangzhi before the battle of Dartsedo. Tang actually lived in Chengdu after he retired in 1701 but did not request permission from the throne until 1709, shortly before his death.[13] The precedents set by Tang Xishun and Yue Shenglong must have encouraged lesser military officials in Sichuan to do the same. Although only a couple of others made formal petitions to the throne, many officers of lower ranks may have simply settled in Sichuan without going through this procedure.[14] It is also notable that most of these military men who settled in Sichuan were from the northwestern frontier—either Shaanxi or Gansu province. Many of them had been Yue Shenglong's longtime subordinates, some even being his fellow villagers. With Yue's protection and promotion of them, a northwestern clique had in fact formed on the Sichuan frontier.

The conspicuous phenomenon that many military men saw Sichuan as an optimum place to make their home in the late Kangxi period contrasted with the civil officials' persistent unwillingness to serve in the province. Despite considerable economic progress achieved in Sichuan, the civil officials in the early eighteenth century continued delaying their arrival at their new posts so that they would be dismissed and then awaited better appointments. As a result, many civil positions in the province were still vacant.[15] Meanwhile, nonmilitary elite members—for example, the gentry families—continued moving out of the province. By 1711 a rule that had been enacted in the early Kangxi period was still in effect, requiring all the officials who came from Sichuan to return home after retirement for the purpose of preventing local elite members from emigrating via their official careers.[16] The stark contrast between the military and the civil elites in Sichuan in choosing their service and retirement places suggests that the province was more agreeable to the military elite.

Another trademark of Kangxi's favorable treatment of his military men was his leniency regarding the military's fortune-seeking activities. In fact, the opportunities for making a fortune provided one of the temptations for the military officials to stay put on the Sichuan frontier. Knowing full well that the economic issue was most vital for the military's morale, the emperor himself helped foster a haven for his officers to further their economic interests. While he was generally harsher in punishing them for appropriating soldiers' stipends and making fraudulent claims as to the size of the armies, Kangxi was more relaxed when it came to their fortune-seeking conduct, often turning his back on the issue of morality. In the late Kangxi period it was a commonplace for military officials to be involved in illicit conduct for economic gains; it was not rare, either, for high-sounding civil officials to impeach their military colleagues for such conduct. Unsurprisingly, incidents happened more frequently in the frontier areas, where the military had more prerogatives. Whenever such a case was brought to his attention, Kangxi tended to be more protective of his military officials. Time and again the emperor exhorted the viceroys who had been appointed to Sichuan not to be overcritical of their fellow military officials. Before Nian Gengyao left for Sichuan in 1709, the emperor gave him the following advice: "The military officials should not be allowed to make trouble. However, they should also be given some latitude [to make money] so that they can raise their families. As the governor, you should be friendly and cooperative with the military officials; do not be overcritical [of them]."[17]

With imperial endorsement and tolerance, the fortune-seeking practice among the military had become widespread in Sichuan by the late Kangxi period. The opportunities were many. It was not unusual for military officials to withhold part of the stipends of their subordinates as capital to start a business, such as running pawn shops and practicing usury. One unique opportunity in Sichuan was the time-honored salt industry. Having been destroyed completely during the Ming-Qing transition, the salt industry began to recover following the Wu Sangui Rebellion, stimulated by the low, or even nominal, gabelle that was started in 1686.[18]

Another opportunity was the border trade in Dartsedo, which resumed following the Qing conquest of the area in 1701. In contrast to the tight control under the Ming dynasty, the Qing only levied a symbolic tariff on the Chinese goods sold to Tibetan merchants but nothing on the Tibetan goods sold to Chinese merchants. Since the time when Yu Yangzhi was the governor of Sichuan, the officials in Sichuan had embezzled the levies on border trade. This practice most likely survived Yu's removal in 1700.

However, the beneficiaries might well have been military officials when more outposts were set up along the highway connecting Chengdu and Lhasa via Dartsedo. Yue Shenglong had been accused of letting his subordinates monopolize the salt business while driving out small salt merchants, and receiving bribes from merchants who sold emaciated horses to his soldiers.[19] For Yue a more convenient way was to "borrow" money from the provincial treasury. Upon his retirement it was found that he still owed 10,000 taels. Although he thought that it was wrong, Kangxi did not penalize Yue, justifying his leniency by saying that Yue "has made many contributions."[20] Kang Tai, a Shaanxi native and the Sichuan provincial military commander from 1712 to 1719, was also found to appropriate soldiers' stipends, which caused the notorious mutiny in 1717 during the mobilizations for the first invasion into Tibet.[21]

Another important way for the military officials in Sichuan to get rich was to invest in land that had been widely available because of the small population. After the Wu Sangui Rebellion the military had seized some arable land in Sichuan whose owners had fled, but did not pay tax. Warning that the trend would continue if no immediate measures were taken, Tuhai, then governor of Sichuan, suggested forcing the military personnel to return the land to their owners upon the latter's return, but allowing them to keep the ownerless land so long as the officers and soldiers registered the land with the local government.[22] It is plausible that this situation persisted into the eighteenth century. In addition to the military colonies, there were several other types of land owned by the military personnel. For one thing the families of the Green Standard troops were allocated land. For another thing some garrisons also owned land as their collective property and rented it out to farmers. The rent collected would then be at the officers' disposal.[23] In addition, military officials had also acquired land despite violating the rules. As was no secret to the throne, Yue Shenglong and his family owned a large amount of land in Chengdu prefecture.[24] Widespread land ownership by the military contributed to the problem of the low rate of land registration relative to the land reclamation that had been well under way. Although the land associated with the military was entitled to certain tax privileges, many preferred not to register their land at all. The fact that the military owned land in Sichuan likely constituted another reason for Kangxi's insistence not to conduct a land survey in the province, in addition to his concern over the stability among the civilian population.

The Yongzheng Period

The late Kangxi period set a precedent for the rest of the eighteenth century in the treatment of the military. When the Yongzheng emperor was enthroned in 1722, he initially attempted to reverse the trend. Deeming the appointment system the key in tightening the central control, Yongzheng paid tremendous attention to it. Being a highly energetic and industrious monarch, he set a high record in constantly reshuffling both civil and military positions in the entire country throughout his short thirteen-year reign. In Sichuan what he attempted to do was to take back the right of appointing lower-rank officials from the provincial authorities. Since the late Kangxi period, it had become a convention for provincial civil and military officials in Sichuan, as well as its two neighbors Yunnan and Guizhou, to fill local vacancies with people they picked from within their province and then report to the central government for approval.

Needless to say, this practice fostered nepotism and weakened central control. In 1724, Yongzheng abruptly rebuffed a request from the governor of Guizhou that local officials in the poor and remote areas of the province be recommended for promotion by the provincial officials, either civil or military. Following this incident, Yongzheng signaled to his courtiers to work out a solution to substitute for this practice. The result was rather ironic: after each national civil service examination, the examinees who failed to pass the examinations would be given an opportunity to serve a sort of internship in those border provinces, including Sichuan. While outstanding performance would win them formal offices in that province upon the recommendation of the provincial officials, they were free to retake the examinations if they so desired.[25] Effective or not, this measure served Yongzheng's purpose in his attempt to take back the right of appointing lower officials in all those border provinces.

Apparently, Yongzheng was not initially impressed with his father's allowing military officials to stay in their positions for an extensive period. In the first five years of his reign, Yongzheng frequently reappointed major military officials in many provinces, including Sichuan, in which the positions of provincial military commander and regional commanders of Chuanbei, Chongqing, and Songpan were mostly affected. As a result, many of the appointees only stayed in their positions briefly, sometimes merely a few months.[26] In the fall of 1723, Yongzheng issued an edict to the Board of War forbidding high-ranking military officials from procuring estates and settling down in their service places. But the edict ruled that military officials below the rank of assistant regional commander would not be restrained by this rule, since Yongzheng thought that the lower officers could not possess large properties and the forced return to their home area would leave some of them in economic difficulties.[27]

Accordingly, the Board of War stipulated that the military officials below the rank of assistant regional commander were to be allowed to own properties in their service places and that they or their families be allowed to settle and change their domiciles when their service was terminated due to retirement, dismissal, or death. The board also stipulated that retired officers should pay taxes once they registered as residents in a place.[28] This new rule revealed that by the late Kangxi reign, it had become a commonplace for military men to purchase estates and settle in their service places, this being far more prevalent in Sichuan. Although this rule prohibited the high-ranking military officials from pursuing wealth and taking root where they served, with green lights turned on to the lower-ranking military officials, it would have been harder to enforce the prohibition on high-ranking officers who would figure out ways to get around the rule. Meanwhile, this compromise to the lower-ranking officers would set up a negative precedent in observing the law of avoidance for all officials, both civil and military.

When Yongzheng started his reign, he inherited from his father a nearly depleted state treasury with the amount of arrears reaching 2.5 million taels of silver.[29] Blaming his father's excessive leniency in supporting the military, the banners and the Green Standard Army alike, for the deplorable situation, Yongzheng was determined to revamp the fiscal system.[30] To be sure, the fiscal breakdown at the end of the Kangxi era was not only caused by military expenditures, which can only be termed as moderate compared with the staggering military spending in the Qianlong era. Among other things, a number of expensive water projects after the Wu Sangui Rebellion and, more important, abuses by officials of all levels taking advantage of the emperor's generosity and leniency, all contributed to the fiscal crisis. While setting up fiscal reforms to generate more state revenues, Yongzheng tried to retrench on military expenditures. He wanted to be less lenient toward the military. In the early years of his reign, Yongzheng showed his determination in a series of moves that were aimed at cutting the military budget: he enjoined that the military expenditures of all provinces be fixed. He admonished Manchu military professionals not to indulge themselves in extravagant lifestyles and made it clear that the state would not increase funds to subsidize Manchu soldiers. He also urged the provincial officials in the northwestern region to submit the accounts of military expenditures to the central government, which had not been done during the Kangxi period. He sent two officials to the Board of Revenue to investigate loans to soldiers.[31]

Nevertheless, Yongzheng's efforts to reverse his father's lenient policy toward the military were soon offset because of the new frontier emergencies in Qinghai and Tibet, even though his fiscal reforms would continue nationwide. After the Lobdzan Dandzin incident Yongzheng had to swiftly resume a power-based stance in frontier affairs. In a few years the Qing launched another expedition to Tibet and soon an all-out war against the Zunghar people in Eastern Turkistan. Meanwhile, numerous military operations were under way in the southwestern frontier, as well as in parts of Sichuan, Hunan, and Guangxi, to impose reform on the ethnic communities. By Yongzheng's fifth year (1727), many signs show that his determination to rein in the military in the frontier areas had largely evaporated. At first, he retreated from his earlier position of recentralizing the official appointment system in the border provinces. In 1726, Yongzheng ruled that the promotion procedures in the border provinces should be directed by specific conditions in each place, thus withdrawing from a wholesale abolition of the *tibu* system in the border provinces.[32] In 1727 he admitted that his policy of forbidding lower officers from being promoted within their own garrisons was not practical, and he stated that the old practice should continue.[33]

When Ortai was sent to the southwestern frontier, Yongzheng yielded even more power to him in the matter of appointing local officials, civil and military alike. As discussed already, Ortai deliberately fostered a clique of his followers in the southwest, recommending a number of his protégés to key positions and even extending his influence to Sichuan. When more and more ethnic communities were brought under the direct Qing rule in the campaign to reform the local chieftain system, it became necessary to set up new rules regarding official appointments to those newly acquired territories. In the fall of 1727, Ortai suggested that officials serving in the remote counties, both newly established ones and those adjacent to the ethnic minorities, should all be qualified for promotion—that is, transferring to better places in three years, instead of five years as in most other areas. Further, he suggested that for those posts, appointees could be selected from among the local officials in the same province. Ortai also requested the application of the same rules to the military officials in those places.[34] Apparently, Yongzheng's rectification of the appointment practice was aborted, given the rapidly changing priorities.

Not only did Yongzheng compromise in official appointments, he also returned to his father's position of being relaxed concerning the economic gains of military men. He soon started following Kangxi's example of lavishing large amounts of awards on soldiers. In 1724 he cancelled the loans of 57,000 taels of silver that the Yunnan troops had borrowed when they were sent to Tibet that year.[35] While he set his hand to pulling down Nian Gengyao in the wake of the Qinghai campaign, Yongzheng did not forget to comfort Nian's troops in the northwestern region; in early 1725 he allocated 200,000 taels from the central treasury to them.[36] Later the same year he turned to the southwest, first granting awards to the troops of Sichuan and Yunnan who had participated in the invasion of Tibet in 1720, and then granting 10,000 taels to Sichuan troops who had followed Zhou Ying to Tibet at the time of the Qinghai crisis.[37] In 1727, when he ordered the expedition to Tibet to quell the riot initiated by the three rebellious Tibetan *kaloon*, he granted the troops a sum to prepare for their equipment, in lieu of loaning money to them as was usually the case.[38] Huang Tinggui, Sichuan's provincial military commander, reported in 1727 that having been spoiled by the favorable treatment in the Kangxi period, the officers and soldiers in Sichuan all competed in showing off their wealth, putting on luxurious silk and satin clothes and borrowing money from others to maintain their extravagant lifestyles, which caused frequent desertion when the soldiers could not pay back their debts. Yongzheng instructed Huang not to try to rectify this problem all at once, but rather to try to change it gradually. He especially said that "it is not convenient for me to give any instructions [on this]."[39] In other words, Yongzheng was noncommittal about solving the problem.

In a similar move, significant concessions were made with regard to the military officials' purchase of properties and settling in their duty areas. Ji Chengbin, a Shaanxi native whose father was Yue Shenglong's comrade-in-arms, followed Yue to Sichuan in 1696 after he became orphaned. First under Yue Shenglong, and then Yue Zhongqi, Ji was promoted in military ranks and set up an extensive family in Sichuan. In 1727, Ji petitioned to Yongzheng to allow him to change his domicile to Chengdu prefecture by citing the aforementioned new rule. Although he was a high military official at this time in Henan province, the highest position he held in Sichuan was below assistant regional commander, Ji argued, so that he was eligible to make Chengdu his home. Ji thus got what he requested.[40] In

1728, shortly before another expedition to Tibet, Yongzheng granted Ma Liangzhu, a brigade commander in Sichuan and a Muslim from Gansu, special permissions as a reward for his participation in the expedition: Ma was allowed to fetch his family from Gansu to Chengdu to settle and to purchase land in his new home area.[41]

Yongzheng's apparently contradictory position would encourage more military officials to breach the rule. As records reveal, at least several other high-ranking military officials settled in Sichuan during the Yongzheng period. One of them was Yang Tianzong, another Shaanxi native. Having distinguished himself as a company commander in the campaign to take Dartsedo in 1701, Yang was promoted to brigade vice commander. It is highly possible that he settled his family in Chengdu around this time. Later he was transferred to a couple of other provinces and was eventually promoted to Yunnan's provincial military commander. When he retired, he returned to his home in Chengdu and officially changed his domicile.[42] In early 1734, Zhao Ru, the regional commander of Jianchang in Sichuan and a Shaanxi native, petitioned the throne and asked that he be allowed to register as a Sichuan resident. Like several others before him, Zhao knew clearly that it violated the rule, but he cited the fact that his family had lived in Sichuan for many years and owned property and that his parents had been buried in Sichuan. Without question, Yongzheng approved Zhao's request.[43] Another military official who settled in Sichuan was Zhou Ying, a veteran general on the Sichuan frontier who had led the first Qing military station in Lhasa after the 1720 invasion and was again sent to Tibet twice in the Yongzheng era. Yang Jinxing, the military commander of Guyuan (Guyuan *tidu*), also settled in Sichuan.[44] Yongzheng went further than his father in that he openly broke the rules that he had set up himself just a few years earlier by endorsing those high-ranking military officials' requests of settling in Sichuan as well as possessing properties there.

The scenario that the military in Sichuan had a great amount of arable land under its control was still a reality during the Yongzheng era. When Ma Huibo, the newly appointed Sichuan governor, tried in 1727 to set his hand to many problems that had accumulated during previous decades, one thing on his agenda was to conduct a land survey.[45] Although he did not venture to extend the survey to the land owned by the military personnel, Ma urged the military personnel, both officers and soldiers, in Sichuan to register their land with the local governments. He suggested setting up rules to punish those who failed to register and the officers who failed to discipline their subordinates.[46] Although no record is available about the follow-up of Ma's motion, most likely many did not report or did not report all of their land. What is interesting in this lone case in which a provincial official exposed the phenomenon of military-owned land to the central government is that Ma Huibo himself was a military man, whose fairly brief tenure as the Sichuan governor, lasting a few months, was marked by his bold attempt to reinvigorate a sluggish and corruption-ridden provincial bureaucracy. Perhaps it was because of his military background that he dared to challenge the military in Sichuan. Not surprisingly, he was soon transferred away from Sichuan.[47]

After having been on the throne for several years, Yongzheng had completely accepted and assumed his father's attitude of partiality toward the military. As is discussed later in this chapter, Yongzheng proved to be a bigger spender in military expenditures than his father. He ventured to institutionalize what his father had pursued in granting economic favors to the military. In so doing, the most radical measure Yongzheng adopted was to officially sponsor the military's involvement in commercial activities. From 1729 to 1730, in three installments, Yongzheng allocated a total sum of 1,183,000 taels to some of the banner garrisons outside of the capital and about a hundred Green Standard garrisons around the country and let his military use the grants as investment capital, "procuring profits through entrepreneurial operation" (*yingyun shengxi*), in Yongzheng's own terms.[48] This policy, by any interpretation, was a radical departure from Kangxi's personal and informal approach in rewarding the military. Altogether, the Green Standard garrisons in Sichuan received nearly 60,000 taels as the capital for investment.[49]

To be sure, the military in Sichuan might not have embraced this opportunity as fervently as in other provinces, where there were not as many opportunities as in Sichuan to receive extra funds from the state. There are only a few records on how the military in Sichuan used these funds. While the Chongqing command opened a pawn shop that had been doing well for some time, most other garrisons commissioned merchants to invest for them or purchased land for rent. The Songpan command in northwestern Sichuan simply distributed the funds to all the soldiers for individual disposition.[50] Meanwhile, the military in Sichuan surely continued in other ways to seek economic gains, mostly illicitly. In 1734, Echang, Sichuan's newly appointed governor, tried to expose to the throne the arrogant manner and illicit conduct of the military personnel in Sichuan, which seemed to be most new appointees' first act. But Yongzheng repudiated his criticism as "absurd comments" (*bujingzhilun*) and further warned him:

"On the frontiers it is best to put the military ahead of the civil bureaucracy, which is secondary."[51] Tantamount to his approval of the military's engagement in illicit businesses, Yongzheng's reaction was indicative of a partial mind-set toward the military in this frontier province.

For the Yue family the Yongzheng period was bittersweet. In the early part of the Yongzheng period, Yue Zhongqi was appointed the governor-general of Sichuan and Shaanxi, which broke the Manchu monopoly on this position but also violated the law of avoidance, as he had been a Sichuanese on paper since 1713. With his ascendancy more family members stepped into the national political arena. Yue Jun, Yue Zhongqi's second son, started his official career in Xi'an prefecture and was directly under his father when Zhongqi became the governor-general of Sichuan-Shaanxi in 1725. At the same time Yue Chaolong, a military officer in Gansu then, was also in Yue Zhongqi's jurisdiction. When Yue Zhongqi asked whether his son and uncle should be transferred to observe the law of avoidance, Yongzheng ruled that Yue Chaolong could stay in the position but promoted Yue Jun to a higher post outside Yue Zhongqi's pale.[52] Soon after, Yue Jun was named Shandong governor, becoming the youngest governor in the entire country. Starting from the early 1730s with Yue Zhongqi's losing imperial favor, the family experienced some difficulties. Nevertheless, none of Yue Zhongqi's relatives was purged because of his case. Yue Jun continued holding his position as Shandong governor, except that Yongzheng no longer treated him with intimacy as before. In Sichuan his family still held most of its numerous estates in the Chengdu area, even though the local officials were supposed to confiscate all Yue's properties. Apparently, the local officials were protective of the Yue family, whose extensive networks remained largely intact.

The Qianlong Period

What unfolded during the long Qianlong reign mirrored the occurrences in the preceding Yongzheng era: in the beginning of his reign, the Qianlong emperor tried hard to rein in the military both in size and in its influence on the Sichuan frontier but had to return to the old track once the frontier emergencies began to arise. By the middle of the Qianlong era—that is, the end of the second Jinchuan war in 1776—the strong military presence in Sichuan became an irreversible reality. Unlike the Kangxi emperor, who tended to give both the Manchu and Chinese generals ample opportunities to move up, Qianlong placed more trust in the Manchus. In Sichuan higher provincial and military positions were often reserved for Manchu or Chinese bannermen, who were hand-picked by the emperor himself. However, the lower military positions in Sichuan were still mostly filled by natives or officers promoted in the province through the *tibu* system.[53] Qianlong did not attempt to limit this practice, partly because of pressure from provincial viceroys who recommended their subordinates to the local positions and partly out of concern that too many officers from outside of the area who were not familiar with the local conditions might impair the frontier's military strength.[54] Consequently, nepotism became prevalent in the area. For instance, at least six of Yue Zhongqi's sons and grandsons held lesser military posts in Sichuan.[55] During the two Jinchuan campaigns most military positions in Sichuan were filled by the people who had earned their promotions in the wars, leaving no vacancies for appointees sent from outside the province by the central government.[56]

Not only did the officials in Sichuan attempt to control the appointment of middle and lower military positions, they also strove to maintain the swollen size of the military establishment. The official size of the Green Standard Army in Sichuan was not noticeably bigger than in other areas: 28,420, compared with 46,180 in Yunnan and 20,243 in Guizhou.[57] But it had greatly expanded during the Yongzheng period, at some points reaching 40,000.[58] The frequent wars throughout the Qianlong era in and near the Sichuan frontier gave the military more opportunities to expand. Usually a seesaw battle ensued between Beijing and the provincial authorities over the military size following each of the wars. While the central government wanted to slim it down, the provincial leaders tried to maintain the status quo so that they would not lose the military funds that they received.

After the first Jinchuan campaign, arguing that demobilizing all those veterans would be harmful to the military, the provincial leaders proposed leaving vacancies in the army unfilled when any appeared but not demobilizing anybody who was currently in service.[59] If this was a passive way to resist disarmament, the active approach was to keep the armies busy. In 1751, two years after the first Jinchuan war, Yue Zhongqi restored annual military field exercises by citing the deterioration of the military strength of his troops.[60] One year later, Yue and Cereng, the governor-general of Sichuan, launched a small campaign against the local chieftain in Zagu, northwestern Sichuan, who had allegedly attacked his neighboring chieftains; they stationed more troops in Zagu after this incident. Despite quick success, Qianlong warned the two viceroys not to drag the state into another onerous and full-scale war by escalating the hostilities, as he knew too well that a campaign of this kind would serve their purposes to receive more funds and maintain the military size.[61]

The call for downsizing the military on the Sichuan frontier was periodically heard at the court; Qianlong himself also tried to do so whenever an opportunity availed itself to him.[62] Nevertheless, a more serious problem took priority in the early 1780s: the apparently swollen size of the Green Standard Army might actually be inflated, as many vacancies had never been filled and the extra stipends had been taken by officers. If this trend continued, the Green Standard Army would be seriously undermined. In 1782, Qianlong authored a drastic reform by ordering the expansion of the "silver to nourish virtue" to all the Green Standard officials in the hope that they no longer needed to embezzle soldiers' stipends. Meanwhile, Qianlong ordered an increase of the Green Standard troops by sixty thousand nationwide to offset the effect of too many vacancies that had existed for years. For this increase the state treasury would pay 3 million taels more each year in feeding its gigantic military buildup.[63] Sichuan got a larger share from this increase than many other provinces, with a total of 4,274 troops being added.[64] Although his earlier concern about oversized military expenditures had not gone away, Qianlong was more inclined to place the quality of his armies ahead of economic concerns, especially in the frontier areas.

While the military land ownership in Sichuan tended to decline during the Qianlong period, the military officials continued seeking to settle in Sichuan.[65] In 1749, in the wake of the first Jinchuan war, Ma Liangzhu, to whom the Yongzheng emperor had given permission to bring his family to Chengdu and purchase estates there in the 1720s, requested that he be allowed to officially change his domicile to Chengdu, where he had already made his home for more than two decades. Knowing that his request was against the rule prohibiting higher-ranking military officials from doing so, he used the conventional excuse that his mother was too old to return to their hometown in Gansu. This excuse easily won Qianlong's approval.[66] In fact, bannermen had been faced with the similar situation as the Green Standard officers had; to be required to return to their banners in Beijing after their service period ended in provincial garrisons was burdensome for many. As Mark C. Elliott has noted, many Chinese bannermen actually purchased properties in their service places. Not unaware of his bannermen's predicament, Qianlong, throughout the 1740s and 1750s, relaxed the rules of forbidding bannermen, Manchu and Chinese alike, from purchasing properties in their service places and obliging all bannermen to return to their banners.[67] Needless to say, this compromise to bannermen would encourage more Green Standard officers in seeking the same. And it might become much less cumbersome for them to realize it starting from the mid-eighteenth century. However, it had been a noticeable phenomenon, up to that point, that many military officials in Sichuan had gone to great lengths to settle there (and in some rare cases in Yunnan).[68]

One important development during the Qianlong period was Yue Zhongqi's return to power in the first Jinchuan war. In 1737, Yue was freed from jail on parole by Qianlong, who thought that Yue should not be blamed for his missteps in directing the war in Eastern Turkistan, since his expertise was in Sichuan.[69] Returning home in Chengdu, Yue named his garden *ansu*, meaning "to be happy with plainness," and his manor *aixian*, meaning "to be fond of leisure." He often spent time reading and gardening. The life he led before his reinstatement in 1748 was uneventful yet comfortable, except for one misfortune: his wife passed away shortly after his return.[70] Yue was obliged to pay 754,600 taels of silver for the damage allegedly caused by his mistakes in the Zunghar campaign, but by 1743 only 27,400 taels had been paid from selling his confiscated properties. Although Sichuan officials reported that all of Yue's properties had been seized and sold, Qianlong voiced his disbelief in 1749, pointing to the fact that the local officials tried to give this family of hundreds of members some protection.[71] After the first Jinchuan campaign Qianlong canceled this old debt himself, however. As later revealed to the throne by Yue himself, the Yue family owned several businesses on top of many land holdings, including a saltpeter workshop and a business of selling firewood that was cut from one of his estates. But Yue admitted to receiving only 400 to 500 taels in annual income from those businesses.[72] With Yue and his family setting an example in going after properties and profits, there is good reason to assume that the other military officials' families also acquired bountiful economic resources, constituting a caste of nouveau riche in this frontier province.

Again proving himself a valuable asset to the empire in the final chapter of the first Jinchuan campaign, Yue was showered with imperial favors. Among other things, he was granted the third rank of duke and had two of his sons entitled as junior guardsmen at the imperial court.[73] Back in Sichuan, Yue was quick to reclaim his fame and power, although they had never really vanished. To reinforce the networks within both the military and civil bureaucracies that Yue Zhongqi had carefully built, he promoted more of his old subordinates, some of whom were still facing corruption charges.[74] Most interestingly, Yue immediately repaired a shrine in Chengdu in dedication to Yue Fei, the Chinese hero of the Song dynasty who had fervently fought the Jurchen, the ancestors of the Manchus. The shrine had been destroyed during Zhang Xianzhong's occupation and had not been repaired since.[75] While the fictitious connections between Yue Fei and Yue Zhongqi had placed him in a dangerous situation in 1728, when Yue was implicated in the Zeng Jing incident, he was confident enough in 1749 to overtly pay homage to Yue Fei, which amounted to an acknowledgment of the blood bond between the ancient hero and the most powerful Chinese general of the time.[76]

Knowing that Yue's influence could also be at the cost of the central government's authority, Qianlong admonished Yue not to be haughty but to keep a good relationship with the governor-general and to discipline his family members.[77] More important, Qianlong repeatedly warned Yue to be discreet in using force against the ethnic peoples in the borderlands, as those conflicts could be costly to the empire but lucrative for frontier generals.[78] Despite his possession of the title of duke, Yue had not been further promoted. As the provincial military commander of Sichuan, he reported to a Manchu governor-general, Cereng. When Cereng led another expedition to Lhasa in 1750, Qianlong deliberately stopped Yue from going to Tibet.[79] He did not let Yue act in Cereng's capacity, either, even though Yue had been in the position of a governor-general back to the 1730s. Instead, the emperor gave the responsibility to Yinjishan, a Manchu and the governor-general of Shaanxi and Gansu. This instance clearly suggested that Qianlong's favor to Yue had a limit.

In the spring of 1754, Yue Zhongqi died at sixty-eight shortly after his son, Yue Jun, had died prematurely in 1753. On the same day on which the emperor issued a condolence that posthumously entitled Yue the duke of *xiangqin*, meaning "assistance with diligence," Qianlong appointed Yue Zhonghuang, Yue Chaolong's son and Zhongqi's cousin, to the position left by Zhongqi, the provincial military commander of Sichuan.[80] Being another open breach of the law of avoidance, Zhonghuang's taking this position prolonged the family's dominance in the province. Nevertheless, Zhonghuang's tenure was largely uneventful, lacking the glorious moments that were envied by every military leader: he did not participate in the campaigns to eliminate the Zunghar empire in Eastern Turkistan in the late 1750s; neither did he march to Tibet, as Zhongqi did several times, to quell a riot or expel invaders. Therefore, even though he held the position of the chief military commander in Sichuan for thirteen years (he died in 1767), and acted as governor-general of Sichuan briefly in 1759, he did not further the fame of the family. For the rest of Qing times Yue Zhongqi was remembered by his offspring, but the degree of power he held was not passed down: none of his descendants ever reached the position and influence comparable to that of Yue Shenglong and Yue Zhongqi.[81]

Throughout the eighteenth century the three successive emperors—Kangxi, Yongzheng, and Qianlong—all made considerable concessions to the military in Sichuan, either breaching rules to accommodate their needs or acquiescing in their self-seeking conduct. Although both Yongzheng and Qianlong had tried at the beginning of their reigns to reverse this practice, the emperors returned to Kangxi's policy of treating the military with leniency and flexibility when they had to count on the military's service on this key frontier. To a large degree, the state compromised its high vigilance against the regional strongmen in these borderlands that had been a priority since the Wu Sangui Rebellion. The Yue family's long dominance on the Sichuan frontier testifies to the state's shift of position. However, Yue Zhongqi's up-and-down career and the abrupt halt of the family's fortune after Yue Zhonghuang's death also show that the tension between the center and the regional power had never really disappeared: the central government was ever watchful. With more and more Manchus taking the key positions in Sichuan in the latter part of the Qianlong period, suffice it to say that it became unlikely to have another Chinese general rise to prominence, which was a relief for the Qing state. As the Manchu generals lived in their isolated garrison compound without many ties with the local society, and no other Yue Zhongqi–type of Green Standard general emerged, Sichuan's military elite began withering in the late Qianlong period, making room for a slowly growing gentry class.

THE MILITARY AND THE LOCAL ECONOMY

Over the course of the eighteenth century the military forces in the Sichuan frontier enjoyed considerable privileges and freedom in expanding their economic interests.[82] These military forces included more than thirty-eight thousand to forty thousand Green Standard troops who were stationed in their garrisons throughout the province and Tibet, as well as more than two thousand Manchu and Mongol troops who were mainly in the Chengdu garrison. During frontier campaigns more troops were deployed from afar, among whom were often Manchu and Mongol bannermen. It was not an isolated case for hundreds of thousands of troops to be assembled in this key strategic area during wartime. This section examines the role that the military and warfare played in the local economy. Quite contrary to conventional wisdom that military operations were usually detrimental to the local economy, what unfolded in the eighteenth century on the Sichuan frontier was that Qing frontier operations helped invigorate the economy, expanding the market for local products and integrating the area into national commercial networks.

The Pouring of Military Funds into Sichuan

The most important factor in understanding the relationship between the military and economic development in Sichuan was that this frontier was fully supported with the funds allocated from the state and transferred from either the central treasury or other provinces. In contrast to the situation in the key economic areas, where the military garrisons were usually funded with the revenues levied locally, it was not Qing policy to squeeze more resources from the local residents in Sichuan, the key strategic area, to meet the ever-increasing demands of the military and frontier wars. The dependency on outside financial support had its origins in the conquest era. At that time the young Qing dynasty had to earmark a fairly big portion of its income to support the war to conquer Sichuan and the southwestern region.[83]

Following the conquest, Sichuan, along with its two southwestern neighbors, remained on the receiving end of state funding, as the revenues in the province were too small to cover the expenses of the military garrisons. By 1685 the total revenue in cash that was collected from Sichuan was only 32,211 taels, but the military expenses in the provinces well exceeded this amount. In 1688, seven years after the Wu Sangui Rebellion, the province spent 115,563 taels in stipends and food rations for the Green Standard garrisons.[84] In 1693 the military expenses, however, jumped to 688,625 taels, while the land taxes and capitation together only produced a sum of about 100,000 taels.[85] So the province had had to depend on the so-called *xiexiang* ("fund for subsidies") that were diverted from the revenues collected in other provinces.[86] The fund for subsidies often came from Shanxi and Shaanxi provinces during the Kangxi period, and mainly from Hubei, Hunan, and Jiangxi provinces (occasionally also from Guangdong and Zhejiang provinces) during the Yongzheng and Qianlong periods. In Sichuan those subsidies went mainly to cover military expenditures.

In the 1670s Sichuan needed more than 800,000 taels of fund for subsidies annually.[87] By 1698, Sichuan received about 600,000 to 700,000 taels of such funds each year.[88] Nevertheless, needs in the province were to rise to new heights entering the eighteenth century. In 1729, Sichuan earmarked 926,400 taels as the military budget, of which more than 763,000 taels were fund for subsidies diverted from Jiangxi province and Liang-Huai salt taxes; the rest was levied locally.[89] In a few years the fund for subsidies from outside rose to nearly 1 million taels.[90] In 1733 total military expenditures in Sichuan were more than 1.1 million taels despite the fact that only a smaller sum of fund for subsidies was received that year.[91] During the early Qianlong period, with the pressure of downsizing the area's military, the state lowered the amount of fund for subsidies for Sichuan to only 200,000 to 300,000 taels a year.[92] Nevertheless, in 1744, Sichuan actually received 916,691 taels of fund for subsidies from other provinces.[93] To be sure, this was still in the period of "peace interlude," shortly before the Zhandui incident in 1745. Once frontier wars came one after another, the scale of military expenses would soon increase. In 1776, the last year of the second Jinchuan war, Sichuan received more than 1.1 million taels of fund for subsidies.[94]

The increase of the state funds flowing into the Sichuan frontier occurred hand in hand with the Qing expansion toward Tibet. After the battle of Dartsedo in 1701, an additional sum of 100,000 taels was added in annual fund for subsidies to Sichuan.[95] At first more money was needed for setting up new outposts and garrisons in the conquered Dartsedo area and for paying soldiers who were recruited to fill them. The building of barracks and other military facilities was also immensely costly, providing the provincial authorities numerous grounds for funding. In early 1728, as the second Tibetan expedition was under way and efficient communication between the center and the frontier became imperative, Yongzheng ordered that the postal stations connecting Sichuan and Yunnan with Tibet be supported by the regular tax income of Sichuan and Yunnan, which made the postal system between Tibet and the two provinces a permanent institution.[96] In 1730 the governor of Sichuan proposed building fifty-five relay-horse stations in the Dartsedo area, each of them including barracks for garrison soldiers and beacon towers.[97] Although the governor did not mention the budget for this project, it would not be an insignificant figure, given the difficult transportation conditions to Dartsedo from the core area of Sichuan. Similar projects were launched throughout the eighteenth century.

Another often-used excuse for more funding was the increasingly wide use of the native soldiers of the local chieftains in the expansion. Having been adopted during the war against Wu Sangui, the use of ethnic soldiers became more common after the Qing conquest of Dartsedo. They were either assigned to join the actions of the Qing military or were stationed in the outposts in the border areas. Although it had been considered more economical to use the native soldiers (as they were usually paid less than the regular Green Standard soldiers), they also gave a good excuse for extra funds. For instance, Nian Gengyao had requested paying the native soldiers in the area west of Dartsedo a subsidy (*yancaiyin*, or "salt and vegetable allowance") that had been only issued to the regular troops in wartime.[98] It was another matter, of course, whether the native soldiers were the true beneficiaries when the state provided these extra funds.

When the Qing started its military station in Lhasa and set up the outposts along the highway from Dartsedo to Lhasa in the wake of its first invasion of Tibet in 1720, one more expense was added to the total military budget of the Sichuan frontier.[99] Even though the size of the military station in Tibet had never been too large—a few thousands in Lhasa and a few hundreds in each of the outposts—it turned out to be an extremely hefty burden.[100] Although the troops from other provinces were deployed on the occasions of military expeditions to Tibet, the garrison troops in Tibet had always been from Sichuan, with only one exception: the garrison in Chamdo had been staffed with troops from Yunnan during the Kangxi and Yongzheng period, but they were replaced by the troops from Sichuan in the early Qianlong period.[101] In Sichuan there was no military unit specially designated for the Tibetan station. Instead, the troops to be sent to Tibet were transferred each time from different garrisons all over the province, as far as Kuizhou prefecture in the eastern tip of Sichuan.

Before leaving for Tibet, they rendezvoused in Dartsedo and underwent reorganization and equipping. Since their station in Tibet was rotated every three years, each year many parts of the province might have experienced the shuttling of the troops to and from Tibet, which meant another large expenditure for the province, including boarding services and hiring draft animals and laborers to carry the luggage of the troops. Given the scarcity of foodstuffs and commodities that were easily acquired in China, coupled with the high altitude and inclement weather, going to Tibet was not deemed agreeable. To maintain morale, the Qing state had to provide more incentives. Besides occasional awards to the troops in Tibet, the state would pay for equipment, horses and horse outfitting, camping tools, and cooking utensils, whereas some of those expenses were funded at the soldiers' own expense in other places and on other occasions.

In addition, deployed officers and soldiers could borrow money from the state for personal furnishings. During the Kangxi and Yongzheng periods chances were that the loan would be exempted sooner or later as a favor of the throne. During the long Qianlong period this practice came to be systematized: the loan was completely exempted if one stayed three years in Tibet, the full tenure; it was 60 percent exempted if one stayed two years; and it was 40 percent exempted if one only stayed one year.[102] Meanwhile, the loan amount was also regulated according to the ranks of military personnel.[103] Furthermore, to be stationed in the area beyond Chamdo was regarded as service "outside of the border" (*kouwai*), so that the soldiers were entitled to additional subsidies, such as *yancaiyin*.[104] Initially, all those expenses were allotted from Sichuan's military budget. Again during the Qianlong period a special account, *Xizang taifeiyin* or *taiZangyin*, meaning "account of military station in Tibet," was set up in Sichuan for all the expenses relating to military station in Tibet.

Moreover, the provisions and cash salaries had to be transported to all the garrisons in Tibet as far as Lhasa. Because highland barley, Tibet's native staple foodstuff, was not consumed by the Chinese soldiers, rice and other foodstuffs had to be transported there year-round. Given the difficult conditions along the Dartsedo-Lhasa route, the cost was tremendous. During the first invasion into Tibet the central government deposited a large fund in both Sichuan and Yunnan, so that the Qing forces stationed in Tibet could be provided with both cash and grain in a timely manner. Yet it was still an onerous task to send the cash to Tibet. When Yunnan needed to send 143,300 taels of silver from this sum to Tibet for the salaries of the Yunnan soldiers in 1723, 160 soldiers were deployed to escort the money to Lhasa; they were again entitled to various subsidies.[105] Although the transportation beyond Chamdo was normally conducted by the Tibetans, the Qing presumably paid for their labor. As all soldiers' salaries usually consisted of two parts, the cash part and the grain ration, it was a problem for the troops in Tibet when the grain ration was not enough, because the prices of rice and other foodstuffs were much higher even in Dartsedo, let alone beyond that point.[106]

During the Yongzheng period the military officials in Tibet and the provincial officials in Sichuan once conflicted over this issue. While the military officials demanded raising the proportion of the grain ration so that their troops in Tibet would not have to buy food at the market, the governor of Sichuan insisted that it was too difficult and costly to hire laborers and transport all the provisions first to Dartsedo and then to Tibet. When the issue was presented to the central government, the Yongzheng emperor ordered either an increase in pay to the troops so that they would be able to purchase rice locally from merchants at a higher price or an increase in the wages to the hired laborers so the supply of rice to the garrisons beyond the border could be guaranteed.[107] For Yongzheng priority was to guarantee the supplies to the garrisons but not to save money, given that the state coffers paid more in either case. Throughout the rest of the eighteenth century the same outcries for an increase in pay to soldiers or an increase in the grain ration could be heard time and again, as the food prices in the border marches and beyond became higher and higher with the passage of time.[108]

An alternative to transporting rice all the way from the core area to Tibet was to build military granaries in the borderlands. This method was first adopted during the invasion into Tibet in 1720, when Gao Qizhuo, the governor-general of Yunnan and Guizhou, suggested building a grain storehouse in Adunzi at the northern tip of Yunnan.[109] In 1728, during another expedition to Lhasa, this method was followed for both Sichuan and Yunnan routes. From Jianchuan, in northern Yunnan, to Chamdo forty-two grain storehouses were set up. In Sichuan a series of grain storehouses was set up along the road from Dartsedo to Chamdo, with Dartsedo serving as the logistical hub. When the armies marched to Lhasa, a considerable portion of them was left to guard those storehouses, which most likely remained in service for the rest of the eighteenth century.[110] After the first Jinchuan campaign the Qianlong emperor endorsed 1 million taels of silver from the unused war funds to fill those storehouses.[111] Nevertheless, it was not cost-effective to store grain beyond Dartsedo—grain rotted more quickly because of Kham's wet climate. Due to logistical difficulties and costs, the numbers of the Qing troops in Tibet were reduced a couple of times in the late Yongzheng period.[112] During the Qianlong era the size of the military station was raised to the level before the reductions, but it had never been an option for the Qing to drastically enlarge its garrisons in Tibet, even at the time when the Tibetan political situation necessitated a reinforced military presence there.

Besides military expenses, the diplomatic missions and envoys to and from Tibet were also included in the expenses of Tibetan affairs for Sichuan. Almost all Qing envoys to Lhasa first stopped in Chengdu, receiving numerous and handsome subsidies from the provincial treasury and being provided with interpreters, equipage, and camping equipment. In 1726 when Oci, the Qing envoy to Lhasa, stopped in Sichuan, his equipage of seventy-nine people claimed more than 16,800 taels from Sichuan for draft animals, supplies, labor, and awards.[113] In 1727, when the Mongols who had lived in Tibet were ordered to be transferred to Qinghai, Yongzheng earmarked 10,000 taels of silver from the Sichuan treasury to pay for this move.[114] In 1749, to curb the high cost of the diplomatic missions to Tibet, the central government promulgated *Xining guitiao* (Xining regulations) to regulate the subsidies provided to the envoys, by which envoys' official ranks were used as criterion for the amount of the subsidies. Hence, when Labdun, one of the *amban* who was killed in the 1750 riot, was sent to Tibet in early 1750, he only received 1,125 taels from Sichuan. Like the budget for the Tibet military station, this expenditure was at first also allocated from Sichuan's military funds but was later covered by the account of *Xizang taifeiyin*.[115] Although the diplomatic expenditures were no longer part of Sichuan's budget in the latter part of the eighteenth century, for Sichuan the obligations of receiving and equipping the envoys still stood as a ready pretext for requesting state funds.

Yongzheng's initiative to reform the local chieftain system opened another broad avenue for state funds to flow into Sichuan. As violence often accompanied the reform, the Qing had to allot funds first to pacify revolts and then, more important, to set up new military outposts to maintain peace, of which the latter was sometimes more expensive, since many ethnic communities were in mountains or other perilous and distant locations. In most cases the revenues paid by the ethnic communities were only symbolic, unable to offset the high costs to keep the areas in order, but the prices of food and other things there were often much higher than in the core area, so that the state had to pay more to soothe the military personnel stationed in those new outposts. If one takes a closer look at the distribution of the military funds in the province, one fact is clearly recognizable: the funds assigned to the garrisons in the core area had been kept relatively constant while the funds to those in the peripherals rose more sharply during the Yongzheng period, when the full-scale expansion into the non-Han communities started in earnest.[116] Given all of the above factors combined, the Sichuan frontier consumed even in peacetime a fairly large amount of funds in supporting the military, both within its borders and in Tibet. Never completely letting go of their apprehension concerning the growth of a powerful satrap in any frontier, the Qing state was, however, firm in its commitment to support the military in the Sichuan frontier at all costs.

Ever-Increasing Wartime Expenditures

As in peacetime, the Qing state followed the principle that the state treasury was responsible for meeting all the financial needs of the military in wartime, not grafting the burden on the people. During the war against the Wu Sangui Rebellion the Kangxi emperor learned that abundant financial support was the key to securing a victory. From that time he had made the military needs a high priority in state spending and was never tight-fisted in financing military operations. If the war expenditures already tended to rise in the Kangxi and Yongzheng eras, they certainly skyrocketed in the Qianlong period. Throughout the eighteenth century the Sichuan frontier experienced more wars than any other frontier, and therefore it received the largest amounts of wartime funds. The first Jinchuan war cost more than 7 million taels of silver.[117] But the most cited example of the high war cost is the second Jinchuan war on which 61.6 million taels were spent in five years.

To contain the ever-increasing war expenses, the Qing state tried hard to regulate war expenditure. Shortly after the conclusion of the second Jinchuan war in 1776, by the order of the Qianlong emperor, a sizable committee was set up to regulate wartime spending. As a result, a set of detailed wartime regulations (*junxu zeli*) was promulgated in 1785 to provide guidelines for wartime expenditures such as soldiers' wartime subsidies and awards, pay to military laborers, compensations to the injured and dead, and the cost in acquisition of munitions and building infrastructure in wartime.[118] Nevertheless, it failed to rein in expenditures in the wars that the Qing would engage in for the remainder of the eighteenth century. In the second Gurkha war, which lasted only a year, 2.8 million taels of silver were spent.[119] At the turn of the nineteenth century the financial expenses of the two domestic campaigns against the Miao Rebellion in Guizhou and western Hunan and the White Lotus Rebellion in Sichuan, Hubei, and Shaanxi crowned the records of war expenses by claiming more than 200 million taels altogether; the abundant state treasury was emptied.[120]

The enormous war spending was incurred, in the first place, by the fact that massive troops were deployed from long distances, involving many provinces in supplying the movements of the armies. As the main Manchu corps was stationed in either Beijing or Manchuria, both over a thousand miles away from Sichuan, the scale of mobilization was always considerable. Besides the bannermen, the Green Standard troops from other provinces were also deployed for the wars on the Sichuan frontier. Although some wars, such as the expeditions to Tibet in 1728 and many smaller operations against the revolting native ethnic communities, only involved the military forces of the province, most major frontier wars, if they escalated, had outside forces deployed. In the 1750 expedition to Tibet eight thousand troops were first sent from Shaanxi to Sichuan and then joined the five thousand troops deployed from Sichuan for the expedition.[121] During the second Jinchuan war from 1771 to 1776, about 129,500 Qing troops, including the bannermen, were sent to western Sichuan from all over the country. The second Gurkha war from 1791 to 1793 necessitated the last deployment of the banner corps to Sichuan from afar for a frontier operation. About eleven hundred bannermen traveled from Manchuria and Mongolia to Lhasa via Qinghai, and then marched across Central Tibet to invade Nepal.[122] In connection with the deployment of troops, hundreds of thousands of military laborers were hired to transport the provisions and war matériel, which consumed a great portion of the total war funds. More on this is discussed later in the chapter.

Another factor that contributed to the high war expenditures is that the Qing state granted its troops multiple wartime subsidies and awards that were not typically given in peacetime. As mentioned earlier, to get their equipment ready, the soldiers could borrow money from the state each time before their deployment. More often than not, the state would later exempt the repayment by the soldiers after a war. Therefore, the commanders would sometimes request to lend more money to soldiers on those occasions. Before the garrison troops in Sichuan joined the first invasion of Tibet in 1719, Nian Gengyao requested to lend cavalrymen 10 taels of silver each and infantry troops 8 taels each, and give five horses to every two cavalrymen, and three horses to every two infantry troops, each horse being assigned 12 taels for maintenance.[123] Altogether, this single expense would cost nearly 100,000 taels, given that about three thousand Green Standard troops were deployed.

Similar scenarios would be repeated in the rest of the eighteenth century. It eventually became an established rule by which the troops deployed were granted a subsidy before their departure. This subsidy came to be known as *xingzhuangyin* (equipage allowance). At the end of the Qianlong period the "equipage allowance" became a regular wartime income for soldiers, which could be as high as their cash stipends for two and a half months.[124] Another wartime subsidy the soldiers and officers received was *yancaiyin* (the "salt and vegetable allowance"), which had been in place from the beginning of the Qing. This subsidy was supposed to pay for the expenses of purchasing any foodstuffs other than grain, such as meat, vegetables, and salt, as well as other necessities during the military operations. The Qing logistical system had never been fully responsible for all the needs of its troops in wartime and purposely left some supply needs to the private sector—that is, merchants—to take care of. The "salt and vegetable allowance" was always paid in cash and amounted sometimes to a soldier's one-month cash stipend. As a special favor to the deployed troops, the throne would raise the rate of this allowance on a case-by-case basis.

Another source for soldiers' wartime income was the awards the throne granted to them during or after a war. Besides the monetary awards from the throne, soldiers would also receive other wartime bonuses from their direct superiors. In addition, the state bore the responsibility to grant allowances to the families of killed military personnel if the families did not have another able-bodied man to inherit the vacancy left by the killed soldier. The allowance was typically half of the killed soldier's stipend.[125] After the first Jinchuan campaign Sichuan paid about 10,000 taels a year to the families that were supposed to receive such pensions.[126] Due to all these subsidies and awards, soldiers received higher pay during wartime.

Given the favorable treatment of the military ranks during wartime, it should come as no surprise that military mutiny was a rarity in the many wars in and near the Sichuan frontier throughout the eighteenth century. There were several severe cases of mutiny in the late seventeenth century, especially during the war suppressing the Wu Sangui Rebellion and in its wake, when reduction of military size was implemented. Nevertheless, during the entire eighteenth century only one small-scale mutiny was reported on the eve of the first Qing invasion of Tibet in Sichuan. As mentioned earlier in this chapter, it was due to the appropriation of soldiers' award money and was subdued before it caused any serious consequences. In wartime it was not uncommon for soldiers to desert their units. In fact, many deserters fled with their pockets full of award silver and materials. But collective mutiny that resulted from mistreatment or underpay was almost unheard of throughout the eighteenth century on the Sichuan frontier. While it is true that officers, especially high-ranking ones, benefited more from all those war bonuses, the rank-and-filers also had reason to be satisfied.

It is almost certain that the war spending was not subject to the close supervision of the central government. Although there was an auditing procedure following each war to check if all the expenses were legitimate, the state could do very little during wartime to forestall misspending. What the state usually did was no more than send additional funds to the front once previously allocated funds had been either embezzled or wasted. At the beginning of the Qianlong period, the campaign against the Miao rebellion in Guizhou claimed a prodigious amount of money, as abuses were serious. In one incident, Zhang Zhao, who was in charge of this campaign before Qianlong was enthroned, squandered most of the 1 million taels of funds allocated for the campaign. To remedy this abuse, the Qianlong emperor simply allocated another 1 million taels to Guizhou to finish the campaign, even though Zhang Guangsi, the new field commander, only requested 800,000 taels.[127] This was a pattern that was repeated time and again: the central government was not in a position to carefully examine the requests for more financial support. Instead, it had to endorse what had been asked for or even give more. At no time during the eighteenth century did the Qing state leave its armies to live off the land within the empire's borders by not furnishing them sufficient funds.

Military Consumption Boosts the Local Market

The generous financial support given by the state to its military would double the effect of the state policy of trying to preserve wealth in Sichuan society in stimulating the local economy, for the military was a reliable and sizable market for local agricultural products and other commodities.[128] In general, there were two levels of military spending. At the collective level the military purchased grain, chiefly rice, from the local market for soldiers' food rations. At times it also needed to purchase construction materials to build, expand, and repair barracks in garrisons and outposts. It might also commission local businessmen for some weapons and munitions, even though the records do not shed much light on it. In wartime the military would significantly augment its spending, albeit temporarily. The deployment of massive troops, sometimes in the hundreds of thousands, resulted in great demands for foodstuffs. Merchants who usually shipped surplus rice to the lower Yangzi valleys could cash in by selling their inventories to the military locally. Besides foodstuffs, the military also purchased widely other commodities in great quantity in wartime, as revealed in a recently published document that was compiled in the Qing dynasty on military expenditures of the second Jinchuan campaign.[129]

The military purchased items that not only were apparently military-related, but also numerous other commodities that were no more than ordinary household items. The items that the military purchased in large quantity for equipping troops in the second Jinchuan war included jackets with military badges, winter coats of fur and leather, hats of fur and leather, and straw hats. The purchased munitions materials included pig iron, copper, lead, saltpeter, sulfur, firebricks, coal, charcoal, cannon wheels and other accessories, hemp ropes (used as fuses), straw, salt, oil, oil cloth, and brushes of palm fiber. An extremely large expenditure was to purchase materials used for setting up camps and equipping them. Those included tents of different kinds and sizes, yurts, canopies, decorative accessories for tents, stakes of iron and wood, mats, ropes and bags of all kinds, door curtains and their accessories, doors and their accessories, water containers of various sizes, trunks of palm fiber, cloth, rugs, woks of various sizes and kinds, wok accessories, other cooking utensils, candles, lanterns, scales, brooms, and bins. Each tent could use dozens of yards of cloth. What is more striking was that all those tents were built in an extravagant manner, so that many decorative tent accessories were on the shopping list that were expensive and intricate. The military also needed a large variety of tools, including axes, spades, hammers, hoes, shovels, files, and nails of all kinds. Also on the list were horse accessories (such as saddles, reins, and removable trays) as well as materials to equip and maintain boats (such as boat accessories, poles, ropes, lime, and tung oil and oiler). In addition, stationery such as papers of all kinds and writing brushes of different sizes were purchased in large quantity.[130] Given that all those materials were purchased in a wholesale manner by the military logistical function, a good portion of them most likely went unused or was wasted. The vendors, however, would have been happy to have such a chance to boost their businesses.

On another level, the individual level, the officers and soldiers depended on the market for many of their needs in both peacetime and wartime. Since the grain ration that the soldiers received as part of their stipend was often not enough to feed both the soldiers and their families, most soldiers had to purchase foodstuffs from the local market in peacetime by spending a part of their cash stipend. They relied on the market for other daily necessities and part of their equipment, such as banners, arrow bags, armor, and even some of their weapons of a traditional type, such as knives, daggers, spears, and so on. Although it was fairly common for military officials to appropriate soldiers' pay, with the flow of large amounts of money into the Sichuan frontier from the state treasury and other provinces' treasuries and periodic awards on special occasions, the military ranks were basically better off economically. The example cited earlier in this chapter that the soldiers in Sichuan had been habitually showing off their wealth from the late Kangxi period and the Yongzheng period demonstrates that the military ranks had enough money to spend at the market even in peacetime when they did not receive generous wartime subsidies.

During wartime, with many kinds of subsidies and awards, soldiers had even more cash to spend, which made it lucrative for merchants to go to the battlefield. As early as the 1690s, during the expeditions into the steppe to fight with the Zunghar empire, led by the Kangxi emperor himself, crowds of merchants had followed the Qing forces, traveling long distances and trading with the troops. Not in any way subject to the control of the Qing logistical officials, those merchants were certainly welcomed by the military. Some of them lost their lives due to illness, shortages of food and water, and so on during the long and difficult trek in the steppe. But high profits would encourage more to go on. Since then, it had become an expected scenario in the frontier campaigns that teams of merchants would swarm to the frontline to do business with the armies.

During the many wars in and near Sichuan in the eighteenth century, those merchants played a significant role in keeping the troops supplied. Soldiers and officers could get from merchants not only their main foodstuffs, but also salt, vegetables, meat, clothes, and other daily necessities. In fact, the frontier campaigns drew people from different areas to shape new business networks. One interesting anecdote in the second Jinchuan war is that a merchant from Shaanxi commissioned some artisans in Kunming, the capital of Yunnan province, to make swords for self-defense, then transported them to Dartsedo to sell to the laborers who were hired to serve the military.[131] Taking advantage of being essentially the only source of supplies on the frontline, where commercial networks had often not reached, the merchants raised their prices for high profits, usually largely exceeding their costs, including transportation. In response to the hiked prices, the military would request increments in pay to the soldiers so they could afford to trade with the merchants. Besides the military ranks, another sizable clientele of those merchants was a large body of military labor force that constituted another regular scenario in the Qing frontier wars, as is detailed later in this chapter. Often largely outnumbering the troops deployed, the military laborers depended even more on the merchants for almost all their needs, since they did not normally receive any food rations other than being paid in cash.

As throngs of merchants trailed the military to the war zone, they sometimes turned the entire frontline into a bustling market place. At the end of the second Jinchuan campaign one official noted that "the merchants are crowded along all the routes of the campaign like clouds gather together." Centered around hundreds of grain stations that had been set up from Chengdu to the Jinchuan front, tens of thousands of businessmen set up their tents and booths to live and trade.[132] In the Qing documents, places with bigger crowds were referred to as "commercial streets" (*maimaijie*).[133] The merchants not only sold food and daily necessities, they also carried luxuries to the frontline, such as silk, liquor, tobacco, dried seafood, and so on, since they sensed the consumption appetite of the military was insatiable. Thanks to them, the generals were able to hold banquets on a regular basis, enjoying all kinds of liquor and rare delicacies.

During the second Jinchuan war the spectrum of the merchandise available at the frontline even amazed the Qianlong emperor, in whose imagination the Jinchuan area was bereft of even basic supplies, let alone luxuries.[134] On several occasions Qianlong became concerned that the soldiers would go bankrupt by spending their stipends on tobacco, liquor, and other luxuries, and that they would lose their fighting capacity when they became drunken and involved in gambling. Qianlong tried but failed to ban drinking and smoking on the front. At one time the field commanders persuaded him to back down on his strict position by telling him that liquor could actually enhance the soldiers' performance.[135] Without any forceful intervention of the state to curb the excessive wartime consumptions, they became more rampant in the late Qianlong period. In the campaigns suppressing the Miao Rebellion and the White Lotus Rebellion, not only did the practice of banqueting continue but the entertainment business also found its market with the military—opera troupes offered performances at the frontline.[136]

Major nonmilitary commodities that were often purchased in large quantities by the military officials were silks and satins of different kinds, which were used as awards and gifts to soldiers. Referred to as *shanghao*, meaning "materials for reward," this practice had long existed in the Qing military. In the first Qing invasion of Tibet from 1718 through 1720, Nian Gengyao had bought silks to reward his soldiers, allegedly with his own salary.[137] It was during the first Jinchuan campaign that Fuheng, the royal commissioner, lavished *shanghao* awards on the military ranks, setting up a precedent of spending excessively on *shanghao*. Although he made others believe that he had used his own allowance, Fuheng was actually given 100,000 taels of silver by the throne for this use.[138] Since then, the practice became widespread in wartime. Instead of digging into their own pockets, military officials would freely make use of the war budget to purchase luxuries, chiefly silks and satins, but sometimes tea, tobacco, liquor, and meat, for rewarding their subordinates.

Since the *shanghao* awards were in addition to the awards, usually in silver, issued by either the state or the chief commanders, this practice dramatically increased the wartime expenditures.[139] The most notorious case was that of the second Jinchuan campaign, in which it was claimed that about 76,600 taels of silver were spent on unjustifiable awards, as was found in the postwar auditing procedures; but this figure does not include the amount spent that was deemed acceptable. The central government was not aware of the enormous scale of the *shanghao* practice until the last stage of the campaign. In early 1776, Qianlong was shocked to learn that tens of thousands of taels had been spent on the *shanghao* items, which he had never heard about.[140] To try to impose some check on it, Qianlong ordered that the spending on *shanghao* be registered with bookkeepers and rules be set for future wars. However, there were numerous loopholes in regulations for wartime spending. The *shanghao* practice continued to cost the Qing state dearly in the wars ahead, even though the second Jinchuan war stands as an extreme case.

For big merchants the frontier campaigns represented a good chance to expand their fortunes, for it was enormously lucrative to be contracted by the military to transport foodstuffs and other supplies to the front, regardless of the risks and hazards. Known as *shangyun* (transportation by merchants), this method started in Kangxi's Zunghar campaigns of the 1690s and continued throughout the Zunghar campaign of the 1720s and 1730s. While commissioning merchants proved to be far more effective in keeping the troops supplied, it was much costlier than managing the logistics through the bureaucratic system. On the Sichuan frontier this method was used in the two Jinchuan wars as well as the second Gurkha war. At the time they were contracted, the merchants received a sum of money to purchase livestock and carts and to hire laborers. In some cases they were also responsible for purchasing the military supplies that they transported, such as grain and construction materials. Then they were obliged to have the matériel delivered to the assigned destinations and to register with the Qing officials there. In the second Jinchuan war, of 2.9 million *shi* of rice supposedly transported to the front, more than 2.6 million *shi* was commissioned to merchants. The costs were also high, claiming 32.2 million taels in total, which was more than 50 percent of the total cost of the campaign, 61.6 million taels.[141] As one might expect, merchants' embezzlement of war funds was widespread, some swallowing the funds without delivering the cargo. After the second Jinchuan campaign several hundred merchants were put in jail for their arrears.[142]

It is highly possible that most of the merchants, either trading with the military or being contracted by the military, were from outside of the frontline and many were from outside of Sichuan, given that the Qing records always used the term "guest" (*ke*) in referring to these merchants, such as *maoyi kemin*, meaning "guest people who do business," and *kemin fucou*, meaning that "guest people" congregated in crowds. More particularly, those well-established merchants who had been contracted for the transportation tasks were almost all from other provinces, especially Shanxi and Shaanxi. As the experience of working for the military likely whetted their interest in the peripheral areas of the province, some started their own business even before the war ended. After the war some of those "guest people" might have either settled down or set up a branch of their business in Sichuan. It is well known among historians that commercial enterprises in Sichuan during the nineteenth and early twentieth centuries were mainly controlled by outsiders—namely, merchants who were still based in other provinces, chiefly Shaanxi and Shanxi.[143] According to an investigation that had been done in the beginning of the Jiaqing reign (1796–1820), in Chongqing, the most important commercial hub in Sichuan, about 98 percent of brokers of various commodities were outsiders.[144] Although it is not confirmed by case studies, it might be that many founders of those businesses were first drawn to Sichuan by wartime opportunities in the eighteenth century.

At the rural level the military's wartime spending also played a role in promoting the commercialization of the local economy. One record in the gazetteer of Hejiang county footnotes this important development: "At the beginning of the Qing times, settlers lived in something like a wilderness. In the Shunzhi and Kangxi periods the land was empty and the population small. Commerce was primitive and simple. In the Yongzheng and

Qianlong reigns military campaigns were conducted in the southwest. The treasury disbursed coins and brought money in from outside the province. A mint was established; money became widely used in commerce and industry."[145] If this was true in Hejiang county, which was not located on the periphery, the effect of the wartime military consumptions on the local economy of the relatively more remote and sparsely populated places might have been even greater. Even the Qianlong emperor acknowledged that "myriads of commodities have begun to circulate [in Sichuan] since the pacification of Jinchuan."[146]

To be sure, the war mobilizations were not as beneficial to every individual in the area as to the merchants. At the local level it was not uncommon for magistrates and *yamen* (local government bureau) clerks to take advantage of the war to exact extra levies from the ordinary people in addition to the regular taxes, even though it was against state policy. Almost without exception, the war situation unleashed price hikes in the market, which surely affected the lives of less affluent people who did not have the capital for a business but struggled for their survival.[147] One of the few documents from the Qianlong period housed in the Municipal Archives of Chongqing is a deed by a farmer to sell his land in the latter part of the eighteenth century, in which the seller cited the unbearable financial burdens during the second Jinchuan war as the reason for him to give up his land.[148] The sufferings of ordinary people during wartime were also recorded by Chinese Catholic priest Li Ande (Andreas Ly) in his diary at the time of the first Jinchuan war. According to Li, people complained about such public burdens as labor and tribute; their boats, horses, mules, and donkeys had been commandeered by the military. However, he mentioned several times that local merchants ventured to the Jinchuan front to do business, including some people he personally knew, although some were killed there.[149]

Employment Opportunities with the Military

If the frontier wars proved to be opportune for the established merchants and speculating peddlers—if they were not killed in the war—but not as promising for the ordinary farmers who detested being away from their land to serve the troops or pay additional dues, there was another group of people who welcomed wars: the landless and jobless, as frontier campaigns generated enormous employment opportunities. From the Kangxi period the Qing state had started paying for all labor in its public projects, including military operations. Therefore the growing military buildup and operations on the Sichuan frontier were an important economic source for some civilians. In peacetime the construction of barracks and postal stations, as well as the transportation of provisions and soldiers' cash stipends to the outposts in Tibet and other peripheries, all demanded a huge pool of laborers. Having been a recipient of "fund for subsidies" from other provinces from the time of the Qing conquest, Sichuan received dramatically increasing funds over the course of the eighteenth century. At times more than 1 million taels of silver were transported from outside to Chengdu yearly, via either eastern or northern Sichuan, which required about a thousand laborers to be hired.[150]

In times of frontier wars the need for military laborers would escalate, creating a massive albeit temporary labor market. The main task of these laborers was to transport foodstuffs and other war matériel, but they were also assigned to other duties, such as carrying the casualties, building camps, roads, and bridges, guarding the grain stations, and providing other services to the troops. Besides laborers, the military was also in need of professionals and craftsmen, such as doctors, veterinarians, carpenters, masons, blacksmiths, ferrymen, mariners, boatmen, herdsmen, painters, painting mounters, and so on.[151] During the second Gurkha war the military hired hands in Sichuan to sew ox hides wrapped around ammunition containers for protecting them against the elements while trekking through the Tibetan plateau and all the way to Nepal. Sitting in their comfortable offices in Beijing, the financial officials, while scrutinizing the accounts of the war expenses, were at a loss—it was difficult for them to imagine how many different ways labor was needed in supporting the military on frontiers.[152]

In wartime the military laborers always largely outnumbered the armies, usually being three times that of the combat forces deployed. In the first Jinchuan campaign the Qing state recruited approximately 200,000 laborers; in the second Jinchuan campaign the number reached 462,000 (there were many who could have been hired more than once, so the actual number of people involved should be smaller).[153] The Qing claimed that the payments for the military laborers were "very high and generous" (*kuanyu youwo*).[154] In fact, this was largely true. The transportation laborers were paid either by workload or by time. Their wages varied from case to case and changed from time to time. In general, if a laborer worked every day in a month, he could earn a wage of 1.5 taels of silver, equivalent to or more than a Green Standard soldier's monthly cash stipend in peacetime, which was 1–2 taels.[155]

In addition to regular wages, the laborers were also given extra pay for various reasons, such as bad weather, difficult routes, or dangerous situations. With some exceptions the laborers were not given food rations in kind but instead were paid cash, in addition to their wages, for them to buy food from the merchants. In the first Jinchuan campaign the laborers began to receive one sum of pay at the time they were hired, known as *anjiayin* (the "family allowance"), which was meant to compensate for their absence from their family, land, or other business.[156] In the second Jinchuan campaign the rate of this allowance was raised to as high as 3 taels. In addition, the laborers were paid this allowance each month, instead of one time at the time of hiring. Even the drifters who had no families received this allowance. The craftsmen and professionals were paid at a higher rate. The doctors and painters, who probably drew maps for the military, were treated especially well. They each received 5 taels of silver "family allowance" and 3 taels as a monthly wage. They were also assigned horses and one or two laborers to serve them.[157] A pension was also issued to their families if the officially hired laborers died during wartime, of which the rate for long-term laborers (*changfu*) who died in action would be 4 taels, and the rate for relay laborers (*beifu* or *lifu*) who died of illness during the war would be 2 taels.[158] Taking all the above into consideration, it is no surprise that a great portion of the total war expenses went to paying laborers.[159]

Even though the pay was not scanty, farmers and the people who had regular livelihoods still shunned being enlisted, given the hardship and risk of being killed. The hiring of the laborers was at first the work of an ad hoc logistical bureau, known as Junxuju, that was typically headed by a governor and staffed with the civil officials of middle-to-lower ranks and even clerks. The hiring of laborers was first carried out by setting up a quota according to the taxation rate. During the second Jinchuan war the logistical bureau conducted four rounds of hiring in this manner. In the first round every 100 taels of tax was assigned ten laborers, and the number of laborers decreased each time until three laborers for every 100 taels of tax in the final round.[160] However, this method soon became problematic, as many officially hired laborers fled or hired others to go for them, if they were well-to-do. The logistical officials once had a debate on whether they should do away with the officially hired laborers, who were referred to as *guangu renfu*, and hire laborers directly from the labor market, since tens of thousands of people swarmed to the grain stations for hiring, most of them being landless and jobless. In fact, they had been hired there by the officials.[161]

Although the use of the officially hired laborers had never been formally abolished, it was the local labor market that furnished the majority of needed laborers in most of the wars. To be sure, the decent pay and seemingly favorable bonuses that a laborer would receive were attractive to many people who struggled to make ends meet, such as the landless and new migrants who had not found any livelihood. As the news of the employment opportunities spread, more people came from other provinces to the war zone to get hired. To distinguish those hundreds of thousands of new arrivals from the locally recruited laborers, the former were thus called "guest laborers" (*kefu*). Evidently, many of those guest laborers stayed put once the war ended and they were discharged. During the second Jinchuan campaign more than half of the 462,000 laborers who were hired were not natives of Sichuan province, or only new arrivals. When the pay to laborers went higher and higher, the front authorities also hired non-Han peoples as laborers, as they were usually paid less than Han Chinese laborers.

Border Trade Is Stimulated

The unfolding of the frontier operations also worked to accelerate the physical connectedness between the Sichuan frontier and other parts of the country by improving the infrastructure, which ultimately helped transregional commerce and border trade develop. In Sichuan the most important hub for border trade between the Chinese and the Tibetans was Dartsedo (Dajianlu in Chinese). At the turn of the eighteenth century, when Yue Shenglong had first came to Sichuan, Dartsedo was not yet a town in a strict sense and had a very small population. Having served as the headquarters of Qing logistical affairs in the Tibetan operations for decades, Dartsedo had been thoroughly transformed, becoming a sizable commercial town nicknamed "small Chengdu." Starting from the first Qing invasion of Tibet from 1718 to 1720, each time following the Qing military operation in Tibet, more merchants from both sides went to Dartsedo to trade. During the Seventh Dalai Lama's exile in the annexed Kham area from the 1720s through the 1730s, first in Lithang and then in Taining, both near Dartsedo, numerous pilgrims went there to pay homage and trade. This drove more Chinese merchants to both Taining and Dartsedo. To accommodate the enlarged scale of trade and administrative tasks, Yazhou county, where Dartsedo was located, was upgraded to a prefecture known as Dajianlu ting in 1729.[162]

After another Qing expedition into Tibet to quell the political riot in 1750, Cereng reported that Tibetan merchants came to Dartsedo to trade in increasingly large numbers, so that it became necessary to set up some rules to take control of the crowds in Dartsedo. He suggested that all Tibetan merchants register with the Qing officials and be issued licenses.[163] Nevertheless, the customs house in Dartsedo did not become profitable even after those measures were adopted. In 1755 and 1756 the total levies from this customs house only amounted to less than 20,000 taels.[164] Given that the Qing state had never been aggressive in maximizing financial gains from taxing the border trade in Dartsedo, the mediocre performance at this customs house cannot be used as evidence of a sloppy market there. Rather, it could be taken as another proof of the laissez-faire economic policy toward this frontier.

In the two Jinchuan wars Dartsedo, approximately sixty-five miles south of the Jinchuan area, served as a major transfer station for the southern route of the Qing forces and thus attracted numerous merchants. At the end of the war in 1776, the old town of Dartsedo was destroyed by a flood. A new town was quickly rebuilt, however, perhaps owing to the presence of a big crowd of outside merchants. After this, a group of rich merchants from Shaanxi raised 30,000 taels of silver to build a grand restaurant named Gongyiyuan (meaning "public righteousness garden"). This luxurious restaurant mainly served the sojourning merchants as a meeting and entertaining place, and remained in business until 1938.[165] After the second Jinchuan campaign Chinese and Chinese Muslim merchants established the first commercial companies in the area; they took advantage of the fact that some new roads to the Gyalrong area had been opened to facilitate the military and that more Chinese had settled in the area as the result of the installation of the military colonies. Meanwhile, lodge business developed as the result of many sojourners, merchants, and porters traveling back and forth between the borderland and the core area; numerous inns mushroomed in Dartsedo and along the road leading to Chengdu.[166]

Thanks to Dartsedo's growth, the other towns in eastern Kham also thrived. Approximately 285 miles northwest of Dartsedo, Chamdo— a Tibetan town near the Sichuan-Tibet border and the highway leading to

Lhasa—started its sprawling when the Qing garrison was installed there in the wake of the first invasion of Tibet.[167] When Yongzheng sent another expedition to Tibet in 1728, Chamdo was already a sizable and bustling commercial hub full of merchants from Sichuan and Yunnan. With much troubles caused by the overflow of troops and merchants in the town, the Qing commanders had to leave a thousand troops from Yunnan in Chamdo to keep order.[168] As the people from Sichuan and Yunnan were most active in the growth of the town, the influence of these two places is fairly visible in Chamdo today.[169]

Between Chamdo and Dartsedo was Bathang, the commercial center for the merchants from Yunnan to trade with the Tibetans. East of Dartsedo, Yazhou, the site of the Yazhou prefect, became another hub in the transregional trade. Tea bricks, as the staple commodity exported to Tibet, were grown and produced in the places adjacent to Yanzhou and wholesaled to merchants in Yazhou. South of Yazhou, a road led to Dali, Yunnan province. From there the road continued to Yongchang and Tengyue, which led to Bhamo in Myanmar. During the mid-nineteenth century some English goods were brought in from Myanmar to Chengdu via this passage.[170] Visiting this part of Sichuan in the late nineteenth century, Baron Ferdinand von Richthofen, a German geographer, was impressed with the extremely heavy loads of tea packs that the laborers carried en route from Yazhou to Dartsedo: 18 packs, or 324 catties. It took them twenty days to get to their destination via the mountainous path, which was about 170 miles.[171] Richthofen's observation is reminiscent of the military laborers walking on this same road who undertook the equally hard work in the eighteenth century. One of the differences was that laborers in Richthofen's time did not mix with the troops on their way to and from Dartsedo as much as in the eighteenth century.

Fertile Ground for Corruption

The century-long frontier operations and the schema of putting strategic importance before economic gains had a profound impact on the behavioral patterns of Sichuan's military and civil bureaucrats. Not surprisingly, the influx of money from the state coffers into Sichuan helped foster an impression that it was attainable to request funds as long as the local officials appealed in the name of frontier defense or military need. As early as the onset of the frontier operations in Sichuan, corruption was its innate companion. Taking advantage, Nian Gengyao had repeatedly asked for more pay to the military in all garrisons in Sichuan, regardless of whether they were directly involved in Tibetan affairs. When Huang Tinggui complained in 1727 that the soldiers in Sichuan were "haughty and self-indulgent," he attributed it to the fact that they had been spoiled by the too generous awards that Nian had requested for them.[172] Yet Nian's subordinate revealed, after he fell from power, that Nian had misused 300,000 taels and falsely reimbursed another 200,000 taels during the Qinghai campaign against Lobdzan Dandzin. Yongzheng once acknowledged that it was no secret to him that the war funds had been largely misused and embezzled ever since the start of the military operations on the western frontier.[173]

During the Qianlong period the many wars in and near Sichuan turned the area into a breeding ground of corruption. As the urgent needs of the battlefield allowed no time for the central government to deliberate on requests for financial support, it always tended to allocate more money than was needed to the front. While misappropriation of military funds was common in both wartime and peacetime, the most notorious case of military corruption during the Qianlong period is the second Jinchuan war, during which enormous amounts of the funds were appropriated by the military commanders and the officials in charge of the logistical networks. By campaigning in the Jinchuan area for a few years, many officials and officers were able to send home both cash and cartloads of such materials as silks. For instance, Fude, a Manchu general, sent home two carriages of silk and silver and bought 7–8 *qing* of land with the sum.[174] The same Fude was also accused of giving his soldiers *shanghao* worth 30,000 taels of silver without justification.[175]

Another big loophole in this war was in contracting merchants for transporting the provisions; hundreds of thousands of taels were spent without proper bookkeeping. After the war ended in 1776, a sizable committee was formed, consisting of the provincial officials and the commissioners sent from the capital, to audit all the accounts. It turned out to be an extremely painstaking and long-winded process, due to the extensive misuse of military funds. After having spent years combing through the accounts, the committee still could not figure out exactly how much money had been spent illicitly. Ultimately, the state had to yield to the fait accompli. Between 1778 and 1785 the throne exempted, in several installments, a total of 6.8 million taels of various debts owned by officials, soldiers, merchants, and military laborers, which amounted to a tenth of the total expenses of the second Jinchuan campaign—that is, 61.6 million taels.[176] When the audit committee concluded its rather loose scrutiny, almost all debts were either canceled or put into an open-ended process of repayment.[177] Not a single official was punished for embezzlement or misuse as a result of the auditing, even though many of them were charged with corruption and cashiered or punished during the war.[178] The only people who were put in jail were hundreds of merchants and their family members who failed to pay off their debts. But after their properties had been confiscated, they were released in 1779 with almost 1 million taels of debt unpaid.[179]

To a large extent, the results of the Jinchuan auditing sent a message that the state did not intend to be draconian in closing all the loopholes in the frontier expenditures. The priority had always been the frontier's security and the military's efficiency, instead of high moral standards. As a result, the military commanders and local officials in the Sichuan frontier did not hesitate in continuing to appropriate military funds in the last two decades of the Qianlong period, during which time corruption cases from Sichuan were abundant.[180] It was not uncommon, either, that the officials elsewhere who were charged in corruption cases had once served in various positions in Sichuan, especially during the second Jinchuan war. In the late Qianlong reign what became especially scandalous were the excessively high expenses in maintaining the military colonies in the Jinchuan area. Although the initial plan for the military colonies in Jinchuan was to let them become self-sufficient to a certain degree, if the state still gave them some financial support, the expenses of maintaining the colonies escalated dramatically. In 1779 the emperor was startled to find out that the military colonies in Jinchuan had cost more than 700,000 taels in three years. Deeming it "not understandable," he could not hide his frustration, stating that the establishing of the military colonies in Jinchuan "does not make any sense at all," if they were so expensive to maintain.[181] Besides paying for labor, stipends to native soldiers, transportation of provisions, and so on, which were all expensive, the military officials in Jinchuan built extravagant *yamen* and mansions for themselves. Later it was found that the costs for building them well exceeded what had been allowed by the rules.[182] In fact, it was commonplace in Jinchuan for the military officials to misappropriate funds in the name of building facilities of all kinds.[183]

Being the last frontier war that marked the end of the Qing expansion, the second Gurkha war did not rank among the most expensive wars in the Qing times. Several factors contributed to it. First, only fifteen to sixteen thousand troops were mobilized for this war, among whom eleven hundred were the bannermen deployed from the north—a small force of bannermen compared with other wars, but about half of which were the native soldiers called from Tibet and western Sichuan. Second, Qianlong was more parsimonious when it came to the spending in this war, even demanding the Tibetans to pay for the expenses of the Tibetan soldiers who joined the expedition to Nepal. Third, the transportation of the provisions by paid military laborers was only to Chamdo, the border between Sichuan and Tibet; a considerable portion of the provisions needed by the Qing expedition in Tibet and Nepal was obtained locally.

Yet misspending was common in this war. As the chief commanders, Fukang'an and Helin spent money in an unrestricted manner. In the wake of the war, Sun Shiyi, who was in charge of the logistical function for the war and then the head of the auditing committee, insisted on retaining in Sichuan both Fukang'an and Helin, for they were chiefly culpable for the many abuses in the spending of war funds.[184] However, the audit of the accounts of this war had never been completed, as the eruption of the Miao Rebellion in 1795 sent all those generals, including Sun, either to battlefields or logistical works. In the new wars against the Miao Rebellion and the subsequent White Lotus Rebellion, which started in 1796, the scenario in which the military commanders and the logistical officials misused and misappropriated war funds only became worse, although in a somewhat different pattern.[185] By the time peace was eventually restored in 1804, the state treasury had been depleted. The Jiaqing emperor later harshly criticized Fukang'an for his abuses in the many campaigns, ordering the removal of his tablet from the shrine honoring the ancestors and heroes of the Qing dynasty.[186] But the malpractices in both peacetime and wartime had been widespread within the military and among the civil officials who were involved in the logistical services, in which the too generous treatment of the Qing toward its military played a large part.

7 THE BENEFIT AND COST OF IMPERIAL STRATEGY

> *Jiangsu and Zhejiang have always been dependent on the grain shipped down from Huguang, whereas Huguang has long been dependent on [the grain cargos from] Sichuan.*—THE YONGZHENG EMPEROR, 1724

AS A CONSEQUENCE OF FRONTIER WARS AND MILITARY OPERATIONS, the Sichuan frontier underwent vigorous growth, and the state was challenged to choreograph its relationship with local society in a situation in which wartime mobilization constituted a major theme in social life. The Qing empire never pursued a unified policy in managing its various frontiers, being more tight-fisted and high-handed elsewhere while preserving a laissez-faire policy in Sichuan. Although at times the state desired to extract more resources from Sichuan, frontier affairs and military operations often forced a sacrifice of possible economic gains in return for stability.

Two outstanding phenomena emerged from the Sichuan frontier, thanks to the Qing state's flexible and generally clement treatment of the region. One was continuous migrations to the area, which completely changed the local population landscape throughout the eighteenth century. Another was the state's support of and active participation in the local grain market. Although the conventional interpretation treats this market as a natural result of economic recovery and development, its formation and evolution are directly related to Qing frontier strategy and operations. In the last two decades of the eighteenth century, when the expansion era was near its end, the more detrimental aspect of the Qing management of the Sichuan frontier became fully evident; many social problems that were either directly or indirectly caused by the century-long frontier operations had eroded the social order and prepared a large pool of potential rebels for the forthcoming White Lotus Rebellion at the turn of the nineteenth century. Although the first uprisings occurred in Hubei, the center of the White Lotus Rebellion soon moved to eastern Sichuan. The prolonged war against the rebels, which turned out to be the most scandalous campaign that the Qing dynasty ever conducted, threw parts of the province into disarray and exposed many structural problems of the Qing military.

THE LAISSEZ-FAIRE POLICY CONTINUES

By the end of the Kangxi reign it was no secret that Sichuan was undergoing tremendous economic recovery and growth. For many in the Qing bureaucracy the extremely low taxes in the province were no longer reasonable but absurd. Moreover, the absence of accurate registration in land ownership also fostered numerous disputes and conflicts among farmers, leading to the multiplication of lawsuits over land and water facilities.[1] Nevertheless, for fear of upsetting the status quo and disaffecting the military in the area, the ailing Kangxi emperor had never intended to do anything about it. It was the start of the Yongzheng reign that sent chilling news to Sichuan: the new emperor was poised to change his father's laissez-faire policy as part of his ambitious agenda to overhaul financial institutions nationwide. As he started setting his hands on the country's more affluent areas, he came under increasing pressure from his officials, who urged him to also wield his ax in Sichuan, the province in which tax evasion was the most prevalent.[2]

In his eight-point plan in 1727 to reform Sichuan's financial and administrative system, Ma Huibo, the newly appointed governor of Sichuan and an outspoken person, enumerated five points related to the abuses in land registration. According to him, ever since the Wu Sangui Rebellion, the provincial government had been extremely lax on land reclamation and registration, which served the purpose of attracting settlers but gave rise to multiple malpractices regarding land registrations. For example, one entire clan had registered under one person's name; they had not changed registration when land changed hands, and they had interlocked cultivated and uncultivated land so that no accurate estimation could be made.[3] Perhaps spurred by Ma's candid exposure of the seriously unruly situation in the land registration in Sichuan, later that year Yongzheng made up his mind to conduct the land survey in Sichuan that his father had persistently avoided. Of course, he paid lip service to assure the tax payers in the province that his purpose was not to increase the taxes but to acquire accurate information about reclamation.

The Sichuan land survey started in early 1728.[4] Anticipating that some unrest would be aroused, given that a drastic increase in taxes seemed inevitable, Yue Zhongqi, then the governor-general of Sichuan and Shaanxi, requested that court officials be sent to Sichuan to help with the survey.[5] It turned out that this project was grimly difficult and took more than three years to complete. Having enjoyed almost nominal taxes for decades since the 1680s, it was only natural that farmers, especially the ones who had migrated to Sichuan early and in the places far away from cities and towns, were not willing to relinquish this advantage.[6] In Chongqing prefecture the hilly landscape added another difficulty for measuring: most paddies on hills and slopes were often small and irregular. During the survey some local officials calculated land by big tracts including the areas that were not arable, such as rocky slopes and cemeteries. In other cases the officials made rough estimations without actually measuring the land or forced farmers to subscribe for higher rates.

Well-known for their bellicose temperaments, the people in Chongqing prefecture staged protests against this unfairly conducted survey. In the summer of 1729 farmers in Dianjiang county kidnapped a *yamen* clerk, interrogated him, and then released him on ransom. Later the same year farmers in Wanxian swarmed to the local *yamen* by the thousands and protested against the high rates of the new land tax. Under a huge banner displaying the slogan "Ten thousand people reporting their grievance," they besieged the *yamen* for days. A similar case also occurred in Zhongzhou, where several hundreds of farmers were involved in a protest.[7] More seriously, a politically ambitious figure, Yang Chengxun, tried to take advantage of the people's grievances against the survey to transform this protest into an anti-Qing uprising. Claiming that he possessed the imperial seals of the past dynasties, and that a younger brother of his was destined to be the king, Yang's propaganda catchphrase was: "The disaster was originated in the year of *wushen* (1728), when the land survey was carried out at the emperor's order."[8]

Although the provincial authorities managed to clamp down on all the protests in association with the land survey, some officials became concerned with long-term stability and sought to forestall a drastic hike of tax rates.[9] Meanwhile, a more important factor set in: the Qing forces in Sichuan and Yunnan were mobilized for another expedition to Tibet in 1728. Around the time of this expedition Yongzheng made two critical moves in his Tibetan strategy that affected Sichuan. First, he placed a large part of Kham under Sichuan's jurisdiction. Second, he kept the Seventh Dalai Lama a virtual hostage in western Sichuan. Both moves added hefty responsibility to Sichuan. A year later Yongzheng launched a new war against the Zunghar people. Sichuan was again mobilized to support this war. In addition, the massive *gaitu guiliu* campaign had been under way in the southwest and parts of Sichuan.

Undoubtedly, all these undertakings reshaped Yongzheng's view of priorities on the Sichuan frontier. He had probably come to realize that it was not in the empire's best interests to try to increase revenue collection at the cost of stability when this frontier was shouldering many a task critical for the overall imperial strategy. Typical of his volatile disposition, Yongzheng made a subtle retreat from his initial objective of rooting out the problem of tax evasions in Sichuan. In 1729, using the excuse of supporting the Tibetan expedition and the smaller campaigns to suppress the local chieftains' resistance against the *gaitu guiliu* reform, Yongzheng exempted the 1730 taxes for five provinces—Gansu, Guangxi, Guizhou, Sichuan, and Yunnan.[10] For Sichuan it could be taken as an appeasement in response to the loud protests. Although the land survey was not brought to a halt until 1731, it continued without the same momentum as when it first started, which contrasted sharply with the harshly executed campaigns in other provinces targeting tax evasions and arrears. In Jiangnan and Zhejiang tens of thousands of people, including many gentry members, were arrested and interrogated. A similar scenario also occurred in Shandong and Hubei, where the campaign to recover the tax arrears was carried out with high intensity.[11] In Sichuan, where tax fraud would have been the most widespread, however, no single person was held responsible and no one was punished, except that some protest leaders were reportedly arrested.

Under the double pressures of popular unrest and frontier emergencies, the state had to lower its expectations of this land survey. While wrapping it up in early 1731, Yongzheng instructed the reduction of the tax rates in some areas if they were set higher than those in neighboring areas, which signaled his willingness to make a concession to the extensive tax evasions in Sichuan.[12] Consequently, the rates that were appraised higher than what was thought reasonable by the local residents were reduced in Chongqing prefecture. In Chengdu prefecture the amount of taxable land in many counties in which tax rates had been in general much lower than in eastern Sichuan was also reduced.[13] In addition, Yongzheng warned the provincial officials not to levy a high rate of surcharges in the name of subsidizing administrative expenses—he knew that it had been the case in Sichuan for the local officials to impose excessive surcharges on farmers.[14] In an attempt to secure credit for himself, Xiande, the governor of Sichuan, proposed that some rules be set to punish the people who failed to report newly reclaimed land, as well as the officials under whom such an act occurred. But Yongzheng categorically rejected these suggestions, calling them "nonsense." Thinking that this move would "add more troubles for now," he insisted that the issue be left to the future when the circumstances became receptive to changes.[15]

Clearly, Yongzheng had returned to his father's laissez-faire position by this time. Therefore it is no surprise that the results of the land survey were far short of having all cultivated land in Sichuan registered. Although the total registered land in Sichuan was more than doubled, increasing from 215,000 *qing* to 450,000 *qing*, and the cash revenues from Sichuan were raised from 225,535 to 656,426 (but the tax in kind decreased from 57,119 *shi* to 13,440 *shi*), they were only a fraction of the total agricultural output from the province. Moreover, they would remain at this level until the mid-nineteenth century (land tax in cash increased slightly to 660,801 during the Qianlong era). This land survey and subsequent tax increase did not alter the reality that the taxes in Sichuan were still the country's lowest.

At the same time that Yongzheng endorsed the land survey, he also paid attention to the issue of migration in Sichuan. In 1727, Yue Zhongqi first reported that migration to Sichuan had become a considerable population movement, with hundreds of thousands of households coming from Huguang, Jiangxi, Guangdong, and Guangxi each year. With no desire of stopping the migration, Yue, however, requested the central government to help subsidize poor immigrants by allocating 10,000 taels of silver from the state treasury. Yongzheng agreed to give this sum to Sichuan but ordered the magistrates in the places from which people migrated to Sichuan to pay for this subsidy, rather than allocating it from the central coffers. Apparently, he tried to check the migration wave by putting more pressure on the local governments of the provinces from which migrants came. Meanwhile, the emperor instructed the local magistrates in Sichuan to be stricter in controlling the new settlers by discerning between the lawful and the unlawful when registering them.[16] Nevertheless, neither the emperor nor the provincial officials, such as Yue Zhongqi, saw the migration as harmful. Having observed this phenomenon for a while, Yongzheng concluded that the reasons for so many people to be so eager to go to Sichuan were that there were huge amounts of unclaimed land, that the rice prices were lower, and that, more important, both poor and well-to-do people were charmed with the rumors that the life was easy and everybody could be wealthy in Sichuan. He continued: "How can one not think that the reason for the price of food in Sichuan to be low is that the territory is huge and population is small. The people who consume are fewer, therefore the price is lower. If people in other provinces all gush into this one province, there would be more mouths to feed, how can one still expect the low expenditures as before?"[17]

The emperor was correct in seeing that the major motivation for migration was the prospect of a better life in Sichuan, which propelled both the poor and the well-to-do to move. While not intending to stop the migration, Yongzheng expected that it would come to an end when the province was fully populated and all the arable land was cultivated. What he failed to realize was that the low taxes in Sichuan had yielded a large amount of agricultural surplus, which would keep food prices in the province consistently lower than in its neighboring provinces.[18] In addition, grain measures in Sichuan were in general larger than those in other places, which made the food prices even lower if the difference in measures was considered.[19] Therefore migrants would still come even when there was no land available for newcomers. For the time being, Sichuan's provincial officials did not foresee this scenario, either. Responding to the emperor's call to put a tighter control on the newcomers, they only tried to come up with more vigorous methods in this regard. Xiande reported that he had sorted the immigrants into two groups, the lawful and the unlawful, and let the former stay but expelled the latter. Then he further divided the "lawful" immigrants into two groups: the poor and the affluent. Among the former, only extremely poor people were eligible for subsidies from the government. They would also be assigned ownerless land when the land survey was finished.[20]

According to what was later reported, some poor immigrants did receive land and cash subsidies from the government.[21] One may have grounds to suspect that these measures to subsidize new settlers, no matter under what conditions, only gave a more heated incentive to the ever higher migration waves. However, when more and more migrants came, the provincial government might not be able to provide them with subsidies. Although accurate statistics are lacking, it is plausible to assume that Sichuan had been considerably populated and cultivated during the short Yongzheng period. For one thing the provincial government felt the need of restoring many county governments that had been abolished in the early years of the Kangxi reign when the province was first taken by the Qing. In 1729, fourteen out of the seventeen abolished county governments were restored, most of those counties being located in the core areas of Sichuan.[22]

TABLE 7.1 LAND TAXES IN 1766

Province	*Land tax in-kind* (shi)	*Land tax in cash* (tael)
Jiangsu	2,085,451	3,255,236
Zhejiang	1,386,700	2,821,483
Jiangxi	899,836	1,939,126
Anhui	694,316	1,707,123
Shaanxi	31,948	1,555,518
Guangdong	348,174	1,260,933
Hunan	277,949	1,178,357
Hubei	286,537	1,121,043
Sichuan	13,440	660,801
Guizhou	135,250	121,282
Yunnan	167,938	105,784

SOURCE: Liang, *Zhongguo lidai hukou, tiandi, tianfu tongji*, 396.

Entering the Qianlong era, the migration to Sichuan continued. It is truer then that population pressure played a larger role in sending migrants to Sichuan.[23] But the attractiveness of Sichuan remained the chief motivation—the Qianlong administration showed no sign of reversing the lax tax policy in the province. Unlike his father, Qianlong did not even try to conduct another land survey in Sichuan during his sixty-year reign. Besides the factor of low taxes, the opportunities brought in by the many frontier wars certainly constituted another catalyst, stimulating the continuous migration waves to the province. Contrary to the situation in the earlier period, when few bureaucrats were willing to take posts in Sichuan, many would find Sichuan an ideal place to serve their official terms then. Some even sought to stay put after their terms ended, as the military officials had chosen to do for some time. The example set by these bureaucratic settlers would further invigorate popular migration.[24]

As in the previous Yongzheng period, it is also impossible to reach an accurate estimation of the immigrants to Sichuan in the Qianlong era.[25] One of the rare quantitative records was made by Zhang Yunsui, the longtime governor-general of Yunnan and Guizhou, who reported in 1749 that more than 243,000 people from Guangdong and Hunan had migrated to Sichuan via Guizhou during the six-year span of 1743 to 1749.[26] Li Rulan, the provincial administrative commissioner of Sichuan, said in 1747 that the immigrants in Sichuan had increased "a hundred times" in recent years.[27] It was during the Qianlong era that more newcomers were forced to spread to the peripheries of the province, as well as to Yunnan and Guizhou. According to the very incomplete and problematic state records, the total number of adult males in Sichuan increased from 409,310 in 1724 to 2,506,780 (the total population) in 1749. In Yunnan it increased from 145,240 (the total adult males) in 1724 to 1,946,173 (the total population) in 1749. In Guizhou it increased from 21,388 (the total adult males) in 1724 to 3,075,111 (the total population) in 1749.[28]

Meanwhile, the provincial officials in Sichuan became alarmed by the mounting crime rates in their jurisdictions. They turned back some migrants by using the excuse that they did not have official documents issued by the governments in their hometowns to prove their being good citizens.[29] They also proposed to the central government that it curb migration into Sichuan. Nevertheless, the Qianlong emperor, who had sensed the population pressure nationwide, had no intention of halting the migration, as he hoped that it would alleviate population pressure in other parts of the country. He reiterated that the government should not place a ban on migration, for it was spurred by the natural desire for survival. For instance, in 1767, Qianlong repudiated the suggestion of the governor-general of Sichuan, Aertai, of imposing a ban on migration as "not reasonable." Qianlong further commented: "As for the jobless poor who trekked through long distance and came to [Sichuan], it is because Sichuan province has vast land and abundant food that they came to seek a livelihood. If this province no longer has spare land to till, and it becomes difficult to survive there, [the migration] will stop without an official ban. If food prices in the place are lower [than in other places] so that they can support their lives, how can it be stopped?"[30]

Clearly, Qianlong knew that the incentives for people to move to

Sichuan were mainly the low cost of living and the highly hopeful livelihood, which were largely generated by the state's light taxation policy. If this policy were to stay in place, the migrations would continue until, as Qianlong estimated, there was neither land nor employment opportunity available for newcomers. As the migration movement to Sichuan was not a state-sponsored one, except in the periods when the province was first conquered and immediately after the Wu Sangui Rebellion ended, the termination of this movement in the early nineteenth century was not due to the intervention of the state, either. Rather, it was a natural response to the realities that Sichuan had been overpopulated, and it was not easier to make a living there than in other places. Although scholar-officials and merchants continued choosing to take residence in Sichuan during the nineteenth century, the large-scale migrations of the lower classes slowed by the late Qianlong period and stopped in the wake of the White Lotus Rebellion.

To some degree, the nonintervention position of the Qing state toward the migrations to Sichuan might have been influenced by the experience of the illegal migrations to Manchuria. Despite a strict ban on Chinese migrations in Manchuria, the extremely low tax obligations and vast fertile arable land, as well as the opportunity of ginseng digging, gave generations of Chinese farmers great incentives to risk violating the official ban.[31] The continuous illegal migrations to Manchuria eventually convinced the Qing that the ban was not feasible so long as the opportunities there were abundant and that it might have been more practical to acquiesce to the new settlers. Given the case of Manchuria, the Qing state knew that a forced ban on migration would not work, but it was best to wait and see the migrations to Sichuan to fall away naturally when the incentive itself perished.

THE GRAIN MARKET ON THE SICHUAN FRONTIER

One important phenomenon in the economic life of eighteenth-century China was the hefty circulation of commercial grain. A national grain market emerged as merchants traveled long distances and transported grain from one province to another. While much attention has been paid to the grain markets in the lower and middle Yangzi valleys, the upper Yangzi valley grain market in Sichuan is only mentioned briefly in the relevant literature.[32] Although scholars are aware of the existence of this important grain market in Sichuan, the explanation of its formation is inclined to be superficial. It is commonly held that because of massive migrations and reclamation of deserted land, surplus grain became available and therefore was shipped down to the lower Yangzi valley and other areas.[33] This interpretation treats the emergence of the upper Yangzi valley grain market as a natural result of economic recovery and development, but it does not take into consideration the historical context and especially the role played by the Qing state and its policy toward the Sichuan frontier. By placing the formation of the Sichuan grain market within the context of Qing frontier undertakings and correlating its evolution and fluctuation with Qing frontier operations, it becomes clear that the upper Yangzi valley grain market was an abnormality. It was not simply a product of natural economic development, but rather, it was fostered to maturity by the Qing special taxation policy toward Sichuan that was prescribed by the Qing frontier strategy.

The Formation of a Grain Market

In the early eighteenth century a national grain circulation system came into existence as the result of serious grain shortages in some areas of the country. In general, two factors contributed to the grain shortages: population increase and the Qing taxation structure. Population pressure became tangible nationwide during the late Kangxi period, for which one conspicuous indication was higher grain prices in the regions of dense population. Kangxi himself first noticed this problem in 1699.[34] Ironically, the area that suffered the most serious grain shortages was none other than the most productive region of the country: Jiangnan, the empire's key economic area. Since the beginning of the Qing, the state had been extremely tight-fisted toward Jiangnan in collecting taxes. The central government often granted tax deductions and exemptions to various areas because of bad harvests or other reasons, but it was strict in forcing Jiangnan to fulfill its taxation obligations, even in the bad years. Jiangnan alone shouldered more than half of the tribute grain obligation, which was not exemptible according to the Qing rule.[35] More specifically, four prefectures of Jiangsu province—Changzhou, Songjiang, Suzhou, and Zhenjiang—took on a third of the total tribute grain obligations.

As has been known by scholars for years, the area could no longer feed its population with the local agricultural output after it fulfilled the heavy tax obligations. The people in the lower Yangzi valley had become dependent on imported grain, referred to as *kemi* (meaning "guest rice" or "imported rice"), for consumption since the turn of the eighteenth century.[36] Some scholars point out that a good portion of the population turned to handicraft industries, which resulted in the increase in demand for commercial grain.[37] If the fact that more people turned to industries resulted from the increase of agricultural productivity as is argued by the same scholars, the commercial grain that they consumed should have been supplied locally by the people who stayed with agriculture. Nevertheless, the grain market in the Jiangnan area was not an internal one. The grain, mainly rice, that was traded on the markets in the Jiangnan region was mostly shipped from outside; it could be expensive—sometimes as high as 1.4 tael per *shi* (approximately 100 liters).[38]

Where did the grain on the Jiangnan grain market come from? As was clear to the throne and everybody else at the end of the seventeenth century, it was from the middle Yangzi valley—namely, Hubei, Hunan, and Jiangxi provinces. Kangxi acknowledged in 1698: "Huguang and Jiangxi have always been abundant in grain. Both Jiangnan and Zhejiang are dependent on the rice from these two places."[39] There was a popular saying: "When the provinces of Hunan and Hubei have good harvests, all the people in the country are fed" (*Huguang shu, tianxia zu*). In 1706 even Kangxi cited it when he attributed the high grain prices in Jiangnan to the fact that the middle Yangzi valley had suffered poor harvests.[40] In fact, Jiangnan was not the only area that became dependent on imported grain. Guangdong also suffered from food shortages due to the rapidly increasing population and became largely dependent on rice imported from Guangxi, another province that enjoyed low tax rates but was abundant in rice production.[41] But Guangxi itself imported rice from Hunan at times. Meanwhile, Shandong and Henan shipped some of their surplus rice to Beijing via the sea route.[42] Evidently, a grain circulation system was taking shape, thanks to the population growth and the unbalanced distribution of tax obligations under the Qing. Not surprisingly, this system of grain circulation was initiated and manipulated by the private sector—namely, merchants. However, the merchants had to risk all the odds associated with a contraband business, since until the early eighteenth century the Qing forbade exporting grain from the middle Yangzi valley. In addition, some local powerful figures also tried to prevent the local surplus grain from being shipped out of their areas so that stable grain prices could be maintained in their own areas.[43]

With the exacerbation of the rice shortage in Jiangnan, the Qing state had to adopt some measures to ensure that the people there were fed.

Nevertheless, its solution was not to lighten the tax burden so that more agricultural output could be consumed in the area, but to make use of the market system to send grain from outside. In 1704, with Kangxi's endorsement, Cao Yin, the superintendent of imperial silk manufacturing in Jiangning (who also functioned as Kangxi's informant), sent people to Hubei, Hunan, and Jiangxi to purchase 15,800 *shi* of rice when grain prices fell there. Although it is not clear how this stock of rice was to be used, it suggests that the state began to participate in the market.[44] On another occasion Kangxi ordered that 300,000 *shi* of the tribute grain that had been collected from Jiangxi be sold in Jiangnan to relieve a food shortage. To make up its tribute grain obligation, the Jiangxi provincial government would buy this amount of grain from Hubei in the following year, as instructed by the emperor.[45] Meanwhile, the state banned rice exports to Southeast Asia, as it believed that the rice shortages in Jiangnan and the southeastern coastal areas were largely caused by overseas rice trade.[46]

Ultimately it became necessary for the state to officially endorse the hitherto contraband grain trade in the country. In 1708, at the request of Yu Zhun, the governor of Jiangsu, Kangxi ordered the lifting of the ban on rice exportation in the middle Yangzi valley provinces, such as Hubei, Hunan, and Jiangxi.[47] Thereupon more official representatives from the grain-importing provinces went to the middle Yangzi valley to purchase rice at lower prices and sold it in their home provinces at the regular prices. Meanwhile, the throne warned provincial officials in Hubei, Hunan, and Jiangxi not to try to prohibit private merchants from purchasing and shipping out grain in their jurisdictions. In 1709 and 1710 grain transactions at the markets in the middle Yangzi provinces dramatically increased, whereas the high grain prices instantly fell in Jiangnan.[48] With the lifting of the ban on grain trade, not only did grain prices fall and remain at a normal level in Jiangnan, but a loud outcry against the heavy tax obligations there also abated. The scheme to place tight exactions on the key economic areas while leaving some of other areas with surplus grain could continue.

At this point what was obscure to the central government, however, was that a substantial portion of rice on the middle Yangzi grain market was actually transported from Sichuan, a place that had not yet been highly regarded for its economic capability, even though its strategic importance had been recently recognized. Not until 1711 was the potential of the upper Yangzi grain market revealed to the central government by Nian Gengyao, the governor of Sichuan. In his seven-point plan on reforming Sichuan's administration and financial system, of which one point was to set up public granaries in Sichuan, Nian reported: "Sichuan province is on the western periphery and surrounded by mountains on all sides, so it is not possible to have transportation routes to everywhere [in the country]. As the province has had a good harvest for many years, there are numerous [merchants] who transport rice out of Sichuan. When the lower Yangzi areas suffer from a poor harvest, they can count on the rice from Sichuan. But when Sichuan suffers from a poor harvest, it is absolutely impossible for the rice in the lower valley areas to go up the river to Sichuan."[49]

This is likely the first time that the central government was informed by its officials about an embryo grain market in Sichuan. If what Nian said was true that merchants had been shipping rice from Sichuan for several years, it provides grounds to assume that the Sichuan grain market took shape about the same time as the national grain circulation system was sanctioned by the Qing state in 1708. In 1712, Nian Gengyao reported again that the rice prices in Sichuan were at a low level as there were not many shipments of rice by merchants to the lower Yangzi valley that year because of good harvests in Huguang and Jiangnan the previous year.[50] He thus suggested that the grain prices in Sichuan had been affected by the voluminous exportation of rice down the Yangzi River.

Yet grain prices in Sichuan were still much lower than in the lower Yangzi valley areas due to low tax responsibilities and continuous good harvests. By the late Kangxi period rice cost only 0.33 taels of silver per *shi* in Sichuan, which was equal to the price about twenty years earlier in Tongcheng county, Anhui province.[51] But in Beijing in 1709, 1 *shi* of millet cost 1.2 tael, and wheat cost 1.8 tael per *shi*. Compared with these prices, Sichuan was definitely an ideal place for merchants to speculate. At one time Kangxi expressed his concern that the rice price was too low in Sichuan and it might hurt the interests of the farmers in the province.[52] Other than this concern, there is no record showing that Kangxi attempted to either make use of the market or regulate it. Before long, however, both the central and provincial governments were fully drawn into the war against the Zunghar invaders in Tibet. The need for provisions became overwhelming, especially when those outposts along the route to Lhasa were set up and started to store grain. Although the military's response to the emergency in Tibet was not satisfactory initially, Kangxi might have been content to see that his lenient tax policy did a timely service to the operation: no report on the shortage of provisions came from Sichuan.

The Start of State Intervention during the Yongzheng Period

The formal state intervention into the Sichuan grain market started with the enthronement of the Yongzheng emperor in 1722. Given the fact that Nian Gengyao had kept in frequent contact with the future Yongzheng emperor, his patron and then one of the possible heirs to the throne, during his governorship in Sichuan since 1709, the latter must have long been familiar with the situation of grain surpluses in Sichuan and the merchants' entrepreneurial activities surrounding them. From the beginning of his reign, Yongzheng showed that he would continue what had been initiated by his father: the use of the market to relieve food shortages in some areas in the country. In 1723, the first year of his reign, the new emperor issued an order to forestall provincial governments from obstructing the passage of grain cargos in their jurisdictions. In the late summer of 1724, a tsunami swept the coastal areas of Jiangnan, damaging some rice crops. To ensure the region's rice supply, Yongzheng issued an edict especially to the provincial officials in Sichuan to alert them not to try to stop the rice cargos of merchants, as he knew that this had happened in the past. In this edict Yongzheng clearly revealed that he was well informed of the importance of the grain market in Sichuan: "Jiangsu and Zhejiang have always been dependent on the grain shipped down from Huguang, whereas Hugaung has long been dependent on [the grain cargos from] Sichuan."[53]

In the same edict the emperor also mentioned that Nian Gengyao had always facilitated the transporting of commercial grain by Sichuan merchants to the lower valleys. Trying to prove that he did not interfere with the grain cargos from Sichuan, Wang Jinghao, the governor of Sichuan at that time and a protégé of Nian Gengyao, reported that the rice shipments from Sichuan had been made on a considerable scale that year. He described to the emperor what had been told to him by the prefect of Kuiguan, which was located at the western end of the Three Gorges of the Yangzi River and was considered the gateway from Sichuan to Hubei via the Yangzi River: "After the autumn harvest [in 1724], about a dozen to twenty rice cargo vessels carrying about 1,000 to 2,000 *shi* of rice passed [Kuiguan] each day, going down to Hubei."[54]

The rice exports from Sichuan became increasingly indispensable in relieving grain shortages in the lower Yangzi valley, as they became more serious in the Yongzheng period. As Qing documents repeatedly indicated, even in the years of good harvests, rice was short in Jiangnan. While not compromising on the high taxation rates and the heavy tribute grain obligation assigned to Jiangnan, the state endeavored to guarantee a sufficient food supply to the grain market in Jiangnan. Compared with other grain-exporting provinces, the price of rice from Sichuan was much lower.[55] With the emperor paying personal attention, the Sichuan grain market was brought into the spotlight, becoming an integral and important component in the national grain market. In a similar move Yongzheng also lifted a ban on rice exportation from Taiwan in 1725, so the surplus grain in Taiwan could be shipped to Fujian, Zhejiang, and elsewhere.[56] Encouraged by the state, more provincial governments sent agents to Sichuan to purchase rice and ship it back to their own provinces that they either sold on the market immediately or stored in local granaries to sell at a fair price when a rice shortage occurred. Those governmental purchases were always in large quantities.[57]

In Sichuan the hub for grain transaction was Chongqing, the area's most important commercial center. The surplus grain was first transported to Chongqing via several rivers, such as the Jialing River, and then reloaded to vessels that navigated the Yangzi River. Up to this point the rice cargos from Sichuan to the middle and the lower Yangzi valleys had been completely free from taxation, even though there was a customs house at Kuiguan, which charged taxes on other commodities such as salt, cotton, and lumber passing in and out of Sichuan. Taking advantage of no tax being levied on the grain cargos, merchants also loaded other commodities, even contraband, in the ships that carried rice. As a result, the levies at the Kuiguan customs house dropped.[58] Meanwhile, local officials along the Yangzi River also took the opportunity to blackmail the grain merchants for bribes. It seemed necessary for the state to intervene. In the fall of 1727, Yue Zhongqi took the initiative to propose levying taxes on grain cargos at the Kuiguan customs, so that the smuggling could be stopped and the revenues increased. Yue argued that this measure would benefit the local governments in overseeing the rice trade and protect merchants from being blackmailed by the local officials. With some hesitation at first Yongzheng finally endorsed it.[59] Therefore the Kuigaun customs house started taxing rice cargos in 1728, a few decades after the Sichuan grain market had taken shape. This change soon provided the Qing state with a handsome income.[60]

Besides increased revenues, levying taxes on rice shipments in Kuiguan gave the Sichuan provincial government yet another convenience: it could place a ban on grain exportation whenever it became necessary by simply checking the cargos at the Kuiguan customs. Above all, the underlying reason for a lenient taxation policy in the province was to make sure military needs were satisfied, especially in time of war. In 1731, Sichuan was shouldering a number of military responsibilities, as discussed in chapter 4. Meanwhile, the harvest from the previous year was poor, and the weather indicated another scanty harvest in 1731. As a result, the grain prices were hiked in Sichuan. In early 1731, Xiande, the governor of Sichuan, placed a ban on exporting rice to Hubei, citing that military needs should take priority.[61]

This was the first time, so far as the available records reveal, in which the local authorities enforced an embargo on the grounds of supporting military operations in Sichuan and beyond. There was, of course, a vested interest for the provincial authorities to prolong the ban of rice exportation. A year passed and the ban was still in place, even though the rice price in Sichuan had fallen. Consequently, revenue collection at Kuiguan plummeted, as not only did grain cargos cease, but other cargos also declined.[62] Worse than that, the embargo triggered price hikes at the grain market in Hubei, thus discouraging merchants from buying grain and shipping it to the lower Yangzi valley, which had suffered from poor harvests in the previous year due to several natural disasters.[63] At this point the central government intervened. Yongzheng issued an edict in early 1733:

> The province of Sichuan is one of the rice-producing regions. [The government] has long allowed merchants to transport rice via the Yangzi River to Hubei to sell in order to meet the demands of the neighboring provinces. In the ninth year of the Yongzheng reign (1731), the governor of Sichuan Xiande petitioned to place a temporary embargo on the rice trade due to the slight hike of rice prices in Sichuan and the military provisions being purchased in the province. This was only an expedient. Xiande should have requested to lift the ban in the tenth year of the Yongzheng reign (1732) when the harvest in Sichuan was good so that the rice prices lowered. But the ban is still in effect today. Thus rice cannot be circulated, and Hubei province cannot benefit from the rice from Sichuan. This is not a fair way for high officials to do their job. Moreover, the prefectures and the counties in Jiangsu and Zhejiang which are short of rice are looking to Hubei for relief. But if this governor does not allow the rice of Sichuan to go to Hubei, then what can the neighboring provinces expect?[64]

The emperor ordered Xiande to lift the embargo immediately.[65] When this news reached the lower Yangzi valley, it aroused a spasm of excitement. Some officials even posted this edict throughout their towns to let people know that relief was on its way.[66] Once the ban was lifted, the grain prices in Hubei fell instantly; and the levies at the Kuiguan customs in 1733 climbed to 92,900 taels, even more than the normal years in the past.[67] This case clearly demonstrates that the Qing state not only endorsed the grain circulation system in the country, which was by and large under the control of private merchants, but also acted proactively at some crucial moments to guide the operation of the system.

The mechanism of the market economy became a complementary part of the Qing state's economic policy. More important, this document suggests that the state was counting on Sichuan's surplus rice to remedy food shortages in the lower Yangzi valley. This scheme had aroused suspicion among contemporary dissidents such as Zeng Jing, who was arrested in 1728 after his uprising plan was intercepted by Yue Zhongqi. In his confession Zeng accused Yongzheng of being greedy "to let people purchase rice in Sichuan and then sell it in Suzhou of Jiangnan."[68] Zeng's accusation, however, might have had some grounds. Besides sending agents to deal in grain on the market, a portion of the revenue collected at the Kuiguan customs house went to the Imperial Household Department, the privy purse of the emperor.[69]

A More Mature Stage of State Intervention during the Qianlong Period

Although Qianlong had attempted to retreat from the Yongzheng emperor's frontier activism when he was first enthroned in 1735, he certainly found that Yongzheng's strategy of keeping Sichuan as a source of grain supply was very useful in equipoising the economic order in the country. He readily inherited it and applied it more skillfully to meet his empire's changing needs at different times. As argued previously in this book, the major reason for the Qing state to apply a fairly low taxation rate to Sichuan was to retain the resources locally in case of any frontier emergency. By the time of the Qianlong reign this rationale was so rooted that no further justification was needed. It had become a common understanding that "it is bound to store resources in the frontiers" (*biandi liyi beizhu*), and that "Sichuan is on the frontier, so that it is imperative to store [grain]" (*Chuansheng dichu bianjiang, jichu jinyao*).[70] In addition to its low taxation policy, the state continued granting tax deductions and exemptions to Sichuan from time to time during the Qianlong period. With more agricultural surpluses in private hands, commercial rice from Sichuan also began to flow to the two southwestern neighbors, Yunnan and Guizhou, neither being abundant in grain output.[71] The importation of rice from Sichuan to these two provinces was facilitated by the two waterway projects in the early Qianlong era: the Jinsha River project and the Chishui River project.[72] Although neither project was fully successful, they helped the surplus rice of Sichuan find new markets in these two neighbors.[73]

Meanwhile, this period did not witness any relaxation in extracting resources from Jiangnan—the state was as harsh as before in pursuing the clearance of the arrears from the area. Therefore the dependence on "guest rice" in Jiangnan was still a reality.[74] Since the beginning of the Qianlong period, the central government had become more active and sophisticated in regulating the national grain market, however. First, the state tightened control over the interior customs houses along the Yangzi River and used them as levers to monitor the direction, volume, and speed of grain circulation.[75] During typical times the government levied fixed duties on all grain traffic. But they would stop levying duties on grain when shipments were heading to a disaster area or a place suffering from food shortages, as regulated by the Qing authorities in 1737 and 1738, although the customs houses would still levy tax on vessels.[76] This method became instrumental in encouraging the private sector's participation in disaster relief and was enforced throughout the Qianlong period except during 1742 through 1748, when all duties on grain were exempted.[77]

Second, the state became more skillful in using its purchasing power to control grain prices at different times of the year. Since the surplus grain was mainly in private hands, the state purchasing power would counterbalance the merchants' manipulation over the grain market. This method had dual effects: On the one hand, the state purchases kept the market strong when it was a buyer's market, such as in the harvest seasons, so that farmers who sold their surplus grain would not lose too much profit to merchants who tried to buy grain at a low price.[78] On the other hand, the government would sell the grain stored in the public granaries to balance the price and to maintain social order when grain prices began to rise.[79] This usually happened on two occasions. One was several months before a harvest. Another was when other regions suffered from a serious grain shortage. At these times the sudden increase in demand on the market would bring the price up. By using the state purchasing power adeptly, the Qing dynasty was no less conversant with the market system than a government in a modern capitalist country.

Third, the state tried to engage merchants in its efforts to balance the grain supply in the country. Whenever a region suffered a natural disaster, the state would urge merchants to go to the disaster-inflicted place by providing information and exhorting them to put disaster relief ahead of profit making. For example, Hubei had a rice shortage in 1751 due to waterlogging while Jiangnan was suffering a drought. Merchants who shipped rice from Sichuan and Hunan were not willing to stop in Hankou and sell rice, since they knew that the prices in the lower Yangzi valley were higher. The Hubei officials had to persuade the passing merchants to sell part of their cargo in Hubei at the local prices.[80] Similar to the situation during the Kangxi and Yongzheng periods, the local governments also hired boats to transport grain from the grain-exporting provinces to their own jurisdiction to help in relieving food shortages. Those government-hired cargo fleets would also set an example for merchants, luring them to do the same.

In addition to using these various methods, state intervention in Sichuan focused on the public granaries.[81] As the surpluses of Sichuan were such an important source for the national grain market, the state wished to see all the granaries in Sichuan constantly full so that the grain garnered in them was ready to be transported in large quantities to any area at any time.[82] Not to disturb the local market in Sichuan, the throne sometimes ordered the provincial government to handle the matter in secret.[83] Filling those granaries might not be in the best interests of the provincial government, since it had to allot funds from its budget to purchase grain to fill the granaries. In fact, the granaries in Sichuan were often empty during the Yongzheng period despite abundant surplus grain on the local market. In 1731, Yongzheng was surprised at the report that the public granaries were short of rice by 600,000 *shi*. To make up the shortage, he allowed the provincial government to use the duties collected from the Kuiguang customs house, as well as the levies on the tea and salt trade, to purchase rice to fill them.[84] To a great degree, the state policy to try to store more resources, mainly grain, on the Sichuan frontier was interpreted by some provincial officials as to leave more resources in private hands, rather than store them in the public facilities.

Entering the Qianlong era, more pressure came from Beijing to keep those granaries full. As a result, Sichuan's provincial government found a not-too-novel but cost-effective way of filling granaries with surplus grain in society: luring the affluent to "donate" grain in exchange for either honorific titles or merely tablets commending their patriotic deed. In the beginning, officials of all ranks in Sichuan were encouraged to "donate" to the granaries. But it does not seem that the officials responded to the call enthusiastically.[85] In 1753, after Sichuan sent 150,000 *shi* of husked rice from its granaries to Jiangnan, it was brought to the emperor's attention how to quickly refill Sichuan's granaries that had become empty. At this point Sichuan's provincial officials pushed the central government to allow them to use the method of *juanna*—namely, to call for commoners of some means to donate grain in exchange for the government's commendation, as "Sichuan is an important frontier area, the granaries cannot be left unfilled for too long."[86]

In addition, they suggested that sojourning merchants in Sichuan could also be encouraged to donate.[87] With Qianlong's approval, Sichuan began to accept donated grain from commoners. In one year more than 34,000 *shi* of grain were donated. In the following year, the provincial government demanded more: they requested that people who donated more than 400 *shi* of grain be entitled with an honorific eighth official rank. This was also approved.[88] Once started, this practice—a covert way to tap surplus grain in this affluent province—continued until the late Qianlong era.[89] To follow the suit of the provincial government, the local governments in Sichuan also encouraged the residents to set up "charitable granaries" (*yicang*), which also accepted donated grain.[90]

What became interesting was that the central government went into conflict more frequently with the provincial government in Sichuan over exporting the surpluses to the lower valleys in the Qianlong period. At times the provincial officials were only lukewarm in encouraging the exportation of the surpluses to other areas. Having their own interests to guard, the Sichuan provincial officials occasionally complained to the throne that the coming of the crowds of grain merchants to Sichuan caused price hikes, and they proposed a ban on the exporting of rice from Sichuan. The officials from other grain-exporting provinces also made the similar plea to the central government.[91] Each time, Qianlong categorically dismissed these complaints and blamed the provincial officials as selfish. Nevertheless, the provincial governments would find ways not to comply with the will of the central government, obstructing exportation of the grain by merchants under their jurisdictions. The action to prevent merchants of other areas from buying grain on the market was customarily referred to as *edi*, meaning "to hinder grain transaction." In this case *edi* also meant to ban the exportation of grains to other areas.

Not surprisingly, Qianlong was against *edi*. He reiterated his position on many occasions. On January 6, 1756, the emperor issued the following statement, criticizing the action of *edi*:

> The harvest is different from province to province each year. It is up to merchants and peddlers to transport [grain] from the place of surplus to the place of dearth in order to help in relief [of shortage]. The local officials have always been selfish and only consider earning credits for themselves, without concern for the general interest [of the country]. Although [I] have forbidden [the local officials] from preventing merchants from buying rice [under their jurisdiction], there always are some officials who only pay lip service to the rule, but violate it in action. Jiangsu and Zhejiang provinces are both suffering from minor disasters this year. Since the local output of grain is less, the two provinces would expect to receive assistance from neighboring provinces. I am indeed worried that some base officials would turn their backs on the principles of relieving disaster and helping neighboring provinces and inhibit merchants from purchasing rice in their areas. If this is the case, the shopkeepers in the disaster area would be more inclined to hoard rice, and the local bullies would make trouble, so that it will be more difficult for the people in the disaster area to get fed. Thus I order that the governors-general and governors in Sichuan, Huguang, Jiangxi, Henan, and Shandong provinces strictly restrain their subordinates and make it known that all merchant shipments, no matter how big in size, be allowed to load and pass freely, that *edi* be forbidden, and that any local miscreants who would interfere with the transportation be seriously punished. You governors-general and governors should enforce the above matters with real efforts, in compliance with my intention to treat every area of the country with equal benevolence.[92]

Qianlong ostensibly played the role of the protector of the private merchants in this case, albeit for the purpose of disaster relief. One should not, however, be under the misapprehension that Qianlong always held this open-minded attitude toward the market. For one thing this attitude was not applicable in another agriculturally productive area, Manchuria, which produced mainly soybean and sorghum but also rice. As the birth place of the Manchus, Manchuria had been specially treated since the founding of the dynasty. The surplus crops of Manchuria were under much tighter control by the Qing state. To keep the grain prices low in Manchuria, the state forbad merchants from shipping the grain from Manchuria to other places, except on a few occasions when Zhili or Shandong province was inflicted with a natural calamity. In each of these cases a special permit had to be acquired from the central government.[93] Therefore the Qing policy toward Sichuan's surplus rice should not be interpreted as evidence that the Qing state was suddenly under the influence of certain liberal trends in supervising the economic order of the country in the mid-eighteenth century.[94] It was always a pivotal principle for the Qing state to treat different areas differently. The Qing state was never hostile in general to the marketing system, but it did tend to tailor its policy to the different political and economic needs at different times.

Although the surplus rice of Sichuan played an important role in disaster relief, it was designed to prepare for frontier emergencies. This method was fully exploited during the frontier campaigns of the Qianlong period. When a campaign started in Sichuan or an expedition was sent to Tibet, sometimes hundreds of thousands of troops and laborers moved to the province. The need for provisions ran high. At these times the state imposed an embargo on grain exportation and forced all merchants to sell grain to the armies. Since most grain cargo was exported through the water route of the Yangzi River, the provincial authorities simply instructed the Kuiguan customs to stop the outflow of grain vessels. When the campaigns ended, the ban would be lifted. State intervention thus worked effectively to direct resources from private hands into serving the frontier wars. During the first Jinchuan campaign grain prices went high due to the enormous demands of the military and military laborers. Thus the provincial government imposed a grain embargo and sold grain that had been garnered in the granaries to lower prices. In 1749 no sooner had the war ended than merchants started preparing cargos to ship down the river. At this point Sichuan lifted the ban.[95]

The same scenario was repeated during the second Jinchuan campaign. On October 4, 1772, when the war was gaining momentum, Qianlong issued an edict ordering an embargo of rice from Sichuan:

> According to Wenshou's memorial on the matter of purchasing 300,000 *shi* of rice to garner in the official granaries in order to prepare for military needs, both summer and autumn harvests in Sichuan are bountiful. So it is bound to buy rice on time to fill the granaries that have been depleted. Back in the seventh month, Zhou Huang reported to me when he was given an audience that Sichuan was well-known for its abundant production of rice, that the provinces in the lower river valleys all benefited from the rice from Sichuan, and that merchants and peddlers transported a great amount of rice out of Sichuan. [He proposed that] it seemed necessary to put some sort of restriction on the circulation. At that time I thought that we had never forbidden the exportation of rice from Sichuan to other provinces, for it is a principle to cut off the excess

> and make up the deficiency. Therefore, it was not a good idea to conceive of anything like an embargo on behalf of the livelihood of the people in a single province. Nevertheless, now I think that the harvests are good in Huguang, Jiangxi, and Jiangnan so that rice is not in short supply, and they do not count on the rice from Sichuan. It is not necessary for merchants to ship it around. More important, both western route and southern route armies in the Jinchuan campaign are purchasing the provisions; the county and prefecture governments are also obliged to purchase 300,000 *shi* of rice. If we continue to allow merchants to transport rice out, I am afraid that the local rice dealers would hoard up rice and raise the price to take advantage, and that the people's daily lives would be affected. Under such a circumstance, the surplus rice has to be retained in Sichuan province. I therefore order Wenshou to carefully manage to impose an embargo in Kuizhou, Hanzhong and other passes, and not to allow merchants and peddlers to transport rice to other provinces to make profits, in the hope that this measure would be beneficial to both the civilians and the military in Sichuan.[96]

This document demonstrates the Qing strategy toward the surplus rice in Sichuan par excellence. According to it, the strategy had two major components: First, the Qing state encouraged the private sector (namely, merchants) to transport the surplus rice of Sichuan to join the national grain circulation in peacetime. Second, during times of emergency the state would have no difficulty in imposing an embargo and forcing merchants to trade only with the military in the war zone. As argued in chapter 6, wartime proved to be a more stable and bigger opportunity for merchants to make profits, so that the embargo would not hurt their interests in general.

Nevertheless, an embargo would hurt the people who relied on the rice supply from Sichuan, typically those in the lower Yangzi valley, which was a drawback of the Qing grain circulation strategy. Once a grain market with stable sources had formed, a considerable amount of the population would count on it for food supply; a wartime embargo certainly brought grain prices up, inflicting great hardship on those people.[97] Not unaware of this dilemma, the state would urge the Sichuan provincial government to immediately lift the embargo once a war ended, sometimes shortly before it. At the end of the first Jinchuan war Qianlong gave such an order.[98] When the second Jinchuan war approached its end, however, an interesting turn occurred.

In 1775 a drought hit Jiangnan, which gave the throne enough reason to worry about a possible rice shortage there. At the same time, however, Wenshou, Sichuan's acting governor-general, stepped up the embargo by also banning all other foodstuffs (*zaliang*), such as wheat and beans, from being shipped out of Sichuan. Wenshou's parochialism enraged the emperor, who ordered an immediate termination of the embargo on the other grains in addition to a harsh chastisement against Wenshou.[99] In view of the fact that the campaign was near its end, Qianlong also ordered in the same edict a lifting of the embargo on rice once the war ended.[100] This time Wenshou showed that he fully grasped the emperor's intent: he started letting rice shipments go down to the lower valleys in December 1775 but did not officially lift the embargo until March 1776, when the war ended.[101] The timely arrival of the Sichuan rice assured the supply on the Jiangnan market despite the previous year's drought. Pleased and relieved, Qianlong composed a poem to record this event, in which he could not but betray his contentment with his skillful maneuvering of Sichuan rice, as well as his satisfaction with Wenshou's adroit handling this time.[102] With this credit Wenshou won an instant promotion to become the formal governor-general of Sichuan.[103]

The Sichuan Grain Market Dwindles

Coincident with the most eventful period in the Qing frontier expansion, the first four decades of the Qianlong reign turned out to be the peak time for the Sichuan grain market. According to an estimation, yearly exportation could reach 1–2 million *shi*.[104] After the second Jinchuan war the Qing state kept counting on the surplus rice of Sichuan to relieve rice shortages in the lower Yangzi valleys and other places, despite some early signs of weakness of this market. In his later years Qianlong composed a number of poems showing his concern over the harvests and the grain market in Sichuan. There were three critical occasions, in the final two decades of the Qianlong reign, in which rice shipments from Sichuan played an important part in disaster relief and meeting military needs. The first time was in 1778 and 1779, when Anhui province was hit by a serious flood and Hubei province suffered drought in some areas. The central government, as in previous instances, ordered the Sichuan provincial government to send the grain stored in the official granaries to Anhui. Meanwhile, it exhorted Hubei and other provinces along the Yangzi River not to stop rice shipments from Sichuan to the lower valley. As Jiangnan was more important than Hubei from the state's perspective, only Auhui, which was part of the Jiangnan area, was designated to receive the relief rice from Sichuan, while the state directed relief grain to Hubei from other areas.[105]

The second time was in 1785, when Zhejiang and Jiangsu suffered from poor harvests and Hubei province also had a bad year. On this occasion the throne took pains to orchestrate the relief efforts to guarantee that both Jiangnan and Hubei received sufficient rice supplies. As in the last instance, the rice from Sichuan was reserved exclusively for Jiangnan, but rice from Jiangxi and Hunan provinces was ordered to go to Hubei.[106] The third time was during the Lin Shuangwen Rebellion in Taiwan in 1787. Sichuan rice was sent to Taiwan and Fujian to support the campaign against the rebellion.[107] Fortunately for the Qing, there was no major military operation in Sichuan during those years.

Things started to change, however: the grain market in Sichuan had begun to dwindle. In 1780, Sichuan felt for the first time the weight of exporting the large quantity of rice to the lower valleys. In that year a slack market hiked grain prices and precipitated a decline of purchases. To lower the prices, 40 percent to 100 percent of the grain stored in the public granaries in Sichuan was sold on the local market, which contrasts with the ratio of 30 percent for selling grain in the granaries in typical years.[108] Accordingly, the tariffs collected that year at the customs house in Jingzhou, Hubei province, went down.[109] Not unaware of the declining capacity of the Sichuan grain market, the Qing state adopted a new measure: it began to drop its prohibition on the export of surplus crops, including rice, from Manchuria, which were shipped to Henan, Shandong, and Zhili by sea. To smooth the functioning of this new market, the state had to warn the provincial authorities of Manchuria, from time to time, not to hinder the exportation, which was not dissimilar to what it had done to the Sichuan provincial government in previous decades.

Then came the two Gurkha wars in the late 1780s and early 1790s. The Sichuan frontier was once again mobilized to support these wars far into Tibet and Nepal. The needs of frontier warfare again outweighed the task of relieving rice shortages in the lower valleys. During the first Gurkha campaign the slow transportation of provisions from Sichuan to Tibet impeded a timely repulse against the invaders, even though the Qing expedition quickly entered Tibet from Sichuan. Therefore right after the campaign the emperor ordered a study of the feasibility of storing rice in the Qing outposts alongside the route connecting Dartsedo and Lhasa.[110] If this motion were to be realized, a considerable portion of the surplus rice in Sichuan would go to its western borderland, and the expenses in transporting the rice to these outposts would be tremendous.

So after deliberation the provincial government and the *amban* in Tibet asked the throne to allow the storage of wheat and highland barley, which were produced locally in the areas where the outposts were located.[111] It is possible that the Sichuan provincial government had sensed more keenly the bleak future of the local rice reservoir. A few years later the second Gurkha war cast a bigger shadow on the grain market. To prepare for the Qing invasion of Nepal via Tibet, the logistical authorities based in Sichuan managed to store more than 105,700 *shi* of various grains in Tibet by the early summer of 1792.[112] Although a large quantity, which consisted of mainly wheat and highland barley, had been purchased inside of Tibet, the grain stored in Sichuan's public granaries was also used. Sichuan's grain market had to be again subjected to military need. Because of the decrease of the shipments going out of Sichuan, rice prices obviously became higher in Hubei during 1791 through 1793.[113]

The end of the second Gurkha war did not bring good news, however; fewer rice shipments arrived in the lower Yangzi valleys, and the customs tariffs levied at the Jingzhou customs house declined year by year.[114] Then the customs houses in Jiujiang (Jiangxi province) and Hushuguan (Jiangsu province) also reported the same problem due to fewer rice shipments from the upper valley.[115] Meanwhile, the grain prices rose in some areas of Sichuan.[116] During the early part of the White Lotus Rebellion, Hubei province, which had been hit by many uprisings, turned to Sichuan for its grain supply. Sichuan proved not to be a reliable source this time.[117] Entering the third year of the rebellion, Sichuan had to ask for importing grain from other provinces such as Hunan and Gansu to support the massive military forces that had been called on from its neighboring provinces.[118] At this time Sichuan's public granaries were more than 75 percent empty due to supporting the war against the Miao Rebellion in Guizhou and Hunan in 1795 through 1797 and provisioning the armies in the current war against the White Lotus rebels.[119]

The single most important cause for the decline of the Sichuan rice market was overpopulation. Wang Di has concluded that the total population in Sichuan exceeded ten million by the late Qianlong period. One major consequence of Sichuan's overpopulation was a decrease in arable land per capita. According to Wang's study, in 1728 arable land per capita in Sichuan was 13.69 *mu*. In 1753 it was 9.51 *mu*. By 1783 it was only 4.90 *mu*. Given the level of productivity of the time, 4 *mu* of land could provide the minimum grain for one person each year. By these figures the arable land in Sichuan did not produce much more than was needed to maintain minimum subsistence of the existing population in the province by the late Qianlong period.[120] By the 1760s the impact of overpopulation had become apparent in the local economy. All land had been used, even hills having been built into terraced paddies.[121] Prices of daily necessities, including that of rice, had risen sharply.[122] The reason that there was still a considerable amount of surplus rice put into the market for circulation nationwide probably lies in the fact that many people were living in poverty. As Catholic missionaries observed during the 1770s and the 1780s, some peasants in the province, especially in hilly areas, led substandard lives, relying largely on corn and sweet potatoes as their main foodstuffs.[123] Needless to say, a large crowd of jobless drifters in Sichuan had to fight for their survival on a daily basis.

The dwindling of the rice market continued after the Qianlong period. During the first half of the nineteenth century, Sichuan gradually lost its capacity to export large quantities of rice to the lower Yangzi valley while its own population kept increasing at a striking rate. By the mid-nineteenth century rice was no longer an export commodity in Sichuan.[124] The circulation of grain became an internal one. This was witnessed by two Westerners who visited Sichuan in the late nineteenth century. The German geographer Baron von Richthofen observed in 1871 that from the Chengdu plain "rice and wheat are sent in large quantities down the river, and distributed through the eastern portions of the province."[125] About the same time an American missionary, Rev. Virgil C. Hart, gave a similar observation: "Rice [in the Chengdu plain] is a staple product, and in good years the ample supply allows it to be exported to the East [of the province]."[126] Despite the dwindling and eventual vanishing of the rice market, the commercial networks and mechanisms that had been built during the peak time of the rice trade would continue to nourish economic prosperity in Sichuan.

Thanks to the grain trade starting in the early eighteenth century, other local products of Sichuan also found markets through the same outlet, which stimulated a more specialized and market-oriented economy in the province, fostering the commercial networks both within and outside of the province.[127] It would not be an exaggeration to assert that the high level of commercialization of Sichuan's economy in the nineteenth century and beyond owed its foundations to the eighteenth century, in which the area's unique strategic position won itself an optimum environment for the commercial economy.[128] To the Qing state, the flourishing of the Sichuan grain market was an unexpected bonus of its special economic policy toward this frontier. But it did not expect that the same policy also encouraged continuous migration to Sichuan, which eventually helped exhaust agricultural surplus there.

THE FERMENT OF A REBELLION

So far this book has emphasized that the Qing state had persistently deemphasized revenue collection from Sichuan for the purpose of facilitating frontier operations. In a similar manner the state did not impose tightfisted control over other aspects of the social life in the area, as its failure to prevent incessant migration to the province demonstrates. Unlike the state's low-taxation policy, its relaxed social control in the province was not a deliberate choice, however, but an inevitable consequence of decades of intensive military operations. By the end of the Qianlong era the social order in Sichuan had severely deteriorated, which paved the way for the eruption of the uprisings during the White Lotus Rebellion. Many historians have pointed to the incessant and massive migration to Sichuan as a cause for the uncontrollable tension in society.[129] While not attempting to challenge this argument, this section places emphasis on the side effects of the frontier campaigns on the local society. These effects unwittingly helped foster the escalating growth of many social problems that had come with the formation of a migrant society, further leading into the ferment for a rebellion.

With so large a percentage of the Sichuan population being immigrants—in some places, such as Chengdu and Chongqing prefectures, as high as 80 percent of the total population—a migrant society with many unique characteristics was coming into existence.[130] Manpower was no longer scarce. Land was reclaimed, first in the core and plain area, then in small plots on hills and in the peripheral areas. New settlers in large numbers changed the layout of the countryside, in which the villagelike structure was a rarity, as the immigrants chose to live by their land, instead of grouping together in a village as was the case in most other places in the country.[131] Meanwhile, more than a thousand marketing towns linked cities and the countryside and became the vital components in the area's economic life.[132] Without traditional lineage and clan structures at the grassroots level to provide some order and mediation, it was the numerous immigrant organizations, which were usually called *huiguan* (meaning "society halls") that functioned as the apparatus of self-governance and mutual aid.[133]

Serving to preserve the common geographic and cultural bonds, *huiguan* could be formed by the people from the same county, the same prefecture, or even the same province, and sponsored worship of their respective native gods, local festivals, and entertainment of their hometown origin. In most cases the patrons of *huiguan* were well-to-do merchants.[134] In the countryside, where immigrants with different geographical origins intermingled, people were more inclined to use mutual contracts to resolve conflicts over various matters. For instance, in Baxian of Chongqing prefecture several farmers reached an agreement regarding irrigating their interlocking rice paddies and chiseled the agreement on a stele.[135]

The unique economic environment also had an impact on the pattern of social mobility in Sichuan. Like the situation in the late seventeenth century, Sichuan still did not excel in the civil service examinations throughout the eighteenth century, only yielding a tiny number of highest degree holders.[136] While the people who could afford to provide their youngsters with education were not lacking, they preferred another path to social prestige—a path through their wealth, not scholarship.[137] As discussed earlier, making donations to the public granaries had been a common way of achieving fame and prestige. So had been some public projects, such as repairing the city wall, for which the local authorities also accepted donations to raise funds.[138] It was not uncommon for the rich to offer donations of either grain or money to the military when there was a campaign in either Sichuan or Tibet in exchange for honorific titles. During the second Jinchuan campaign the state reinstated the practice of *juanna* in the hope of mitigating the skyrocketing cost of the war. It was estimated that the income from *juanna* reached 10 million taels.[139] For the local officials, soliciting for donations was a convenient way to tap the resources from this affluent province that had not been heavily taxed by the state. As was often the case, the income from this source could be easily manipulated by them without the strict surveillance of the central authorities.

A migrant society usually had two seemingly contradictory characteristics: On the one hand, it displayed a considerable capacity for self-governance. On the other hand, it was a hotbed of crime and disorder. For the government it was the second characteristic that aroused constant concern. While many wealthy merchants, small peddlers, and craftsmen came to Sichuan, and many farmers obtained land and established their families, a considerable portion of the newcomers consisted of jobless paupers with whom dangerous elements such as secret society members or sectarian agitators were often mixed. As it was imperative to fill the vast country with cultivators in the wake of the Qing conquest of the area in the late seventeenth century, the desperate provincial officials welcomed all kinds of people. In 1668, Zhang Dedi, the governor of Sichuan, had petitioned to allow the landless, paupers, and drifters to settle in Sichuan, regardless of whether they had household registration in other provinces. This was tantamount to an invitation to the outlaws.[140] It is conceivable that the marginal people might have been more motivated to migrate. As Robert E. Entenmann has shown, many a criminal or fugitive did go to Sichuan and start their lives anew there.[141]

During the Yongzheng period preventing the outlaws from going to Sichuan had been the major reason for the emperor to try to exert some control over the hitherto unfettered migration movements. When the early part of the Qianlong period witnessed even greater migrations to Sichuan, a considerable portion of newcomers consisted of drifting mendicants. Some other newcomers also became beggars when they could no longer find either land or jobs in Sichuan. Meanwhile, many unemployed single males took refuge in Buddhist temples. Having no commitment to Buddhism, and without shaving their heads, their congregation in the temples became one of the sources of disorder.[142] By the end of the Qianlong reign it was said that mendicants were everywhere and in big crowds in Sichuan. They swarmed to weddings, funerals, and other ritual occasions, extorting food and drink, and turned from begging to theft and looting.[143] At this point the provincial government started to resort to using force to send back newcomers, although it was unable to reverse the tide.[144]

In addition, the unbalanced sex ratio among the new settlers, many of whom were single males, gave increased opportunities for crimes.[145] As early as the Yongzheng period, taking advantage of the situation that women were in great demand, tribal women in Sichuan's northwestern border areas, such as Maoxian, Wenchuan, Zagu, and Jinchuan, where both the Qiang and Tibetan peoples lived, went to the cores of Sichuan to look for a livelihood along with male members of their families, as the agricultural yields from their home places, which were hilly and barren, were only enough to support them half a year. Referred to as *xiaba* (meaning "going down to the plain"), their sojourn was seasonal: they left home each fall after the agricultural season ended and returned home the next spring. The huge crowds, sometimes in the tens of thousands, spread to different parts of Sichuan as far as Chongqing and Kuizhou prefectures.

While the men did odd jobs, the women set up brothels and received their guests.

Although some officials voiced their concerns, this phenomenon might have been in place throughout the Yongzheng period.[146] It might have helped alleviate the tension in society caused by the overwhelming number of single males. Starting from the late 1720s, many migrants returned to their home places and brought their families and relatives back to Sichuan.[147] Although some males reunited with their families, more single males followed suit to go to Sichuan when the returned settlers spread the word about the easy living in their new home province. Therefore the unbalanced sex ratio was still a reality by the latter part of the Qianlong period. At the same time cases of adultery and rape were numerous, often resulting in the murder or the suicide of the women involved.[148] Correspondingly, there was a sharp increase in the number of "chaste women," a title posthumously granted by the state to those women who committed suicide in an attempt to guard their chastity, in Sichuan from this period.

During the latter part of the Qianlong period frequent frontier wars and mobilizations in society served to exacerbate some of the underlying problems in this migrant society. The frontier wars attracted hundreds of thousands of people to the battlefield to be hired as military laborers or servicemen to the armies. Many of the hired laborers were landless and jobless drifters who regarded the hiring by the military as a decent, albeit temporary, employment opportunity. Such was also the case with many new immigrants who could not find any livelihood in Sichuan. Therefore the wars served to alleviate population pressure in Sichuan to some degree, creating an illusion that the area was full of opportunities that would encourage more people of the lumpen proletarian type to come. Nevertheless, each time the wars ended, military laborers would be sent back to society, suddenly heightening the already serious problem of overpopulation. To make things worse, the military did not adopt any measures to help settle the dismissed laborers, even though it provided a compensation package that was anything but meager for the injured and dead soldiers and laborers. Taking into consideration the people who lost their livelihoods as an indirect result of the ending of the wars, such as unemployment due to the downsizing in lodging, transportation, and other businesses, the total number of people whose lot had been reduced could have been fairly high.

Besides laid-off laborers, another threat to social order in Sichuan and its neighboring provinces was the thousands of soldiers who deserted during those wars. In the five-year second Jinchuan war thousands of Green Standard soldiers fled their camps and dispersed into society. In 1779, three years after the campaign ended, the state claimed that 1,241 deserters were still at large, although this may well be a much reduced number since it was widespread in the Green Standard system for officers to conceal soldiers' desertion to collect their stipends.[149] In the following few years, Qianlong issued many orders to oblige the local officials in Sichuan to bring those deserters to justice. However, positive results were few and far between. After having repeatedly changed the deadline, in 1784 the state had to call off the fruitless campaign of rounding up the deserters. In 1785, in an evaluation of officials, only 40 out of 150 officials in Sichuan were not penalized for the unsatisfactory handling of the matter of deserters.[150] But in a few years the two Gurkha wars started, which would send new deserters into society.

Frequent frontier engagements preoccupied the attention of the local governments so that the social order tended to deteriorate further with each campaign. Once a war was under way, a large portion of the bureaucracy in Sichuan, including both officials and clerks, was mobilized to staff the ad hoc logistical system. Sometimes officials from other provinces and even Beijing were also sent to help. To fill the vacancies left by those enlisted officials, lower officials were ordered to take over their superiors' positions. Sometimes one magistrate had to take care of two counties that might not even be adjacent to each other. Some counties were left unattended.[151] At the time of the first Jinchuan war the gates of the city wall in Chengdu had to be closed during nighttime, for there were not enough soldiers to guard them.[152] Even worse, many local officials and clerks could not return to their posts immediately after a war ended, since they had to stay in Chengdu to undergo the time-consuming audit process, which sometimes lasted for years.[153]

After the first Jinchuan war Emin, Sichuan's judicial commissioner, complained that "for years, criminal cases such as looting and killing increased several times from before." With cases backlogged for years, he had hundreds to deal with all at once after the war.[154] Cereng, the governor-general, also had the same headache. When he was to lead an expedition to Lhasa in 1750, only one year after the end of the first Jinchuan war, he requested that Yinjishan, the governor-general of Shaanxi and Gansu, take care of daily routines in Sichuan, since the latter was in Sichuan to be in charge of logistics for the expedition.[155] After the second Jinchuan war a similar situation recurred. The local officials were stunned to find out that the local society had been largely taken over by a group of bandits, known as *guolu* or simply *guo* (the individual members were referred to as *guoluzi*).[156]

The *guolu* banditry emerged in Sichuan as early as the Yongzheng period, even though it did not constitute a major threat until the Qianlong era. In 1727, Huang Tinggui, the provincial military commander at that time, reported that because of the local governments' crackdown on prostitution by the ethnic women from northwestern Sichuan, non-Han women could no longer be allowed to join their men in their yearly sojourn in the core areas of Sichuan. Huang also said that those single males, without being accompanied by their women, were more inclined to commit crimes: some went pillaging and thieving.[157] Even though there was no formal gang that had emerged from those ethnic sojourners, they could well have been the embryonic form of the *guolu* society, as suggested by a Qing author.[158] This early episode tended to be forgotten, however, when more Han Chinese drifters joined its ranks. In 1739, when a provincial official exposed the *guolu* problem to the central government, he only indicated that the *guolu* bandits were composed of the jobless immigrants and suggested to set up a communal surveillance system (*baojia*) in Sichuan.[159]

In 1745, Qingfu, the governor-general of Sichuan and Shaanxi, confirmed again that "most of the *guolu* bandit members in Sichuan are vagrants from Fujian, Guangdong, Huguang, Shaanxi provinces and so on."[160] Yue Zhongqi also reported in 1749 that they consisted of "drifting folks from other provinces."[161] Echoing the earlier call for setting up the *baojia* system, Chen Hongmou, a senior provincial viceroy, also recommended the use of this method to tackle the *guolu* problem. In addition, he suggested that the provincial government try to undermine the social foundation of the banditry by helping the poor to gain a livelihood.[162] Judged from their behaviors, mainly involving pillage and pillage-related killing, the *guolu* banditry was simply driven by a subsistence crisis but was not a politically motivated movement, as some have claimed.[163]

In the latter part of the Qianlong era the frontier wars and the subsequent layoffs certainly helped swell the bandit ranks by sending the deserters and dismissed laborers to them. Since those people, including some of the military laborers, had undergone military training, their joining would add an edge of violence to the group.[164] Indeed, the *guolu* problem in Sichuan was drastically exacerbated starting in 1781, five years after the second Jinchuan war had ended. The bandits went on armed pillage, sometimes in groups of hundreds.[165] Alarmed by the frequent reports of pillage cases, Qianlong ordered that the provincial government take decisive action and extinguish the bandits. To enjoin the local officials and to show his determination, the emperor dismissed Wenshou from his position as the Sichuan governor-general and exiled him to Ili, for he was ineffective in taking charge of the matter.[166] To boost the campaign to crack down on the banditry, Fukang'an was transferred from Yunnan to be the governor-general of Sichuan.

In 1782, Fukang'an proposed fifteen measures, such as strengthening the *baojia* system, escorting mendicants back to their home provinces, and checking on all drifters at all the gateways to Sichuan.[167] More important, he resorted to harsh punishment. Since the early 1780s, the capital punishments in Sichuan had been much more numerous than in other provinces.[168] In 1785, Li Shijie, Fukang'an's successor, requested to provide more formal military training to selected local militia members (*minzhuang*), as the Green Standard garrisons were not sufficient to keep order in the local communities.[169] Despite all the efforts on the Qing part, cases of pillaging and killing did not decline in the succeeding years. Meanwhile, the spread of gangsters to Yunnan and Guizhou caused the rise of crime in those provinces.

Parallel to the *guolu* problem, the expansion of the White Lotus sectarian movement constituted another hazard threatening social order in Sichuan. During its long evolution since its first appearance in the Southern Song dynasty (1127–1279), White Lotus sectarianism had become an amalgam of Buddhism, Taoism, Confucianism, Manicheism, and other religious elements, with distinctive millenarian characteristics as well.[170] Meanwhile, its mechanism of mutual aid, the equal chance for women to participate, and its eschatological ideology were all instrumental in its growth. Despite the official ban on any White Lotus activity under both the Ming and Qing dynasties, a spate of the White Lotus sects, under extremely diverse names, had emerged. In Sichuan and Yunnan, White Lotus groups had long been active. In 1746, Zhang Baotai, a White Lotus leader, led a sizable uprising in Yunnan, which was the first time that the Qing state became seriously alarmed by White Lotus sectarianism.[171] After this incident Qianlong ordered an investigation into White Lotus groups in both Yunnan and Sichuan, confiscating all the sectarian gathering halls and burning all their sutra and other printed materials.[172] The first Jinchuan war soon started in 1747, and since then, the provincial authorities had not paid sufficient attention to the issue of sectarian activities in Sichuan, as frequent frontier emergencies had taken priority.

In 1774, another White Lotus uprising in Linqing, Shandong, aroused again the attention of the Qing authorities.[173] At that time, however, Sichuan was fully engaged in the massive second Jinchuan war, which did not end until 1776. In 1775, Qianlong commented on Wenshou's proposals to prevent White Lotus groups from expanding in Sichuan in such a manner: "Carry out these measures forcefully. But it is not the urgent matter in Sichuan at this moment."[174] In fact, the local government in Sichuan had hardly been able to deal with the routines in wartime, let alone make the extra effort to bring sectarian groups under control.[175] The last frontier wars, the two wars with the Gurkhas in Tibet and Nepal from 1788 to 1793, once again demanded the full energy and attention of the Sichuan provincial authorities. At the height of the second Gurkha war many prefects and magistrates from all over Sichuan went to Chamdo and beyond to help administer logistical affairs.[176] When the Qing expedition triumphed in that last, far-flung expedition, those officials returned to their respective posts, only to find themselves faced with a country that had been ruled by bandits and criminals.[177] In eastern Sichuan, Dazhou, which was about 130 miles northeast of Chongqing, had been the center of the White Lotus movement in Sichuan. Since those White Lotus teachers were affluent, living in spacious mansions, they came to host many *guolu* members in their own households when the local governments intensified their crackdown on the banditry.[178] In 1794, the Qing state that had been freed from its century-long frontier operations decided to take a preemptive move by arresting key sectarian leaders in both Hubei and Sichuan. As was the case historically with many uprisings by sectarian groups, heightened pressure from the state—abuses by officials in this campaign were widespread and extreme—served as the fuse for the eruption of a rebellion.

Meanwhile, an intensified campaign to crack down on illegal minting also served to exacerbate the tension in society. In the last two decades of the eighteenth century, devalued coins had been in wide use in Sichuan and its neighboring provinces.[179] While vigorous commercial activities and slack governmental control in Sichuan all contributed to their extensive circulation, the expansion of copper and lead mining in Yunnan and Guizhou also stimulated illegal minting when a large quantity of state-monopolized metals were smuggled into the hands of illegal minters.[180] The coins cast in the illegal mints were lighter in weight and of poorer quality, but they were popular in the local society. Although the whole country encountered the problem of devalued coins, nowhere was it more serious than in Sichuan.[181] To acquire more profits, some official mints in

Sichuan and the two southwestern provinces also cast devalued coins with the acquiescence of the local governments. Sometimes coins made by the official mints were of even poorer quality than those made by the illegal mints. When the central government became alarmed by the seriousness of the issue in the last few years of the Qianlong reign, things had gone too far to reverse them overnight, but a crackdown was ordered anyway.[182] The suddenly tightened control on illegal coin-minting, as feared by the throne, added one more catalyst to the already agitated society on the eve of the White Lotus Rebellion, for many people who had lived on this illegal business lost their means of livelihood.[183]

In 1796, the first year of the new Jiaqing reign (1796–1820), White Lotus groups started uprisings in western Hubei, which kindled sectarian uprisings in Dazhou and Dongxiang, a few dozen miles northeast of Dazhou. Despite the fact that the White Lotus rebels lacked clear strategic goals and had never been well organized, the rebellion lasted for almost a decade in the eastern and northeastern parts of Sichuan. By 1800 the Qing forces were able to drive main rebel forces to the peripheries and restored peace in many affected areas. No longer capable of attacking major cities or holding any stretch of territory, the rebels resorted to guerrilla tactics. They scattered in smaller groups, some starting to penetrate into the deep mountains in the border region astride Sichuan, Hubei, and Shaanxi—the so-called "three-border area"—taking advantage of the fact that the Qing forces were largely province-based, being content to clear only their own jurisdiction. Despite their dwindling size, their mobility and ability to coerce civilians into their ranks gave the rebels an edge over the Qing forces, which merely pursued their enemies at a distance and fought with them sporadically without eliminating them. Not until late 1804 was the Qing state able to proclaim final victory over the rebels.[184]

Suzuki Chusei has maintained that religious commitment was instrumental in the White Lotus Rebellion by pointing to the intellectual quality of its leaders.[185] Nevertheless, the rank-and-filers of the rebellion in Sichuan were mainly filled by the *guolu* bandits and other marginal elements, such as salt smugglers, illegal minters, and jobless drifters.[186] After the Miao Rebellion was put down in Guizhou and western Hunan in 1797, some of the dismissed military laborers were also drawn into the ranks of the White Lotus rebels.[187] It was this composition of the rebel forces that gave rise to a conspicuous feature of the rebellion: the rebels maintained their banditlike behaviors throughout the conflict, pillaging the local households everywhere they went and coercing hundreds of thousands of civilians, including women and children, to swell their ranks.

In the end, the religious persuasions of the sectarian leaders largely gave way to sheer predatory desires. As in other cases, the predatory propensity of the rebels was paralleled by the protective strategy of the property owners, who scrambled to form militias to guard their lives and properties from the onset of the rebellion, as the Qing forces had ever been insufficient in providing protection to all the local residents and they themselves were not well-disciplined.[188] To a degree, the unfolding of this war in Sichuan echoed a long-standing and acute social problem in society: a wide gap between the affluent and the paupers. As this chapter has demonstrated, Qing frontier operations in this key strategic area did not result in a reinforced control of the local society. On the contrary, the success in Qing imperial strategy was at the cost of social stability in some parts of the Sichuan frontier.

EPILOGUE

Sichuan is the most important province in the western territory of the country, with difficult topography and wealthy residents. It has always been deemed critical in the security of the country. . . . If Sichuan is lost, then Yunnan, Guizhou, and Guangxi could no longer expect any military funds, Hubei and Hunan could no longer collect lijin on commodities from and to Sichuan, and Shaanxi and Henan would also be in a dangerous position and exposed to [rebels'] attack.

—LUO BINGZHANG, 1860

ALTHOUGH IT WAS THE WHITE LOTUS REBELLION THAT EFFECTIVELY deprived the Qing empire of the capacity to continue its expansion—after its once-abundant treasury was depleted by the costly campaign—the 1792 invasion into Nepal had already foreshadowed the end of the Qing expansion era. No longer threatened by a dangerous enemy from outside, but faced with increasingly formidable domestic problems, the Qing state felt more keenly the tremendous financial costs and psychological strains that far-flung military operations would entail. Shortly after the second Gurkha war, in late 1792, the Qianlong emperor composed an essay, *Yuzhi shiquan ji* (In commemoration of the ten complete victories), attempting to immortalize his military accomplishments.[1] By labeling both successful and failed frontier campaigns as victorious, Qianlong ventured to rewrite history in order to create a glorious facade for his legacy. However, by summing up his éclat into the auspicious "ten" victories, he alluded to the end of the expansion era. Looking back, he must have been content with the fact that the territories of the Qing empire had been significantly enlarged and that the entire frontier had been secured.

Stimulated by territorial expansion, the Qing monarchs had conducted projects of exploring and charting their vast territories. While several nationwide efforts had been made to map the empire, the Qing expansion into Tibet aroused curiosity about the land that had largely remained inaccessible to the Chinese.[2] As the Yellow River originated from the Tibetan-Qinghai plateau, several exploration missions were sent by Kangxi and Qianlong to locate the sources of the Yellow River, which had hitherto remained unclear.[3] Meanwhile, the consolidation of the grip of the ethnic communities of the southwestern frontier throughout the eighteenth century also spurred enhanced interest in the cultures of the non-Han peoples. No longer regarding all of them as one kind—the "Miaofan"—the Qing state had acquired a considerable amount of knowledge about those ethnic peoples through more intensified interactions, peaceful and forceful, with them.[4] Contrary to common belief that the Qing state assumed an imperialistic stance in its acquisition of knowledge of the ethnic peoples, this author would like to see this development in a more positive light. For better or worse, the eighteenth-century expansion of the Qing empire and all those state-sponsored projects brought with it an unprecedented interest in the places and cultures that had been unfamiliar to the Chinese who had lived in the core of the empire for centuries.

Nevertheless, the vigor and activism in exploring and documenting the empire would soon evaporate with the advent of the new era. Without state sponsorship, geographic and ethnological research and writing became only the endeavors of interested individual scholars and officials. The transition from the Qianlong era to the Jiaqing era was marred by the eruption of two rebellions—the Miao Rebellion that started in 1795 and the White Lotus Rebellion a year later. During the campaigns against these two large-scale rebellions, the Qing dynasty lost a number of experienced military leaders. In 1796, Fukang'an died of illness while commanding the war against the Miao rebels. A few years earlier, his longtime deputy, Hailancha, had died. Shortly after Fukang'an's death, Sun Shiyi died in Sichuan while coordinating the logistics for the campaign against the White Lotus Rebellion. At the end of the year, Helin, the governor-general of Sichuan, also died of illness in the Guizhou campaign. In the following year, another major military leader of the Qianlong era, Agūi, passed away shortly after he retired from the positions of chief grand councilor and grand secretariat. Then in 1798 the longtime viceroy of Sichuan and the commander-in-chief of the two Gurkha campaigns, Ehui, died. Without doubt, the demise of almost a whole generation of veteran military leaders hindered the Qing efforts in the two ongoing wars against the rebellions. It took a while for the Qing to adjust its military mechanism, which was predominantly oriented for frontier operations, to domestic campaigns against ethnic and sectarian rebellions, but the new military leaders emerging from the campaign to put down the White Lotus Rebellion proved to be disappointing. A new era had come. Qianlong had the chance to witness its dawn from his retirement, but he soon passed away himself in 1799 at the age of eighty-seven.

With the death of the Qianlong emperor and his many decorated generals, the Qing frontier strategy descended into a stage that was characterized by inward-looking defensiveness. Among other changes, the Qing state in the nineteenth century was no longer as proactive in safeguarding Tibet as it had been during the eighteenth century. In the beginning of the nineteenth century, strained by the prolonged and expensive campaign against the White Lotus rebels, Sichuan failed, for the first time, to send funds in time to Lhasa for the Qing garrisons, so that the Qing *amban* had to borrow money from the Dalai Lama and Panchen Lama, time and again.[5] Over the course of the nineteenth century the ever-present anti-Qing sentiments among the Tibetans grew even stronger. Meanwhile, Qing suzerainty over Tibet became increasingly nominal, the Qing *amban* often failing to impose their will over the Kashag, the Tibetan governing council. More important, the Qing dynasty was no longer able to provide military assistance when such was needed in Tibet.[6] When the British intensified their inroads into Tibet in the mid-nineteenth century, the Qing state yielded them the right of entry. In 1904, Youtai, the powerless *amban* of the Qing dynasty, was the first one who greeted Col. Francis Younghusband, the leader of the British expedition, after he had crushed the Tibetan resistance and made his way forcefully into Lhasa.[7] In 1905 the Tibetans in Bathang revolted against the Qing garrison troops and Chinese settlers, which epitomizes the weakening of the Qing grip on the Kham area that had been annexed into Sichuan in the first half of the eighteenth century.[8]

While the Qing state had passed the peak of its frontier agenda, its domestic affairs were also plagued with inertia and indecision in the postrebellion era. Had the Jiaqing emperor and his successor, the Daoguang emperor (r. 1821–50), been the equals of their predecessors of the eighteenth century in vision and ability, they might have embarked on a sweeping fiscal reform to relieve the empire from the serious financial crisis brought about by the decade-long exhausting campaign against the White Lotus rebels. Nevertheless, this scenario did not occur in the wake of the White Lotus Rebellion. The taxation structure that had been set up in the formative years of the Qing dynasty, and lasted through the expansion era, remained largely unchanged.[9] In this framework the Jiangnan area continued to shoulder the extremely heavy burden of high taxes and a large portion of the tribute grain as it had been doing for many centuries. The outcry for fiscal reform was raised periodically but always dribbled away in the ocean of inertia. Meanwhile, the Sichuan frontier's fiscal advantages that had been underpinned by the state's strategic considerations had not been taken away, even though the area's strategic importance began vanishing at the turn of the nineteenth century. The annual land tax in cash of Sichuan remained at only 660,000 taels of silver, one of the lowest in the entire country.

The nearly absurd low tax quotas for Sichuan did not go by without arousing questions. In 1814, Baoxing, the governor-general of Sichuan, proposed levying a surcharge of 2 taels of silver for each tael of regular tax in Sichuan for the purpose of raising funds for border defense. Baoxing might have felt that the unreasonably low taxes in Sichuan would cost both the central and provincial governments a great amount of revenue, which would have helped strengthen their financial capacity. Ironically, this proposal was not welcomed at the central government. He Linghan, the minister of the Board of Revenue of the time, rebutted Baoxing's suggestion. He argued that even though this surcharge would not mean a big burden for the people in Sichuan, given that the taxes in the province were the lightest in the country (*tianfuzhiqing, jiayu tianxia*), it ran counter to the principle of preserving the wealth among the people (*cangfuyumin*). Therefore the suggestion should not be taken into consideration. The throne backed He's position.[10] The taxation status quo was thus resanctioned by the central government. As this book has shown, "preserving the wealth among the people" had been the Qing's justification for adopting a lenient attitude toward revenue collection from the Sichuan frontier, even though economic recovery and further growth in the core area of Sichuan had long been recognized by the central authorities. During the entire eighteenth century a wealthy Sichuan was essential for the Qing frontier enterprise, supporting the many frontier wars in and outside the area as well as the Qing military station in Tibet. Meanwhile, the Qing state would utilize the surplus grain of Sichuan province to equipoise the grain supply in the nation, as is discussed in chapter 7.

Having been a successful policy, "preserving the wealth among the people" became largely obsolete and a liability for the Qing dynasty in the postexpansion era. When the German geographer Ferdinand von Richthofen visited Sichuan in 1871, he was impressed with the light tax obligation of the Sichuan farmers: "The taxes which the farmer in Sz'-chwan [Sichuan] has to pay are merely nominal, and make him almost a free owner of the soil. The favoured position which Sz'-chwan enjoys in this respect is an heirloom from the time when, after the devastation of the province perpetrated by the first Manchu Emperors, they desired to offer inducements to settlers, and it is very creditable to the government that the privileges which it then granted have never been withdrawn."[11] Richthofen was right that the privilege was an heirloom from early Qing times, but he failed to point out that in addition to serving as an incentive to migrants, there was another reason, and a more important one, for the Qing state never to withdraw the favor: the need to support the military station and operations in the area, as has been discussed throughout this book.[12]

Richthofen was certainly not the only one unaware of the violent eighteenth century. The longtime peace and inaction on the Sichuan frontier throughout the nineteenth century had left the province with little of the ethos of a frontier stronghold that it used to feel in the eighteenth century. The noneventful decades quietly transformed the area. By the mid-nineteenth century it was widely known that Sichuan was one of the most productive and abundant places in the country. For outsiders such as Richthofen it was the extravagance of the urban life in Chengdu, the provincial capital, that stood for the character of this province.[13] At the same time one has to dig deep in the gazetteers or search over the breached and torn steles in the shrines in honor of the killed in frontier campaigns to recover a recent but forgotten past. In Chengdu only one street, Tidu jie ("the boulevard of provincial military commander"), in the center of the city in which the *yamen* of the provincial military commander was located, suggested that the military officials used to enjoy great power and prestige in this province.[14] West of the city, the compound of the Manchu and Mongol bannermen's garrison became decayed and overshadowed by bustling urban life in Chengdu, even though the population in the compound had multiplied to nearly thirty thousand at the end of the dynasty.[15] Li Jieren, a twentieth-century novelist of Chengdu, has vividly depicted the isolated and out-of-date life within the Chengdu banner garrison at the turn of the twentieth century.[16]

After the military elite gradually phased out, a gentry class rose to prominence in its place. Consisting chiefly of civil officials who had chosen to settle in this wealthy province after their official tenures had ended, this class consummated their enjoyment of the legacy of the eighteenth century by investing in both land and commerce, as both proved extremely profitable when land taxes were low and the marketing system had been largely free from exactions of the state. They had created a new gentry culture that was in a sense a replica, with modifications, of the gentry culture in Jiangnan, as many new official migrants were originally from that area.[17] Northwest-born soldiers and generals no longer loomed large in society. Rather, visitors would see the Sichuanese as "most gentle and amiable in character, and the most refined in manners."[18] And they viewed Chengdu as "une ville des mandarins" (a city of Mandarins).[19] At the lower level of society the low taxes left a considerable amount of wealth with the commoners despite the fact that overpopulation in Sichuan had counteracted the fruits of economic development to some degree. Plus, the wealth in Sichuan was more evenly distributed among property owners without the great gap between the rich and the poor, which was characteristic in many other areas of the country.[20]

One legacy of the eighteenth century, however, remained a reality until at least the end of the Qing dynasty, which was that outsiders controlled the commercial life in Sichuan.[21] Although merchants from many different provinces had their businesses in Sichuan, it was merchants from Shaanxi and bankers from Shanxi who became most dominant in the economic life of Sichuan.[22] In Chongqing, the major commercial hub of the province, sixteen out of seventeen banks were affiliated with Shanxi businessmen in the late nineteenth century.[23] Choosing not to settle in Sichuan, many of those merchants and bankers from the two provinces were merely sojourners; they kept their families in their own home towns and invested in real estate there, while spending most of their time in Sichuan taking care of their businesses. Over time the gentry class in Sichuan also built close ties with those outside merchants and bankers by investing in their businesses. Not a phenomenon unique to Sichuan, the prospering of those outside merchants in Sichuan had its origins in the eighteenth century during which time Sichuan was inviting to businessmen, given the favorable taxation situation, the laissez-faire attitude of the authorities toward commerce, and the opportunities in the frontier wars.[24]

The taxation advantage that Sichuan had enjoyed did not last forever. The outbreak of the Taiping Rebellion in the mid-nineteenth century upset the status quo and forced the Qing dynasty to reshape the map of fiscal obligations of the different areas. After the Taiping rebels took the tri-cities of Wuhan in the beginning of 1853, two years after the rebellion started in Guangxi province, the whole lower Yangzi valley was open to the formidable advance of the rebels. Lacking preparedness and morale, the Qing troops abandoned the vast and critical areas between Wuhan and Nanjing to the rebels with little resistance. In the spring of 1853 the Taiping rebels seized Nanjing. Shortly after, the Taiping rebels sent an expedition across the Yangzi River and took the city of Yangzhou, paralyzing the Grand Canal, the only north-south waterway, which had been the main transportation route for the tribute grain to Beijing. Although the Taiping rebels did not launch an offensive to the eastern part of Jiangsu and Zhejiang province until 1860, for the first time in Qing history, Jiangnan, the key economic area, could not be counted on for the state's revenue income and possible new levies to support the extensive and expensive war against the Taiping rebels and others. It was against this backdrop that the Qing state had to turn to Sichuan, another granary in which the wealth was largely in the hands of the private sector, or "preserved among the people," for financial resources.

Right after the Taiping Rebellion erupted in early 1851, Sichuan was designated as one of the "province for assistance" (*xiejisheng*), which was a reversal of its position as a recipient of both funds and matériel from other provinces in the seventeenth and eighteenth centuries. It was now Sichuan's turn to send money, matériel, and even troops to the battleground provinces. As the insightful contemporaries in the camp defending the Qing dynasty were keenly aware, it was extremely vital to keep Sichuan safe and stable. Hu Linyi, the governor of Hubei province and one of the founding figures of the Hunan Army, emphasized the significance of Sichuan in 1859: "The wealth of Sichuan is five times that in the Huai River valley, ten times that in Jiangxi province, and twenty times that in Hubei province. If Sichuan is lost to the rebels, then it would be difficult for anybody to eliminate this rebellion in the near future . . . it is a great disaster to lose Sichuan, and a great blessing to keep Sichuan in safety."[25]

Holding an upper river valley usually gives a military advantage regarding the lower valleys. In this case, however, it was Sichuan's wealth that took priority in the determination of the Qing military leaders to prevent this province from falling to enemies. In fact, this had been a shared conviction for the Qing state and the emerging generation of provincial strongmen throughout the upheavals of the mid-nineteenth century. To ensure strong leadership of the province, the Qing state frequently reshuffled the governor-general of Sichuan between 1853 and 1860, leaving each governor-general appointed only approximately one year in this position. Having an eye on the rich resources in Sichuan, the leaders of the

Hunan Army were eager to send a deputy of their own to the province, even entertaining the idea of placing Zeng Guofan, the Hunan Army's founding father, in that position. In 1860, when Sichuan was under attack by a group of rebels from Yunnan led by Li Yonghe and Lan Chaoding, the throne appointed Luo Bingzhang, the governor of Hunan at the time and one of the patrons of the Hunan Army, to this critical position. Luo's coming to Sichuan in 1861 materialized the long-harbored intent of the Hunan Army that they could make the resources in this wealthy province within their reach.

To further facilitate the transfer of Sichuan's wealth to the Hunan Army, Luo later recommended Liu Rong, a leading general of the Hunan Army, to the position of the administration commissioner of Sichuan—his chief responsibility was to manage the province's fiscal matters. During Luo Bingzhang's six-year stay in Sichuan, he spared no effort to repulse and defeat rebels who tried to infiltrate into the province. In 1859 and 1862 he drove Li Yonghe and Lan Chaoding to Shaanxi province. Then between 1861 and 1863 he successfully entrapped the estranged Taiping general, Shi Dakai, and his army consisting of veteran rebels at the bend of the Dadu River, eliminating a dangerous enemy for both Sichuan and the Qing dynasty. While all its neighbors, including both Yunnan and Guizhou, were engulfed by rebellions, Sichuan was largely intact in the catastrophic era, which sharply contrasts with its experiences during the Ming-Qing transition, the Wu Sangui Rebellion, and the White Lotus Rebellion. Consequently, the economic order in Sichuan had not been disturbed by warfare, by and large.

While the Qing took pains to defend Sichuan, it recklessly tapped its wealth to support the massive and protracted civil war. At first the land taxes were virtually doubled, although the dramatic tax increase took the form of a surcharge—namely, 1 tael surcharge being added for every tael of regular land tax.[26] Besides, the taxpayers in Sichuan were forced to make a "donation" (*juanshu*) in exchange for honorable official titles that were good for nothing in most cases. Although this method had been applied in Sichuan, referred to as *juanna*, during the second Jinchuan war and the campaign against the White Lotus Rebellion, it amounted to another levy on all taxpayers this time, as the "donation" was collected involuntarily along with the land tax. Sometimes it was as high as five times the regular land tax.[27]

Another important way to exact money from the province was through the *lijin* system. First installed in Yangzhou in the lower Yangzi valley in

1853, the *lijin* system was introduced to other parts of the country shortly after. Although long overdue, the new system of taxing on commerce, by which numerous custom stations on transportation routes levied a 1 percent transit tax on all commodities in transportation, proved to be instrumental in supporting the war against the rebellions. In Sichuan *lijin* began to be levied in 1856. Due to the high level of commercialization of its economy, Sichuan soon became one of the most important contributors of *lijin* income for the Qing state; about 1 million taels of silver were collected annually from Sichuan during the era of the Taiping Rebellion.[28]

On top of all the new levies, Sichuan had to support the local militias that had mushroomed all over the province by the order of the Qing state and more than sixty thousand troops, including the troops of the Hunan Army brought into Sichuan by Governor-General Luo. During the civil war more than ten thousand Green Standard troops were sent from Sichuan to other provinces to fight; their expenses were all supplied by Sichuan.[29] To fulfill his tacit agreement with the Hunan Army, Luo also managed to supply the Hunan Army with what he tapped from Sichuan during his tenure.[30] As recognized by both the Qing throne and many contemporaries, Sichuan played a critical role in saving the Qing dynasty in the avalanche of the mid-nineteenth century. Meanwhile, the people in Sichuan acutely felt the pain of being relentlessly squeezed by the state, which was a complete reversal of the state's lenient fiscal policy in the previous two centuries.

The end of the war against the Taiping rebels did not bring relief to Sichuan, however. For the Qing state the economic gains from this affluent province were too valuable to give away. During the postwar era Sichuan continued to function as a "province for assistance," sending millions of taels to the central government and other provinces for a variety of uses, including suppressing the remainders of rebellions and supporting expensive projects of state-run modern industries. Therefore, all those new levies in the form of surcharges, forced donations, and *lijin* continued. The reform movement at the turn of the twentieth century only created new financial burdens for the people in the province. Lacking clear rules to follow on the specifics of those new levies, abuses by and corruption of local officials became rampant and serious.[31] Having only spent a few months in Sichuan in 1871, Richthofen had noticed the absurd charges on commodities by numerous *lijin* stations in Sichuan, deeming it the biggest obstacle to further development of commerce in the province.[32]

The abrupt deprivation of the longtime privilege in tax obligation had a profound impact on the collective consciousness of the people in Sichuan.

Having enjoyed almost nominal taxes for two centuries, the Sichuanese—elite classes and well-to-do commoners alike—reacted strongly against the sharply increased financial burden from the mid-nineteenth century. The bitter feelings turned into fertile soil for both popular protests and the anti-Manchu revolutionary undercurrent that began to gain momentum in the last decade of the Qing dynasty. During the Constitutional Movement of the 1900s, what resurfaced in Sichuan was a strong tendency toward regionalism, championing more autonomy for the province. In the propaganda that was penned by reformers and revolutionaries from Sichuan, one common and outstanding feature is the poignant criticism of the Qing's exacting the wealth of Sichuan since the era of the Taiping Rebellion, even though almost all those documents shunned mentioning the revenue collection before that time.[33] When the historical Railroad Right Recovery Movement started in Sichuan in the early summer of 1911, defending the economic interests of the residents in Sichuan became a rallying point for this extremely strenuous across-all-walks-of-life protest. Although it was not its initial purpose, the movement was translated into popular uprisings in its latter part, which served as a harbinger of the 1911 Revolution later that year. Indeed, the revolutionaries in Wuchang might not have acted in October 1911 if the Qing military forces in the city had not been weakened by the deploying of three battalions to Sichuan to put down the uprisings there.

Even though the Qing efforts, hasty and indiscreet, to transform Sichuan into another key economic area starting from the mid-nineteenth century fatally backfired, the Qing policy to keep Sichuan in the position of a key strategic area during the eighteenth century was essentially successful, given that all the frontier wars and other military operations had been adequately supplied and supported. Being an empire that was primarily rooted in its military prowess, the Qing dynasty displayed high vigor and a number of distinctive characteristics in ruling the empire in its prime. Among them was its ability to manage a vast empire by hierarchicalizing different areas and adopting different policies toward them. The story of Sichuan's ascendancy in the empire's strategic consideration attests to this quality of the Qing. It took a long time for the Qing state to finally confirm the vital importance of the Sichuan frontier after having gone back and forth in separating the province from and combining it with the northwestern frontier in administrative terms.

Finally, by the mid-eighteenth century, the state came to the conclusion that the Sichuan frontier had to shoulder an exclusive and critical task—to support the Qing engagement in Tibet. More specifically, Sichuan was the base area for the military station in Lhasa and all the outposts along the artery between Chengdu and Lhasa (a minor portion of supporting the outposts was undertaken by Yunnan province) and was the launching pad for far-flung wars outside the borders of Sichuan. Apparently, the Qing state had been led by pragmatism in responding to its frontier crises but had not let itself be restrained by any preset and dogmatic principle. In configuring the Sichuan frontier, what came to be grasped by the dynasty's ruling elite was that the key strategic areas deserved special attention and support at all costs.

The story of the Sichuan frontier demonstrates how the state in imperial China could reshape an area—either defined by administrative scope, geographic boundaries, or strategic significance—by applying specially designed policies to it. Although Sichuan had been low in status in both economic and strategic terms, the Qing state quickly adjusted its position toward the area and began to search for the best policy to govern it, once the province's potential significance began to come to light. Throughout the eighteenth century the Qing state had given up a considerable amount of revenue that could have been levied from Sichuan and persisted in its policy of "preserving the wealth among the people." In fact, this policy became the pivotal lever in the change of the economic landscape of the area. Thanks to this policy, migrants swarmed in and repopulated the area that had been severely depopulated during the protracted Ming-Qing transition; merchants came to purchase and transport surplus grain to the lower Yangzi valleys and set up commercial networks to connect this area with outside markets; and the military elite first, and the scholar-officials second, chose to settle down and created new cultures in the core part of the area.

By the mid-eighteenth century economic affluence had been achieved in Sichuan. Unlike in Taiwan, where the state had tried but failed to increase revenues locally to achieve fiscal balance on the frontier, freeing the state from supporting it financially, it simply did not occur to the Qing central government to let the Sichuan frontier achieve fiscal autarky throughout the eighteenth century, even though Sichuan's core area was no less fertile and productive than Taiwan in the latter part of the eighteenth century.[34] Despite the fact that this area had never been a significant revenue contributor to the Qing state before the mid-nineteenth century, the Sichuan frontier had constantly been at the receiving end of the state funds. At times, the state allocated the more-than-needed funds to the area, especially during frontier wars, to lubricate the military operation and the function of the frontier. What prohibited the central authorities from increasing taxes was that attempts to upset the fiscal status quo would disturb stability on this frontier. Although it was an empirewide scenario for the Qing dynasty to have failed to raise taxes in accordance with the increased productivity at its prime time, the Qing state demonstrated a more than usual degree of leniency toward Sichuan, which could only be explained in the context of the strategic significance of the area.

In addition, one important form of state policy, waging wars in and near this frontier, provided vital stimuli to economic development. Conventional wisdom holds that military operations are harmful to the local economy, upsetting the normal rhythm of social life and increasing people's economic burden. It might be the case if an area became an actual battleground or the military forces were not sufficiently supplied by the state (as occurred during the protracted Ming-Qing transition and the Wu Sangui Rebellion), or if the discipline of the troops was problematic (as happened in the Miao area of Guzhou, Guizhou province, in the last years of the Yongzheng period). On those occasions the military operations caused depopulation and the destruction of the economy.

Nevertheless, the Qing frontier undertakings and wars during the eighteenth century did not adversely affect the economy in general on the Sichuan frontier. It was not unknown in history that military operations brought about prosperity, of which the prerequisites should be that all the wars did not occur in the core part of the area, that the war destruction was minimal or even nonexistent in the core areas, and that the wars were solely yet generously financed by outside sources, not by squeezing the local society. This was exactly the case for the Sichuan frontier during the eighteenth century. As the experience of the Qing expansion in this part of the empire shows, war, a vital political agent, would often transgress any boundary that was set by either nature or human beings, generating transregional movements, such as deployment of troops, mobilization of military labor, congregation of merchants, and migration of military families and ordinary people. To facilitate wars and consolidate newly conquered territories, the state freely exercised its power to cede and combine territories, regardless of their traditional—that is, ecological, ethnic, and cultural— boundaries.

War also brought in the steady influx of state funds and redirected economic resources to new territories that had not been within the usual caliber of the marketing system. More important, military needs overrode the rules of market. As additional transportation costs were compensated for by high profits and sometimes state subsidies, merchants were motivated to go to the peripheries and barely accessible places, some of them thereby finding new business opportunities in the long-term. Involving both political and socioeconomic activities, warfare is one of the human activities that can drastically reshape society in a relatively short time, as seen in the case of the Sichuan frontier during the eighteenth century, when the occurrence of war was hardly sporadic but frequent. During the first Jinchuan campaign, when Fuheng was sent to Sichuan to direct the campaign, the Qianlong emperor hinted of his desire to stop the war as quickly as possible. Qianlong suggested that Fuheng use the excuse that the people in Sichuan were suffering from the war and the local economy was impaired. When Fuheng arrived in Sichuan, however, he felt it was difficult to use this excuse, since in his opinion people's suffering in the province was not caused by the war.[35] Perhaps he had grasped the vigor the war had instilled into society despite the strains it caused on the local bureaucracy and some segments of the population.

In treating the Sichuan frontier, another noteworthy tendency that the Qing state demonstrated was its open-mindedness toward the market mechanism, as exemplified in the case of the Sichuan grain market. Thanks to the lenient taxation policy, a grain market took shape in Sichuan in the beginning of the eighteenth century which absorbed the surplus grain that had been left with the people in this productive province. Contrary to what many scholars used to believe, that the imperial state in China always stood as an obstacle to marketing systems, the Qing state did not interfere in the market through political means most of the time; rather, it actively participated in the system to facilitate the circulation of the surpluses to the lower Yangzi valleys to relieve rice shortages.[36] When grain prices rose in the areas of grain shortages, merchants were stimulated to transport the surpluses from Sichuan to the lower Yangzi valleys. At those moments the Qing state adeptly exercised its influence through economic means, such as using inland customs, to lever the operation of the market. When there were frontier wars in Sichuan or Tibet, the state could use its political power to temporarily suspend the natural movement of the commercial grain to supply its frontier wars. If the Qing state did not anticipate the formation of the grain market in the upper Yangzi valley as one of the outcomes of its light taxation policy toward the area, they did not hesitate to take advantage of this market in equilibrating the economic life in the country. From the Yongzheng period through the Qianlong period the Qing state skillfully maneuvered the surplus grain from Sichuan to suit its changing needs on different occasions. This shows that the Qing state was conversant with the terms and rules of the marketing systems and was testing new ways in directing the national economic life.

One should not reach the opposite conclusion, however: namely, that the Qing state was suddenly enlightened by some liberal trends and became a promoter of capitalism. This book has emphasized that the Qing state pursued different policies and rationales in ruling different areas. It is critical to note that the treatment the Sichuan frontier, a key strategic area, received was not applied to other areas, especially to the key economic areas, where the Qing state never relented in exacting high taxes, either in cash or in kind. In so doing, the Qing state created a dual policy in governing the economic life in the country. For the key economic areas, such as Jiangnan, it would not give up the high rate of taxes and leave more surpluses for the market, which inevitably hindered the further development of the economy in the area, no matter how productive this area was as warranted by its superior natural and human conditions.

On the Sichuan frontier, although the single most important objective was to guarantee support to the military and the frequent wars, the state had no intention of hindering the marketing systems. On the contrary, it showed its sophisticated skill in employing market means to facilitate the subsystem of grain circulation. The apparent inconsistency in the Qing's attitude toward the market economy was determined by the different role each area played in the strategic map of the Qing empire. As surplus rice exported from Sichuan weighed significantly in the country's economic life, the Qing state paradoxically found an adroit yet awkward way to administer the economic life in the country—with its key economic areas supplied with commercial grain from its key strategic area but without loosening its grip on the revenue exactions from its key economic areas.

In sum, the Qing state could be "liberal" in some cases and to some areas but more "traditional" in other cases and to other areas. In addition, the state failed to adjust its revenue strategy when the chief reason for the leniency toward the Sichuan frontier had disappeared. In this matter it was not as rational as it had been during the expansion era. Failure to adjust to the changed environments could have been caused either by lack of vision or lack of strength. For the Qing dynasty in the early nineteenth century, both contributed to unwisely maintaining the taxation status quo in Sichuan. When the state rushed to Sichuan for extra revenues in the midst of the Taiping Rebellion, it went much further than achieving fiscal balance. Sichuan was turned into one of the key economic areas by the state when it exacted excessive amounts of surcharges in various names from the province in the dynasty's last sixty years of life, which shows further that the "liberal" stance of the Qing state was conditional and changeable.

Starting from the end of the seventeenth century, the Sichuan frontier had been a hotbed for powerful satraps and military leaders, given the area's rising importance and frequent frontier wars. Ever since the suppression of the Wu Sangui Rebellion, the state had paid considerable attention to controlling provincial viceroys and chief military commanders in the southwestern frontier as well as in Sichuan. The state would often find itself in a dilemma, however: on the one hand, it had to please those satraps and generals by compromising many bureaucratic rules and principles. On the other hand, it had to keep a constant vigilance against the strongmen on the frontier. The rise and fall of several frontier satraps in the Sichuan frontier—such as Nian Gengyao, Yue Zhongqi, and Zhang Guangsi—attest to these dynamics. Sometimes the throne purposely allowed one overlord to extend his purview outside of his jurisdiction and interfere in other area's affairs. The cases such as Nian Gengyao's overtaking of the northwestern region and Ortai's extending his influence into Sichuan were the result of this scheme.

Overall, the state would try not to create a situation in which contention between the center and a region was more prone to occur. During the Qianlong period there was a tangible change in managing the Sichuan frontier: the emperor tended to appoint more Manchus to the area's key positions. Despite the fact that most of them were the empire's prominent frontier leaders—such as Fukang'an, Ehui, Helin, and Sun Shiyi, a lone non-Manchu strongman from the Sichuan frontier in the late eighteenth century—they did not develop deep roots in the area. The story of Yue Zhongqi's family occupying the chief military position in Sichuan for more than a half century was not repeated in the latter part of the eighteenth century. It proved that the Qing central government was essentially successful in preventing powerful provincial strongmen from emulating Wu Sangui's example. Nevertheless, the state also paid a price: it yielded too many financial concessions to the military leaders on the frontier. In the end the state was forced to the verge of bankruptcy in the war against the White Lotus Rebellion, as it was impossible for the state to withhold economic favors to the military during a war, but they became simply too expensive and excessive.

Thus the situation on the Sichuan frontier contrasted with that in the areas that did not belong to the category of strategically important areas; it also differed from the situation in other strategically important areas. As John Robert Shepherd has argued in his monumental book on the Taiwan frontier during the first half of the Qing dynasty, Taiwan's location was strategically critical as the Qing holding of Taiwan would prevent pirates and foreign powers from using the island for activities that might be harmful to the Qing empire.[37] Nevertheless, throughout the eighteenth century, Taiwan had not experienced the same intensity of mobilization and frequent wars as the Sichuan frontier had undergone. The only sizable war that occurred in Taiwan was an internal one, the war suppressing the Lin Shuangwen uprising in 1787 and 1788. As Shepherd has convincingly demonstrated in his work, the size of the military in Taiwan had been kept constant, by and large, and the only increments were direct responses to local problems, such as rebellions.[38]

Along this line the Qing authorities strengthened their surveillance over the local society in the wake of the Lin Shuangwen Rebellion. On the Sichuan frontier most wars were against the enemies on the other side of the border or the outsiders within the border, such as the Jinchuan tribes or non-Han ethnic communities in the peripheries of the province. Unlike Taiwan, where local stability was the primary goal of the military lineup, the main tasks of the military stationed on the Sichuan frontier were the security of Tibet and the expansion of the empire. Therefore the frequent mobilization and reinforcement of military strength did not necessarily heighten the Qing control over the core area and inner borders of Sichuan, which had been within the traditional jurisdiction of the Chinese empire. On the contrary, the local control could even be weakened by those war mobilizations, as the civil bureaucracy became so preoccupied by the task of supporting the military that it had no adequate capacity to police the local society.

By the end of the eighteenth century, when the Qing empire was successful in securing all its frontiers, the local authorities in Sichuan were faced with a severely deteriorated social order. Fed by dismissed military laborers and deserting soldiers, banditry and sectarian movements expanded and eventually became out of control. Compounded with the problem of overpopulation, which was encouraged by the light tax obligations in Sichuan, the province was ripe for an eruption of rebellion in the mid-1790s. Having said this, it is important to note that it might not have been the intention of the Qing dynasty to leave the local society unattended while being engaged in war and military deployment. But the mechanism of its frontier operations certainly lacked a link in ensuring political and social control over the local society.

More particularly, a virtual anarchy came into being in the border areas between Sichuan, Hubei, and Shaanxi provinces over the course of the expansion era. The unfolding of the frontier undertakings finally placed Sichuan, the key player in the Qing Tibetan strategy, in a fixed position relative to its traditional partners, Shaanxi and Gansu and sometimes Hubei. In other words Sichuan was no longer attached to any of these neighbors. As the position of the governor-general of Sichuan and Shaanxi was abolished, first in the Yongzheng period and then in the Qianlong period, the two areas of the Sichuan frontier and the northwestern frontier, chiefly Shaanxi and Gansu, were no longer subject to the concerted supervision of one governor-general. By the same token, Hubei became separated from Sichuan in the early Kangxi period, when the position of the governor-general of Sichuan and Huguang was abolished. Later, when a banner garrison was set up in Chengdu during the first invasion of Tibet, the banner garrison in Jingzhou of Hubei was no longer responsible for any task in Sichuan as it had been before that time. Such a development might have contributed to the relaxation of political control in the large mountainous areas astride the borders between Sichuan, Hubei, and Shaanxi, unwittingly facilitating the formation of a de facto haven for the people who had been deprived of regular means to live, such as landless farmers, soldiers who had deserted, demobilized laborers, bandits, and other jobless drifters.

In 1698, when Yue Shenglong started his expansion toward Tibet in the western borderland of Sichuan, he transferred a great portion of the Green Standard garrison that was located northeast of Chongqing to Dartsedo by arguing that it was not necessary to have a large military presence in eastern Sichuan, where the chance of using military force was small.[39] This incident clearly illuminates a trend throughout the expansion era that reinforcing the peripheries that bordered Tibet was sometimes at the cost of political and military control in the core areas and areas that bordered on heartland provinces. As a result, the interior borderlands were turned into soft spots at the end of the expansion age. Ironically, it was in eastern Sichuan that the White Lotus Rebellion thrived and grew into a prolonged and grave crisis for the Qing. Surprised at first, the Qing state might well have regretted its neglect of the inner borderlands while devoting most of its resources to the outer borders.

ABBREVIATIONS USED IN NOTES AND BIBLIOGRAPHY

GZDQL	*Gongzhongdang Qianlongchao zouzhe* (Secret palace memorials of the Qianlong period)
JCFL	*Pingding Jinchuan fanglüe* (Chronicle of the first Jinchuan campaign)
JCLA	*Pingding liang Jinchuan junxu li'an* (Collected records and precedents related to the military expenditures of the second Jinchuan campaign)
KXHW	*Kangxichao Hanwen zhupi zouzhe huibian* (Complete collection of the memorials in Chinese with the emperor's comments of the Kangxi period)
KXMW	*Kangxichao Manwen zhupi zouzhe quanyi* (Complete translation of the memorials in Manchu with the emperor's comments of the Kangxi period)
LJCFL	*Pingding liang Jinchuan fanglüe* (Chronicle of the second Jinchuan campaign)
MQDA	*Ming Qing dang'an* (Archives of the Ming and Qing dynasties)
NGDK	*Neigedaku dang'an* (Archives of the cabinet of the Qing dynasty)
NMH	*Nian Gengyao Man Han zouzhe yibian* (Collection of Nian Gengyao's memorials in Manchu and Chinese, with the Manchu ones translated into Chinese)
QSG	*Qingshigao* (Draft history of the Qing dynasty)

QSLKX	*DaQing lichao shilu, Shengzuchao* (Veritable records of successive reigns of the Qing dynasty, the Kangxi reign)
QSLQL	*DaQing lichao shilu, Gaozongchao* (Veritable records of successive reigns of the Qing dynasty, the Qianlong reign)
QSLSZ	*DaQing lichao shilu, Shizuchao* (Veritable records of successive reigns of the Qing dynasty, the Shunzhi reign)
QSLYZ	*DaQing lichao shilu, Shizongchao* (Veritable records of successive reigns of the Qing dynasty, the Yongzheng reign)
SCTZ	*Sichuan tongzhi* (Gazetteer of Sichuan)
SYD	*Qianlongchao shangyudang* (Edicts of the Qianlong period)
SMFL	*Qinzheng pingding shuomo fanglüe* (Chronicle of the Kangxi emperor's expeditions to pacify the steppe)
XZDA	*Yuan yilai Xizang difang yu zhongyang zhengfu guanxi dang'an shiliao huibian* (A collection of historical archives concerning the relationship between Tibet and the central government since the Yuan times)
YZHW	*Yongzhengchao Hanwen zhupi zouzhe huibian* (Complete collection of the Chinese memorials with the emperor's comments of the Yongzheng period)
YZMW	*Yongzhengchao Manwen zhupi zouzhe quanyi* (Complete translation of the Manchu memorials with the emperor's comments of the Yongzheng period)

NOTES

1 INTRODUCTION

Epigraph: Chongxiu Chengdu xianzhi (Revised gazetteer of Chengdu county), *juan* 1.

1 The four rivers were the Min, the Lu (Jinsha), the Luo (Tuo), and the Ba (Jialing).

2 Kokonor was the region that falls into today's Qinghai province and part of Gansu province of China. "Kokonor" is Mongolian, meaning "blue lake." Although the main residents in Kokonor were Mongols and Tibetans, some Chinese and other peoples also lived there (Yang Ho-chin, *Annals of Kokonor*, 7).

3 Ho Ping-ti considers that the core part of Sichuan, Jiangnan, and northern Zhejiang had been "relatively fully developed in the agricultural sense" since early times in Chinese history (Ho, "Early-Ripening Rice in Chinese History").

4 *Chongxiu Chengdu xianzhi, juan* 1.

5 The Baoye passage was located in the southwestern part of today's Shaanxi province. Winding in deep mountains of Mount Qinling, it was built along the two rivers, the Bao and the Ye, running about 150 miles. Its southern end was to the north of Hanzhong and its northern end was at the Wei River valley, the gateway to Xi'an.

6 Chen Ziang, "Treatise Arguing against War against the Untamed Qiang People in Yazhou," in *Qinding quanTangwen* (Imperial-sanctioned collection of proses of the Tang period), vol. 5, 2716–18.

7 The An Lushan Rebellion (755–63) was a large-scale revolt by the military magnates from the Tang's northern frontiers. It became the turning point for the Tang dynasty, triggering its downturn both politically and economically.

8 Skinner, "Regional Urbanization in Nineteenth-Century China," 212.

9 Besides the governors-general of Zhili and Sichuan, the other governors-general were those of Shaanxi-Gansu, Huguang, Liang-Guang, Liang-Jiang, Fujian-Zhejiang, and Yunnan-Guizhou. Shanxi and Henan provinces were not under any governor-general's control. For discussion on the distinction between a governor and a governor-general in rank, function, and scope of power, see Guy, "Inspired Tinkering," chapter 3.

10 Chi, *Key Economic Areas in Chinese History*.

11 After the Han dynasty collapsed in 220, China was first divided by three kingdoms. Then several nomadic peoples set up their own competing regimes in the north. Meanwhile, successive Chinese dynasties ruled the south in the Yangzi River valley and largely developed the region. After the Sui dynasty (581–618) reunified the country in 589, the lower Yangzi River valley remained to be the most productive area.

12 For Sichuan's position as a key economic area in the Tang times, see Feng Hanyong, "Tangdai Jiannan dao de jingji zhuangkuang yu LiTang de xingwang guanxi" (The relationship between the economic situation of Jiannan circuit and the rise and fall of the Tang dynasty). For Sichuan's hefty economic contribution to the central government in the Song times, mainly through the state's monopoly of the tea industry, see Paul Smith, *Taxing Heaven's Storehouse*.

13 On Sichuan's separatist tendency, see Chi, *Key Economic Areas in Chinese History*, 31–33; and Liang Qichao, *Yinbingshi quanji* (Collected works of Liang Qichao), 37/51. Foreign observers also reached the same conclusion. One of them stated: "In short, Sz-Chuan is a wonderful section of the empire,—an empire of itself, independent in a great measure of outside help" (Hart, *Western China*, 281). The two most prominent historical instances for Sichuan as an independent power competing with other parts of China are the Shu Kingdom (221–263) of the Disunion period and the states of the Former Shu (907–925) and the Later Shu (934–965) during the interregnum period after the collapse of the Tang dynasty.

14 Guy, "Imperial Powers and the Appointment of Provincial Governors in Ch'ing China."

15 The most recent work is Peter C. Perdue's *China Marches West*. The earlier works on the northwestern frontier include James Millward's *Beyond the Pass*. In Chinese literature the most prominent recent works include those by Ma Ruheng and Ma Dazheng (*Elute Menggu shi lunji* [Collected studies on the history of the Eleuth Mongols] and *Qingdai de bianjiang zhengce* [Frontier policy of the Qing dynasty]) and Yuan Senpo (*Kang Yong Qian jingying yu kaifa beijiang* [The Qing governance and explorations of the northern frontiers during the Kangxi, Yongzheng, and Qianlong periods]).

16 The recent studies on the southwestern frontier during the Qing include Laura Hostetler's *Qing Colonial Enterprise*; C. Patterson Giersch's *Asian Borderlands*; Donald Sutton's "Ethnicity and the Miao Frontier in the Eighteenth Century" and

"Ethnic Revolt in the Qing Empire: The Miao Uprising of 1795–1796 Reexamined"; and John E. Herman's *Amid the Clouds and Mist*. For the Taiwan frontier the major works include John Robert Shepherd's *Statecraft and Political Economy on the Taiwan Frontier*; and Emma Jinhua Teng's *Taiwan's Imagined Geography*.

17 For the Manchuria frontier recent works include James Reardon-Anderson's *Reluctant Pioneers*, and Christopher M. Isett's *State, Peasant, and Merchant in Qing Manchuria*.

18 Adshead, *Province and Politics in Late Imperial China*, 105. Earlier in the same work, S. A. M. Adshead claims that only at the end of the Qing "Szechwan became for the first time a leading viceroyalty, organizing projects for the empire, spending more than half its revenue within its own borders, receiving subsidies from other areas" (ibid., 74).

19 There are only a few English-language works on Sichuan during the early Qing period, among which is Robert Entenmann's "Migration and Settlement in Sichuan." There are several Chinese-language general histories of Sichuan, including Wang Gang's *Qingdai Sichuan shi* (A history of Sichuan during the Qing dynasty) and some specialized studies such as Sun Xiaofen's work on the migration to Sichuan (*Qingdai qianqi de yimin tian Sichuan* [Migration to Sichuan during the early Qing period]), Hu Zhaoxi's studies on the massacres by Zhang Xianzhong (*Zhang Xianzhong tu Shu kaobian* [A study of Zhang Xianzhong's alleged massacres in Sichuan]), and Wang Di's works on the socioeconomic structure of Sichuan (*Kuachu fengbi de shijie* [Striding out of a closed world]).

20 Luciano Petech's *China and Tibet in the Early Eighteenth Century* remains the major English-language work in this regard. Tsepon W. D. Shakabpa's *Tibet* also has a section on the eighteenth century.

21 In his manuscript "State and Economy in Southwest China, 1250-1850," James Z. Lee emphasizes the role the state played in the economic growth in the southwest. Both Millward (*Beyond the Pass*) and Perdue (*China Marches West*) treat the economic development in Eastern Turkistan as an integral part of the Qing conquest and rule of that region. Giersch (*Asian Borderlands*) also pays close attention to the commercial activities within and across Yunnan's borders that occurred side by side with Qing southwestward expansion.

22 For example, the Number One Historical Archives of China reprinted all memorials of the Yongzheng period that are extant, including the ones housed in the National Palace Museum in Taipei, in a forty-volume compendium, *Yongzhengchao Hanwen zhupi zouzhe huibian* (Complete collection of Chinese memorials with the emperor's comments of the Yongzheng period). Another important source for this study is *Qianlongchao shangyudang*, a collection of the edicts by the Qianlong emperor, also edited by the Number One Historical Archives of China.

23 The compendia in point are *Kangxichao Manwen zhupi zouzhe quanyi* (Complete translation of the memorials in Manchu with the emperor's comments of the Kangxi period) and *Yongzhengchao Manwen zhupi zouzhe quanyi* (Complete transla-

tion of the Manchu memorials with the emperor's comments of the Yongzheng period). Both were translated and edited by the Number One Historical Archives of China in Beijing. A collection of all Nian Gengyao's memorials, including the translation of those in Manchu, *Nian Gengyao Man Han zouzhe yibian*, also proved indispensable for this book.

1 A HUMBLE BEGINNING, 1644–1696

Epigraph: *DaQing lichao shilu, Shengzuchao* (Veritable records of successive reigns of the Qing dynasty, the Kangxi reign, hereafter QSLKX), 160/1b-2b.

1. On the Qin conquest of these two kingdoms and its relationship to the Qin unification, see Sage, *Ancient Sichuan and the Unification of China*.
2. The effectiveness of this tactic has been recently challenged. See Herman, "Mongol Conquest of Dali."
3. During the Yuan-Ming transition Sichuan was taken by Ming Yuzhen, one of many rebel leaders of the time, who set up an independent kingdom, Xia, there.
4. The land tax quota of Sichuan in 1578 was 1,028,544 *shi* of grain, only higher than Guangdong, Guangxi, Guizhou, and Yunnan provinces (Ray Huang, *Taxation and Governmental Finance*, 164).
5. On the number of the Manchu troops, see Fang, "Technique for Estimating the Numerical Strength." On the Southern Ming regimes, see Struve, *Southern Ming*.
6. *DaQing lichao shilu, Shizuchao* (Veritable records of successive reigns of the Qing dynasty, the Shunzhi reign, hereafter QSLSZ), 15/27b-28a.
7. On the anti-hair-shaving movement in Jiangnan, see Wakeman, *Great Enterprise*, 646–74.
8. Payment of tribute grain was initiated in the Ming dynasty. Seven provinces paid such tribute to the state in the Ming times (Henan, Huguang, Jiangxi, North Zhili, Shandong, South Zhili, and Zhejiang) and eight in the Qing period (Anhui, Henan, Hubei, Hunan, Jiangsu, Jiangxi, Shandong, and Zhejiang).
9. About the Zhang Xianzhong Rebellion, see Parsons, *Peasant Rebellions of the Late Ming Dynasty*, especially 17–19, 142–60, and 167–85. See also Pih, *Le Père Gabriel de Magalhães*, 34–35.
10. Buglio (Li Leisi) went to China in 1637. De Magalhães (An Wensi) went to Goa in 1634 and arrived in China in 1640. Both men went to Sichuan a few years before Zhang's arrival.
11. Pih, *Le Père Gabriel de Magalhães*, 37–42.
12. Ibid., 36; and Parsons, *Peasant Rebellions of the Late Ming Dynasty*, 171.
13. *Ming Qing dang'an* (Archives of the Ming and Qing dynasties, hereafter MQDA), A3-43; and QSLSZ, 21/18a-b.
14. QSLSZ, 23/9a-10b. On Haoge's life and his conflict with Dorgon, see several of his biographies in *Zhuangao*, Nos. 7580, 7471, and 7306; these unpublished biog-

raphies of the Historiography Institute of the Qing dynasty are housed in Taipei's National Palace Museum.

15 According to de Magalhães, only four hundred troops marched to Sichuan (Pih, *Le Père Gabriel de Magalhães*, 53–60). This may be a false claim, for Haoge might have sent dispatches away, and de Magalhães only counted troops accompanying Haoge himself. According to another source, there were "thousands" of Manchu troops with Haoge (MQDA, A4-232), but this still was not a sufficient force.

16 MQDA, A3-43.

17 Ibid., A4-232.

18 QSLSZ, 29/8b-9a.

19 Xie, *NanMing shilüe* (A brief history of the Southern Ming regimes), 178–79.

20 Fu, *Wuma Xiansheng jinian* (Chronicle of Monsieur Wuma), 119; Gu Shanzhen, "KeDianshu" (A narrative of my stay in Yunnan), 100; and Pih, *Le Père Gabriel de Magalhães*, 54–55.

21 MQDA, A7-66.

22 Entenmann, "Migration and Settlement in Sichuan," 48–49; and Peng and Wang, *Qingdai Sichuan nongcun shehui jingji shi* (A socioeconomic history of rural Sichuan in the Qing times), 71.

23 Li Guoying accused many officials of being unworthy and doing nothing good but exacting people, seizing others' wives, gambling, and so on (MQDA, A9-66).

24 QSLSZ, 33/19b-20a.

25 De Magalhães also thought that Haoge should not have divided his expedition into smaller dispatches and that he should have made northern Sichuan his base, as the supplies were abundant there (Pih, *Le Père Gabriel de Magalhães*, 54–55).

26 Haoge's subordinates could not help but spread disheartening stories about Sichuan upon their return. One Manchu officer named Neikun was dismissed from office and given a hundred lashes for his loud complaints about the hardships in Sichuan (QSLSZ, 36/11b).

27 The leading work of this kind is Hu Zhaoxi's *Zhang Xianzhong tu Shu kaobian* (A study of Zhang Xianzhong's alleged massacres in Sichuan).

28 Shen, *Shunan xulüe* (A sketch of the disasters in Sichuan), 107; Parsons, *Peasant Rebellions of the Late Ming Dynasty*, 172; and Pih, *Le Père Gabriel de Magalhães*, 43–54.

29 Entenmann, "Migration and Settlement in Sichuan," 37–38.

30 For a study of those accounts, see Ren, "Guanyu Zhang Xianzhong shiliao de jianbie" (An examination on the material relating to Zhang Xianzhong).

31 MQDA, A8-10.

32 One of the rebel leaders, Yang Zhan, made Jiading in southern Sichuan his base and set up military agricultural colonies to supply his troops and the residents who stayed with food (Fei, *Huangshu* [A book on devastation], 444).

33 Quite a few of Luo's memorials are included in MQDA, A1-A8.

34 MQDA, A8-10, A8-140, A7-176, and A9-143.

35 About the Southern Ming regime in Guilin, see Struve, *Southern Ming*, 139–95.

36 Lombard-Salmon, *Un exemple d'acculturation chinoise*, 55.

37 Some accounts of the devastation in the region can be found in Struve, *Voices from the Ming-Qing Cataclysm*.

38 Strongest among Zhang's remnants, Sun Kewang had long attempted to acquire a title from the Southern Ming court in Guilin. See Wakeman, *Great Enterprise*, 990n5 and 1030; and Struve, *Southern Ming*, 73–75, 86–88, and 116–19.

39 For Hong Chengchou's role in conquering the southwestern area, see Wang Chen-main, *Life and Career of Hung Ch'eng-ch'ou*, 183–96.

40 Ibid., 193; and Struve, *Voices from the Ming-Qing Cataclysm*, 149–50.

41 Wang Chen-main, *Life and Career of Hung Ch'eng-ch'ou*, 199–200, and 202–3.

42 QSLKX, 6/11a-b. Zhu was surrendered to Wu Sangui by the Myanmar king and executed by Wu in 1662. See Struve, *Voices from the Ming-Qing Cataclysm*, 239–60.

43 In 1662 the capital of Sichuan was temporarily moved to Chongqing, when the major battlegrounds had shifted to eastern Sichuan (QSLKX, 6/20b-21a).

44 There is no concensus on the population figures before and after the Ming-Qing transition. Although the total population in the Ming dynasty might be between one hundred million and two hundred million, it remains a question whether it was reduced by half in the early Qing (Peterson, "Introduction: New Order for the Old Order," 5).

45 In the same year, 117,522 adult males were registered in Yunnan and 13,839 in Guizhou (*DaQing huidian* [Collected statutes of the Qing dynasty], Kangxi period, *juan* 23, 3b-4a).

46 Fei, *Huangshu*, 437; and Entenmann, "Migration and Settlement in Sichuan," 49.

47 In a census of 1659 only twenty-three households were registered in Wenjiang county, with thirty-one men and twenty-three women (*Wenjiang xianzhi* [Gazetteer of Wenjiang county], *juan* 3).

48 QSLSZ, 134/2a-b; and QSLKX, 7/21b-22a.

49 In 1664 an official in the Board of War suggested that the surrendered rebel chiefs be dispatched to posts all over the country, to alleviate the pressure on Sichuan. This was still enforced in 1673 (QSLKX, 11/8b and 43/10a).

50 QSLKX, 22/3b-4a.

51 *Qingchao wenxian tongkao* (General history and examination of Qing institutions and documents), *juan* 19.

52 QSLKX, 24/30b; and *Huangchao jingshi wenbian* (Statecraft writings of the Qing period), *juan* 72. In 1724 there were about fifty-seven thousand *mu* (100 *mu* equals 1 *qing*) of the military colonies in Sichuan. During the Qianlong period the amount further went down until all the military colonies disappeared (*Qingchao wenxian tongkao*, *juan* 10).

53 QSLKX, 27/19a.

54 MQDA, A 38-40.

55 *Sichuan tongzhi* (Gazetteer of Sichuan, hereafter SCTZ), *juan* 64. Zhang Dedi was

rewarded in 1670 with an honorable title for his achievements in calling people back to Sichuan (QSLKX, 33/14b).

56 The site of the governor-general of Huguang was later moved to Wuchang, Hubei.

57 Parts of this long memorial are included in QSLKX, 36/7b-8b.

58 Ibid., 40/4b-5a.

59 Entenmann, "Migration and Settlement in Sichuan," 79.

60 Deng Xiaoping's ancestors were persuaded by Li Xian'gen, an official in Guangdong and a Sichuan native, to move back in 1671 to their original hometown, Guang'an county, in eastern Sichuan (Maomao, *Wode fuqin Deng Xiaoping* [My father Deng Xiaoping], 26).

61 Zhou Xun, *Shuhai congtan* (Miscellanea of Sichuan), 20; and Sun, *Qingdai qianqi de yimin tian Sichuan* (Migration to Sichuan during the early Qing period), 30.

62 Sun, *Qingdai qianqi de yimin tian Sichuan*, 5 and 30; Hu, *Zhang Xianzhong tu Shu kaobian*, 90; and Mori, "Shindai Sisen no imin keizai" (The migration economy in Sichuan during the Qing Dynasty).

63 QSLSZ, 124/14b-15a.

64 Wakeman, *Great Enterprise*, 1036.

65 Kessler, *K'ang-hsi and the Consolidation of Ch'ing Rule*, 78; and Wakeman, *Great Enterprise*, 1099.

66 Kessler, *K'ang-hsi and the Consolidation of Ch'ing Rule*, 77. MQDA, A38-49 and A38-51; QSLKX, 108/16a-b and 108/17a-b; and Ma Yao, *Yunnan jianshi* (A brief history of Yunnan), 162.

67 QSLKX, 15/14b and 97/5a-b.

68 Ibid., 18/18a, 19/1b, and 19/10b.

69 For more on the Wu Sangui Rebellion, see Wakeman, *Great Enterprise*, 1066–1127.

70 Entenmann, "Migration and Settlement in Sichuan," 59. While Entenmann holds that about one million original residents remained in Sichuan in 1680, a demographical historian estimates that there were approximately five hundred thousand people left in Sichuan at the time (Li Shiping, *Sichuan renkou shi* [A demographic history of Sichuan], 155).

71 *DaQing huidian* (Kangxi period), 23/7a-b.

72 Kangxi interviewed the officials from those provinces to gather information and monitor the situation there. Some of the conversations were not included in his daily record, *Qijuzhu*, if they were confidential (Kessler, *K'ang-hsi and the Consolidation of Ch'ing Rule*, 131).

73 QSLKX, 19/18b-19a.

74 But Kangxi did not show any mercy if the non-Han chieftains rebelled against the Qing. He once ordered to extirpate these chieftains if they did not respond to the Qing call to surrender when the Qing forces campaigned in the southwest (ibid., 97/3a-b).

75 *Zhuangao*, No. 7267. It is also included under a different title in *Huangchao jingshi wenbian*, 86/3b-5a.

76 QSLKX, 106/18a-b.

77 Ibid., 106/18b-19a.

78 Ibid., 108/11a and 113/17a.

79 Ibid., 124/4b-5a.

80 Ibid., 124/16b-17b and 124/19b-20b.

81 The author of Cai's biography agrees that Cai's removal from his position in Yunnan was due to his hard line in the affairs of the non-Han peoples (Hummel, *Eminent Chinese of the Ch'ing Period*, 734–36).

82 Cai Yurong, *Pingnan jilüe* (A brief account of the campaign pacifying the South).

83 QSLKX, 126/1b-2a.

84 Ibid., 129/12a-13a.

85 Junchen was son of the duke of Zhou, who became the regent to the king of the Zhou dynasty after his father died. Zhaobo was also a member of the Zhou imperial household and thus shared some power with the duke of Zhou. Both figures stand for competent statesmen with the potential to rule.

86 QSLKX, 155/19a-a, 155/22a-b, 158/19a-20a, and 158/20a-b. Also Zhao Erxun, *Qingshigao* (Draft history of the Qing dynasty, hereafter QSG), *juan* 276.

87 *Zhuangao*, No. 7103.

88 Fan's father, Fan Wencheng, had surrendered to the Qing before its conquest of China and played an instrumental role in the conquest era. His elder brother, Fan Chengmo, the governor-general of Fujian, had been jailed by Geng Jingzhong during the Wu Sangui Rebellion and died in jail. A detailed account of Fan Chengmo's story is in Wakeman, *Great Enterprise*, 1105–15.

89 QSG, *juan* 232. When Fan went to the capital for an imperial audience in 1693, in a rare show of his approval, Kangxi bestowed upon Fan an outfit of furs of his own (QSLKX, 161/3b-4a).

90 QSLKX, 156/4a-b.

91 Kangxi once mentioned in 1717 that he had never heard of any bad weather report from these four provinces (QSLKX, 272/5a). Not until 1692 did Sichuan receive its first tax exemption.

92 As late as 1706, appointed officials to Yunnan, Guizhou, and Sichuan still delayed their arrivals (QSLKX, 193/22b). In 1685 Zhao Hongcan, a high-ranking officer in northern Sichuan, requested to be transferred by citing the inclement climate there. He was subsequently reappointed to Zhili province (ibid., 121/3a-b).

93 Ibid., 96/27b-28a.

94 Ibid., 113/9a. In the early Qing both provinces used to be listed as ones for which the stipend was of the border standard. Sichuan was changed to inland standard in 1663; Guangxi was changed in 1669.

95 *Zhuangao*, No. 7103; and QSG, *juan* 274.

96 In 1691, when it was proposed that the retired officials be allowed to choose their

place for retirement, the emperor approved the motion but with the exception that the officials from Sichuan and Fengtian were still obliged to return to their home provinces (QSLKX, 150/15b-16a). In 1716, when Bai Huang, the acting governor of Guizhou, requested the application of this rule to Guizhou, he cited Sichuan as precedent (KXHW, vol. 7, 362–64).

97 Li Yu, "Social Change during the Ming-Qing Transition."

98 QSLKX, 149/15a.

99 Li Yu, "Social Change during the Ming-Qing Transition." Just over sixty *jinshi* degree holders were from Sichuan during the entire Kangxi period (calculated according to the data provided in Li Chaozheng, *Qingdai Sichuan jinshi zhenglüe* [Brief biographies of *jinshi* degree holders from Sichuan during the Qing Dynasty]).

100 Kessler, *K'ang-hsi and the Consolidation of Ch'ing Rule*, 95.

101 QSLKX, 124/21b-22a and 130/2b-3a.

102 Ibid., 126/24b and 136/7b-8a.

103 For a good example of the hesitation on the part of the provincial officials to request funds from the central government, see a memorial by Wang Yan, the governor of Guizhou. Wang said that he understood that it was difficult for the state to grant any financial support to his province (cited in Lombard-Salmon, *Un exemple d'acculturation chinoise*, 352–53).

104 QSLKX, 160/1b-2b.

105 Hart, *Western China*, 281.

2 A STRATEGIC TURN FROM THE STEPPE TO TIBET, 1696–1701

Epigraph: DaQing lichao shilu, Shengzuchao (hereafter QSLKX), 185/11b.

1 This section on the history of Tibetan Buddhism, the Yellow Sect in particular, is based on a number of general histories of Tibet and the works on the Sino-Tibetan relationship and Tibetan Buddhism. Among them are *Tibet*, by Tsepon W. D. Shakabpa; *A Cultural History of Tibet*, by David Snellgrove and Hugh Richardson; *Tibetan Nation*, by Warren W. Smith Jr.; "China's Relations with Inner Asia," by Suzuki Chusei; *Chusei Chibetto shi kenkyu* (Studies on the medieval history of Tibet), edited by Sato Hisashi; *Zangzu shiyao* (Highlights of Tibetan history), by Wang Furen and Suo Wenqing; *The Tibetan Assimilation of Buddhism*, by Matthew T. Kapstein; and *The Annals of Kokonor*, translated by Yang Ho-chin.

2 For the rise of the Tibetan empire, see Beckwith, *Tibetan Empire in Central Asia*.

3 Backus, *Nan-chao Kingdom and T'ang China's Southwestern Frontier*, 24.

4 For a refreshing study of the Mongol embrace of Tibetan Buddhism before and during Qing times, see Johan Elverskog's recent work, *Our Great Qing*.

5 For the Mongol Yuan's patronage of the Sakya sect, see Petech, *Central Tibet and the Mongols*.

6 The Tumed Mongols were dominant in southern Mongolia in the sixteenth cen-

tury and frequently attacked the northern borderlands of the Ming dynasty.

7 But C. R. Bawden holds that Altan Khan was converted to Buddhism in 1573, a few years before his meeting with Sonam Gyatso (Bawden, *Modern History of Mongolia*, 28–29). As Elverskog has pointed out, Altan's conversion to Tibetan Buddhism was not meant to bring the Mongols into the Tibetan cultural and religious sphere. Instead, he attempted to create an independent "Mongolian Buddhism" (Elverskog, *Our Great Qing*, 101–4 and 123–26).

8 "Dalai" is Mongolian for "ocean" and "lama" is Tibetan for "superior master."

9 Bergholz, *Partition of the Steppe*, 152–72; Bawden, *Modern History of Mongolia*, 41–47; and Di Cosmo, "Military Aspects of the Manchu Wars against the Čaqars."

10 While the Tumed Mongols belonged to the "Eastern Mongols," the Oirat Mongols were known as the "Western Mongols." During the fifteenth century, Esen, the legendary leader of the Oirat, frequently attacked the northern marches of the Ming. In 1449 he captured the Zhengtong emperor of the Ming in Tumubao, Hebei province. Esen did not fully take advantage of his exploit, however, failing to establish a viable nomadic state during his prime year. Therefore, when he was killed in a revolt by his chieftains in 1454, it ended the Oirat's dominance over China's northern frontier. For the Tumu incident, see Mote, "T'u-mu Incident of 1449," and Du and Bai, *Ximenggu yanjiu* (Studies on the Western Mongols), 88–98.

11 Gushri Khan's name was Thoripeihur. "Gushri" was a title conferred on him by a Yellow Sect lama and the leaders of the Khalkha Mongols in 1606, which meant "great teacher of the state" (Yang Ho-chin, *Annals of Kokonor*, 35). About Gushri Khan's life and involvement in Tibet, see Ma Ruheng and Ma Dazheng, *Elute Menggu shi lunji* (Collected studies on the history of the Eleuth Mongols), 1–18; and Luo Lida, "Mingmo Qingchu de Meng-Zang guanxi he GushiHan ruZang shijian" (Mongolian-Tibetan relations during the Ming-Qing transition and the incident of Gushri Khan's invasion of Tibet).

12 The Khalkha Mongols came to Kokonor in 1634 and defeated the Tumed Mongols there. Then the Khalkha persecuted the Yellow Sect in Kokonor (see Ma Ruheng and Ma Dazheng, *Elute Menggu shi lunji*, 10; and Bergholz, *Partition of the Steppe*, 48).

13 Shakabpa, *Tibet*, 111.

14 On a map from the late Ming, the area of Tibet is marked as *Menggu fandi* (Mongol barbarians' territory). The map is now kept in the National Palace Museum in Taipei.

15 Farquhar, "Origins of the Manchus' Mongolian Policy."

16 Some records of those early contacts between the Tibetans and the Manchus are collected in *Yuan yilai Xizang difang yu zhongyang zhengfu guanxi dang'an shiliao huibian* (Collection of historical archives concerning the relationship between Tibet and the central government since the Yuan times, hereafter XZDA), vol. 2, 213–22.

17 *Aochao* in Chinese, it is usually translated as "the collective tea party to monks." It was an important religious ceremony in Tibetan Buddhism.

18 About the Dalai Lama's visit, see XZDA, vol. 2, 224–37.

19 Shakabpa, *Tibet*, 116.

20 *DaQing lichao shilu, Shizuchao* (Veritable records of successive reigns of the Qing dynasty, the Shunzhi reign, hereafter QSLSZ), 74/18a-19a.

21 The Manchu rulers were greatly saddened by his death, for he was believed to be truly loyal to the Qing (XZDA, vol. 2, 245).

22 Elverskog, *Our Great Qing*, 104–9.

23 Kessler, *K'ang-hsi and the Consolidation of Ch'ing Rule*, 152–53.

24 It also stipulated that Tibet would not levy any charges or duties on goods imported from Nepal (Shaha, *Modern Nepal*, vol. 1, 29). Tibet was rich in silver deposits but lacked the means to mint coins.

25 As many scholars have argued, it is apparent that the Qing ruling elite became sincerely interested in Tibetan Buddhism later, especially during the Qianlong period. See Zito, *Of Body and Brush*; Rawski, *Last Emperors*, 257–58; Wang Xiangyun, "Qing Court's Tibet Connection"; and Hevia, "Lamas, Emperors, and Rituals."

26 *DaQing lichao shilu, Taizongchao* (Veritable records of successive reigns of the Qing dynasty, the reign of Hung Taiji), 18/13a.

27 *Kangxi qijuzhu* (Diaries of action and repose of the Kangxi emperor), KX 12/10/09, vol. 1, 127.

28 Ma Ruheng and Ma Dazheng, *Elute Menggu shi lunji*, 34.

29 Yuan Sengpo, *Kang Yong Qian jingying yu kaifa beijiang* (The Qing governance and explorations of the northern frontiers during the Kangxi, Yongzheng, and Qianlong periods), 314–16. Petech also points out that Kangxi's interest in Tibet was merely "religious-political" (Petech, *Central Tibet and the Mongols*, 9–10).

30 Some of the records about the intricate triangular relationship between the Qing, Lhasa, and Wu Sangui, including archives in Mongolian, are in XZDA, vol. 2, 251–61. As told by Shakabpa, the Dalai Lama took "an impartial view" of the rebellion (Shakabpa, *Tibet*, 121).

31 QSLKX, 54/16a-17b. On the eve of the Qing victory the Dalai Lama admitted that he was wrong in urging the Qing to show leniency toward Wu (XZDA, vol. 2, 261).

32 QSLKX, 90/5a; and XZDA, vol. 2, 260–61.

33 QSLKX, 90/9b-10a.

34 Ibid., 96/16a-b.

35 The first *desi* was appointed by Gushri Khan in 1642 (Shakabpa, *Tibet*, 111).

36 It was believed in Tibet that Sangye Gyatso was the Fifth Dalai Lama's biological son. In 1652, before his trip to Beijing, the Fifth Dalai Lama stayed one night in an aristocrat's home, just north of Lhasa. The hostess accompanied the Dalai Lama to bed. The following year, Sangye Gyatso was born in this family (Wang

Yao, "Diba Sangjie Jiacuo zakao" (A study on *desi* Sangye Gyatso); Petech, *Central Tibet and the Mongols*, 9; and Shakabpa, *Tibet*, 125–32).

37 Shakabpa, *Tibet*, 121–22.

38 The major literature on the Zunghar Mongols includes Perdue, *China Marches West*; Bergholz, *Partition of the Steppe*; Pallas, *Sammlungen historischer Nachrichten über die Mongolischen Völkerschaften* (Historical material on the Eleuth Mongols); Du and Bai, *Ximenggu yanjiu* (Studies on the Western Mongols); and Ma Ruheng and Ma Dazheng, *Elute Menggu shi lunji*.

39 Bergholz, *Partition of the Steppe*, 31–43, 44–45.

40 Ibid., 47–48.

41 Yet there were contacts between Ba'atur and the Qing court in the 1640s and 1650s (Ma Ruheng and Ma Dazheng, *Elute Menggu shi lunji*, 52–71). For Ba'atur's relationship with the Russians, see Bergholz, *Partition of the Steppe*, 48–60.

42 Bergholz, *Partition of the Steppe*, 244.

43 Galdan also acquired firearms, among other things, from the Russians (ibid., 245–48).

44 About the origins of the internal strife among the Khalkha Mongols and the Zunghar attacks against them, see ibid., 255–64; and Bawden, *Modern History of Mongolia*, 47–80.

45 With Lhasa's backing, a *kuriltai* was summoned at Khurin-Bilchir in Mongolia in October 1686, and an agreement was reached between the conflicting parties of the Khalkha Mongols; however, it was soon broken (Bergholz, *Partition of the Steppe*, 258–59).

46 Kangxi elucidated the correlation between his acceptance of the Khalkha Mongols and the Zunghar problem in *Qinzheng pingding shuomo fanglüe* (Chronicle of the Kangxi emperor's expeditions to pacify the steppe, hereafter SMFL), 44/40b-41a. Also see Bergholz, *Partition of the Steppe*, 263–64; and Bawden, *Modern History of Mongolia*, 77–80.

47 About the Sino-Russian relations of the time, see Kessler, *K'ang-hsi and the Consolidation of Ch'ing Rule*, 97–103; Mancall, *Russia and China*, chapters 2–5; and Yuan Sengpo, *Kang Yong Qian jingying yu kaifa beijiang*, 36–58.

48 Bergholz, *Partition of the Steppe*, 255.

49 For the Qing expeditions against Galdan, see Perdue, *China Marches West*, 133–209.

50 As Sengge's son, Tsewang was Galdan's enemy by default. Galdan had killed two of Tsewang's brothers, and Tsewang himself barely escaped murder by Galdan. In addition, Galdan took Tsewang's fiancée as his own concubine in 1679 (SMFL, 27/9b-10a). Also see Bergholz, *Partition of the Steppe*, 279–80; and Yuan Sengpo, *Kang Yong Qian jingying yu kaifa beijiang*, 83.

51 Zhuang Jifa, *Qingdai Zungaer shiliao chubian* (Collected Qing archives on the Kangxi emperor's expeditions against the Zunghar), 215–21 (also in *Kangxi chao Manwen zhupi zouzhe quanyi* [Complete translation of the memorials in Manchu with the emperor's comments of the Kangxi period, hereafter KXMW], 182–83).

Later Kangxi claimed that Galdan committed suicide by taking poison (QSLKX, 183/7a-8b), which is an overt fabrication.

52 SMFL, 26/4b.

53 In 1695, Sangye allegedly told Galdan: "It is auspicious to stage a southern expedition." Galdan regretted this after his rout in 1696: "It was not my own desire to thrust into the Kerulen River valley. It was because the Dalai Lama told me that it was greatly auspicious if I conducted a southern expedition. The Dalai Lama killed me whereas I killed you people!" (SMFL, 26/5a).

54 Ibid., 33/44b-45a; and Bergholz, *Partition of the Steppe*, 293.

55 SMFL, 25/41a-b.

56 Ibid., 26/4b.

57 Ibid., 26/55a; and Bergholz, *Partition of the Steppe*, 288–89.

58 SMFL, 27/60b, 27/9a-11b, and 26/5a-b.

59 Bergholz, *Partition of the Steppe*, 282–83.

60 QSLKX, 163/7b; and SMFL, 13/33a-35a and 26/55a.

61 SMFL, 13/33b.

62 The primary sources for this section are mainly from SMFL, a compendium recording Kangxi's expeditions against Galdan in 1696 and 1697 that was completed in 1708. Compared with QSLKX, which was compiled during the Yongzheng era, SMFL provides more truthful and complete documentation of the making of the early Qing Tibetan policy. The records in QSLKX had apparently been pruned.

63 SMFL, 28/23a.

64 Ibid., 26/55b.

65 Ibid., 28/22b-23a.

66 Ibid., 28/23b. Panchen Lama was the title given posthumously by the Fifth Dalai Lama to his teacher, Lobsang Chokyi Gyaltsen, the abbot of the Tashilhunpo monastery near Shigatse upon the latter's death (three deceased lamas were posthumously entitled the First, Second and Third Panchen Lama). The Fifth Dalai Lama also recognized Lobsang Yeshe as Lobsang Chokyi Gyaltsen's incarnation and the Fifth Panchen Lama. Although the Fifth Panchen Lama did not obtain the position of the next highest authority in the Yellow Sect hierarchy until 1713, this policy had actually been conceived long before 1713.

67 SMFL, 28/29a.

68 Ibid., 28/37a.

69 Ibid., 31/21b and 31/38b.

70 Ibid., 36/16b-21a and 37/12b-18b.

71 Ibid., 37/19a-21b.

72 In the Western way of calculations the Dalai Lama had been dead for fifteen years and the new Dalai Lama was fourteen years old.

73 Ibid., 39/9b-10a and 40/1a-3a.

74 Ibid., 39/53b.

75 Ibid., 39/55a-56b.

76 Ibid., 40/1a-6b.

77 Ibid., 40/27a-31a. In pinning the blame on the lamas, Kangxi said the following: "It is useful to raise a dog, as it barks at strangers. But it is not useful to provide for those lamas" (ibid., 40/30a-31a). Those lamas were later interrogated and punished (ibid., 45/16a-22a).

78 Ibid., 47/12a-17b. Later it was decided that the Panchen Lama would visit Beijing in the spring of 1699 (QSLKX, 192/8a-9a). Despite this, he had not made a visit before he died in 1737.

79 LCangskya Khutuktu was criticized by court officials for his kowtowing to Sangye during his Tibetan mission, but Kangxi pardoned him (QSLKX, 190/11b-12a).

80 XZDA, vol. 2, 304–6.

81 QSLKX, 187/3a-5b.

82 SMFL, 36/40a.

83 Ibid., 44/23b-24a; and QSLKX, 83/23b.

84 Cited in Xiao, *Qingdai tongshi* (A complete history of the Qing dynasty), vol. 1, 842.

85 QSLKX, 185/11b.

86 *Kangxichao qijuzhu*, KX 35/07/14 (unpublished, in the National Palace Museum in Taipei); and QSLKX, 174/21b.

87 SMFL, 18/10a-11a and 18/29b-30a. Yue, *Yue xiangqingong xinglüe* (A brief biography of Yue Zhongqi).

88 On one occasion Kangxi ordered the giving of extra horses to Yue and his escorting team as their alternating riding vehicles (SMFL, 20/37b).

89 Ibid., 23/8a.

90 Ibid., 28/6a-b.

91 See Yue Shenglong's unpublished biography, *Zhuangao*, No. 6409 (1-3). About the rarity of the prestigious title given to the Green Standard generals, see Zhaolian, *Xiaoting zalu* (Miscellanea at Xiao pavillion), 24–25 and 177.

92 Only three other military officials' secret memorials from this period are extant. Altogether, there are only about a dozen people's memorials before 1706 that are extant, all of which are in the first volume of KXHW, although it is possible that many other memorials have been lost. This privilege was extended to more officials after 1706. For the system of secret memorials, see Silas Hsiu-liang Wu, *Communication and Imperial Control in China*.

93 *Kangxi qijuzhu*, KX 24/09/11, vol. 2, 1353.

94 *Kangxichao qijuzhu*, KX 35/07/14 (unpublished, in the National Palace Museum in Taipei).

95 KXHW, vol. 1, 23.

96 Although Dajianlu must be a transliteration from its original Tibetan name Dartsedo, there was also a legend on its origins. It was said that Zhuge Liang, an outstanding statesman and military strategist of the Three Kingdoms era

(220–280), had set up a workshop to forge weapons there during his westward campaigns, thus the place was named Dajianlu, literally meaning "furnace for arrow-forging."

97 Also referred to as Eastern Tibet, Kham bordered Sichuan and Yunnan. The other parts of Tibet are U, Tsang, Ngari or Western Tibet, and Amdo (Kokonor). .

98 *Kangding xianzhi* (Gazetteer of Kangding county), 607.

99 Shakabpa, *Tibet*, 113.

100 *Kangding xianzhi*, 360.

101 SMFL, 13/10b-11a.

102 Smith, *Taxing Heaven's Storehouse.*

103 Chen Yishi, "Qingdai Chuanchaye de fazhan jiqi yu Zangqu de jingji wenhua jiaoliu" (The development of the tea industry in Sichuan and the economic and cultural exchanges with the Tibetans during the Qing dynasty). For more on the tea-horse trade of the Ming times, see Wu Ren'an, "Mingdai ChuanShaan chamamaoyi qianshuo" (On the tea-horse trade in Sichuan and Shaanxi during the Ming dynasty).

104 Meanwhile, the state-controlled tea-horse trade as a whole tended to decline and was completely phased out in the latter part of the eighteenth century. See Lin, "Qingdai de chamamaoyi" (Tea-horse trade during the Qing dynasty).

105 Since ancient times two extremely difficult and dangerous routes maintained the tiny stream of commercial exchanges between the Tibetans and the Han Chinese. One was the Yunnan-Tibet route—from Kunming, via Gyelthang (Zhongdian in Chinese), Deqing, and Chamdo to Lhasa. The second was the Sichuan-Tibet route—from Yazhou, via Dartsedo, Bathang, and Chamdo to Lhasa. In terms of the volume of transactions, the latter route had been more important. After the Qing conquest of Yunnan in the 1660s, the Fifth Dalai Lama requested the opening of trade in Beishengzhou, northern Yunnan (QSLKX 4/9b-10a). With the Qing endorsement the trade was officially opened in 1665, which mainly benefited Wu Sangui, the feudatory of Yunnan. When Wu's rebellion was put down, the Qing forces occupied Gyelthang, a lodge place for the Tibetan merchants. To expel the Tibetan officials who were still stationed in Gyelthang, Cai Yurong, then governor-general of Yunnan and Guizhou, closed down the border trade (ibid., 104/23a-b).

106 Ibid., 194/9b-10a.

107 In fact, the Ming did not consider that Dartsedo was within its jurisdiction. According to *Mingshi* (A history of the Ming dynasty), it was located "outside of Sichuan" (*zai Sichuan jiaowai*). See Zhang Tingyu, *Mingshi*, 331/19b.

108 QSLKX, 176/7a-b.

109 The Liangshan-Wanxian garrison was located in eastern Sichuan between Chongqing and Kuizhou. It had had 575 men in total. But Yue thought that it was overstationed, given the relatively secure location of the outpost (ibid., 188/15a-b). Also see Yue Shenglong's unpublished biography, *Zhuangao*, No. 6409 (1-3).

110 QSLKX, 194/3b-4a.

111 Ibid., 193/16a-b; and *Qianlong chao shangyudang* (Edicts of the Qianlong period; hereafter SYD, vol. 12, 495–96).

112 QSLKX, 194/3b-4a and 194/9b-10a. SYD, vol. 12, 485–86.

113 Yu Yangzhi exposed that Yue Shenglong had tried to control the salt business in Sichuan and took the benefits to fill his own pocket. He also said that Yue had appropriated officers and soldiers' salaries, a prevalent misconduct among military officials (QSLKX, 193/15b-16a; and SYD, vol. 12, 495–96).

114 QSLKX, 194/7a. The two officials were Luocha, a vice minister of the Board of Works, and Butai, a grand secretariat.

115 Ibid., 198/9b-10a and 198/10a-11a.

116 Yu was exiled to Manchuria in 1704 (ibid., 216/19b). Although he was ultimately pardoned from death, his political career was over.

117 Ibid., 202/16b-17a.

118 Ibid., 199/14a-b. But according to *Kangding xianzhi*, only fifty troops led by a squad leader (*bazong*) were transferred from the Hualin garrison to Dartsedo this time (*Kangding xianzhi*,360).

119 QSLKX, 199/23b-24b.

120 Ibid., 201/26a-b.

121 Ibid., 202/10a-11a.

122 Ibid., 203/8a.

123 Ibid., 210/8a-b.

124 Ibid., 203/16b.

125 Ibid., 210/7b.

126 They were Mubaseerji, a lama; Shutu, director (*langzhong*); and Tietu, vice director (*yuanwai*). Ibid., 207/5b-7a.

127 *Kangding xianzhi*, 360.

128 *Sichuan tongzhi* (Gazetteer of Sichuan, hereafter SCTZ), 13/1a-2b; and QSLKX, 225/19a-b.

129 *Zhuangao*, No. 6409 (1-3).

130 It was obviously an excuse to make room for Yue Shenglong to come back to this position. QSLKX, 206/8a.

3 THE FORMATIVE ERA, 1701–1722

Epigraph: Kangxichao Manwen zhupi zouzhe quanyi (Complete translation of the memorials in Manchu with emperor's comments of the Kangxi period, hereafter KXMW), 1350.

1 Wei Qingyuan holds that the major reason for the Ming to levy high taxes from Jiangnan was to meet its military needs in the dynasty's early years (Wei Qingyuan, "Mingchu Jiangnan diqu jingji zhengce de ruogan wenti" [Some issues

concerning the economic policy toward the Jiangnan area in the early Ming times]).

2 *DaQing lichao shilu, Shizuchao* (Veritable records of successive reigns of the Qing dynasty, the Shunzhi reign, hereafter QSLSZ), 16/9b-10a.

3 Between late 1646 and early 1648 he sent eighteen cargos totaling 737,030 taels of silver to the capital (*Ming Qing dang'an* [Archives of the Ming and Qing dynasties, hereafter MQDA], A7-48).

4 Being able to clear arrears became a major criterion in the evaluation of officials in Jiangnan in 1658 (QSLSZ, 118/8a-10a).

5 Based on the taxes levied from Anhui, Jiangsu, and Zhejiang provinces (Liang Fangzhong, *Zhongguo lidai hukou, tiandi, tianfu tongji* [Statistics of households, land, and taxation in Chinese history], 387, 389).

6 Kessler, *K'ang-hsi and the Consolidation of Ch'ing Rule*, 33–34, 102–8.

7 Dennerline, "Fiscal Reform and Local Control."

8 QSLSZ, 112/7a.

9 Ibid., 112/7b.

10 Ibid., 6/9a-11a.

11 Many of the reports in this regard can be found in MQDA, A1-A9.

12 *DaQing lichao shilu, Shengzuchao* (Veritable records of successive reigns of the Qing dynasty, the Kangxi reign, hereafter QSLKX), 192/21b.

13 Ibid., 224/6b-7a.

14 On the Qing aid and relief to the Mongols, see Yuan Sengpo, *Kang Yong Qian jingying yu kaifa beijiang* (The Qing governance and explorations of the northern frontiers during the Kangxi, Yongzheng, and Qianlong periods), 462–72.

15 *Kangxi qijuzhu* (Diaries of action and repose of the Kangxi emperor), KX 24/09/18, vol. 2, 1357; and QSLKX, 122/7b.

16 *Kangxichao Hanwen zhupi zouzhe huibian* (Complete collection of the memorials in Chinese with the emperor's comments of the Kangxi period, hereafter KXHW), vol. 1, 23.

17 QSLKX, 204/14a-15a.

18 Ibid., 254/26a-27a.

19 Zhang Tingyu, *Mingshi* (A history of the Ming dynasty), 309/32b.

20 For a study of the literature on Zhang Xianzhong and his alleged massacres, see Ren, "Guanyu Zhang Xianzhong shiliao de jianbie" (An examination on the material relating to Zhang Xianzhong). Ren Naiqiang has questioned the truthfulness of many of the accounts in this kind of literature.

21 For example, Wei Yuan, a historian of the early nineteenth century, readily adopted this assertion (*Wei Yuan ji* [Collected works of Wei Yuan], 388).

22 Kangxi did sometimes try to allocate more money to Sichuan in small amounts. In 1698, when Yu Yangzhi requested 2,000 taels of silver each year for hiring hands to transport military funds from other provinces to Sichuan, Kangxi

reversed the negative decision made by the Board of War and endorsed his request (QSLKX, 187/13b-14a).

23 Ibid., 210/9b.

24 Yue Shenglong lost his eyesight in 1711 and then retired. He passed away in 1713 (KXHW, vol. 3, 259–63 and 409). Ma Jibo, a regional commander from the northwest, succeeded him (QSLKX, 247/17a).

25 QSLKX, 239/13b-14a.

26 *Nian Gengyao Man Han zouzhe yibian* (Collection of Nian Gengyao's memorials in Manchu and Chinese, with the Manchu ones translated into Chinese, hereafter NMH), 180.

27 Ibid., 172–74.

28 Ibid., 179–83.

29 QSLKX, 256/14b.

30 In 1703, 1,724 *qing* of land was registered in Sichuan; in 1711, 15,380 *qing* of land was registered (QSLKX, 221/5a and 248/26a). In 1717, Nian Gengyao reported that 9,111 households, 1,752 *qing* and 58 *mu* land, and 1,130 adult males were registered in the Chengdu plain area (ibid., 272/14b-15a).

31 Ho, "NanSong zhijin tudi shuzi de kaoshi he pingjia" (An examination and evaluation on the statistics of arable land since the Southern Song dynasty); Perkins, *Agricultural Development in China*, 7 and 200; Myers, "Usefulness of Local Gazetteers for the Study of Modern Chinese Economic History"; Skinner, "Sichuan's Population in the Nineteenth Century"; and Wang Di, "Qingdai Sichuan renkou, gengdi ji liangshi wenti" (Problems of population, arable land, and grain in Sichuan during the Qing dynasty).

32 QSLKX, 207/5b-7a.

33 NMH, 174.

34 Yue Shenglong observed in late 1696 that northern Sichuan was still very scarcely populated, but the Chengdu area and southern Sichuan were in the process of being populated (KXHW, vol. 1, 23).

35 Ibid., vol. 5, 336–37.

36 This was the case in Hunan. In 1700, Hunan was still referred to as having "sparse population and vast land" (*minxi diguang*) (QSLKX, 197/18b-19a). It still had 46,100 *qing* of deserted land by 1714 (ibid., 260/7b-8a). For economic recovery in Hunan after the Wu Sangui Rebellion, see Perdue, *Exhausting the Earth*, 72–75.

37 QSLKX, 211/5a. About Zhao's efforts in dealing with the problem of illegal surcharges and his other reforms in Hunan, see Perdue, *Exhausting the Earth*, 80–87.

38 KXHW, vol. 5, 336–38.

39 Sun, *Qingdai qianqi de yimin tian Sichuan* (Migration to Sichuan during the early Qing period), 2 and 17–24; and Peng and Wang, *Qingdai Sichuan nongcun shehui jingji shi* (A socioeconomic history of rural Sichuan in the Qing times), 6. In "Migration and Settlement in Sichuan," Robert E. Entenmann takes a more balanced approach by pointing to the change of the state policy toward the migra-

tion to Sichuan—namely, it was more encouraging in the earlier periods but shifted to a policy that tried to place the spontaneous migration under the government's control.

40 It is not unlikely that the local officials embezzled the subsidies to new settlers. In 1698 it was revealed that Wuhe, the governor-general of Sichuan and Shaanxi, had appropriated 400,000 taels of silver from the funds of an agricultural loan (QSLKX, 189/5a).

41 KXHW, vol. 6, 613.

42 Peng and Wang, *Qingdai Sichuan nongcun shehui jingji shi*, 113–15.

43 QSLKX, 250/17b; and Entenmann, "Migration and Settlement in Sichuan," 124.

44 QSLKX, 271/16b; and KXHW, vol. 7, 805–6.

45 Zhou Xun, *Shuhai congtan* (Miscellanea of Sichuan), 20.

46 Liang Fangzhong, *Zhongguo lidai hukou, tiandi, tianfu tongji*, 393.

47 According to Wang Di, the population in Sichuan in 1786 reached 10.21 million (Wang Di, *Qingdai Sichuan renkou, gengdi ji liangshi wenti*). Therefore, it was unlikely the real population figures in the 1720s were that low.

48 QSLKX, 293/4b-5a and 293/4b-5a.

49 Ibid., 240/3b-5b.

50 KXHW, vol. 4, 525.

51 NMH, 181.

52 More discussion on this issue is in chapter 6 of this book.

53 Lee, "State and Economy in Southwest China," 198.

54 Pallas, *Neilu Yazhou Elute lishi ziliao* (Historical material on the Eleuth Mongols in Inner Asia), 42–43.

55 Lajang poisoned his brother, Vangjal, and took the position for himself (Petech, *China and Tibet in the Early Eighteenth Century*, 9).

56 For the conflict between Lajang Khan and Sangye Gyatso, see Petech, *China and Tibet in the Early Eighteenth Century*, 10–13; Shakabpa, *Tibet*, 129–33; Wang Yao, "Diba Sangjie Jiacuo zakao" (A study on *desi* Sangye Gyatso); and Yang Ho-chin, *Annals of Kokonor*, 44.

57 QSLKX, 227/9a-b. Tsangyang Gyatso was rescued on his way to Beijing by Tibetan monks near Drepung monastery, but he walked out toward the Qing force, attempting to stop the fighting that had left scores killed. Tsangyang died of illness in southern Kokonor in early 1706. Some believed, however, that he was murdered by his escorts (Wang Yao, "Diba Sangjie Jiacuo zakao"; Yang Ho-chin, *Annals of Kokonor*, 45; and Petech, *China and Tibet in the Early Eighteenth Century*, 15–17).

58 About this "soul boy," see Petech, *China and Tibet in the Early Eighteenth Century*, 20–24.

59 Tsering Wanggyia (Cerenwangjie), *Poluonai zhuan* (Biography of Pholhanas), 135–37.

60 QSLKX, 259/4b-5a.

61 Ibid., 253/7b. Its Tibetan version is in *Xizang lishi dang'an huicui* (A collection of historical archives related to Tibet), No. 36.

62 QSLKX, 263/4b-5b. A conflict between the Tibetans and the Mongols in Kokonor occurred in early 1716 for controlling the soul boy. Under the Qing military threat the Mongol leaders eventually agreed to send him to Kumbum (ibid., 265/13a-b, 266/17a-18a, and 268/4b-5b).

63 Ibid., 264/19b-20a.

64 Ibid., 265/15a-b and 271/3b-4a.

65 Ibid., 273/15b-17a. Tsering Dondup started from southwestern Ili, bypassed the grand Gobi, went across the western part of the Kunlun Mountains, then reached Tengrinor (Namco in Tibetan), which connects Nearer Tibet (Xiao Yishan, *Qingdai tongshi* [A complete history of the Qing dynasty], vol. 1, 833–34).

66 QSLKX, 273/7b-9a and 273/23a-b.

67 Ibid., 278/20a. About the Zunghar raid and occupation of Tibet, see also Petech, *China and Tibet in the Early Eighteenth Century*, 32–73; and Shakabpa, *Tibet*, 135–57.

68 See epigraph of this chapter (KXMW, 1350).

69 Ibid., 1302–4.

70 A detailed narrative of Erentei's last battle can be found in Yinti's memorial, KX 58/05/12, in Manchu, whose Chinese translation is in KXMW, 1392–94. Also see QSLKX, 281/13b-14a; unpublished biography of Erentei (*Zhuangao*, No. 5656); Tsering Wanggyia (Cerenwangjie), *Poluonai zhuan*, 182. In the following year, Tsering Dondup released about five hundred Qing prisoners of war, most of whom made their way back to the Qing (NMH, 206).

71 NMH, 204.

72 KXMW, 1350–53.

73 QSLKX, 282/10b-11a.

74 KXHW, vol. 8, 167 and 331–32. NMH, 197–99, 202–4, and 205–7.

75 QSLKX, 285/16a-18a.

76 NMH, 202.

77 KXMW, 1351.

78 NMH, 203.

79 *Zhuangao*, No. 6409 (1-3).

80 Ibid. However, Galbi did not mention at all Yue's contribution in his own account of the expedition (*Sichuan tongzhi* [Gazetteer of Sichuan], hereafter SCTZ, 192/9b-13a).

81 QSLKX, 289/13b-15a, 289/16b-17a, and 289/20a-b; SCTZ, 192/9b-14b; and Petech, *China and Tibet in the Early Eighteenth Century*, 66–73.

82 The second Sixth Dalai Lama who had been installed by Lajang Khan was escorted to Beijing and died there in 1725 (Petech, "Dalai-Lamas and Regents of Tibet"). By calling the new Dalai Lama the Seventh Dalai Lama, both the Tibetans and the Qing recognized the legitimacy of Tsangyang Gyatso as the true Sixth Dalai Lama.

83 QSLKX, 289/2a-3a.

84 Ibid., 291/11b-12a.

85 Petech, *China and Tibet in the Early Eighteenth Century*, 74–90.

86 Jeanne Mascolo de Filippis, "The Western Discovery of Tibet," in Pommaret, *Lhasa in the Seventeenth Century*, 7.

87 Lattimore, *Inner Asian Frontiers of China*, 233; Lattimore, *Studies in Frontier History*, 526–57; and Bergholz, *Partition of the Steppe*, 307–8.

88 KXMW, 1350.

89 The Jingzhou garrisons were staffed with the Manchu troops, but the Guangzhou and Fuzhou garrisons were staffed with Chinese bannermen.

90 QSLKX, 273/23a-b.

91 NMH, 192–3; KXHW, vol. 7, 1068–70 and 1135–9; and QSLKX, 274/6b-7a, 274/15b-16a, 274/19a-b, and 276/19b.

92 QSLKX, 281/19b-20a; and KXMW, 1341.

93 QSLKX, 280/12b-13b.

94 Ibid., 280/12b-13b.

95 Ibid., 282/15b.

96 Ibid., 274/20a-b.

97 Shakabpa, *Tibet*, 96.

98 KXHW, vol. 8, 72; and QSLKX, 277/4a-b. Those Manchu soldiers were not all disciplined, often seizing properties from the local residents and killing and eating the Tibetans' yaks that had been hired to transport supplies (NMH, 204–5).

99 QSLKX, 279/7a-8b and 283/17a-18a.

100 Ibid., 284/19a-20a; SCTZ, 81/5a; and Yue, *Yue xiangqingong xinglüe* (A brief biography of Yue Zhongqi).

101 NMH, 208–9.

102 QSLKX, 291/1b-2b.

103 Ibid., 299/5b-6a.

104 Ibid., 285/14b-15a; and Petech, *China and Tibet in the Early Eighteenth Century*, 66.

105 At the same time Yongning prefecture was merged into the new Yongbei prefecture (QSLKX, 190/14b-15a).

106 Ibid., 191/25a-b.

107 Ibid., 98/3a-b.

108 KXHW, vol. 4, 200–6.

109 Like the Manchu troops dispatched to Dartsedo, those Manchu officers who later were stationed in Dali were also troublemakers. They were accused of seizing women, drinking, brawling, and fighting each other (KXMW, 1331–32).

110 QSLKX, 288/10b. On the development of the relay horse system in Yunnan, see Pasquet, *L'évolution du système postal*.

111 NMH, 200–1.

112 QSLKX, 281/19b-20a and 281/21b-22a.

113 Ibid., 292/20b.

114 Ibid., 292/17a.

115 KXHW, vol. 3, 859–60.

116 Nengtai, the governor of Sichuan from 1704 through 1709, and Bian Yongshi, the provincial administrative commissioner, illicitly levied heavy surcharges, each taking more than 20,000 taels. Both men were charged. While Bian died of illness, Nengtai was given the death penalty (QSLKX, 247/17b).

4 REALIGNMENT IN THE YONGZHENG PERIOD, 1723–1735

Epigraph: Yongzhengchao Hanwen zhupi zouzhe huibian (Complete collection of the Chinese memorials with the emperor's comments of the Yongzheng period, hereafter YZHW), vol. 18, 1028.

1 Feng Erkang, *Yongzheng zhuan* (Biography of the Yongzheng emperor), 47–79; and Huang Pei, *Autocracy at Work*, 51–80.

2 *DaQing lichao shilu, Shizongchao* (Veritable records of successive reigns of the Qing dynasty, the Yongzheng reign, hereafter QSLYZ), 1/9a-10a, 3/31b-32a, 3/49a-50b, and 4/1b-2a. Yinti was put in prison in 1726 and was not released until the Qianlong reign.

3 QSLYZ, 3/2b-3b; and Petech, *China and Tibet in the Early Eighteenth Century*, 92–94. However, Yongzheng ordered a thousand Sichuan soldiers stationed to Chamdo.

4 Sato, "Robuzandanjin no hanlan ni tsuide" (On Lobdzan Dandzin's revolt); and Ma Ruheng and Ma Dazheng, *Elute Menggu shi lunji* (Collected studies on the history of the Eleuth Mongols), 36–51.

5 *Qinzheng pingding shuomo fanglüe* (Chronicle of the Kangxi emperor's expeditions to pacify the steppe, hereafter SMFL), 48/1a-2a.

6 Yang Ho-chin, *Annals of Kokonor*, 48–49.

7 *Gongzhongdang Yongzhengchao zouzhe* (Secret palace memorials of the Yongzheng period, vol. 1, 188.

8 Ma Ruheng and Ma Dazheng, *Elute Menggu shi lunji*, 41–42.

9 *Ming Qing dang'an* (Archives of the Ming and Qing dynasties, hereafter MQDA), A40-30; and QSLYZ, 12/2a-3a and 12/3a-5a.

10 *Yuan yilai Xizang difang yu zhongyang zhengfu guanxi dang'an shiliao huibian* (A collection of historical archives concerning the relationship between Tibet and the central government since the Yuan times, hereafter XZDA), vol. 2, 342–43. Zhou Ying arrived in Lhasa in early 1724 and did not return to Sichuan until the fall of 1725 (ibid., 343–44, 362–64).

11 For the most detailed account of Yue's expedition to Tsaidam, see *Zhuangao* (Unpublished biographies of the Historiography Institute of the Qing dynasty), No. 6409 (1–3).

12 During this period there were dozens of Tibetan tribes in the region (Huang Fensheng, *Zangzu shilüe* [A short history of the Tibetans], 229–30; and Chen Guangguo, *Qinghai Zangzu shi* [A history of the Tibetans in Qinghai], 352–90).

13 Yang Ho-chin, *Annals of Kokonor*, 49–50.

14 In a thirteen-point proposal Nian Gengyao detailed methods for controlling this newly conquered land (*Nian Gengyao Man Han zouzhe yibian* [Collection of Nian Gengyao's memorials in Manchu and Chinese, with the Manchu ones translated into Chinese, hereafter NMH], 280–94; and QSLYZ, 20/26b-29a).

15 Meaning "blue lake" in Chinese, Qinghai is used subsequently to refer to the area. During the Yongzheng period Xihai or "western lake" was also used to refer to this region.

16 *Zhongdian xianzhi* (Gazetteer of Zhongdian county), 1997, 45.

17 The original comments can be found in YZHW, vol. 33, 397. The forged one is in *Yongzheng zhupi yuzhi* (Collected edicts of the Yongzheng emperor), vol. 4, 2199, which was compiled at Yongzheng's order and published in 1738. Also see Yang Qiqiao, *Yongzheng di jiqi mizhe zhidu yanjiu* (A study on the Yongzheng emperor and his secret memorial system), 273.

18 *DaQing lichao shilu, Shengzuchao* (Veritable records of successive reigns of the Qing dynasty, the Kangxi reign, hereafter QSLKX), 263/18b-19a.

19 QSLYZ, 52/29b-30b; and Tsering Wanggyia (Cerenwangjie), *Poluonai zhuan* (Biography of Pholhanas), 255–69.

20 QSLYZ, 38/2a-3b; XZDA, vol. 2, 364–66, 370–72; and *Sichuan tongzhi* (Gazetteer of Sichuan, SCTZ), 191/1b-2a.

21 The annexed area was mainly under Yazhou prefecture, which was promoted from Yazhou independent department or *zhili zhou* in 1729 with the seat of Yazhou prefect in Ya'an. Within Yazhou prefecture the Dartsedo area was placed under Dajianlu subprefecture or Dajianlu ting (Zhao Erxun, *Qingshigao* [Draft history of the Qing dynasty, hereafter QSG], *juan* 69). Some of the annexed territories were also placed under the Songpan guard (which became Songpan subprefecture, or Songpan ting) and Ningyuan prefecture.

22 XZDA, vol. 2, 374–80.

23 Ibid., vol. 2, 381–86; and Petech, *China and Tibet in the Early Eighteenth Century*, 113–16.

24 QSLYZ, 60/24b-25a and 61/6a-b; and SCTZ, 192/15a.

25 QSLYZ, 60/25a.

26 XZDA, vol. 2, 393.

27 Pholhanas was associated with Lajang Khan in his early years. He led an army and fought against the Zunghar Mongols when the Qing expeditions had approached Lhasa in 1720. He was appointed the fifth *kaloon* in 1723. Pholhanas had long manifested his pro-Qing position. For his early years, see Petech, *China and Tibet in the Early Eighteenth Century*, 26–29. For more detailed accounts on the civil war in Tibet and the Qing second invasion of Tibet, see Tsering Wanggyia, *Poluonai zhuan*, 270–345; and Petech, *China and Tibet in the Early Eighteenth Century*, 116–44.

28 QSLYZ, 62/21b-22a.

29 Ibid., 75/18a-b; and SCTZ, 192/15a-19a.

30 XZDA, vol. 2, 414–19.

31 Initially, the Qing intended to let Pholhanas only rule Further Tibet and leave Nearer Tibet to other people recommended by Pholhanas. But Yongzheng eventually decided to let Pholhanas take charge of all Tibet except Kham (QSLYZ, 76/4a-b and 76/13a-14a).

32 Jalangga proposed leaving ten thousand Qing troops in Lhasa. The number was first reduced to five thousand, then to two thousand, upon Pholhanas's persistent request. The Qing garrison troops were led by three military officials—Mailu, Zhou Ying, and Ma Jishi—and were to be accommodated in civilian homes in Lhasa (QSLYZ, 72/18a-b; XZDA, vol. 2, 419–21 and 425; and Tsering Wanggyia, *Poluonai zhuan*, 349–51).

33 XZDA, vol. 2, 426–27.

34 Ibid., vol. 2, 380. There is no evidence to prove that the three rebel *kaloons* were associated with the Zunghar Mongols. The three also accused Khangchennas, who was killed by them, of having connections with the Zunghar. These accusations could be regarded merely as political vilifications. Petech, *China and Tibet in the Early Eighteenth Century*, 149–51.

35 XZDA, vol. 2, 380; and *Zhanggu congbian* (Collected historical documents), No. 4, Ortai's memorials: On Tibetan affairs No. 1.

36 Tsering Wanggyia, *Poluonai zhuan*, 346–49.

37 For the documents concerning the Dalai Lama's move to Lithang, see XZDA, vol. 2, 426–40).

38 QSLYZ, 76/7b-8a and 76/9b.

39 Mancall, *Russia and China*, 211–15. Widmer, *Russian Ecclesiastical Mission in Peking*, 70–87; and Bergholz, *Partition of the Steppe*, 330–40.

40 The eighteenth- and nineteenth-century scholar Peter Simon Pallas believes that Tsewang Rabdan was murdered by the Yellow Sect clergymen under him, as they resented his invasion of Tibet in 1717 (Pallas, *Neilu Yazhou Elute lishi ziliao* [Historical material on the Eleuth Mongols in Inner Asia], 42–44).

41 For this campaign, see Perdue, *China Marches West*, 250–55.

42 Feng Erkang, *Yongzheng zhuan*, 412–16.

43 Due to Japan's cutting its export of copper to China by 50 percent in 1715, the Qing seriously considered to explore the copper deposit in the southwestern frontier. For the copper mining in Yunnan, see Lee, "State and Economy in Southwest China, 1250–1850," specifically chapter 8. Also see Smith, "Ch'ing Policy and the Development of Southwest China," 180–219; and Dunstan, "Safely Supping with the Devil."

44 Kent C. Smith first linked Ortai's reform in the southwestern frontier with the Zunghar campaign and Qing engagement in Tibet in his groundbreaking study of Ortai's governorship in the southwest: "The Tibetan and Central Asian campaigns gave impetus to much reorganization of the territory lying along the

Yunnan-Szechwan border, especially to revision of the relationships between tribal chieftains and Imperial officialdom there" (Smith, "Ch'ing Policy and the Development of Southwest China," 118–19).

45 Backus, *Nan-chao Kingdom and T'ang China's Southwestern Frontier*, especially chapters 2 and 4.

46 About Yongzheng's obsession with omens, see Feng Erkang, *Yongzheng zhuan*, 495–506; and Chen Hsi-yuan, "Propitious Omens and the Crisis of Political Authority."

47 On the personal relationship between Yongzheng and Ortai, see Feng Erkang, *Yongzheng zhuan*, 476–481 and 544–48; Smith, "Ch'ing Policy and the Development of Southwest China," 16–18; and Guy, "Inspired Tinkering," chapter 11.

48 Yongzheng clearly stated this opinion in 1724, but he did not seem to be ready to do anything about it at that point (QSLYZ, 20/17b-18a).

49 There were two meanings for *gaitu guiliu*. One was to replace the local chieftains with regular officials. Another meant to confer Qing titles or ranks on the existing local chieftains, making them responsible for collecting symbolic taxes and keeping order in the local communities. The latter method was more commonly adopted during the Yongzheng period. There has not been a systematic treatment of Ortai's *gaitu guiliu* campaign in the southwestern frontier. The scholarship that covers this event and its consequences includes Wei Yuan, *Shengwuji* (Chronicle of imperial military campaigns), *juan* 7; Smith, "Ch'ing Policy and the Development of Southwest China"; Lombard-Salmon, *Un exemple d'acculturation chinoise*, 211–28; Feng Erkang, *Yongzheng zhuan*, 390–402; Huang Pei, *Autocracy at Work*, 273–301; Wu Xinfu and Long Boya, *Miaozu shi* (A history of the Miao nationality), 323–40; Ma Yao, *Yunnan jianshi* (A brief history of Yunnan), 166–70; Gong, *Zhongguo tusi zhidu* (The native chieftain system in China); and Herman, "Empire in the Southwest."

50 QSLYZ, 23/26a-b.

51 The Kangxi emperor reiterated in 1721 that he had never intended to carry out the *gaitu guiliu* reform in the southwest (QSLKX, 1486/43a-b).

52 The revolt was triggered by misconduct of the Qing garrison in the spring of 1735 and soon spread to involve hundreds of thousands of people. It was not completely put down until the second year of the Qianlong reign, in 1737. See Wei Yuan, *Shengwuji*, *juan* 7; Wu Xinfu and Long Boya, *Miaozu shi*, 341–49; and Lombard-Salmon, *Un exemple d'acculturation chinoise*, 171–76, 231–36.

53 QSLYZ, 74/10b-11a.

54 In one year after the Qinghai campaign Nian was given several hereditary titles, one higher than another, until he received the first rank of *ashan i hafan*, meaning "baron" (QSLYZ, 12/9a, 17/11a-b, and 26/22a-b).

55 At the end of 1724, Yongzheng vented his grudges against Nian: "I am not a teenage emperor, [there is] no need of waiting for Nian Gengyao's instructions" (*Yongzhengchao qijuzhu* [Diaries of action and repose of the Yongzheng emperor],

YZ 02/11/15). For details of Nian Gengyao's alleged abuse of his power and other misconduct, see Xiao Shi, *Yongxianlu* (Records from the Yongzheng period), *juan* 3.

56 Most of his crimes were relative to corruption, such as appropriating military funds; dealing in illegal salt, tea, and horse trade; and making trivial errors in etiquette (QSLYZ, 39/6b-12a). For Nian Gengyao's case, see Feng Erkang, *Yongzheng zhuan*, 104–30. Also see Huang Pei, "Qing Shizong yu Nian Gengyao zhi guanxi" (The relationship between the Yongzheng emperor and Nian Gengyao), and his *Autocracy at Work*, 102–7. Nian's sister, Yongzheng's concubine, died of illness in 1725.

57 QSLYZ, 21/8a, 31/10b-11a, 33/7a-b, 34/8b, 34/14a, 36/2a, and 36/5a.

58 Fuge, *Tingyu congtan* (Miscellanea at Tingyu hall), 65–66.

59 One of few people to pay attention to the rivalry between Yue and Ortai is Smith (Smith, "Ch'ing Policy and the Development of Southwest China," 120–43).

60 QSLKX, 191/20b.

61 Ortai's predecessor, Gao Qizhuo, had proposed so (Smith, "Ch'ing Policy and the Development of Southwest China," 117).

62 In 1726, Chang Deshou, the administrative commissioner of Yunnan, again proposed the transfer of Dongchuan to Yunnan (YZHW, vol. 6, 894–95).

63 Lee, "State and Economy in Southwest China, 1250–1850," 233.

64 Some documents related to Ortai's taking over Wumeng and Zhenxiong can be found in YZHW, vol. 9, 78–80, 204, 235–39, 252–55, and 514–55.

65 For Yongzheng's advice to Ortai, see QSLYZ, 42/14a-b.

66 Yongzheng seemed to have anticipated that Yue would propose to give the two prefectures to Yunnan. He had written to Ortai about it even before he received Yue's memorial, judging from the dates of their correspondence.

67 Yongzheng forwarded to Ortai Yue's memorials, which did reveal some ill feelings toward Ortai, but he did not forward Ortai's to Yue (YZHW, vol. 10, 74–77).

68 QSLYZ, 71/30a.

69 YZHW, vol. 19,102–4, 224–25, 272–73, 390–91, and 527; vol. 20, 261–63, 312–15, and so on. For a detailed account of this campaign, see Smith,"Ch'ing Policy and the Development of Southwest China," 101–79 passim.

70 *Eertai zoushu* (Ortai's memorials), 6a, 8a, 23b, 32a, 32b, 46b, 50a, 57a, 74a, and 114a.

71 *Eertai zoushu*, 50a.

72 YZHW, vol. 19, 527.

73 Ibid., vol. 18, 1028.

74 Ibid., vol. 21, 100–2.

75 Hummel, *Eminent Chinese of the Ch'ing Period*, 921.

76 Tan, *Yuan Shaanxi Sichuan xingsheng yan'ge kao* (An examination of the evolution of Shaanxi province and Sichuan province during the Yuan dynasty).

77 XZDA, vol. 2, 395.

78 QSLYZ, 47/16a.

79 YZHW, vol. 20, 106–7.

80 QSLYZ, 109/15b-17a.

81 Ibid., 112/26b-27a.

82 XZDA, vol. 2, 438–40; and SCTZ, 13/8a-10a.

83 YZHW, vol. 33, 1014–15.

84 QSLYZ, 82/31a-b; and YZHW, vol. 33, 863.

85 QSLYZ, 103/8a-b. Although some officers from other provinces were still sent to lead troops in Tibet during the 1730s, it gradually became a practice during the Qianlong period that most officers appointed to Tibet were from Sichuan.

86 But Yongzheng sent an officer from Hubei to lead the two thousand troops from Sichuan, as he did not want to weaken the military leadership in Sichuan (YZHW, vol. 21, 487–91, 710, and 808–10; and QSLYZ, 108/8a-b). Those troops were only away for about a year before they were sent back to Sichuan (QSLYZ, 125/18b-19a).

87 YZHW, vol. 20, 221; and QSLYZ, 103/31a-32b. The governor-general of Shaanxi later became governor-general of Shaanxi and Gansu.

88 QSLYZ, 110/23a-b.

89 YZHW, vol. 20, 261–62.

90 Yue Chaolong was a brigade commander in Sichuan during the late Kangxi period. In 1722 he was transferred to Qinghai because his nephew Yue Zhongqi was promoted to Sichuan's provincial military commander. The Qing rule forbade relatives to serve in superior-subordinate positions. See Wei Xiumei, *Qingdai zhi huibi zhidu* (The avoidance system of the Qing dynasty), 72–74.

91 YZHW, vol. 19, 499.

92 Zeng Jing was a scholar in Hunan and an admirer of Lü Liuliang, a renowned scholar and anti-Manchu nationalist. In 1728, Zeng sent a student of his to Chengdu and tried to instigate Yue Zhongqi to rebel against the Qing. For an exclusive study of Zeng Jing's case, see Spence, *Treason by the Book*.

93 En route to the front, Yue Zhongqi submitted a memorial to Yongzheng detailing ten advantages that the Qing forces possessed for a victory (QSLYZ, 82/5a-6a).

94 Ibid., 103/16b-18a.

95 Ibid., 104/17a-b.

96 Ibid., 114/13b-14a.

97 Ibid., 124/26a-27a.

98 Hummel, *Eminent Chinese of the Ch'ing Period*, 349–50.

99 These appointees were Ji Chengbin and Yan Qingru. Ji was ordered to commit suicide due to his responsibility in the Qing defeat in 1730. Yan retired after returning from the Zunghar campaign. He was another person with a Sichuanese domicile to be appointed the provincial military commander of Sichuan, but he had never taken the position.

100 QSLYZ, 108/36b.

101 One of them, Wang Tingzhao, was soon appointed by Yongzheng to act as

regional commander of the Chuanbei command (Chuanbei zhen) (YZHW, vol. 25, 52–53).

102 Echang allegedly indulged himself in drinking so that he was often fatuous and muddleheaded (QSLYZ, 156/5b-6b).

5 THE SHAPING OF INDEPENDENCE IN THE QIANLONG PERIOD, 1736–1795

Epigraph: DaQing lichao shilu, Gaozongchao (Veritable records of successive reigns of the Qing dynasty, the Qianlong reign, hereafter QSLQL), 1388/23b.

1 On Qianlong's modification of Yongzheng's policies, see Feng Erkang, *Yongzheng zhuan* (Biography of the Yongzheng emperor), 555–61; and Guy, "Personnel Policy in the Early Qianlong Reign."

2 QSLQL, 5/42a-b. On the evolution of the Grand Council, see Bartlett, *Monarchs and Ministers.*

3 QSLQL, 422/6a.

4 The Tibetans built new barracks in northern Lhasa for the Qing troops, who had previously been accommodated in private Tibetan homes, which led to many soldiers starting their families during their station (Tsering Wanggyia [Cerenwangjie], *Poluonai zhuan* [Biography of Pholhanas], 418–20; and *DaQing lichao shilu, Shizongchao* [Veritable records of successive reigns of the Qing dynasty, the Yongzheng reign, hereafter QSLYZ], 129/1a-2a).

5 *Yuan yilai Xizang difang yu zhongyang zhengfu guanxi dang'an shiliao huibian* (Collection of historical archives concerning the relationship between Tibet and the central government since the Yuan times, hereafter XZDA), vol. 2, 448–54, 484.

6 QSLQL, 17/17a-b.

7 Ibid., 52/3a-b; and MQDA, A84-112.

8 Tsering Wanggyia, *Poluonai zhuan*, 395–97 and 418–20.

9 While the regular number for *amban* was two, there were four or five of them in Tibet in the late Yongzheng period (Wu Fengpei and Zeng Guoqing, *Qingchao zhu-Zangdacheng zhidu de jianli yu yan'ge* [The establishment and evolution of the Qing *amban* system in Tibet], 21).

10 QSLQL, 106/28b; and XZDA, vol. 2, 472–74 and 475–76.

11 QSLQL, 8/7a-b.

12 Huang was appointed a commissioner of the imperial procession guard. Later he became first the regional commander of Tianjin and then the governor of Gansu.

13 For example, after Yinjishan was appointed the governor-general of Sichuan and Shaanxi, Fang Xian, the governor of Sichuan, specially reported to the throne that he personally respected the new governor-general and was very happy about his coming (ibid., 119/30b-31a). That the governor took this unusual step actually betrays some problem in their relationship.

14 Guy, "Personnel Policy in the Early Qianlong Reign."

15 Zhao Erxun, *Qingshigao* (Draft history of the Qing dynasty, hereafter QSG), *juan* 297.

16 In a poem composed for Jishan upon his new appointment to Sichuan, Qianlong mentioned his father's death and expressed his high expectations of Jishan (*Sichuan tongzhi* [Gazetteer of Sichuan, hereafter SCTZ], 15/1a). Jishan was later sent to Tibet again as an *amban* in 1749. In 1751 he was ordered to commit suicide for his failure to adopt forceful and timely measures to discipline Pholhanas's son, Gyumey Namgyal (XZDA, vol. 2, 574).

17 Guy, "Imperial Powers and the Appointment of Provincial Governors in Ch'ing China."

18 The military colonization in Hami went into high gear after this time. For the Qing military colonization in Eastern Turkistan, see Perdue, *China Marches West*, 342–53.

19 QSLQL, 37/22b-23a.

20 About Nian's thirteen-point proposal, see *Nian Gengyao Man Han zouzhe yibian* (Collection of Nian Gengyao's memorials in Manchu and Chinese, with the Manchu ones translated into Chinese, hereafter NMH), 280–94.

21 Lee, "Migration and Expansion in Chinese History."

22 QSLQL, 165/14a-b.

23 Huang proposed to send seven hundred soldiers to the nearby Hualin garrison, which had had only three hundred soldiers, and another hundred soldiers to Fuhe brigade. He also proposed creating several positions for the officers of Taining. Thus most of the military personnel that were subject to demobilization were retained in service (QSLYZ, 155/3a-b).

24 In 1742, Zhang Yunsui, Yunnan's governor-general, overtly voiced his unwillingness to reduce Yunnan's military force. He only agreed not to refill 1,160 positions when they became vacant (QSLQL, 173/11a-12b). Zhang Guangsi, Guizhou's governor-general, proposed exactly the same in reducing Guizhou's military force (ibid., 236/7b-8b).

25 QSG, *juan* 303; and Hummel, *Eminent Chinese of the Ch'ing Period*, 503.

26 QSLQL, 225/18a-20a.

27 The following account of the Zhandui incident is mainly based on ibid., *juan* 239–80. Also see Herman "National Integration and Regional Hegemony," 237–54.

28 Yongzheng once chastised the Sichuan officials for their reckless and haphazard manner in dealing with the Zhandui problem ("*qianjiu hanhu, caoshuai jiean*") (*Yongzhengchao Hanwen zhupi zouzhe huibian* [Complete collection of the Chinese memorials with the emperor's comments of the Yongzheng period, hereafter YZHW], vol. 21, 1–3).

29 XZDA, vol. 2, 487–88.

30 QSLQL, 239/4a.

31 When this conspiracy was exposed during the first Jinchuan campaign, Qingfu was ordered in 1749 to commit suicide for his cheating; Li Zhicui, Sichuan's provincial military commander, was executed in 1750. Bangun later went to Tibet but was caught and killed by Fucing, the Qing *amban* stationed in Lhasa.

32 XZDA, vol. 2, 484–89.

33 This section on the first Jinchuan campaign is based on QSLQL, *juan* 284–353; *Pingding Jinchuan fanglüe* (Chronicle of the first Jinchuan campaign, hereafter JCFL); Wei Yuan, *Shengwuji* (Chronicle of imperial military campaigns), *juan* 7; Cheng Muheng, *Jinchuan jilüe* (A history of the first Jinchuan war); and Zhuang, *Qing Gaozong shiquan wugong yanjiu* (Studies on the Qianlong emperor's "ten military achievements"), 116–28.

34 Gyalrongwa is Tibetan, meaning "the people who live in the valleys close to the Chinese." Their language, Gyalrong, was similar to Tibetan but "differed substantially from the dialects of Tibet proper" (Fletcher, "Ch'ing Inner Asia c. 1800," 94). Today, most Gyalrong communities are located in Aba (Ngawa in Tibetan) zhou, Sichuan province.

35 Wang Chang, *Shujiao jiwen* (A memoir of the second Jinchuan campaign). This was also the practice of the Qiang people in Songpan prefecture. For more on this, see chapter 7 in this book.

36 The Sui dynasty (581–618) set up a county in Jinchuan. The Ming installed a Zagu *anfusi* (pacification agency) that had the two Jinchuan valleys in its jurisdiction (Gu Yanwu, *Tianxia junguo libing shu* [A study on advantages and disadvantages of all parts of the country], 20/24b).

37 Wei Yuan held that Small Jinchuan submitted to the Qing in 1666 (Wei Yuan, *Shengwuji*, *juan* 7). But according to QSG, Small Jinchuan did so in 1650, and Jinchuan did so in 1667 (QSG, *juan* 69).

38 The chieftain's title was called *solobun* in Gyalrong. It was translated as *shaluoben* or *seleben* in Chinese.

39 In the beginning of the first Jinchuan war, Qianlong even referred to the Jinchuan people as Miaofan (Miao barbarian), as he could not distinguish them from the Miao people in Guizhou. But he abandoned this usage later in the war.

40 In early 1748, Bandi, the minister of the Board of War who was taking charge of the logistical affairs in Jinchuan, suggested in private to the emperor that he reinstate Yue Zhongqi to help the campaign.

41 Necin's grandfather, Ebilun, was one of the regents of the Kangxi emperor. After becoming the chief grand councilor in 1737, Necin had been trusted by Qianlong.

42 Shortly before he called both Necin and Zhang Guangsi to the capital, Qianlong had an audience with Ma Liangzhu, a veteran officer of Sichuan, from which Qianlong must have learned firsthand information about the campaign.

43 Zhang Guangsi was executed in early 1749 in Beijing. Necin was escorted back to Jinchuan to be executed in front of the Qing armies. But he was executed en route

in early 1750 because the war had ended (QSLQL 333/19a-b; and QSG, *juan* 301).

44 For somewhat dramatized details of this episode, see Yue Jiong, *Yue Xiangqingong xinglüe*. The chieftain of Jinchuan agreed to surrender the people who had started the feud to the Qing authorities, give away arms, and pay symbolic tribute to the Qing.

45 John Herman has thoroughly spelled out this point (Herman, "National Integration and Regional Hegemony," 255–83).

46 QSLQL, 331/31b and 335/20b-21a.

47 Luciano Petech gives high marks to Pholhanas (Petech, *China and Tibet in the Early Eighteenth Century*, 194–97). So do the authors of *A Cultural History of Tibet*, David Snellgrove and Hugh Richardson, who think that his rulership helped preserve Tibetan independence in the face of Chinese overlordship (Snellgrove and Richardson, *Cultural History of Tibet*, 219). But Tsepon W. D. Shakabpa thinks that Pholhanas's pro-Qing position provided grounds for China's claims of overlordship in Tibet then and in the future (Shakabpa, *Tibet*, 147).

48 XZDA, vol., 2, 492; Petech, *China and Tibet in the Early Eighteenth Century*, 193–94; and Shakabpa, *Tibet*, 147.

49 QSLQL, 280/3b-5a.

50 XZDA, vol., 2, 496; and QSLQL, 296/10a.

51 *Gongzhongdang Qianlongchao zouzhe* (Secret palace memorials of the Qianlong period, hereafter GZDQL), vol. 1, 323–25; Shakabpa, *Tibet*, 148; and Ding Shicun, *ZhuZangdachen kao* (A study of the Qing *amban* in Tibet), 41.

52 XZDA, vol. 2, 499–503 and 505–7.

53 Ibid., vol. 2, 519–22; SCTZ, 193/21a-23a; Petech, *China and Tibet in the Early Eighteenth Century*, 216–19; and Shakabpa, *Tibet*, 148–49.

54 *Junjidang* (Archives of the Grand Council, the Qianlong period), No. 006234 and No. 006289.

55 Qianlong first cut the expedition to two thousand troops from Sichuan, then downsized it further to eight hundred troops (*Junjidang*, No. 006289).

56 Ibid., No. 006383.

57 XZDA, vol. 2, 523–55; and QSLQL, 385/13a-19b. Also see Petech, *China and Tibet in the Early Eighteenth Century*, 198–216.

58 For a detailed study on the Qing conquest of the Zunghar homeland in Eastern Turkistan, see Perdue, *China Marches West*, 270–89.

59 Forêt, *Mapping Chengde*, 159.

60 For Qianlong's war against the Muslim tribes in the late 1750s, see Perdue, *China Marches West*, 289–92.

61 For the unsuccessful Myanmar war, see Yingcong Dai, "Disguised Defeat."

62 The main sources on the second Jinchuan war include *Jinchuan dang* (Archives of the second Jinchuan campaign); *Junjidang*; *Pingding liang Jinchuan fanglüe* (Chronicle of the second Jinchuan campaign, hereafter LJCFL); and QSLQL, *juan* 880–1009. Prominent among the narratives of the war include Wang Chang, *Shujiao*

jiwen; Wei Yuan, *Shengwuji*, *juan* 7; and Zhuang Jifa, *Qing Gaozong shiquan wugong yanjiu*, 129–81.

63 Qianlong gave instructions on the tactic of "attacking the barbarians with the barbarians" to the officials in Sichuan many times (QSLQL, 562/1b-2a, 565/21a-22b, 675/2b-4b, 716/17b-18b, and 763/1b-4b).

64 One can find many edicts in QSLQL, *juan* 890 and 891, of this nature. Aertai was later dismissed twice and was ordered to commit suicide in early 1773 for alleged embezzlement of war funds.

65 Yingcong Dai, "Disguised Defeat."

66 QSLQL, 1002/27b-29a.

67 XZDA, vol. 2, 558–59.

68 QSLQL, 1017/18b. However, the Bon belief remains influential even today in the area (*Aba Zangzu Qiangzu zizhizhou zhi* [The gazetteer of Ngawa autonomous zhou of Tibetan and Qiang nationalities], 591–92).

69 To mark his victory in conquering the Jinchuan area, Qianlong later changed Meinuo into Maogong, meaning "great triumph."

70 QSLQL, 1075/25b-26a and 1277/7b.

71 Ibid., 1418/5b-6b. *Kuoerka dang* (Archives of the Gurkha wars), QL 57/12/06, 9–10; and Marchal, *Vie de M. L'Abbé Moÿe de la Société des Missions-Étrangères*, 198–99.

72 The native Jinchuan soldiers were sent to Gansu to suppress the New School Muslim Rebellion in 1782 and 1784, to Taiwan to suppress the Lin Shuangwen Rebellion in 1787, and to Tibet to join the two Gurkha campaigns in 1788 and 1792. Despite their many contributions, they were only paid half of what was paid to the Green Standard soldiers, sometimes even less.

73 The material for this section include *Kuoerka dang*, a collection of the archives of the two operations, XZDA, vol. 2, 618–724; QSLQL, *juan* 1312–19 and 1385–1419; Wei Yuan, *Shengwuji*, *juan* 5; Sato, "Daiichiji Guruka Sensô ni tsuide" (On the first Gurkha war) ; Shaha, *Modern Nepal*, vol. 1, 54–71; Regmi, *Modern Nepal*, vol. 1, 435–87; Shakabpa, *Tibet*, 151–72; and Zhuang Jifa, *Qing Gaozong shiquan wugong yanjiu*, 417–91.

74 QSLQL, 1292/25b-26a. In 1786, when Sichuan planned to repair the Huiyuan monastery, which had been built for the Seventh Dalai Lama but was seriously damaged by an earthquake, Qianlong had the plan downsized, for he thought that this refuge for the Dalai Lama was no longer useful after the Zunghar threat had been annihilated (ibid., 1249/1a-2b).

75 From western Nepal the Gurkha people began to rise to power in the sixteenth century. About the founding of the Gurkha dynasty, see Regmi, *Modern Nepal*, vol. 1, 18–57 and 198–224; and Shaha, *Modern Nepal*, vol. 1, 23–28.

76 Shaha, *Modern Nepal*, vol. 1, 29 and 39; and Regmi, *Modern Nepal*, vol. 1, 427–28.

77 Shaha, *Modern Nepal*, vol. 1, 33–35.

78 For a detailed account of Bogle's mission, see Younghusband, *India and Tibet*,13–25.

79 Regmi, *Modern Nepal*, vol. 1, 390–92; and Younghusband, *India and Tibet*, 26–32.

80 Shaha, *Modern Nepal*, vol. 1, 60–61. About the role the British played in the Gurkha wars, also see Lamb, *Britain and Chinese Central Asia*, 22–31; and Feng Mingzhu, *Jindai Zhong Ying Xizang jiaoshe yu Chuan-Zang bianqing* (Relationships between China, Britain, and Tibet and the border affairs between Sichuan and Tibet), 27–76.

81 In 1779 the Sixth Panchen Lama started his trip to Beijing after the Qing court had invited him for years. During his stay in Rehe and Beijing he received numerous gifts from the Qianlong emperor. After his death his remains and the gifts in thousands of packs were sent back to Tashilhunpo in 1781. About records on the Panchen Lama's visit to Beijing and his death, see XZDA, vol. 2, 583–617.

82 Having arrived in Tibet ahead of the main force from Sichuan, both Ehui and Chengde, the provincial military commander of Sichuan, were prepared for a fight, but they were stopped by Bazhong, who had ordered the return of the expedition to Sichuan (*Qianlong chao shangyudang* [Edicts of the Qianlong period, hereafter SYD], vol. 18, 121–23).

83 It was "1,000 silver ingots," according to the original agreement. Conversion to taels is from Xiao Yishan, *Qingdai tongshi* (Complete history of the Qing dynasty), vol. 2, 142.

84 In 1788 and 1789 the Qing sent an expedition into Vietnam and tried to keep the reigning dynasty, the Le dynasty (1427–1788), in place in the face of a rebellion. The war was unsuccessful but was settled when the new ruler of Vietnam accepted the status of a vassal to the Qing. For a concise account of this incident, see Alexander Woodside, "The Ch'ien-lung Reign," vol. 9 of *Cambridge History of China*, edited by Willard J. Peterson, 230–309 (Cambridge: Cambridge University Press, 2002).

85 QSLQL, 1388/22a-24b, 1389/7b-11b, and 1403/29a-30a; and *Kuoerka dang*, QL 56/10/06, 64, and QL 56/10/18, 111.

86 Qianlong agreed to send three thousand Green Standard troops from Sichuan and another three thousand to four thousand native soldiers from western Sichuan to Tibet. So the total number of the Qing forces in Tibet increased to about fifteen thousand to sixteen thousand before the invasion of Nepal (*Kuoerka dang*, QL 57/04/03, 3–13).

87 Ibid., QL 56/09/28, 52.

88 QSLQL, 289/45a-b and 286/15b-16a.

89 Ibid., 299/26a-b.

90 Ibid., 234/1b-2a; and XZDA, vol. 2, 470–72, 476–77, 478–81.

91 QSLQL, 298/14a-15a.

92 Ibid., 305/6a.

93 Ibid., 329/59a-60b.

94 Ibid., 329/58a-b.

95 After the first Jinchuan war Bandi brought the seal of the governor of Sichuan to the capital in late 1749, thus marking the end of this office in Sichuan (ibid., 331/ 6b).

96 SCTZ, *juan* 23.

97 QSLQL, 803/2b.

98 Ibid., 593/28b-30a.

99 Ibid., 627/3a-b.

100 Ibid., 989/24b-25a. Also see XZDA, vol. 2, 558–64.

101 There were thirteen Manchu generals in the Qianlong period who were stationed in Chengdu, Fuzhou, Guangzhou, Hangzhou, Heilongjiang, Ili, Jiangning, Jilin, Jingzhou, Ningxia, Shengjing, Suiyuancheng, and Xi'an. For the policy of letting the Manchu generals take charge of the Green Standard Army, see Ding Yizhuang, "Youguan Qingdai baqi yu lüying guangxi de liangge wenti" (On two issues relating to the relationship between the Eight Banners and the Green Standard Army in the Qing dynasty).

102 QSLQL, 1004/24a-27a.

103 Zhou Xun, *Shuhai congtan*, 126–27; and SCTZ, *juan* 24.

104 Before 1772 only one Chinese bannerman, Wang Zhiding, had served in this position during the Wu Sangui Rebellion. The Manchus who served in this position since the second Jinchuan war were Chengde, Fengshen, Guancheng, Guilin, Lebao, Mingliang, Mukedeng'e, and Qishiwu. Only one Chinese, Peng Chengyao, was briefly in this position in 1793 (SCTZ, 107/1a-3a).

105 QSLQL, 1295/2a-b.

106 Ehui, who began his military career as a lower-ranking officer in Sichuan, was promoted from the post of provincial military commander of Yunnan to that of the Chengdu general in 1777. Later he was appointed an *amban* in Tibet and then governor-general of Sichuan. Techeng'e was appointed the Chengdu general in the late 1770s. After that he was acting governor-general of Sichuan three times. Fukang'an served as the governor-general of Sichuan twice and the Chengdu general once. Chengde served as the provincial military commander in the 1780s and later became the Chengdu general. Guancheng was the provincial military commander in 1791 and soon appointed the Chengdu general in 1793. Helin served as the Chengdu general first and was transferred to Tibet as an *amban* in the wake of the Gurkha war and finally to the post of governor-general of Sichuan in 1794.

107 XZDA, vol. 2, 638–39.

108 Ibid., vol. 641–54; its summary is in QSLQL, 1333/28a-35a. In 1789, Ehui and Chengde sent a letter to the Tibetan government to order the training of Tibetan soldiers to staff the twelve outposts between Lhasa and upper Tibet (*Xizang lishi dang'an huicui* [A collection of historical archives related to Tibet], No. 46).

109 XZDA, vol. 2, 653–54.

110 *Kuoerka dang*, QL 56/12/25, 107–9.

111 Ibid.

112 Its title in Chinese is "Qinding Zangnei shanhou zhangcheng ershijiutiao," and its Chinese version can be found in *WeiZang tongzhi* (Gazetteer of Tibet), *juan* 12.

For its Tibetan version, see *Xizang lishi dang'an huicui*, No. 50

113 According to Articles No. 4–7 in "The Twenty-Nine Article Ordinance of Government," Tibet was to set up a new army consisting of three thousand men with 50 percent of them being equipped with firearms under the supervision of Qing officers; Tibet was also to produce arms and ammunition locally.

114 *Kuoerka dang*, QL 56/09/28, 52–54, and QL 57/01/05, 32–34. A similar discussion was repeated many times in the edicts issued in 1791 and 1792.

115 Ibid., QL 57/09/16, 76–78. For Qianlong's tight-fisted disposition of the war expenses, also see ibid., QL 56/10/06, 65–66, and QL 56/10/20, 136.

116 The Qing disinterest frustrated the Nepali attempt to procure diplomatic gains between adroitly dealing with the two powers surrounding it, China and British India (Shaha, *Modern Nepal*, vol. 1, 700). Meanwhile, the Qing also ignored the British, who were proactive in infiltrating into Tibet from British India. In 1793 both the Gurkha tribute mission and the George Macartney mission came to the Qing court. While the former was eager to repair the relationship with the Qing, Macartney intended to explain to the Qianlong emperor that Britain did not side with the Gurkhas in the conflict, but he did not have a chance to do so due to the notorious kowtow controversy. (When Macartney met with Qianlong, he refused to perform the kowtow ritual to the emperor and failed to convince the emperor to open the country for trade. This incident became a frequently cited case of cultural conflict between China and the West. For an anthropological study on the Marcartney mission, see Hevia, *Cherishing Men from Afar*.) (Shaha, *Modern Nepal*, vol. 1, 61, and Feng Mingzhu, *Jindai Zhong Ying Xizang jiaoshe yu Chuan-Zang bianqing*, 37–45).

6 THE MILITARY PRESENCE IN SOCIETY AND ECONOMY

Epigraph: Yongzhengchao Hanwen zhupi zouzhe huibian (Complete collection of the Chinese memorials with the emperor's comments of the Youngzheng period, hereafter YZHW), vol. 27, 142–43.

1 Some of the content in this section is drawn from an article of mine, Yingcong Dai, "To Nourish a Strong Military."

2 *DaQing huidian* (Collected statutes of the Qing dynasty, hereafter DQHD) (Yongzheng period), 135/3b-4a.

3 *DaQing lichao shilu, Shengzuchao* (Veritable records of successive reigns of the Qing dynasty, the Kangxi reign, hereafter QSLKX), 232/19b. The *tibu* practice had been used since the beginning of Qing times. However, there were concerns among bureaucrats over its wide use once the conquest era was near its end (*Huangchao jingshi wenbian* [Statecraft writings of the Qing period], 70/9a). In 1671, Cai Yurong requested that the chief provincial officials in Sichuan, both military and civil, have the power to appoint military officers stationed in strategic points in Sichuan (QSLKX, 36/10a). In 1672, Kangxi agreed to let the provincial military

commanders in some provinces recommend outstanding military officers to the positions within their provinces, including Yunnan and border commands in Sichuan province (DQHD, YZ, 135/1b-2a). Because of the widespread use of the practice during the war against Wu Sangui, the central government restricted, in 1678, the use of *tibu* to the provinces that were still at war (QSLKX, 71/22b-23a).

4 QSLKX, 282/9a-b.

5 Ibid., 297/5a-b. The court officials suggested abating the *tibu* for the civil officials save for several remote prefectures in Guangxi and Yunnan provinces and in Taiwan prefecture. But *tibu* would still be used for appointments of military officials below the rank of regional vice commander (ibid., 297/12a-b).

6 Right after the Wu Sangui Rebellion, Kangxi clearly pointed out that it was not ideal to let military officials stay in one place for too long (ibid., 109/2a-b).

7 *Kangxichao qijuzhu* (Diaries of action and repose of the Kangxi emperor), KX 50/10/11, National Palace Museum, Taipei.

8 Ibid., KX 52/04/20; and QSLKX, 254/28a-b.

9 *Qianlongchao shangyudang* (Edicts of the Qianlong period, hereafter SYD), vol. 495–96.

10 Yue Chaolong was later transferred to Qinghai, when Yue Zhongqi became Sichuan's provincial military commander (*Qingshigao* [Draft history of the Qing dynasty, hereafter QSG], *juan* 296).

11 He was later buried in the Chengdu area (*Sichuan tongzhi* [Gazetteer of Sichuan, hereafter SCTZ], 11/2a-b).

12 Hummel, *Eminent Chinese of the Ch'ing Period*, 957.

13 SCTZ, 11/4b-5a.

14 *Chongxiu Chengdu xianzhi* (Revised gazetteer of Chengdu county), *juan* 7.

15 QSLKX, 223/4a.

16 *Gongzhongdang Kangxichao zouzhe* (Secret palace memorials of the Kangxi period), vol. 6, 548–49. See also n. 96, chapter 1.

17 QSLKX, 239/14a-b.

18 Zhang Xuejun and Ran Guangrong, *Ming Qing Sichuan jingyan shigao* (A draft history of salt industry in Sichuan during the Ming and Qing periods), 79–83.

19 QSLKX, 193/15b-16a and 198/10a-11a; and SYD, vol. 12, 496.

20 QSLKX, 250/12b; and *Kangxichao Hanwen zhupi zouzhe huibian* (Complete collection of the memorials in Chinese with the emperor's comments of the Kangxi period, hereafter KXHW), vol. 3, 676–77 and 857–60.

21 KXHW, vol. 7, 1135–39. This incident is mentioned in chapter 3 of this book.

22 QSLKX, 96/20b-21a.

23 For instance, in 1727 the provincial military commander of Sichuan, Huang Tinggui, parceled out a military drill ground in Huayang county to farmers for rent, which yielded approximately 200 taels of silver a year, serving as the public funds for the garrison stationed there. By 1750 the size of this piece of land was more than 700 *mu*. In that year the governor-general of Sichuan (Cereng) and

the provincial military commander (Yue Zhongqi) proposed raising the rent to 451 taels. This sum continued to serve as the public funds of the garrison (*DaQing lichao shilu, Gaozongchao* [Veritable records of successive reigns of the Qing dynasty, the Qianlong reign, hereafter QSLQL], 361/23a-b).

24 It was revealed in the Yongzheng period that the Yue family had nearly 100 *qing* of land in several counties in Chengdu prefecture and houses of more than six hundred rooms in the Chengdu area (YZHW, vol. 24, 707–8).

25 *DaQing lichao shilu, Shizongchao* (Veritable records of successive reigns of the Qing dynasty, the Yongzheng reign, hereafter QSLYZ), 22/7a-b.

26 According to the records in ibid., *juan* 5–53.

27 Ibid., 10/6b-7a; and DQHD (YZ), 140/12b-13a.

28 QSLYZ, 10/6b-7a.

29 Ibid., 100/16b.

30 Ibid., 2/24b-26a and 26/13a-14b.

31 Ibid., 6/9a-b, 6/19b-20a, 6/20b-21a, and 6/26a-b.

32 Ibid., 48/23b-24a.

33 Ibid., 63/16a-17a.

34 Ibid., 61/30b-32a.

35 Ibid., 61/12b-13b.

36 Ibid., 29/14a-b.

37 Ibid., 33/4a-b; 37/4a-b.

38 Ibid., 63/1a-3a.

39 YZHW, vol. 10, 17–18.

40 Ibid., vol. 9, 71–73 and 951–52.

41 *Junjidang* (Archives of the Grand Council, the Qianlong Period), No. 004714.

42 SCTZ, 11/4a-b.

43 YZHW, vol. 25, 571.

44 Both Yang and Zhou were buried in the Chengdu area (SCTZ, 44/30b and 44/31a).

45 This land survey is discussed further in chapter 7.

46 YZHW, vol. 9, 674.

47 Ma Huibo was one of the few people who became a high-ranking military official through the military examinations. Before he was promoted to be governor of Sichuan in 1726, he was the provincial military commander of Guizhou (QSG, *juan* 299).

48 Yingcong Dai, "*Yingyun Shengxi*: Military Entrepreneurship in the High Qing Period." The profits from investment were supposed to be used as subsidies to soldiers on the occasions of either a wedding or a funeral in their families, the so-called "red and white celebrations" (*hongbai xishi*), which were considered the major expenditures in a soldier's life.

49 The accurate amount was 59,974 taels (ibid.).

50 *Junjidang*, No. 009732. In the early Qianlong reign the emperor ordered all provinces to return the original capital funds to the central government. By 1753,

Sichuan had only returned 11 percent of its original capital funds, ranking low among all the provinces. Cereng explained that Sichuan had been in wars (at first the Zhandui incident and then the first Jinchuan war), and more money was needed in rewarding soldiers.

51 YZHW, vol. 27, 142–43.

52 Ibid., vol. 5, 71–72.

53 *Ming Qing dang'an* (Archives of the Ming and Qing dynasties, hereafter MQDA), A168-43; A 177-76.

54 QSLQL, 285/8a-b.

55 Yue Jiong, *Yue xiangqingong xinglüe* (A brief biography of Yue Zhongqi).

56 *Pingding liang Jinchuan junxu li'an* (Collected records and precedents related to the military expenditures of the second Jinchuan campaign, hereafter JCLA), 1/56b.

57 DQHD (YZ), 130/4b-7b. The reason that Yunnan had the larger military force was because of the arrangement of Wu Sangui, who had installed ten commands in Yunnan, which were reduced to six after his rebellion. See Cai Yurong's biography (*Zhuangao* [Unpublished biographies of the Historiography Institute of the Qing dynasty], No. 7267). Zhang Dedi, the governor-general of Yunnan and Guizhou, had petitioned to retain twenty-five hundred troops from Shaanxi and recruit the rest from Zhili and Henan to rebuild Yunnan's military force when the war entered its last stage (MQDA, A38-185).

58 YZHW, vol. 22, 491–92.

59 QSLQL, 337/30a-b and 338/17b-18a.

60 *Junjidang*, No. 007348; and QSLQL, 400/14a-15a.

61 QSLQL, 422/4b-7a, 423/2b-3b, 423/4b-6b, 424/4a-5a, 424/25b-28a, and 426/7b-10a.

62 In 1779, Qianlong ordered to reduce military forces in Sichuan to save some funds for the military colonies in Jinchuan that turned out to be more expensive to maintain than expected. But he advised doing it at a slow pace so no unrest would be stirred up (ibid., 1089/12a-13b).

63 Ibid., 1141/21b-24b, 1143/16a-17b, 1147/4a-7a, and 1163/27a-32b; and Luo Ergang, *Lüying bingzhi* (On the system of the Green Standard Army), 66–67. On the background of the expansion of the "silver to nourish virtue" to military officials, see Yingcong Dai, "*Yingyun Shengxi*."

64 QSLQL, 1163/28a-b.

65 By the early Qianlong period 60 percent of the military land had been sold to civilians, and another 20 percent was owned by retired soldiers or their civilian descendants. Jishan, the governor of Sichuan, petitioned in 1746 to convert all military land to taxable land (*Xuzhou fuzhi* [Gazetteer of Xuzhou prefecture], 26/11b).

66 *Junjidang*, No. 004714.

67 Elliott, *Manchu Way*, 263–68.

68 In 1727, Zhao Yaoru, a Shaanxi native and Yunnan regional commander,

requested to change his domicile to Yunnan by citing the facts that his parents had been buried in Yunnan and that he himself had stayed there for almost fifty years. Although Yongzheng granted him the permission, he let Zhao Yaoru process it with the local authorities when he was either transferred to another province or retired (YZHW, vol. 9, 96–97).

69 *Qianlongdi qijuzhu* (Diaries of action and repose of the Qianlong emperor), vol. 2, 158; and QSLQL, 313/13b-14a. In early 1737, Qianlong also appointed Yue Zhonghuang, Yue Zhongqi's cousin and Yue Chaolong's son, to a military position in Sichuan (ibid., vol. 1, 585).

70 Yue, *Yue xiangqingong xinglüe*.

71 QSLQL, 350/24b-25b.

72 *Gongzhongdang Qianlongchao zouzhe* (Secret palace memorials of the Qianlong period, hereafter GZDQL), vol. 1, 638–39.

73 Yue turned down one favor offered by the emperor, however, when Qianlong suggested to give an official position in Sichuan to one of Yue's sons, Yue Chun, a county-level civil bureaucrat. This time, even Yue Zhongqi thought that this was too overt a breach of the law of avoidance (*Junjidang*, No. 004417).

74 QSLQL, 352/2a, 353/6b-7a, and 464/9a-10a; and *Junjidang*, No. 004307, No. 005059, and No. 005074.

75 Yue, *Yue xiangqingong xinglüe*; and *Chongxiu Chengdu xianzhi*, 2/5b-6a.

76 Later the Yues openly acknowledged that they were the descendants of Yue Fei (Yue, *Yue xiangqingong xinglüe*).

77 GZDQL, vol. 1, 638–39.

78 QSLQL, 431/8b-10a and 432/1b-3a.

79 *Junjidang*, No. 006242.

80 QSLQL, 458/13b. At the time he was appointed to Sichuan, Yue Zhonghuang was the provincial military commander of Guangxi.

81 Yue Zhongqi had seven sons and sixteen grandsons, all of whom held only lesser civil or military titles (*Yue xiangqingong xinglüe*).

82 The size of the Green Standard Army in Sichuan fluctuated throughout the eighteenth century. By the end of the Yongzheng era it exceeded forty thousand (YZHW, vol. 26, 800–1).

83 At some points the war expenditures were more than what the state received from taxation. In the early 1660s the final campaign to take Yunnan from the last Southern Ming regime cost more than 9 million taels of silver a year, while the total annual income of the state from regular taxes was only 8.75 million taels. The Board of Revenue complained: "To exhaust the entire revenue income of the country cannot be enough to support one province's expenditure" (QSLSZ, 136/22a).

84 *Kangxichao baoxiaoce* (Fiscal reports from Sichuan of the Kangxi period), KX 25 (1688), No. 1001.

85 Ibid., KX 32 (1693), No. 1850. The reason for a big jump from five years previous

might be the mobilization for the military operations in the steppe against the Zunghar empire, but there is no hard proof for this link.

86 Besides Sichuan, the other provinces that received "fund for subsidies" in early Qing times were Fujian, Guangdong, Guangxi, Guizhou, and Yunnan. I adopt here Wang Yeh-chien's translation "fund for subsidies" for *xiexiang* (Wang Yeh-chien, *Land Taxation in Imperial China*, 18).

87 *Huangchao jingshi wenbian*, 72/13b.

88 QSLKX, 187/13b-14a.

89 *Yongzhengchao baoxiaoce* (Fiscal reports from Sichuan of the Yongzheng period), YZ 7 (1729), No. 3443.

90 YZHW, vol. 22, 491–92.

91 The reason for a smaller sum of fund for subsidies from outside that year was that 500,000 taels of revenues levied from Sichuan in 1732 and 1733 were allocated as military funds in 1733 (*Yongzhengchao baoxiaoce*, YZ 11 [1733], No. 3416).

92 QSLQL, 339/13a-b.

93 MQDA, A138-10.

94 The actual figure is 1,101,650 taels (MQDA, A233-37).

95 QSLKX, 207/25b.

96 QSLYZ, 64/18b-19a. During the first invasion of Tibet from 1718 through 1720, twenty-one postal stations were built from Anningzhou to Tacheng in western Yunnan, which represented the Qing's first effort to connect to this remote province. About the postal system in Yunnan, see Pasquet, *L'évolution du système postal*.

97 QSLYZ, 93/13a.

98 Ibid., 6/13b.

99 Ultimately, six major stations became constant structures in the Qianlong period: Dartsedo, Lithang, Bathang, Chamdo, Lari, and Lhasa, among which the last three belonged to "outside of border" (*kouwai*) stations and were entitled to more subsidies (SCTZ, 196/18b-19b).

100 During the late Qianlong era there were thirty-four hundred troops who were stationed in Tibet and western Sichuan (west of Dartsedo), among whom eighteen hundred were the Green Standard troops but the rest were the native soldiers recruited locally, including Tibetan soldiers (*Kuoerka dang* [Archives of the Gurkha wars], QL 57/08/23, 197).

101 MQDA, A132-63.

102 Ibid., A267-108.

103 The quotas were 300 taels for *youji* (brigade commander), 160 taels for *qianzong* (company commander), 120 taels for *bazong* (squad leader), 30 taels for *waiwei* (detached company commander and detached squad leader), 12 taels for cavalry soldier, and 10 taels for foot soldier (ibid, A105-10 and A267-112).

104 In Sichuan the soldiers who were assigned to places beyond Dartsedo always received this subsidy no matter whether they were engaged in fighting (*Junjidang*, No. 006289).

105 MQDA, A40-1.

106 During this period the rice price in the core area of Sichuan was about 0.2 to 0.3 tael per *dou* (1 *dou* equals 1 decaliter), but in the Dartsedo area it was 0.8 to 1 tael per *dou* (QSLYZ, 95/1b-2b).

107 Ibid., 95/1b-2b.

108 In 1751, Cereng requested to increase food rations for the soldiers in Songpan by citing the rate in the Taining garrison. Because of high food prices there, soldiers' salaries could only afford food for half a year (GZDQL, vol. 1, 523–55).

109 MQDA, A40-2.

110 SCTZ, 192/17b-18a.

111 QSLQL, 335/21a-b.

112 In 1728 the military station in Lhasa was reduced from three thousand to two thousand (QSLYZ, 72/18a-b). In 1733 it was again reduced: Sichuan soldiers in Lhasa and other places were reduced from two thousand to five hundred, and Yunnan soldiers stationed in Chamdo were reduced from one thousand to five hundred (QSLYZ, 129/1a-2a).

113 YZHW, vol. 6, 943–44.

114 QSLYZ, 61/5b-6a.

115 MQDA, A173-143 and A270-4.

116 *Yongzhengchao baoxiaoce*, No. 3312, YZ 1 (1723), No. 3445, YZ 2 (1724), No. 3443, YZ 7 (1729), No. 3416, YZ 11 (1733).

117 QSLQL, 335/20b-21a. Ten million taels were sent to Sichuan (Lai Fushun, *Qianlong zhongyao zhanzheng zhi junxu janjiu* [A study of the logistics of the important campaigns of the Qianlong period], 428).

118 *Qinding Hubu, Bingbu, Gongbu junxu zeli* (Imperial-sanctioned regulations of wartime expenditures concerning the Boards of Revenue, War, and Works). This document comprises three parts: *Qinding Hubu junxu zeli* (Regulations of wartime expenditures of the Board of Revenue), *Qinding Bingbu junxu zeli* (Regulations of wartime expenditures of the Board of War), and *Qinding Gongbu junxu zeli* (Regulations of wartime expenditures of the Board of Works).

119 But the total amount of money that the state had allotted for this war was 6 million (*Kuoerka dang*, QL 57/12/14, 85).

120 The Miao Rebellion in Guizhou and western Hunan at the end of the Qianlong era was triggered by the conflicts between the native Miao people on the one side and the Han Chinese settlers and Qing officials on the other side. Although the rebellion was put down in 1796 after the Qing organized a major suppression campaign by sending massive troops from nearby provinces, including Sichuan, the area was not completely pacified until 1802. For more on the incident, see Sutton, "Ethnic Revolt in the Qing Empire"; Lombard-Salmon, *Un exemple d'acculturation chinoise*, 239–48; and Wu Xinfu and Long Boya, *Miaozu shi* (A history of the Miao nationality), 395–420. On the White Lotus Rebellion, see chapter 7 in this book.

121 Due to the swift restoration of order in Lhasa, only eight hundred troops from Sichuan went to Lhasa.

122 About fifteen thousand troops were mobilized locally from Sichuan, Yunnan, and Tibet to form the mainstay of the expedition to Tibet.

123 *Kangxichao Manwen zhupi zouzhe quanyi* (Complete translation of the memorials in Manchu with the emperor's comments of the Kangxi period, hereafter KXMW), 1272–74.

124 *Qinding hubu junxu zeli* (Imperial-sanctioned regulations of wartime expenditures concerning the Board of Revenue), *juan* 1, *Qinding hubu, bingbu, gongbu junxu zeli* (Imperial-sanctioned regulations of wartime expenditures of the Boards of Revenue, War, and Works), part 1.

125 *Junjidang*, No. 004533.

126 MQDA, A166-129.

127 The state ordered Zhang Zhao and other officials to repay the squandered fund of 1 million taels, but it is not known whether they did it (*Qianlongdi qijuzhu*, vol. 1, 8–9).

128 Parts of this and the next sections are drawn from an article of mine, Yingcong Dai, "Qing State, Merchants, and the Military Labor Force in the Jinchuan Campaigns."

129 *Pingding liang Jinchuan junxu li'an* (Collected records and precedents related to the military expenditures of the second Jinchuan campaign, JCLA), 2/43-66.

130 JCLA was edited by Zheng Qishan, a scholar of the late Qing. The collected archives were not published until 1989.

131 QSLQL, 972/21a–22a.

132 *Jinchuan dang*, QL 41, 1/81; and also QSLQL, 965/14b-15a.

133 *Pingding liang Jinchuan fanglüe* (Chronicle of the second Jinchuan campaign, hereafter LJCFL), 93/10b and 117/7a-b.

134 QSLQL, 913/7a-8b.

135 *Jinchuan dang* (Archives of the second Jinchuan campaign), QL38, 3/224-226, 3/301, and 3/509-510.

136 Fuge, *Tingyu congtan* (Miscellanea at Tingyu hall), *juan* 8, 258–59.

137 *Nian Gengyao Man Han zouzhe yibian* (Collection of Nian Gengyao's memorials in Manchu and Chinese, with the Manchu ones translated into Chinese, hereafter NMH), 210–11

138 *Pingding Jinchuan fanglüe* (Chronicle of the first Jinchuan campaign, hereafter JCFL), 14/12a.

139 QSLQL, 1008/15a-b; and JCLA, 2/142a-b.

140 *Jinchuan dang*, QL41, 1/285.

141 Merchants did not deliver all the rice commissioned. Rice worth the value of 3.1 million taels that was issued to them had never been delivered, which was, however, less than 10 percent of the total amount spent in *shangyun*. JCLA, 2/168a-b;

and Palace Memorials, No. 38162, cited in Lai Fushun, *Qianlong zhongyao zhanzheng zhi junxu janjiu*, 241).

142 JCLA, 2/168a-171b.

143 Madeleine Zelin, "The Rise and Fall of the Fu-Rong Salt-Yard Elite: Merchant Dominance in Late Qing China"; and Adshead, *Province and Politics in Late Imperial China*, 15. Adshead calls those outsider merchants "carpet-bag capitalists."

144 Sun Xiaofen, *Qingdai qianqi de yimin tian Sichuan* (Migration to Sichuan during the early Qing period), 84–85.

145 *Hejiang xianzhi*, cited in Entenmann, "Migration and Settlement in Sichuan," 81.

146 SYD, vol. 18, 132.

147 The records about higher grain prices around the times of frontier wars can be seen frequently in the archives; see, for example, *Neigedaku dang'an* (Archives of the cabinet of the Qing dynasty, hereafter NGDK), No. 073445-001. Also see Cheng Muheng, *Jinchuan jilüe* (A history of the first Jinchuan war), 1/18.

148 Archive No. 0801, in the Municipal Archives of Chongqing, Chongqing.

149 Entenmann, "Adreas Ly on the First Jinchuan War in Western Sichuan."

150 YZHW, vol. 22, 491–93.

151 JCLA, *juan* 2.

152 MQDA, A267-70.

153 JCLA, preface.

154 QSLQL, 321/45a-b.

155 Soldiers with horses received 2 taels a month; those without horses received 1.5 taels. Garrison soldiers only received 1 tael a month. In addition, all soldiers received rice rations at varied rates (Chen Feng, *Qingdai junfei yanjiu* [A study of the Qing military appropriations and expenditures], 110).

156 In the first Jinchuan campaign 2 taels were paid to one laborer at the time of his hiring and 1 tael was paid when the laborer was discharged, even though the second part was subject to the circumstances (MQDA, A154-6).

157 JCLA, 2/69a-b.

158 Ibid., 2/4a.

159 Ibid., 1/3a-3b.

160 Ibid., 2/71b-72a.

161 *Jinchuan dang*, QL38, 4/283-285, and QL39, 1/229.

162 YZHW, vol. 16, 439.

163 GZDQL, vol. 1, 515–16.

164 The figure was 19,419 taels (MQDA, A192-153).

165 *Kangding xianzhi* (Gazetteer of Kangding county), 184–85 and 286.

166 *Maerkang xianzhi* (Gazetteer of Maerkang county), 22; *Aba Zangzu Qiangzu zizhizhou zhi* (The gazetteer of Ngawa autonomous zhou of Tibetan and Qiang nationalities), vol. 2, 1532, and vol. 3, 2328); and *Kangding xianzhi*, 185–86.

167 The Chinese rendering of Chamdo was Chamuduo in Qing times and later became Changdu, meaning "prosperous city."

168 SCTZ, 192/18a.

169 Mu et al., *Dian-Zang-Chuan dasanjiao wenhua tanmi* (An exploration of the cultures in the great delta of Yunnan, Tibet, and Sichuan), 179.

170 Richthofen, *Baron Richthofen's Letters*, 188.

171 Ibid., 189.

172 YZHW, vol. 10, 17–18.

173 Ibid., vol. 3, 761–63.

174 *Jinchuan dang*, QL41, 1/299-301 and 1/355-357.

175 Ibid., QL41, 2/13-14.

176 Records about the audit of the Jinchuan war's accounts are numerous. See QSLQL, *juan* 1070–1219. Also in JCLA, 1/79a-93a and 2/200a-206a.

177 It was ruled that there was a total of 393,679 taels of debts to be repaid by various parties. But by 1785, fourteen years after the campaign, 257,522 taels remained unpaid (JCLA, 2/200a-206a).

178 For instance, Aertai, the governor-general, was dismissed for his mishandling of the war and was also found to have embezzled the military funds. He was ordered to commit suicide (QSG, *juan* 113).

179 The total debts owed by merchants amounted to 3.13 million tael. When all the merchants were released in 1779, it was decided to let the officials who had hired those merchants pay back half of the remaining debts and to withhold the "silver to nurture virtue" of the officials in Sichuan for another half of them (JCLA, 2/168a-171b).

180 Fule, Sichuan's governor-general, was dismissed in 1786 due to his implication in his subordinate's embezzlement (QSLQL, 1254/18a-19b).

181 QSLQL, 1086/14a-15a.

182 MQDA, A269-25.

183 In 1791 the budget for constructing a military drill ground and an arsenal in the Jinchuan area largely exceeded the permissible amount; but Ehui, the governor-general, failed to give an explanation despite being requested to do so three times. Eventually, the Board of Works had to submit the case to the throne. A one-year investigation of the case, however, did not yield any meaningful results (QSLQL, 1379/5b-6b and 1409/15a-16a).

184 But the emperor disapproved (SYD, vol. 18, 176–77; Cai Guanluo, *Qingshi liezhuan* [The biographies of Qing history], 333).

185 For the abuses in the White Lotus war, see Yingcong Dai, "Civilians Go into Battle."

186 Cai Guanluo, *Qingshi liezhuan*, 328.

7 THE BENEFIT AND COST OF IMPERIAL STRATEGY

Epigraph: Yongzhengchao Hanwen zhupi zouzhe huibian (Complete collection of the Chinese memorials with the emperor's comments of the Yongzheng period, hereafter YZHW), vol. 3, 918.

1 About 70 to 80 percent of lawsuits in Sichuan were land-related (YZHW, vol. 9, 675). The local magistrates had to hire more and more clerks and runners dealing with such lawsuits, which explains the overgrowth of the sub-bureaucrat class in Sichuan. For a study of this group, see Reed, *Talons and Teeth*.

2 YZHW, vol. 6, 400, and vol. 19, 652.

3 Ibid., vol. 9, 673–76.

4 An earlier coverage of this survey can be found in Entenmann, "Migration and Settlement in Sichuan," 131–42.

5 *DaQing lichao shilu, Shizongchao* (Veritable records of successive reigns of the Qing dynasty, the Yongzheng reign, hereafter QSLYZ), 63/21b-22a. As a result, more than half a dozen officials from the capital were sent to Sichuan, one of whom, Gao Weixin, later became Sichuan's administrative commissioner.

6 YZHW, vol. 17, 314–16.

7 Ibid., vol. 16, 103–4 and 151.

8 Ibid., vol. 18, 148–49; and QSLYZ, 89/32a-34b and 93/4a-b.

9 For example, Zhao Hongen, Sichuan's administrative commissioner, requested to reduce the newly decided tax rates to alleviate the tension in society (YZHW, vol. 16, 438).

10 QSLYZ, 82/8b-10a.

11 Feng Erkang, *Yongzheng zhuan* (Biography of the Yongzheng emperor), 193–97.

12 YZHW, vol. 19, 652.

13 Ibid., vol. 19, 652–53. In general, the tax increase did not match the increase of registered land. In Xuyong prefecture the registered land before the survey was 21,565 *qing*, and the taxes were 45,183 taels. The survey brought up the registered land to 28,100 *qing*, and the taxes to 51,997 taels. The increased rates were 30 percent and 15 percent, respectively (*Xuyong xianzhi* [*Gazeteer of Xuyong county*], 17/16).

14 YZHW, vol. 18, 728.

15 Ibid., vol. 19, 15.

16 QSLYZ, 61/29a-30b.

17 Ibid., 66/23a-b.

18 The records about low prices of food and other daily necessities in Sichuan in the Yongzheng period are numerous; see, for example, YZHW, vol. 6, 946, and vol. 26, 828–29.

19 Li Wei, the governor of Zhejiang, reported in 1727 that 1 *shi* in Sichuan was about 1 *shi* and 3 *dou* in Zhejiang (ibid., vol. 9, 793–94).

20 QSLYZ, 65/9a-10b.

21 Xiande gave every couple 30 *mu* of rice paddy and 50 *mu* of dry land; for every additional adult male there was an additional 15 *mu* of rice paddy or 25 *mu* of dry land and 12 taels of silver for the cost of equipment and seeds. The tax-free periods for the new settlers were three years for rice paddies and five years for dry land (ibid., 67/25b-26a).

22 YZHW, vol. 16, 842–44.

23 In Hunan there had not been much unused land available by the mid-eighteenth century (Perdue, *Exhausting the Earth*, 86–87).

24 A Han Chinese bannerman, Wang Ji, requested he be allowed to withdraw from the banner and return to his original home, Tongchuan, Sichuan. Wang's grandfather was a Tongchuan native but had joined the Qing army when Haoge came to Sichuan in 1646, as many of his family members had died in the upheavals. He was later adopted by a Cao family of the Han Bordered Blue Banner (*Sichuan tongzhi* [Gazetteer of Sichuan, hereafter SCTZ], 514/6a-7a). To be sure, this occurred when the Chinese bannermen were expulsed from their banners in the Qianlong period. Wang might have lost his bannerman status due to this measure. See Elliott, *Manchu Way*, 337–42.

25 Entenmann, "Migration and Settlement in Sichuan," 223–25.

26 *DaQing lichao shilu, Gaozongchao* (Veritable records of successive reigns of the Qing dynasty, the Qianlong reign, hereafter QSLQL), 311/44a-b.

27 Ibid., 283/23a-b.

28 Liang Fangzhong, *Zhongguo lidai hukou, tiandi, tianfu tongji* (Statistics of households, land, and taxation in Chinese history), 258; and Li Shiping, *Sichuan renkou shi* (A demographic history of Sichuan), 160–63. According to Li Shiping's estimation, the total population in Sichuan in 1724 should be 2,046,555, if it is assumed there were five people in a household.

29 *Junjidang* (Archives of the Grand Council, the Qianlong Period), No. 006215.

30 QSLQL, 784/19a-b. An earlier edict by Qianlong along the same lines was quoted in Cereng's memorial cited above (*Junjidang*, No. 006215).

31 Reardon-Anderson, *Reluctant Pioneers*, 18–70; and Lee, *Manchurian Frontier in Ch'ing History*, 87–90, and 101–15.

32 The recent studies on the Yangzi valley grain markets are Wang Yeh-chien's "Secular Trends of Rice Prices in the Yangzi Delta"; and Wong and Perdue, "Grain Markets and Food Supplies in Eighteenth-Century Hunan."

33 Chuan Han-sheng, *Ming Qing jingjishi yanjiu* (A study on economic history of the Ming and Qing dynasties), 61. A more recent study of Sichuan's economic history during the Qing times points to smaller population as the reason for the availability of surplus grain (Peng and Wang, *Qingdai Sichuan nongcun shehui jingji shi* [A socioeconomic history of rural Sichuan in the Qing times], 137). Abe Takeo's influential work, "Beikoku jyukyuu no kenkyu: Yoseishi no issho toshitemita" (A study on the supply of grain: One chapter of the history of the Yongzheng period), does not go beyond the above interpretation.

34 *DaQing lichao shilu, Shengzuchao* (Veritable records of successive reigns of the Qing dynasty, the Kangxi reign, hereafter QSLKX), 193/19a-b.

35 But exceptions are not absent from the records of the late Kangxi period.

36 On the lower Yangzi valley's dependence on grain transported from the upper

Yangzi valleys since the early eighteenth century, see Chuan and Kraus, *Mid-Ch'ing Rice Markets and Trade*. The Qing documents from this period confirm that the people there had to consume "guest rice" (QSLKX, 233/9a-b).

37 For example, Li Bozhong brings out this point in *Agricultural Development in Jiangnan*.

38 *Kangxichao Hanwen zhupi zouzhe huibian* (Complete collection of the memorials in Chinese with the emperor's comments of the Kangxi period, hereafter KXHW), vol. 2, 181–82.

39 QSLKX, 187/19a. In 1709, Kangxi also told the officials in Jiangxi to explore waterways connecting Jiangxi with Hunan, so that surplus grain in Hunan could be shipped out (KXHW, vol. 2, 606–9).

40 QSLKX, 193/19a.

41 KXHW, vol. 4, 538–39, and vol. 7, 915–16.

42 Ibid., vol. 7, 327–28.

43 This was the case in some prefectures of Jiangxi province (ibid., vol. 2, 944–45).

44 Ibid., vol. 1, 124–25.

45 QSLKX, 233/22b.

46 Ibid., 232/4a-b; and KXHW, vol. 1, 331. Later in the Yongzheng period the Qing authorities realized that the oversea trade was not the cause of the rice shortage in China, because Southeast Asian countries also produced rice (QSLYZ, 54/20a-b).

47 QSLKX, 233/9a-b.

48 There are a number of memorials on this matter from these two years in KXHW, vol. 2. Between 1709 and 1710, 585,449 *shi* of rice and 12,410 *shi* of grain were purchased in and shipped from Jiangxi (KXHW, vol. 2, 944–45).

49 *Nian Gengyao Man Han zouzhe yibian* (Collection of Nian Gengyao's memorials in Manchu and Chinese, with the Manchu ones translated into Chinese, hereafter NMH), 181.

50 KXHW, vol. 4, 379.

51 QSLKX, 272/6b-7a.

52 KXHW, vol. 6, 443.

53 YZHW, vol. 3, 918.

54 Ibid, vol. 3, 917–18.

55 Due to the low prices and larger measures, the rice exported from Sichuan was 4 to 5 *qian* lower than the rice from Jiangxi and Huguang per *shi* (ibid., vol. 9, 793–94).

56 Ibid., vol. 4, 576 and 618–19; also see Shepherd, *Statecraft and Political Economy on the Taiwan Frontier*, 164.

57 For example, the Zhejiang government bought more than 100,000 *shi* of rice in Chongqing at one time in early 1727 (YZHW, vol. 9, 116–17). It again planned to allot 200,000 taels to purchase more rice from Sichuan in 1728. But Yongzheng

cautioned not to trust such a big sum to a few agents. He suggested 40,000 to 50,000 taels instead and stressed that the right people be used in this purchase trip (ibid., 793–94).

58 In 1727, Yongzheng requested the figure of the annual levies at the Kuiguan customs. Although it was reported at first that it was around 20,200 taels, the provincial government had to correct this figure by reporting that it could collect as much as 40,500 taels a year, after the throne ordered an investigation of the matter (ibid., vol. 9, 327–28, 398–99, and 677–78).

59 Ibid., vol. 10, 416; and QSLYZ, 62/5a-b.

60 In the first eight and a half months of 1729, before the high season for rice trade, the Kuiguan customs house had already collected more than 45,000 taels (YZHW, vol. 16, 112).

61 Ibid., vol. 19, 1005.

62 The total revenues collected at the Kuiguan customs house were 27,991 taels in 1730 and 27,850 taels in 1731 due to the embargo. But it was estimated by the superintendent of the customs house that the total revenue income in a normal year could reach as high as over 90,000 taels (ibid., vol. 23, 704–5).

63 Ibid., vol. 23, 911–13 and 965–66.

64 Ibid., vol. 23, 940–41; also in QSLYZ, 127/1b-2a.

65 In fact, the ban had been lifted at the end of 1732 (YZHW, vol. 23, 704–5).

66 Ibid., vol. 25, 71–72.

67 Ibid., vol. 24, 194–95, and vol. 26, 823–24.

68 *Dayi juemi lu* (The narration of the great righteousness and enlightenment), 98.

69 Ever since the late Kangxi period, a portion of the income from the internal customs houses was submitted to the Imperial Household Department (Lai Huimin, "Qing Qianlongchao de shuiguan yu huangshi caizheng" [Customs houses and imperial income under the Qianlong emperor]).

70 QSLQL, 193/7a.

71 Guizhou imported rice from Guangxi before the mid-eighteenth century. Likely for the purpose of safeguarding the rice supply from Guangxi, the military colonies were installed in the Guzhou area (a prefecture in Guizhou province), which was located in the southeastern corner of the province and on the artery of the rice trade, following the suppression of the Miao revolts in the mid-1730s.

72 Zhang Yunsui, the governor-general of Yunnan and Guizhou, initiated the Jinsha River project in 1742, attempting to make the river fully navigable by removing dangerous shoals (QSLQL, 269/47a-b; and Pan, "Qingdai Yunnan de jiaotong kaifa" [Development in transportation in Yunnan during the Qing times]). Shortly after the Jinsha River project was completed in 1748, Zhang started the project to dredge the Chishui River in Guizhou, trying to open a waterway connecting Guizhou with the Yangzi River.

73 In 1749, Zhang Yunsui observed that the Jinsha River project promoted the inflow of Sichuan rice to Yunnan, which helped lower rice prices in Yunnan (QSLQL,

311/46a). About the impact of the Chishui project on Guizhou's economy, see Lombard-Salmon, *Un exemple d'acculturation chinoise*, 197–209; and QSLQL, 311/48a.

74 For example, Zhejiang had to import 2 million to 3 million *shi* of "guest rice" even during the years of bumper harvest (*Gongzhongdang Qianlongchao zouzhe* (Secret palace memorials of the Qianlong period, hereafter GZDQL], vol. 1, 143–45).

75 The most important customs houses along the Yangzi River included Kuiguan in Sichuan, Jingzhou in Hubei, Jiujiang in Jiangxi, and Hushuguan in Jiangsu.

76 QSLQL, 43/11b-12a and 73/3b-4b. In 1741 the governor of Jiangxi suggested exempting tax on vessels as well, but the central government did not approve this motion (*Ming Qing dang'an* [Archives of the Ming and Qing dynasties, hereafter MQDA], A102-21). But in 1758 taxes on vessels were waived for rice shipments from Hubei, Hunan, Jiangxi, and Sichuan to Henan for disaster relief (QSLQL, 555/9b and 559/3b).

77 The reason for this unconditional exemption during these years was that the throne hoped to lower the rising rice prices. But it did not work (ibid., 329/26a-27a).

78 Ibid., 544/5b-6b.

79 Ibid., 507/16b.

80 Ibid., 386/20b-21b.

81 For a comprehensive study of the Qing granary system, see Will and Wong's *Nourish the People.*

82 When eastern Zhejiang suffered a serious drought in 1751, Hubei sent to Zhejiang its grain stored in the granaries by the emperor's order. Meanwhile, Qianlong instructed to have the granaries in Hubei refilled with grain from Sichuan's granaries. Sichuan managed to send 229,000 *shi* of rice to Hubei, despite the increases in rice prices in Sichuan (GZDQL, vol. 1, 200–201 and 501–2). Again in 1753, when the Huai-Yang area in Jiangnan was afflicted with a deluge, Qianlong ordered Sichuan to transport a large quantity of grain from its granaries for disaster relief.

83 Not anticipating a bumper harvest in Zhili in 1744, for example, Qianlong instructed Shuose, the governor of Sichuan, to prepare in secret 300,000 *shi* of rice for possible needs in Zhili. Qianlong told Shuose "not to let others know [of it]" (QSLQL, 215/2a-3b).

84 QSLYZ, 108/40a-41b and 127/1b-2a.

85 In 1731, of approximately 1,523,000 *shi* of all kinds of grains garnered in the granaries, only about 2,300 *shi* were "donated" by more than two hundred officials in Sichuan (MQDA, A132-8).

86 MQDA, A 186-167.

87 Ibid. The practice of *juanna* was first used during the campaign against the Wu Sangui Rebellion. Although the Qing state had tried not to use it again, it used the method a couple of times in Sichuan during frontier wars to raise funds. For

a study of the practice in the Qing times, see Xu, *Qingdai juanna zhidu* (The system of purchasing offices by contributions during the Qing dynasty).

88 For those who donated more than 10 *shi*, some gift was awarded; for those who donated more than 30 *shi*, a door tablet was granted; for those who donated more than 50 *shi*, their names were reported to the central government for awards (MQDA, A187-141).

89 At least until 1767 this practice was still in place, and the above rules were still cited (ibid., A207-69).

90 SCTZ, 198/69a.

91 Chen Hongmou, the governor of Hunan, complained in 1755 about increase in grain prices in his jurisdiction due to too many shipments of rice to Zhejiang (QSLQL, 503/22b-23b).

92 Ibid., 502/10a-b.

93 Ibid., 287/6b-8a and 747/7a-8a.

94 For a discussion on a liberal tendency in the Qing state's economic policy, see Dunstan, "Safely Supping with the Devil." Also see her recent work, Dunstan, *State or Merchant*, 8 and 429.

95 *Junjidang*, No. 4173.

96 QSLQL, 916/17b-18a.

97 Qianlong noted, shortly before the first Jinchuan war ended, that the increase of grain prices in Jiangnan had been caused by the embargo in Sichuan (ibid., 333/25a).

98 Ibid., 337/28b-29a.

99 *Jinchuan dang* (Archives of the second Jinchuan campaign), QL40, 4/115; and QSLQL, 995/25a-26a.

100 *Jinchuan dang*, QL40, 4/115-6.

101 QSLQL, 993/31a and 1002/3b-4a.

102 SCTZ, 16/4b-5a.

103 QSLQL, 1002/11b.

104 Chuan and Kraus, *Mid-Ch'ing Rice Markets and Trade*, 71.

105 QSLQL, 1063/11a-12b, 1064/7a-8a, 1064/15a-16b, 1065/27b, 1066/16a-17a, and 1066/18a-b.

106 Ibid., passim, *juan* 1236– 1263.

107 Ibid., 1286/5a, 1286/18b-19a, and 1291/4a.

108 Ibid., 1101/19a-20a.

109 Ibid., 1114/7a-8a.

110 Ibid., 1326/10a-13a.

111 Ibid., 1328/2a-b and 1331/3b-4a.

112 *Kuoerka dang* (Archives of the Gurkha wars), QL57/04/26, 75.

113 McCaffrey "Living through Rebellion," 59.

114 QSLQL, 1412/33b-35a.

115 Ibid., 1428/11a-b, 1452/10a-11a, and 1467/6a-7a.

116 Ibid., 1490/12a-b.

117 In 1797, Hubei asked Kuizhou prefecture to send in 30,000 *shi* of rice, but only a tenth of the amount requested was delivered (*Qinding jiaoping sansheng xiefei fanglüe* [Imperial-sanctioned chronicle of the campaign to suppress the heretical bandits in the three provinces], 49/32b-33a).

118 Ibid., 71/14a-b and 72/9b-11b.

119 The total storage of grain in the granaries was 2,827,700 *shi*; 426,370 *shi* had been used in the war to suppress the Miao Rebellion, and 1,743,500 *shi* had been used in the White Lotus war (ibid., 72/9b-11b).

120 According to Wang Di, the population in Sichuan in 1786 was 10.21 million; in 1791 it was 11.7 million (Wang Di, "Qingdai Sichuan renko, gengdi ji liangshi wenti" [Problems of population, arable land, and grain in Sichuan during the Qing dynasty]).

121 Peng and Wang, *Qingdai Sichuan nongcun shehui jingji shi*, 9.

122 *Qingdai QianJiaDao Baxian dang'an xuanbian* (Selected archives of Ba county from the Qianlong, Jiaqing, and Daoguang periods of the Qing dynasty), 319.

123 Marchal, *Vie de M. L'Abbé Moÿe de la Société des Missions-Étrangères*, 222.

124 According to Wang Di, there were 20.7 million people in Sichuan in 1812. It had almost doubled from 11.7 million in the early 1790s (Wang Di, "Qingdai Sichuan renko, gengdi ji liangshi wenti").

125 Richthofen, *Baron Richthofen's Letters*, 183.

126 Hart, *Western China*, 278.

127 In the long run, industries such as salt, tong oil, wax, tea, silk, and so on all developed along with the rice trade (Mori, "Shindai Sisen no imin keizai" [The migration economy in Sichuan during the Qing Dynasty]).

128 Madeleine Zelin has noted that the salt industry in Sichuan had enjoyed far more freedom than in other places of the country in the early Qing (Zelin, *Merchants of Zigong*, xiv–xv).

129 The related discussions are in Wei Yuan, *Shengwuji* (Chronicle of imperial military campaigns), *juan* 9; Suzuki Chusei, *Chugoku shi ni okeru kakumeii to shyukyo* (Revolution and religion in Chinese history); and Entenmann, "Migration and Settlement in Sichuan," especially chapter 5, "Migrant Society," and others.

130 Sun, *Qingdai qianqi de yimin tian Sichuan* (Migration to Sichuan during the early Qing period), 36–44.

131 Richthofen, *Baron Richthofen's Letters*, 165.

132 Skinner, "Marketing and Social Structure in Rural China"; and Sun, *Qingdai qianqi de yimin tian Sichuan*, 79–81. According to Sun Xiaofen, some marketing towns specialized in one commodity, such as silk, cotton, or grain.

133 QSLQL, 271/39b-40a.

134 Lü, "Ming Qing shiqi de huiguan bingfei gongshangye hanghui" ("Huiguan" of the Ming and Qing periods were not guilds); and Sun, *Qingdai qianqi de yimin tian Sichuan*, 243–62. Unlike Lü Zuoxie, who thinks that *huiguan* were not guilds of

businessmen but purely immigrant organizations, Sun has shown that some *huiguan* were actually formed by businessmen of the same profession and from the same places. Sun also points out that *huiguan* helped promote the configuration of some marketing towns.

135 *Qingdai QianJiaDao Baxian dang'an xuanbian*, 1.

136 Li Yu, "Social Change during the Ming-Qing Transition." During the entire Yongzheng and Qianlong reigns Sichuan produced fewer than two hundred *jinshi* degree holders, which ranked the province fairly low in the country in production of degree holders (Li Chaozheng, *Qingdai Sichuan jinshi zhenglüe* [Brief biographies of those who hold *jinshi* degrees from Sichuan during the Qing Dynasty], 1–266).

137 One indication of the affluence in Sichuan is that gambling was more widespread than in other parts of the country, according to one provincial official's report (*Neigedaku dang'an* [Archives of the Cabinet of the Qing dynasty, hereafter NGDK], No. 119616).

138 QSLQL, 651/2a-b.

139 In fact, before the state used *juanna*, some big merchants, such as salt merchants in Jiangsu, had donated huge amounts of money to the campaign. They were usually rewarded with honorific titles.

140 MQDA, A 38-40.

141 Entenmann, "Migration and Settlement in Sichuan," 125.

142 QSLQL, 790/10b-11a.

143 NGDK, No. 119616-001.

144 For instance, in 1787 the Sichuan provincial government sent *yamen* clerks to escort some thirty people from Anhui province back home (QSLQL, 1278/31a-32a).

145 For single males' inclination to get involved in rebellious activities, see Perry, *Rebels and Revolutionaries in North China*, 51–52.

146 YZHW, vol. 10, 18–19, and vol. 25, 1017–18.

147 For example, many settlers from Guangdong province returned to bring their families (ibid., vol. 24, 135–36, and vol. 25, 73–76 and 190–91).

148 According to the provincial government, there were fifty-eight fatal cases in 1792, more than half of which involved the death of a woman who either committed suicide in the wake of adultery or was murdered in an attempted rape (MQDA, A268-43).

149 QSLQL, 1074/12b and 1081/7b-9a.

150 Ibid., 1231/2b-3b.

151 Yingcong Dai, "Qing State, Merchants, and the Military Labor Force in the Jinchuan Campaigns."

152 Entenmann, "Andreas Ly on the First Jinchuan War in Western Sichuan."

153 NGDK, No. 119616-001. The overstretch of the local officials in wartime might be another reason for the local governments in Sichuan to hire more clerks and runners than in other provinces.

154 GZDQL, vol. 1, 155.

155 *Junjidang*, No. 006242.

156 There have been a variety of interpretations on the origins of the name *guolu*. Most recently, Barend J. ter Haar has argued that both *guolu* and *gelao* (meaning "the gathering of brothers and elders") were derived from the oral version for the Klau (Gelao in Chinese), an ethnic people who had inhabited eastern Sichuan during the Qing, and used in derogatory terms to label those who gambled and looted in the area (Haar, "Gathering of Brothers and Elders"). Cheng Muheng held that the *guolu* came initially from the non-Han areas in western Sichuan (Cheng Muheng, *Jinchuan jilüe* [A history of the first Jinchuan war]). Careful investigation of the meaning of *guolu* can also be found in works by Hu Zhaoxi, Huo Datong, and Yang Guang ("'Guolu' kaoxi" [An examination of '*guolu*']); Cai Shaoqing ("On the Origin of the Gelao Hui [Kolaohui]"); and Zhuang Jifa ("Qingdai Gelaohui yuanliu kao" [An examination of the origins of the Gelao society in the Qing dynasty]).

157 Huang thus argued to only allow the tribal peoples to go to the Han Chinese areas in families but not to let young women between fifteen and twenty years old come. It seemed that Yongzheng was not very concerned with the problem and thus not impressed with this suggestion (YZHW, vol. 10, 18–19).

158 Cheng Muheng, *Jinchuan jilüe*.

159 QSG, *juan* 380.

160 QSLQL, 251/6a-6b. Also in *Shihuozhi* (Records of economic history of Qing times): *Hukou shiji* (Records on population and households), the eleventh year of the Qianlong reign.

161 According to Yue, the *guolu* bandits normally got together for gambling in the daytime and went out to pillage by night (*Junjidang*, No. 005060).

162 *Huangchao jingshi wenbian* (Statecraft writings of the Qing period), 75/7b.

163 An example of labeling the *guolu* movement as anti-Manchu can be found in Wang Gang, *Qingdai Sichuan shi* (A history of Sichuan during the Qing dynasty), 917–19. But most scholars agree that the *guolu* banditry was not an anti-Qing organization.

164 During the second Jinchuan war, Qianlong gave an order to select physically fit laborers for military training and then assign them to guard the grain stations or to accompany provision teams (JCLA, 2/71a; *Jinchuan dang*, QL38, 4/209-210; and Yingcong Dai, "Qing State, Merchants, and the Military Labor Force in the Jinchuan Campaigns").

165 Zhao Yunsong, *Kanjing jiaofei shulüe* (A brief history of the war to exterminate the White Lotus bandits), 1/3b. Some other people whose livelihoods had been detrimentally affected by the end of the second Jinchuan war might also have chosen to join the banditry. For instance, two owners of a food shop in Chengdu, Liu Laoshi and Luo Tianfu, closed their shop and became *guolu* bandits in 1778, two years after the end of the second Jinchuan war (Perdue, *Exhausting the Earth*,

112–13). A Catholic missionary in Sichuan claimed that the province had become a place of killing and pillage by the followers of the White Lotus teachings since 1775 (Marchal, *Vie de M. L'Abbé Moÿe de la Société des Missions-Étrangères*, 258–59). He might have mistaken the *guolu* bandits for the White Lotus members, as the White Lotus movement remained largely peaceful until 1794, when the Qing seriously persecuted them. Or this could be taken as evidence for the convergence of the *guolu* banditry and the White Lotus groups, as discussed later in this chapter.

166 QSLQL, 1140/13a-14a.

167 NGDK, No. 119616.

168 Fukang'an reported in 1783 that he had condemned 120 *guolu* bandits to either death or exile during his two-year stay in Sichuan (NGDK, No. 147575).

169 QSLQL, 1241/7b-8a.

170 Daniel Overmyer has argued that the syncretism in the elite intellectual trend during the Song and the Yuan dynasties influenced such a development in folk religion (Overmyer, *Folk Buddhist Religion*, 134). The other major works on the White Lotus teachings include Naquin, *Millenarian Rebellion in China*, and "Transmission of White Lotus Sectarianism in Late Imperial China"; Suzuki, *Chugoku shi ni okeru kakumei to shukyo* and *Sennen okoku-teki minshu undo no kenkyu* (A study of popular millenarian movements in China and Southeast Asia); Yu Songqing, *Ming Qing Bailianjiao yanjiu* (A study of the White Lotus teachings during the Ming and Qing dynasties); and Haar, *White Lotus Teachings in Chinese Religious History*.

171 For a study of this uprising, see Suzuki, *Sennen okoku-teki minshu undo no kenkyu*, 243–66.

172 *DaQing shichao Shengxun* (Imperial edicts and instructions of the ten emperors of the Qing dynasty), Qianlong, 251/3.

173 On this rebellion, see Naquin, *Shantung Rebellion*.

174 QSLQL, 977/23a-b.

175 It seems that the local officials in Sichuan did not have a clear idea about the White Lotus movement. They arrested missionaries from Les Missions-Etrangères de Paris and forced them to confess that they were affiliated with White Lotus groups (Launay, *Histoire des missions de Chine*, 149).

176 *Kuoerka dang*, QL 57/02/22, 101.

177 In 1792, the year that the second Gurkha war ended, the crime cases in Sichuan had multiplied. Among the 138 cases in which the perpetrators were caught, 58 involved the death of an individual. All those cases fell into only two categories: pillaging and adultery or rape (MQDA, A268-43). There were additional cases that had not been solved.

178 Zhao Yunsong, *Kanjing jiaofei shulüe*, 1/3b.

179 There are numerous records on the issue of devalued coins in Sichuan (QSLQL, *juan* 1060-1470).

180 According to the Qing rule, 90 percent of copper procured in Yunnan mines had to be purchased by the state at a modest price; only 10 percent could be sold on the market at a higher price (ibid., *juan* 1106/19b-21b).

181 In 1794 more than 1.1 million *jin* or catty of devalued coins were confiscated in Sichuan alone, while only several dozen to several hundred *jin* of them were confiscated in other provinces (ibid., *juan* 1446/23a-24a).

182 Qianlong designated Fukang'an, the governor-general of Yunnan and Guizhou, to be in charge of the campaign to crack down on the illegal minting in Guizhou, Sichuan, and Yunnan. By late 1794, Fukang'an had arrested more than two hundred alleged coin dealers (SYD, vol. 18, 198–99, 290–91, and 864–65).

183 Wei Yuan, *Shengwuji*, *juan* 9; and Suzuki, *Sennen okoku-teki minshu undo no kenkyu*, 310.

184 The existing works on this rebellion include Kuhn, *Rebellion and Its Enemies*; Jones and Kuhn, "Dynastic Decline and the Roots of Rebellion"; and some parts in Suzuki, *Chugoku shi ni okeru kakumei to shukyo* and *Sennen okoku-teki minshu undo no kenkyu*, 308–11. For one aspect of the Qing suppression campaign against the rebellion—that is, the use of the hired militias—see Yingcong Dai, "Civilians Go into Battle."

185 Suzuki, *Chugoku shi ni okeru kakumei to shukyo*, 173.

186 Many scholars agree that the *guolu* bandits were the mainstay of the rebel force in Sichuan (Yan, *Sansheng bianfang beilan* [A collection of documents on the borderlands of the three provinces], *juan* 17; Hu Zhaoxi et al., "'Guolu' kaoxi"; and Haar, *White Lotus Teachings in Chinese Religious History*, 251 and 255–56).

187 Zhao Yunsong, *Kanjing jiaofei shulüe*, 1/3b.

188 About the "predatory" and "protective" strategies, see Perry, *Rebels and Revolutionaries in North China*.

1 EPILOGUE

Epigraph: Luo Wenzhonggong zouyi (Collected memorials by Luo Bingzhang), 16/53b-54a.

1 The ten wars include two against the Zunghar Mongols, one against the Muslim tribes in Eastern Turkistan, two Jinchuan wars, the war in Taiwan to crack down on Lin Shuangwen's rebellion, the Myanmar war, the Vietnam war, and two Gurkha wars. Noticeably, Qianlong purposely excluded from the list several wars against domestic rebellions: a war in Shandong in 1774 against a sectarian rebellion led by Wang Lun and two wars against the Muslim rebellions in Gansu in 1782 and 1784. This essay by Qianlong is included in *Da Qing lichao shilu, Gaozongchao* (Veritable records of successive reigns of the Qing dynasty, the Qianlong reign, hereafter QSLQL), 1414/7b-12a.

2 In 1708, Kangxi began to undertake a project mapping the empire, in which

some Jesuits working for the Qing court were involved. Although Tibet was not included in this project, Heshou, the imperial envoy to Lhasa, was instructed to draw a map of Tibet (Petech, *China and Tibet in the Early Eighteenth Century*, 19). Throughout the eighteenth century more efforts were made to map Tibet, which resulted in the completion of a cluster of maps of Tibet. See Cheng Chongde and Sun Zhe, "Qianlong shidai de jiangyu geju yu 'Neifu yutu'" (The territorial scope of the Qianlong period and the "maps of the inner court").

3 In 1704, Kangxi sent Laxi, an imperial guardsman, to explore the sources of the Yellow River (*Da Qing lichao shilu, Shengzuchao* [Veritable records of successive reigns of the Qing dynasty, the Kangxi reign, hereafter QSLKX], 217/10b-12b). In 1782 the Qianlong emperor sent Amida to explore the origins of the Yellow River again (QSLQL, 1160/34b-43a). Largely based on the results of Amida's exploration, a compendia on the sources of the Yellow River, *Qinding heyuan jilüe* (Imperial-sanctioned account of the sources of the Yellow River), was compiled in 1782.

4 For a study of a group of album paintings of ethnic peoples in Guizhou, see Hostetler, *Qing Colonial Enterprise*.

5 The *amban* borrowed a total of 20,000 taels from the Dalai Lama and the Panchen Lama. When the *amban* tried to borrow from them a second time, the Dalai Lama and the Panchen Lama were reluctant to grant their request. Embarrassed, the Jiaqing emperor noted: "What a shame!" (*Da Qing lichao shilu, Renzongchao* [Veritable records of successive reigns of the Qing dynasty, the Jiaqing reign], 91/6b-7b).

6 On two occasions in the nineteenth century—first in 1841 and 1842 and then in 1855 and 1856, when the Tibetans went into conflict with the Dogra people, an Indian tribe from Jammu, and again with the Gurkhas—the Qing dynasty gave no help (Wu Fengpei and Zeng Guoqing, *Qingchao zhuZangdacheng zhidu de jianli yu yange* [The establishment and evolution of the Qing *amban* system in Tibet]), 78–81; and Shakabpa, *Tibet*, 193–94).

7 Shakabpa, *Tibet*, 192–223; Richardson, *Tibet and Its History*, 73–90; and Deshayes, *Histoire du Tibet*, 217–35.

8 Adshead, *Province and Politics in Late Imperial China*, 66–68.

9 It has been a consensus among the scholars of the Qing that the dynasty lacked timely adjustments in its tax policy. See Wang Yeh-chien, *Land Taxation in Imperial China*, 131; and Shepherd, *Statecraft and Political Economy on the Taiwan Frontier*, 398.

10 *Qingshigao* (Draft history of the Qing dynasty, hereafter QSG), *juan* 374.

11 Richthofen, *Baron Richthofen's Letters*, 180.

12 He also failed to notice that the heavy surcharges on land taxes since the era of the Taiping Rebellion had, at the very least, doubled the tax quotas in Sichuan.

13 Richthofen was enthusiastic in giving detailed accounts of the well-maintained and broad street roads, carefully adorned houses, and well-dressed people in Chengdu (ibid., 183–84).

14 Zhou Xun, *Shuhai congtan* (Miscellanea of Sichuan), 129. This street is still called

Tidu jie today and is full of shops and boutiques selling electronic products.

15 Liu, "Chengdu ManMengzu pianduanshi" (Some anecdotes of the Manchu and Mongol peoples in Chengdu).

16 Li Jieren, *Ripples across Stagnant Water*, 279–80. In the early twentieth century part of the banner compound was converted into a public park, Shaocheng gongyuan, by the last Chengdu general. It remains a park today but has a new name, Renmin gongyuan (People's Park).

17 Again, Li Jieren's trilogy—*Ripples across Stagnant Water*, *Baofengyuqian* (On the eve of a Storm), and *Dabo* (Surges)—would serve as a good footnote for this development. Several characters in his trilogy belonged to the descendants of the official migrants, who originally were from the Jiangnan area and settled in Sichuan after their official tenures because of the bountiful resources, benign climate, beautiful scenery, and easy ways to get rich in the province. By the early twentieth century those official migrants' descendants had fared extremely well in Sichuan, owning large areas of land in the countryside that were all rented out to farmers to till and stately mansions in Chengdu, being all engaged in commercial activities, and holding a position in the bureaucracy through purchase. Having no bond with the military, they would prefer to be referred to as the families of "semi-official and semi-gentry" (*banguan banshen*) and followed the fashion trends of the gentry class in the lower Yangzi valley. In 1936, when Huang Yanpei, the pioneer of Chinese career education and a political activist, visited Chengdu, he also observed striking similarities in social practices and popular culture between Chengdu and the cities in Jiangnan. As he terms it, those two places were consistent in style and culture (*daoyi fengtong*) (Huang Yanpei, *Shudao* [A voyage to Sichuan], 39–40).

18 Richthofen, *Baron Richthofen's Letters*, 163.

19 The Mission Lyonnaise report, quoted in Adshead, *Province and Politics in Late Imperial China*, 20.

20 Hart, *Western China*, 281.

21 Adshead, *Province and Politics in Late Imperial China*, 15; and Richthofen, *Baron Richthofen's Letters*, 164 and 200.

22 Madeleine Zelin has shown that merchants from Shaanxi were most instrumental in Sichuan's salt industry (Zelin, *Merchants of Zigong*, 25).

23 Cited in Adshead, *Province and Politics in Late Imperial China*, 15.

24 William Rowe has noted that the tea trade in Wuhan in the latter part of the Qing era was controlled by non-native businessmen (Rowe, *Hankow: Conflict and Community in A Chinese City*, 134).

25 *Hu Linyi quanji* (The complete collection of Hu Linyi), vol. 6, 45.

26 In the beginning, the provincial government levied the taxes of later years in advance in the name of "borrowing" to meet the huge demands. Before long, the provincial officials of Sichuan had to place some surcharges on regular taxes to stabilize the source for extra income. In so doing, the real tax burden on the

population of Sichuan was suddenly doubled (*Da Qing lichao shilu, Wenzongchao* [Veritable records of successive reigns of the Qing dynasty, the Xianfeng reign], 18/31a-b).

27 *Luo Wenzhonggong zougao* (Collected memorials by Luo Bingzhang), 3/2.

28 This amount includes *lijin* levied on salt, which was a large portion of the total amount of the *lijin* revenue from Sichuan (Luo Yudong, *Zhongguo lijin shi* [A history of the *lijin* system in China], 415–23; and Zelin, *Merchants of Zigong*, 140–44).

29 Wang Kaiyun, *Xiangjun zhi* (A history of the Hunan army), 144.

30 Ibid., 166.

31 For Sichuan's fiscal burdens during the last decade of the Qing, see Adshead, *Province and Politics in Late Imperial China*, throughout and especially 40–42 and 69–70.

32 Richthofen, *Baron Richthofen's Letters*, 180.

33 The most representative of this type of propaganda document can be found in Zhou Kaiqing, *Sichuan yu xinhai geming* (Sichuan and the 1911 Revolution), 4–17.

34 Shepherd, *Statecraft and Political Economy on the Taiwan Frontier*, 181 and 224–25.

35 QSLQL, 333/27b and 37a-b.

36 An example of this kind of accusation concerning the state of late imperial China can be found in Braudel, *Wheels of Commerce*, 136–37.

37 Shepherd, *Statecraft and Political Economy on the Taiwan Frontier*.

38 Ibid., 182.

39 See chapter 2 of this book for details. This scenario was actually repeated several times in the eighteenth century, when the garrison forces in eastern Sichuan were sent to the Tibetan border marches for a variety of tasks.

GLOSSARY

Adunzi 阿墩子

Aergu ting 阿爾古廳

Aertai 阿爾泰

Agūi 阿桂

aixian 愛閑

Ajige 阿濟格

Altan Khan (Anda Han) 俺答汗

anfusi 安撫司

anjiayin 安家銀

An Lushan 安祿山

ansu 安素

An Wensi (Gabriel de Magalhães) 安文思

ashan i hafan 阿思哈尼哈番

Ba 巴

Ba'atur (Batuer) 巴圖爾

Bai Bing 白冰

Bai Huang 白潢

Bandi 班第

banguan banshen 半官半紳

Bangun 班滾

baojia 保甲

Baoning 保寧

Baoxing 寶興

Baoye 褒斜

Bathang (Batang) 巴塘

Baxi 巴錫

Baxian 巴縣

Bazhong 巴忠

bazong 把總

beifu 背夫

beile 貝勒

Beisheng zhou 北勝州

biandi liyi beichu 邊地理宜備儲

bianfeng 邊俸

Booju (Baozhu) 保柱

bujingzhilun 不經之論
Cai Yurong 蔡毓榮
cangfuyumin 藏富于民
canjiang 參將
Cao Yin 曹寅
Cereng (Celeng) 策楞
chama maoyi 茶馬貿易
Chamdo (Chamuduo) 叉木多
Changdu (Chamdo) 昌都
Changcejilie 昌側集烈
changfu 長夫
Chawa 嚓哇
Chaya 嚓雅
Chishui 赤水
Chuanbei zhen 川北鎮
Chuan-Shaan sanbian zongdu 川陝三邊總督
Chuansheng dichu bianjiang, jizhu jinyao 川省地處邊疆,積貯緊要
Cifeidiaoyuan, gaidiaoyaoye 此非調遠,蓋調要也
Cixing shiguan zhongda 此行事關重大
Dadu 大渡
Daguan 大關
Dajianlu ting 打箭爐廳
Dalai Khan (Dalai Han) 達賴汗
Dali 大理
Dartsedo (Dajianlu) 打箭爐
Daxi 大西
Dazhou 達州
Dechen (Deqin) 德欽
desi (diba) 第巴
Dianjiang 墊江
Dodo (Duoduo) 多鐸
Dongchuan 東川
dongnan wei caifu zhongdi, zhen shijia zhennian 東南為財富重地，朕時加軫念
Dorgon (Duoergun) 多爾袞
dou 斗
Dujiangyan 都江堰
duoluo beile 多羅貝勒
Ebilun (Ebilong) 額必隆
Echang 鄂昌
edi 遏糴
Ehai 鄂海
Ehui 鄂輝
Eleuth (Elute) 厄魯特
Emida 鄂彌達
Erentei (Elunte) 額倫特
Esen (Yexian) 也先
Fala 法喇
Fan Chengmo 范承謨
Fan Chengxun 范承勛
Fang Xian 方顯
Fan Wencheng 范文成
Fucing (Fuqing) 傅清
Fude 富德
fudutong 副都統
fufeng 腹俸
Fuheng 傅恆

fujiang 副將
Fukang'an 福康安
gaitu guiliu 改土歸流
Galayi 噶喇依
Galbi (Gaerbi) 噶爾弼
Galdan (Gaerdan) 噶爾丹
Galdan Tsereng (Gaerdan Celing) 噶爾丹策零
Gao Qizhuo 高其倬
Gedun Truppa (Gendun Zhuba) 根敦朱巴
Gelugpa (Gelupai) 格魯派
Geng Jimao 耿繼茂
Geng Jingzhong 耿精忠
Gesitai 葛思泰
Gongyiyuan 公義園
guangurenfu 官僱人夫
guanhu xiangshen 官戶鄉紳
Guihuacheng 歸化城
Guilin 桂林
guo 嘓
guolu 嘓嚕
guoluzi 嘓嚕子
Gurkhas (*kuoerka*) 廓爾喀
Gushri Khan (Gushi Han) 顧實汗
Guyuan 固原
Gyelthang (Zhongdian) 中甸
Gyumey Namgyal (Zhuermote Namuzhale) 朱爾默特那木扎勒
Hailancha 海蘭察
Hami 哈密
Hangyilu 杭奕祿
Hanjun 漢軍
Hanzhong 漢中
Haoge 豪格
Ha Yuansheng 哈元生
He Fu 何傅
Hejiang 合江
Helin 和琳
He Linghan 何淩漢
Heqing 鶴慶
Holohoi (Heluohui) 何洛會
hongbai xishi 紅白喜事
Hong Chengchou 洪承疇
Huairen 懷仁
Hualinping 化林坪
Huang Tinggui 黃廷桂
Huguang shu tianxia zu 湖廣熟，天下足
Huguang tian Sichuan 湖廣填四川
huiguan 會館
Huiyuan 惠遠
Hu Linyi 胡林翼
huohao 火耗
Jalangga (Chalang'a) 查郎阿
Jaranas (Zhaernai) 扎爾鼐
Jialing 嘉陵
Jianchuan 劍川
jiangjun 將軍
Jiangka 江卡
Ji Chengbin 紀成斌
jieshou 解手

jin 斤
Jinchuan 金川
Jingzhou 荊州
Jinsha 金沙
Jishan 紀山
juanna 捐納
juanshu 捐輸
Junchen 君陳
junwang 君王
Junxuju 軍需局
Junxu zeli 軍需則例
Kaita 開泰
kaloon (galun) 噶倫
Kang Tai 康泰
Kata (Gada) 噶達
ke 客
kefu 客夫
kemi 客米
kemin fucou 客民輻輳
Kham (Kang) 康
Khangchennas (Kangjinai) 康濟鼐
Klau (Gelao) 仡佬
kouwai 口外
kuanyu youwo 寬裕優渥
Kuiguan 夔關
Kuilin 奎林
Kuizhou 夔州
Kumbum (Ta'ersi) 塔兒寺
Labdon (Labudun) 拉布敦
Lajang Khan (Lazang Han) 拉藏汗
Lan Chaoding 藍朝鼎
lanling shiwei 藍翎侍衛
Laxi 拉錫
Lebao 勒保
Lewuwei 勒烏圍
li 里
Li Ande (Andreas Ly) 李安德
Liang-Huai 兩淮
Liang Shizheng 梁詩正
Liangshan 梁山
lianxiang 練餉
Li Dingguo 李定國
Lifanyuan 理藩院
lifu 里夫
Li Guoying 李國英
Li Jieren 李劼人
lijin 釐金
Li Laiheng 李來亨
Li Leisi (Louis Buglio) 利類思
Li Lin 李麟
Lingling 零陵
Lin Shuangwen 林爽文
Liping 黎平
Li Shijie 李世傑
Lithang (Litang) 理塘
Liu Jie 劉傑
Liu Rong 劉蓉
Liu Zhaoqi 劉兆琪
Li Xu 李煦
Li Yonghe 李永和

Li Zicheng 李自成

Lobdzan Dandzin (Luobuzang Danjin) 羅卜藏丹津

Lozang Gyatso (Luosang Jiacuo) 羅桑嘉措

Lu 瀘

Luding 瀘定

Lü Liuliang 呂留良

Lumpa (Longbunai) 隆布鼐

Luo (Tuo) 雒 (沱)

Luo Bingzhang 駱秉章

Luo Xiujin 羅綉錦

Ma Huibo 馬會伯

Mailu 邁祿

maimaijie 買賣街

Maizhokunggar (Mozhugongka) 墨竹工卡

Ma Jibo 馬際伯

Ma Jinliang 馬進良

Mala 馬喇

Ma Liangzhu 馬良柱

manja (aochao) 熬茶

Manpi 满丕

Maogong 懋功

Maoxian 茂縣

maoyikemin 貿易客民

Meinuo ting 美諾廳

Menggu fandi 蒙古番地

Meng Qiaofang 孟喬芳

Miaofan 苗番

Mingliang 明亮

Mingshi 明史

Ming Yuzhen 明玉珍

minzhuang 民壯

mu 畝

Muguomu 木果木

Naige 鼐格

nanmu 楠木

Nanzhao 南昭

nei tusi 内土司

Nengtai 能泰

Necin (Neqin) 訥親

Ngabo (Aerbuba) 阿爾布巴

Nian Gengyao 年羹堯

Nikan 尼堪

Ningyuan 寧遠

niru 尼祿

Oboi (Aobai) 鰲拜

Oci (Eqi) 鄂齊

Oirat or Oyirad (Wala) 瓦喇

Ortai (Eertai) 鄂爾泰

Pengba 烹壩

Pholhanas (Poluonai) 頗羅鼐

Qiang 羌

Qinghai 青海

qianjiu hanhu, caoshuai jiean 遷就含糊，草率結案

qianzong 千總

qing 頃

Qingfu 慶復

Ren Guorong 任國榮
ruji 入籍
Sangye Gyatso (Sangjie Jiacuo) 桑結嘉措
sanxiang jiapai 三餉加派
Sengge 僧格
shanghao 賞號
shangyun 商運
Shengzu shilu 聖祖實錄
shi (it is now pronounced *dan*) 石
Shi Dakai 石達開
Shu 蜀
Shunning 順寧
Shuose 碩色
Solobun (Shaluoben) 莎羅奔
Sonam Gyatso (Suonan Jiacuo) 索南嘉措
Songpan ting 松潘廳
Songpanzhen zhongjun youji 松潘鎮中軍遊擊
Songtsen Gampo (Songzan Ganbu) 松贊干布
Sun Kewang 孫可望
Sun Shiyi 孫士毅
Suonuomu 索諾木
Taining 泰寧
taiZangyin 臺藏銀
Tang Xishun 唐希順
Tashilhunpo (Zhashilunbu) 扎什倫布
Techeng'e 特成額
tejian 特簡
Tengrinor (Tenggeernao) 騰格爾腦
Tengyue 騰越
tibu 題補
tianfu zhiqing, jiayu tianxia 田賦之輕，甲于天下
Tianjin zongbing 天津總兵
tianxia caifu, banchu dongnan 天下財富，半出東南
Tidu jie 提督街
Tongzi 桐梓
Tsangyang Gyatso (Cangyang Jiacuo) 倉央嘉措
Tsengasang (Senggesang) 僧格桑
Tsering Dondup (Celing Dunduobu) 策零敦多布
Tsewang Rabdan (Cewang Alabutan) 策妄阿喇布坦
Tsongkhapa (Zongkaba) 宗喀巴
Tubote guowang 吐伯特國王
Tuhai 圖海
Tumubao 土木堡
tusi 土司
Ulaan Butung (Wulanbutong) 烏蘭布通
Wang Ji 王機
Wang Jinghao 王景灝
Wang Lun 王倫
Wanxian 萬縣
Wei Jiqi 衛既齊

Wenchuan 汶川
Wenfu 溫福
Wenjiang 溫江
Wenshou 文綬
Wuge 武格
Wumeng 烏蒙
Wu Sangui 吳三桂
Wu Shifan 吳世璠
xiaba 下壩
Xiande 憲德
xiangqin 襄勤
Xichong 西充
xichui jinyao 西陲緊要
xiejisheng 協濟省
Xierda 希爾達
xiexiang 協餉
Xifo 禧佛
Xihai 西海
xingzhuangyin 行裝銀
Xining *guitiao* 西寧規條
Xinjiang 新疆
Xiwang 西王
Xizang taifeiyin 西藏臺費銀
xunfu 巡撫
Xuyong 敘永
Xuzhou 敘州
Ya'an 雅安
Yalong 雅礱
yancaiyin 鹽菜銀
Yang Bi 楊馝
Yang Chengxun 楊成勛
Yang Jinxing 楊進興
Yang Tianzong 楊天縱
Yang Yingju 楊應琚
Yang Zhan 楊展
Yan Qingru 彥清如
Yansin (Yanxin) 延信
Yao Diyu 姚諦虞
Yazhou 雅州
yicang 義倉
yilaoyongyi 一勞永逸
yiman gongman 以蠻攻蠻
yingyun shengxi 營運生息
Yinjishan 尹繼善
Yinti 胤禵
Yinzhen 胤禛
Yitongzhi 一統志
Yongbei 永北
Yongchang 永昌
yongjue genchu 永絕根除
Yongning *fujiang* 永寧副將
Yongzheng zhupi yuzhi 雍正朱批諭旨
Yonten Gyatso (Yundan Jiacuo) 雲丹嘉措
Youtai 有泰
Yue Chaolong 岳超龍
Yue Fei 岳飛
Yue Jun 岳濬
Yue Shenglong 岳昇龍
Yue Zhonghuang 岳鍾璜
Yue Zhongqi 岳鍾琪

yunqiwei 雲騎尉
Yu Yangzhi 于養志
Yu Zhun 于準
Yuzhi shiquan ji 御制十全集
Zagu 雜谷
zai Sichuan jiaowai 在四川徼外
zaliang 雜糧
Zeng Jing 曾靜
Zeng Ying 曾英
Zhandui 瞻對
Zhang Dedi 張德地
Zhang Guangsi 張廣泗
Zhang Penghe 張鵬翮
Zhang Xianzhong 張獻忠
Zhang Yunsui 張允隨
Zhang Zhao 張照
Zhaobo 召伯
Zhao Ru 趙儒
Zhao Shenqiao 趙申喬
zhen 鎮
Zhenxiong 鎮雄
Zhi turen shu 制土人疏
zhilizhou 直隸州
Zhongdian (Gyelthang) 中甸
Zhongjia 仲家
zhongjun youji 中軍遊擊
Zhongzhou 忠州
Zhou Ying 周瑛
Zhuge Liang 諸葛亮
Zhu Youlang 朱由榔
zhuZangdachen 駐藏大臣
zongbing 總兵
zongdu 總督
Zunmod (Zhaomoduo) 昭莫多
Zunyi 遵義
Zuozhenpingfu, ji'naifengqi
作朕屏輔，濟乃封祁
zuoling 佐領

SELECTED BIBLIOGRAPHY

UNCOMPILED, COMPILED, AND PUBLISHED PRIMARY SOURCES

Aba Zangzu Qiangzu zizhizhou zhi (The gazetteer of Ngawa autonomous zhou of Tibetan and Qiang nationalities). 3 volumes. Chengdu: Minzu Chubanshe, 1994.

Cai Guanluo, ed. *Qingshi liezhuan* (The biographies of Qing history). 3 volumes. Taipei: Qiming Shuju, 1965.

Cai Yurong. *Pingnan jilüe* (A brief account of the campaign pacifying the south). Volume 3, *Qingshi ziliao* (Material of Qing history), 218–22. Beijing: Zhonghua Shuju, 1982.

Cheng Muheng. *Jinchuan jilüe* (A history of the first Jinchuan war). Volume 3, *Xizangxue Hanwen wenxian huike* (Series of the Chinese documents in the Tibetan studies). Beijing: Zhongguo Zangxue Chubanshe, 1994.

Chongxiu Chengdu xianzhi (Revised gazetteer of Chengdu County). 1873. 7 volumes. Reprint, Taipei: Taiwan Xuesheng Shuju, 1971.

ChuanShaanChu shanhou shiyi dang (Achives of the late phase of the campaign against the White Lotus Rebellion in Sichuan, Shaanxi, and Hubei). National Palace Museum, Taipei.

Dai Zhili. *Sichuan baolu yundong shiliao* (Records of the Railroad Rights Recovery Movement in Sichuan). 3 volumes. Beijing: Kexue Chubanshe, 1959.

Da Qing huidian (Collected statutes of the Qing dynasty), Jiaqing period. 10 volumes. Taipei: Wenhai Chubanshe, 1991.

Da Qing huidian (Collected statutes of the Qing dynasty), Kangxi period. 20 volumes. Taipei: Wenhai Chubanshe, 1995.

Da Qing huidian (Collected statutes of the Qing dynasty), Qianlong period. 1 volume. Beijing: Zhonghua Shuju, 1991.

DaQing huidian (Collected statutes of the Qing dynasty), Yongzheng period. 30 volumes. Taipei: Wenhai Chubanshe, 1995.

Da Qing huidian shili (Collected statutes of the Qing dynasty: Precedents). 12 volumes. Beijing: Zhonghua Shuju, 1991.

Da Qing lichao shilu (Veritable records of successive reigns of the Qing dynasty). 1220 volumes. Tokyo: Okura Shuppan Kabushiki Kaisha, 1937–1938. In the chapter notes these records are identified by the particular reign: *Shengzuchao* (the Kangxi reign), QSLKX; *Gaozongchao* (the Qianlong reign), QSLQL; *Shizuchao* (the Shunzhi reign), QSLSZ; and *Shizongchao* (the Yongzheng reign), QSLYZ.

Da Qing shichao shengxun (Imperial edicts and instructions of the ten emperors of the Qing dynasty). 7 volumes. Taipei: Wenhai Chubanshe, 1965.

Dayi juemi lu (The narration of the great righteousness and enlightenment). Volume 4, *Qingshi ziliao* (Material of Qing history), 3–169. Beijing: Zhonghua Shuju, 1983.

Di Cosmo, Nicola, trans. and ed. *The Diary of a Manchu Soldier in Seventeenth-Century China*. Richmond, U.K.: Curzon Press, 2001.

Eertai zoushu (Ortai's memorials). 2 volumes. Beijing: Quanguo Tushuguan Wenxian Suowei Fuzhi Zhongxin, 1991.

Entenmann, Robert E., trans. "Andreas Ly on the First Jinchuan War in Western Sichuan (1747–1749)." *Sino-Western Cultural Relation Journal* 19 (1997): 6–21.

Erongan, Eshi, Ebi, Ening, Exin, and Emo. *Xiangqinbo E Wenduangong nianpu* (A chronicle of Ortai). Volume 2, *Qingshi ziliao* (Material of Qing history), 55–152. Beijing: Zhonghua Shuju, 1981.

Fei Mi. *Huangshu* (A book on devastation). In *Zhang Xianzhong jian Sichuan shilu* (A collection of the writings on Zhang Xianzhong's massacres in Sichuan), edited by He Rui and others, 416–47. Chengdu: Bashu Shushe, 2002.

Fu Diji. *Wuma Xiansheng jinian* (Chronicle of Monsieur Wuma). 1 volume. Chengdu: Sichuan Renmin Chubanshe, 1981.

Fuge. *Tingyu congtan* (Miscellanea at Tingyu hall). 1 volume. Hong Kong: Longmen Shudian, 1969.

Gongzhongdang Kangxichao zouzhe (GZDQL) (Secret palace memorials of the Kangxi period). 9 volumes. Taipei: National Palace Museum, 1976–1977.

Gongzhongdang Qianlongchao zouzhe (Secret palace memorials of the Qianlong period). 75 volumes. Taipei: National Palace Museum, 1982–1984.

Gongzhongdang Yongzhengchao zouzhe (Secret palace memorials of the Yongzheng period). 32 volumes. Taipei: National Palace Museum, 1977–1980.

Guizhou tongzhi (Gazetteer of Guizhou). 24 volumes. 1741.

Gu Shanzhen. "KeDianshu" (A narrative of my stay in Yunnan). In *Hukou yusheng ji* (Records on surviving in tigers' jaws), 77–108. Shanghai: Guangwen Shuju, 1936.

Gu Yanwu. *Tianxia junguo libing shu* (A study on advantages and disadvantages of all parts of the country). Taipei: Taiwan Shangwu Yinshuguan, 1981.

Hart, Virgil C. *Western China: A Journey to the Great Buddhist Centre of Mount Omei*. Boston: Ticknor and Company, 1888.

Huangchao jingshi wenbian (Statecraft writings of the Qing period). 1887. Edited by He Changling. Reprint, Taipei: Wenhai Chubanshe, 1972.

Hu Linyi quanji (Complete colletion of Hu Linyi). 12 volumes. Shanghai: Dadong Shuju, 1936.

Jianzhou zhi (Gazetteer of Jianzhou). 11 volumes. 1853. Reprint, Taipei: Shangwu Yinshuguan, 1966.

Jiaobudang (Achives of the campaign against the White Lotus Rebellion). National Palace Museum, Taipei.

Jiaqing chongxiu yitongzhi (National gazetteer, revised edition of the Jiaqing period). 11 volumes. 1820. Reprint, Taipei: Shangwu Yinshuguan, 1966.

Jinchuan an (A collection of the records relating to the two Jinchuan wars). 1 volume. Beijing: Zhongguo Zangxue Chubanshe, 1994.

Jinchuan dang (Archives of the second Jinchuan campaign). National Palace Museum, Taipei.

Junjichu lufu zouzhe (Copies of the archives of the Grand Council). Number One Historical Archives of China, Beijing.

Junjidang (Archives of the Grand Council, the Qianlong Period). National Palace Museum, Taipei.

Junyingdang (Archives of the military camps, or archives of the Zunghar campaigns of the Qianlong period). National Palace Museum, Taipei.

Kangding xianzhi (Gazetteer of Kangding county). 1 volume. Chengdu: Sichuan Cishu Chubanshe, 1995.

Kangxichao baoxiaoce (Fiscal reports from Sichuan of the Kangxi period). Number One Historical Archives of China, Beijing.

Kangxichao Hanwen zhupi zouzhe huibian (KXHW) (Complete collection of the memorials in Chinese with the emperor's comments of the Kangxi period). Edited by the Number One Historical Archives of China. 8 volumes. Beijing: Dang'an Chubanshe, 1984–1985.

Kangxichao Manwen zhupi zouzhe quanyi (KXMW) (Complete translation of the memorials in Manchu with the emperor's comments of the Kangxi period). Translated and edited by the Number One Historical Archives of China. 1 volume. Beijing: Zhongguo Shehuikexue Chubanshe, 1996.

Kangxichao qijuzhu (Diaries of action and repose of the Kangxi emperor). 211 volumes. National Palace Museum, Taipei.

Kangxi qijuzhu (Diaries of action and repose of the Kangxi emperor). Edited by the Number One Historical Archives of China. 3 volumes. Beijing: Zhonghua Shuju, 1984.

Kuoerka dang (Archives of the Gurkha wars). National Palace Museum, Taipei.

Legendre, A.-F. *Deux années au Setchouen: Récit de voyage, étude géographique, sociale et économique* (Two years in Sichuan: Travel account, and geographical, social, and economic investigation). Paris: Librairie Plon, 1905.

Liang Qichao. *Yinbingshi quanji* (Collected works of Liang Qichao). 4 volumes. Shanghai: Shanghai Dadao Shuju. 1936.

Li Furong. *Yanyu nang* (Sichuan's story [during the Ming-Qing transition]). In *Zhang Xianzhong jian Sichuan shilu*. Edited by He Rui and others, 29–98. Chengdu: Bashu Shushe, 2002.

Li Huan, ed. *Guochao qixian leizheng chubian* (The biographies of the eminent figures of the Qing period, the first part). 65 volumes. Taipei: Wenhai Chubanshe, 1966.

Luo Wenzhonggong zougao (Collected memorials by Luo Bingzhang). 10 volumes. 1891.

Luo Wenzhonggong zouyi (Collected memorials by Luo Bingzhang). 3 volumes. Taipei: Wenhai Chubanshe, 1967.

Lu Zijian, ed. *Qingdai Sichuan caizheng shiliao* (Material relating to financial matters in Sichuan during the Qing dynasty), part 1. 2 volumes. Chengdu: Sichuansheng Shehuikexueyuan Chubanshe, 1984.

Maerkang xianzhi (Gazetteer of Maerkang county). 1 volume. Chengdu: Sichuan Renmin Chubanshe, 1995.

Mian dang (Archives of the Myanmar war). National Palace Museum, Taipei.

Ming Qing dang'an (MQDA) (Archives of the Ming and Qing dynasties). 324 volumes. Edited by Zhang Weiren. Taipei: Institute of History and Philology of the Academia Sinica, 1986–1995.

Ming Qing shiliao (Historical materials of the Ming and Qing dynasties). *Gengbian* (The seventh series). 2 volumes. Taipei: Institute of History and Philology of the Academia Sinica, 1960.

Missionaries' correspondence. Archives des Missions Etangères de Paris, Paris.

Neigedaku dang'an (NGDK) (Archives of the cabinet of the Qing dynasty). Institute of History and Philology, Academia Sinica, Taipei.

Nian Gengyao Man Han zouzhe yibian (NMH) (Collection of Nian Gengyao's memorials in Manchu and Chinese, with the Manchu ones translated into Chinese). Translated and edited by Ji Yonghai, Li Pansheng, and Xie Zhining. 1 volume. Tianjin: Tianjin Guji Chubanshe, 1995.

Pallas, Peter Simon (Palasi). *Neilu Yazhou Elute lishi ziliao* (Historical material on the Eleuth Mongols in Inner Asia; a Chinese translation of the original German-language work, *Sammlungen historischer Nachrichten über die mongolischen Völkerschaften in einem ausführlichen Auszuge*). Translated by Shao Jiandong and Liu Yingsheng. 1 volume. Kunming: Yunnan Renmin Chubanshe, 2002.

———. *Sammlungen historischer Nachrichten über die mongolischen Völkerschaften*. Graz, Austria: Akademische Druck-u. Verlagsanstalt, 1980.

Peng Zunsi. *Shubi* (Bloodsheds in Sichuan). In *Zhang Xianzhong jian Sichuan shilu*. Edited by He Rui and others, 127–82. Chengdu: Bashu Shushe, 2002.

Pingding Jinchuan fanglüe (JCFL) (Chronicle of the first Jinchuan campaign). Beijing:

Quanguo Tushuguan Wenxian Suowei Fuzhi Zhongxin, 1992.

Pingding liang Jinchuan fanglüe (LJCFL) (Chronicle of the second Jinchuan campaign). 2 volumes. Beijing: Quanguo Tushuguan Wenxian Suowei Fuzhi Zhongxin, 1991–1992.

Pingding liang Jinchuan junxu li'an (JCLA) (Collected records and precedents related to the military expenditures of the second Jinchuan campaign). Edited by Zheng Qishan. 8 volumes. Beijing: Quanguo Tushuguan Wenxian Suowei Fuzhi Zhongxin, 1989.

Qianlongchao Junjichu suishoudengjidang (The Grand Council's digests of memorials and edicts of the Qianlong period). Edited by Number One Historical Archives of China. 46 volumes. Guilin: Guangxi Shifandaxue Chubanshe, 2000.

Qianlongchao shangyudang (SYD) (Edicts of the Qianlong period). Edited by Number One Historical Archives of China. 18 volumes. Beijing: Dang'an Chubanshe, 1991.

Qianlongdi qijuzhu (Diaries of action and repose of the Qianlong emperor). Edited by Number One Historical Archives of China. 42 volumes. Guilin: Guangxi Shifandaxue Chubanshe, 2002.

Qing archives. Municipal Archives of Chongqing, Chongqing, China.

Qinding heyuan jilüe (Imperial-sanctioned account of the sources of the Yellow River). Edited by Ji Yun. 1782. Reprint, Taipei: Guangwen Shuju, 1969.

Qinding Hubu, Bingbu, Gongbu junxu zeli (Imperial-sanctioned regulations of wartime expenditures concerning the Boards of Revenue, War, and Works). Haikou: Hainan Chubanshe, 2000.

Qinding jiaoping sansheng xiefei fanglüe (Imperial-sanctioned chronicle of the campaign to suppress the heretical bandits in the three provinces). 69 volumes. Taipei: Chengwen Chubanshe, 1970.

Qinding quanTangwen (Imperial-sanctioned collection of proses of the Tang period). 20 volumes. Tainan: Jingwei Shuju, 1965.

Qingchao wenxian tongkao (General history and examination of Qing institutions and documents). 2 volumes. Taipei: Xinxing Shuju. 1958.

Qingdai Baxian dang'an huibian—Qianlong juan (A collection of archives of Ba county: The Qianlong reign). 1 volume. Beijing: Dang'an Chubanshe, 1991.

Qingdai dang'an shiliao congbian (A collection of the archives of the Qing dynasty), volume 4. Beijing: Zhonghua Shuju, 1979.

Qingdai QianJiaDao Baxian dang'an xüanbian (Selected archives of Ba county from the Qianlong, Jiaqing, and Daoguang periods of the Qing dynasty). 1 volume. Chengdu: Sichuan Daxue Chubanshe, 1989.

Qing Gaozong yuzhi shiwen shiquan ji (A collection of the Qianlong emperor's poems on the ten military campaigns). 1 volume. Taipei: Heji Shilin Shuju. 1963.

Qing zhongqi wusheng Bailianjiao qiyi ziliao (The material concerning the White Lotus Rebellion in five provinces in the mid-Qing period). 5 volumes. Nanjing: Jiangsu Renmin Chubanshe, 1981.

Qinzheng pingding shuomo fanglüe (SMFL) (Chronicle of the Kangxi emperor's expeditions to pacify the steppe). 32 volumes. Beijing: Zhongguo Shudian, 1987.

Richthofen, Ferdinand von. *Baron Richthofen's Letters, 1870–1872*. Second edition. Shanghai: Printed at the North-China Herald office, 1903.

Shen Xunwei. *Shunan xulüe* (A sketch of the disasters in Sichuan). In *Zhang Xianzhong jian Sichuan shilu*. Edited by He Rui and others. Chengdu: Bashu Shushe, 2002.

Shihuozhi (Records of economic history of Qing times). National Palace Museum, Taipei.

Sichuan tongzhi (SCTZ) (Gazetteer of Sichuan). 120 volumes. 1816.

Tsering Wanggyia (Cerenwangjie). *Poluonai zhuan* (Biography of Pholhanas; the Chinese translation of *dPal mi'i dban po'i rtogs brjod pa 'jig rten kun tu dga' ba'i gtam*). Translated by Tang Chi'an. Lhasa: Xizang Renmin Chubanshe, 1988.

Viard, Jules. *Seize ans en Chine: Lettres du P. Clerc, provicaire du Su-tchuen méridional* (Sixteen years in China: Letters of P. Clerc, acting curate of southern Sichuan). Paris: Rene Haton, 1887.

Vigneron, Lucien. *Deux ans au Se-Tchouan (Chine centrale)* (Two years in Sichuan [Central China]). Paris, 1881.

Wang Chang. *Shujiao jiwen* (A memoir of the second Jinchuan campaign). Shanghai: Shanghai Guji Chubanshe, 1990.

———. *ZhengMian jilüe* (A brief account of the Myanmar campaign). Shanghai: Shanghai Guji Chubanshe, 1990.

Wang Kaiyun. *Xiangjun zhi* (A history of the Hunan Army). Changsha: Yuelu Shushe, 1983.

Wang Xianqian. *Shichao Donghua lu* (The records of ten emperors from the archives in Donghua hall). Shanghai: Gongji Shuzhuang, 1899.

Wang Xinheng. *Jinchuan suoji* (Miscellaneous notes on Jinchuan). Beijing: Zhongguo Zangxue Chubanshe, 1994.

Wei Yuan. *Shengwuji* (Chronicle of imperial military campaigns). 1 volume. Shanghai: Shijie Shuju, 1936.

Wei Yuan ji (Collected works of Wei Yuan). 2 volume. Edited by Zhonghua Shuju. Beijing: Zhonghua Shuju, 1976.

WeiZang tongzhi (Gazetteer of Tibet). 2 volumes. Shanghai: Shangwu Yinshuguan, 1937.

Wenjiang xianzhi (Gazetteer of Wenjiang county). 2 volumes. 1921.

Wenxian congbian. (Collectanea from the Historical Records Office). 36 volumes. Beijing: The Palace Museum, 1930–1937.

Wu Han, ed. *Chaoxian Lichao shilu zhong de Zhongguo shiliao* (The accounts relating to China found in the veritable records of the Yi dynasty of Korea). 12 volumes. Beijing: Zhonghua Shuju, 1980.

Xiao Shi. *Yongxianlu* (Records from the Yongzheng period). 1 volume. Shanghai: Zhonghua Shuju, 1959.

Xizang lishi dang'an huicui (A collection of historical archives related to Tibet). Edited by Xizang Dang'anguan (Archives of Tibet). 1 volume. Beijing: Wenwu Chubanshe, 1995.

Xuyong xianzhi (Gazeteer of Xuyong county). 1933. 2 volumes. Reprint, Taipei: Xuesheng Shuju, 1967.

Xuzhou fuzhi (Gazetteer of Xuzhou prefecture). 28 volumes. 1895.

Yan Ruyi. *Sansheng bianfang beilan* (A collection of documents on the borderlands of the three provinces). 12 volumes. Yangzhou: Jiangsu Guangling Guji Keyinshe, 1991.

Yang Ho-chin, trans. *The Annals of Kokonor.* Edited by Sum-pa Mkhan-po. Bloomington: Indiana University Press, 1969.

Yongzhengchao baoxiaoce (Fiscal reports from Sichuan of the Yongzheng period). Number One Historical Archives of China, Beijing.

Yongzhengchao Hanwen zhupi zouzhe huibian (YZHW) (Complete collection of the Chinese memorials with the emperor's comments of the Yongzheng period). 40 volumes. Edited by Number One Historical Archives of China. Nanjing: Jiangsu Guji Chubanshe, 1990.

Yongzhengchao Manwen zhupi zouzhe quanyi (YZMW) (Complete translation of the Manchu memorials with the emperor's comments of the Yongzheng period). 2 volumes. Translated and edited by Number One Historical Archives of China. Hefei: Huangshan Shushe, 1998.

Yongzhengchao qijuzhu (Diaries of action and repose of the Yongzheng emperor). 5 volumes. Edited by Number One Historical Archives of China. Beijing: Zhonghua Shuju, 1993.

Yongzheng zhupi yuzhi (Collected edicts of the Yongzheng emperor). 10 volumes. Taipei: Wenhai Chubanshe, 1965.

Yuan yilai Xizang difang yu zhongyang zhengfu guanxi dang'an shiliao huibian (XZDA) (A collection of historical archives concerning the relationship between Tibet and the central government since the Yuan times). 7 volumes. Edited by Duojiecaidan, Li Pengnian. Beijing: Zhongguo Zangxue Chubanshe, 1994.

Yue Jiong. *Yue xiangqingong xinglüe* (A brief biography of Yue Zhongqi). Volume 4, *Qingshi ziliao* (Material of Qing history) 170–83. Beijing: Zhonghua Shuju, 1983.

Yunnan tongzhigao (Draft of Yunnan gazetteer). 112 volumes. 1835. Edited by Wang Song.

Yunnan tongzhi (Gazetteer of Yunnan). 7 volumes. 1736. Edited by Ortai and Yinjishan.

Zhanggu congbian (Collected historical documents). 10 volumes. Beijing: Gugong Bowuyuan, 1928–29.

Zhang Tingyu. *Mingshi* (A history of the Ming dynasty). 6 volumes. Taipei: Taiwan Shangwu Yinshuguan, 1984.

Zhao Erxun. *Qingshigao* (QSG) (Draft history of the Qing dynasty). 48 volumes. Beijing: Zhonghua Shuju, 1977.

Zhaolian. *Xiaoting zalu* (Miscellanea at Xiao pavillion). Beijing: Zhonghua Shuju, 1980.

Zhao Yunsong. *Kanjing jiaofei shulüe* (A brief history of the war to exterminate the White Lotus bandits). Taipei: Tailian Guofeng Chubanshe, 1970.

Zhongdian xianzhi (Gazetteer of Zhongdian county). Kunming: Yunnan Minzu Chubanshe, 1997.

Zhongzhou zhilizhouzhi (Gazetteer of Zhongzhou subprefecture). 8 volumes. 1826.

Zhou Kaiqing, ed. *Sichuan yu xinhai geming* (Sichuan and the 1911 Revolution). Taipei: Sichuan Wenxian Yanjiushe, 1964.

Zhou Xun. *Shuhai congtan* (Miscellanea of Sichuan). Taipei: Wenhai Chubanshe, 1966.

Zhuangao (Unpublished biographies of the Historiography Institute of the Qing dynasty). National Palace Museum, Taipei.

Zhuang Jifa, trans. and ed. *Qingdai Zungaer shiliao chubian* (Collected Qing archives on the Kangxi emperor's expeditions against the Zunghar Mongols). Taipei: Wenshizhe Chubanshe, 1977.

SECONDARY SOURCES

Abe Takeo. "Beikoku jyukyuu no kenkyu: Yoseishi no issho toshitemita" (A study on the supply of grain: One chapter of the history of the Yongzheng period). In *Shindaishi no kenkyu* (Studies on the Qing dynasty). Edited by Abe Takeo, 411–522. Tokyo: Sobunsha, 1971.

Adshead, S. A. M. *Province and Politics in Late Imperial China: Viceregal Government in Szechwan, 1898–1911*. London: Curzon Press, 1984.

Backus, Charles. *The Nan-chao Kingdom and T'ang China's Southwestern Frontier*. Cambridge: Cambridge University Press, 1981.

Barfield, Thomas J. *The Perilous Frontier: Nomadic Empire and China*. Cambridge: Basil Blackwell, 1989.

Bartlett, Beatrice S. *Monarchs and Ministers: The Grand Council in Mid-Ch'ing China, 1723–1820*. Berkeley: University of California Press, 1991.

Bawden, C. R. *The Modern History of Mongolia*. London: Kegan Paul International, 1989.

Beckwith, Christopher I. *The Tibetan Empire in Central Asia: A History of the Struggle for Great Power among Tibetans, Turks, Arabs, and Chinese during the Early Middle Ages*. Princeton, N.J.: Princeton University Press, 1987.

———. "The Tibetans in the Ordos and North China: Considerations on the Role of the Tibetan Empire in World History." In *The History of Tibet*. Volume 1, *The Early Period: To c. AD 850: The Yarlung Dynasty*. Edited by Alex McKay. London: Routledge Curzon Press, 2003.

Bergholz, Fred W. *The Partition of the Steppe: The Struggle of the Russians, Manchus, and the Zunghar Mongols for Empire in Central Asia, 1619–1758: A Study in Power Politics.* New York: Peter Lang Publishing, 1993.

Braudel, Fernand. *The Wheels of Commerce.* Volume 2 of *Civilization and Capitalism, Fifteenth–Eighteenth Century.* Translated by Siân Reynolds. Berkeley: University of California Press, 1992.

Byon, Jae-hyon. *Local Gazetteers of Southwest China: A Handbook.* Seattle: School of International Studies, University of Washington, 1979.

Cai Shaoqing. "On the Origin of the Gelao Hui (Kolaohui)." *Modern China* 10, no. 4 (1984): 481–508.

Chao Kang. *Man and Land in Chinese History: An Economic Analysis.* Stanford, Calif.: Stanford University Press, 1986.

Chen Feng. *Qingdai junfei yanjiu* (A study of the Qing military appropriations and expenditures). Wuchang: Wuhan Daxue Chubanshe, 1992.

Cheng Chongde and Sun Zhe. "Qianlong shidai de jiangyu geju yu 'Neifu yutu'" (The territorial scope of the Qianlong period and the "maps of the inner court"). In *Qingshi lunji: Qinghe Wang Zhonghan jiaoshou jiushi huadan* (Collection of papers on Qing history—on the occasion of celebrating Professor Wang Zhonghan's ninetieth birthday). Edited by Zhu Chengru, 379–91. Beijing: Zijincheng Chubanshe, 2003.

Chen Guangguo. *Qinghai Zangzu shi* (A history of the Tibetans in Qinghai). Xining: Qinghai Minzu Chubanshe, 1997.

Chen Hsi-yuan. "Propitious Omens and the Crisis of Political Authority: A Case Study of the Frequent Reports of Auspicious Clouds during the Yongzheng Reign." *Papers on Chinese History* 3 (Spring 1994): 77–94.

Chen Hua. *Qingdai quyu shehui jingji yanjiu* (A study on the economy in the macro-regions during the Qing dynasty). Beijing: Zhongguo Renmin Daxue Chubanshe, 1996.

Chen Jiexian. *Qingshi zabi* (Collected articles on Qing history), volumes 1–3. Taipei: Xuehai Chubanshe, 1977.

Chen Yishi. "Qingdai Chuanchaye de fazhan jiqi yu Zangzu de jingji wenhua jiaoliu" (The development of the tea industry in Sichuan and the economic and cultural exchanges with the Tibetans during the Qing dyansty)." In *Qingdai bianjiang kaifa shi* (The history of frontier exploitation during the Qing dynasty). Edited by Ma Ruheng and Ma Dazheng, 305–32. Beijing: Zhongguo Shehuikexue Chubanshe, 1990.

Chi Ch'ao-ting. *Key Economic Areas in Chinese History: As Revealed in the Development of Public Works for Water Control.* New York: Paragon Book Reprint Corporation, 1963.

Chiu Peng-sheng. "Shiba shiji Diantong shichang zhong de guanshang guanxi yu liyi guannian" (The relationship between the bureaucracy and merchants and the awareness of interest in the copper market of Yunnan in the eighteenth century). *Lishi Yuyan Yanjiusuo jikan* (Bulletin of the Institute of History and Philology Academia Sinica) 72, no.1 (2001): 49–119.

Chuan Han-sheng. *Ming Qing jingjishi yanjiu* (Study on economic history of the Ming and Qing dynasties). Taipei: Lianjing Chuban Shiyegongsi, 1987.

Chuan Han-sheng and Richard A. Kraus. *Mid-Ch'ing Rice Markets and Trade: An Essay in Price History*. Cambridge: East Asian Research Center, Harvard University, 1975. Distributed by Harvard University Press.

Ch'ü T'ung-tsu. *Local Government in China under the Ch'ing*. Cambridge: Council on East Asian Studies, Harvard University, 1988. Distributed by Harvard University Press.

Chu, Yung-deh Richard. "An Introductory Study of the White Lotus Sect in Chinese History with Special Reference to Peasant Movement." Ph.D. dissertation. Columbia University, 1967.

Crossley, Pamela Kyle. *A Translucent Mirror: History and Identity in Qing Imperial Ideology*. Berkeley: University of California Press, 1999.

Crossley, Pamela Kyle, Helen F. Siu, and Donald S. Sutton, eds. *Empire at the Margins: Culture, Ethnicity, and Frontier in Early Modern China*. Berkeley: University of California Press, 2006.

Dai Yi. *Jianming Qingshi* (A concise history of the Qing dynasty). Beijing: Renmin Chubanshe, 1980.

Dai, Yingcong. "Civilians Go into Battle: Hired Militias in the White Lotus War, 1796–1805." *Asia Major* 22 (2009).

———. "A Disguised Defeat: The Myanmar Campaign of the Qing Dynasty." *Modern Asian Studies* 38, part 1 (2004): 145–88.

———. "Military Finance in the High Qing Period: An Overview." In *Military Culture in Imperial China*, 296–316, 380–82. Edited by Nicola Di Cosmo. Cambridge: Harvard University Press, 2009.

———. "To Nourish a Strong Military: Kangxi's Preferential Treatment of His Military Officials." *War and Society* 18, no. 2 (October 2000): 71–91.

———. "The Qing State, Merchants, and the Military Labor Force in the Jinchuan Campaigns." *Later Imperial China* 22, no. 2 (December 2001): 35–90.

———. "The Rise of the Southwestern Frontier under the Qing, 1640–1800." Ph.D. dissertation, University of Washington, 1996.

———. "*Yingyun Shengxi*: Military Entrepreneurship in the High Qing Period: 1700–1800." *Late Imperial China* 26, no. 2 (December 2005): 1–67.

De Filippis, Jeanne Mascolo. "The Western Discovery of Tibet." In *Lhasa in the Seventeenth Century: The Capital of the Dalai Lamas*. Edited by Françoise Pommaret, 1–14. Leiden: Brill, 2003.

Dennerline, Jerry. "Fiscal Reform and Local Control: The Gentry-Bureaucratic Alliance Survives the Conquest." In *Conflict and Control in Late Imperial China*. Edited by Frederic Wakeman Jr. and Carolyn Grant, 86–120. Berkeley: University of California Press, 1975.

Deshayes, Laurent. *Histoire du Tibet* (History of Tibet). Paris: Fayard, 1997.

Diamond, Norma. "Defining the Miao: Ming, Qing, and Contemporary Views." In *Cultural Encounters on China's Ethnic Frontiers*. Edited by Stevan Harrell, 92–116. Seattle: University of Washington Press, 1995.

Di Cosmo, Nicola. "Kirghiz Nomads on the Qing Frontier: Tribute, Trade, or Gift Exchange?" In *Political Frontiers, Ethnic Boundaries, and Human Geographies in Chinese History*. Edited by Nicola Di Cosmo and Don J. Wyatt, 351–72. London: Routledge Curzon Press, 2003.

———. "Military Aspects of the Manchu Wars against the Ĉaqars." In *Warfare in Inner Asian History (500–1800)*. Edited by Nicola Di Cosmo, 337–67. Leiden: Brill, 2002.

Di Cosmo, Nicola, and Don J. Wyatt, eds. *Political Frontiers, Ethnic Boundaries, and Human Geographies in Chinese History*. Richmond, U.K.: Curzon Press, 2001.

Ding Shicun. *ZhuZangdacheng kao* (A study of the Qing *amban* in Tibet). Nanjing: MengZang Weiyuanhui, 1943.

Ding Yizhuang. "Youguan Qingdai baqi yu lüying guanxi de liangge wenti (On two issues relating to the relationship between the Eight Banners and the Green Standard Army in the Qing dynasty)." In *Qingshi lunji: Qinghe Wang Zhonghan jiaoshou jiushi huadan*. Edited by Zhu Chengru, 30–43. Beijing: Zijincheng Chuibanshe, 2003.

Dunstan, Helen. *Conflicting Counsels to Confuse the Age: A Documentary Study of Political Economy in Qing China, 1644–1840*. Ann Arbor: University of Michigan, 1996.

———. "Safely Supping with the Devil: The Qing and Its Merchant Suppliers of Copper." *Late Imperial China* 13, no. 2 (December 1992): 42–81.

———. *State or Merchant? Political Economy and Political Process in 1740s China*. Cambridge: Harvard University Asia Center, 2006.

Du Rongkun and Bai Cuiqin. *Ximenggu yanjiu* (Studies on the Western Mongols). Urumchi: Xinjiang Renmin Chubanshe, 1986.

Elliott, Mark C. *The Manchu Way: Eight Banners and Ethnic Identity in Late Imperial China*. Stanford, Calif.: Stanford University Press, 2001.

Elman, Benjamin A., and Alexander Woodside, eds. *Education and Society in Late Imperial China, 1600–1900*. Berkeley: University of California Press, 1994.

Elverskog, Johan. *Our Great Qing: The Mongols, Buddhism, and the State in Late Imperial China*. Honolulu: University of Hawai'i Press, 2006.

Entenmann, Robert E. "Migration and Settlement in Sichuan, 1644–1796." Ph.D. dissertation, Harvard University, 1982.

———. "Sichuan and Qing Migration Policy." *Ch'ing-Shih Wen-T'i* 4, no. 4 (1980): 35–54.

Fang Chao-ying. "A Technique for Estimating the Numerical Strength of the Early Manchu Military Forces." *Harvard Journal of Asiatic Studies* 13, no. 1 (June 1950): 192–215.

Fan Jinmin. "Ming Qing Jiangnan zhongfu wenti shulun (The heavy taxation in

Jiangnan in the Ming and Qing dynasties)." *Zhongguo jingjishi yanjiu* (Studies on Chinese economic history) 3 (1996): 108–23.

Farquhar, David M. "The Origins of the Manchus' Mongolian Policy." In *The Chinese World Order: Traditional China's Foreign Relations*. Edited by John King Fairbank, 198–205. Cambridge: Harvard University Press, 1968.

Feng Erkang. *Yongzheng zhuan* (Biography of the Yongzheng emperor). Shanghai: Sanlian Shudian, 1999.

Feng Hanyong. "Tangdai Jiannandao de jingji zhuangkuang yu LiTang de xingwang guanxi" (The relationship between the economic situation of Jiannan circuit and the rise and fall of the Tang dynasty)." *Zhongguoshi yanjiu* 2 (Studies in Chinese History) (1982): 79–92.

Feng Mingzhu. *Jindai Zhong Ying Xizang jiaoshe yu Chuan-Zang bianqing: Cong Kuoerka zhiyi dao Huashengdun huiyi* (Relationships between China, Britain, and Tibet and the border affairs between Sichuan and Tibet: From the Gurkha wars to the Washington Conference). Taipei: National Palace Museum, 1996.

Feurwerker, Albert. "The State and the Economy in Late Imperial China." *Theory and Society* 13 (1984): 297–326.

Fletcher, Joseph F. "China and Central Asia, 1368–1884." In *The Chinese World Order: Traditional China's Foreign Relations*. Edited by John King Fairbank, 206–24. Cambridge: Harvard University Press, 1968.

———. "Ch'ing Inner Asia c. 1800." In *The Cambridge History of China*. Volume 10, *The Late Ch'ing, 1800–1911*, part 1. Edited by John K. Fairbank, 35–106. Cambridge: Cambridge University Press, 1978.

Forêt, Philippe. *Mapping Chengde: The Qing Landscape Enterprise*. Honolulu: University of Hawai'i Press, 2000.

Franke, Herbert. "The Exploration of the Yellow River Sources under Emperor Qubilai in 1281." In *China under Mongol Rule*. Edited by Herbert Franke, chapter 9, 401–16. Brookfield, Vt.: Variorum, 1994.

———. "Tibetans in Yüan China." In *China under Mongol Rule*. Edited by Herbert Franke, chapter 8, 296–328. Brookfield, Vt.: Variorum, 1994.

Gao Wangling. "QianJia shiqi Sichuan de changshi, changshiwang jiqi gongneng" (Markets and marketing networks, and their functions in Sichuan during the Qianlong and Jiaqing periods). *Qingshi yanjiu ji* (Collection of studies on Qing history) 3: 74–92. Beijing: Zhongguo Renmindaxue Chubanshe, 1984.

Gaustad, Blaine Campbell. "Religious Sectarianism and the State in Mid-Qing China: Background to the White Lotus Uprising of 1796–1804." Ph.D. dissertation, University of California at Berkeley, 1994.

Giersch, C. Patterson. *Asian Borderlands: The Transformation of Qing China's Yunnan Frontier*. Cambridge: Harvard University Press, 2006.

———. "'A Motley Throng': Social Change on Southwest China's Early Modern Frontier, 1700–1880." *Journal of Asian Studies* 60, no. 1 (February 2001): 67–94.

Glanh, Richard von. *The Country of Streams and Grottoes: Expansion, Settlement, and the*

Civilizing of the Sichuan Frontier in Song Times. Cambridge: Council on East Asian Studies, Harvard University, 1987.

Gong Yin. *Zhongguo tusi zhidu* (The native chieftain system in China). Kunming: Yunnan Minzu Chubanshe, 1992.

Gourdin, F. (Guluodong). *Shengjiao ruChuanji* (A history of Catholicism in Sichuan). Chengdu: Sichuan Renmin Chubanshe, 1981.

Greatrex, Roger. "A Brief Introduction to the First Jinchuan War (1747–1749)." In *Tibetan Studies*, volume 1. Edited by Per Kvaerne. Oslo: Institute for Comparative Research in Human Culture, 1994.

Gu Jiegang and Li Guangming. "Mingmo Qingchu zhi Sichuan" (Sichuan during the Ming-Qing transition). *Dongfang zazhi* (Eastern miscellany) 31, no. 1 (January 1934): 171–81.

Guo Meilan. "Liushi Banchan chaojin shimo" (About the Sixth Panchen Lama's visit to Beijing). In *Qingshi lunji: Qinghe Wang Zhonghan jiaoshou jiushi huadan*. Edited by Zhu Chengru, 597–607. Beijing: Zijincheng Chubanshe, 2003.

Guy, R. Kent. "Imperial Powers and the Appointment of Provincial Governors in Ch'ing China, 1700–1900." In *Imperial Rulership and Cultural Change in Traditional China*. Edited by Frederick P. Brandauer and Chun-chieh Huang, 248–80. Seattle: University of Washington Press, 1994.

———. "Inspired Tinkering: The Qing Creation of the Province," University of Washington, 2002.

———. "Personnel Policy in the Early Qianlong Reign: The Ascension of the Qianlong Emperor as a Moment of Crisis." Paper presented at the annual conference of the Association for Asian Studies, 1993.

Haar, Barend J. ter. "The Gathering of Brothers and Elders (Ko-lao hui): A New View." In *Conflict and Accommodation in Early Modern East Asia: Essays in Honour of Erik Zürcher*. Edited by Leonard Blusse and Harriet T. Zurndorfer, 259–83. Leiden: Brill, 1993.

———. *The White Lotus Teachings in Chinese Religious History*. Honolulu: University of Hawai'i Press, 1990.

Harrell, Stevan, ed. *Cultural Encounters on China's Ethnic Frontiers*. Seattle: University of Washington Press, 1995.

Hedtke, Charles H. "Reluctant Revolutionaries: Szechwan and the Ch'ing Collapse, 1898–1911," Ph.D. dissertation, University of California, 1968.

Herman, John E. *Amid the Clouds and Mist: China's Colonization of Guizhou, 1200–1700*. Cambridge: Harvard University Press, 2007.

———. "Empire in the Southwest: Early Qing Reforms to the Native Chieftain System." *Journal of Asian Studies* 56, no. 1 (February 1997): 47–74.

———. "The Mongol Conquest of Dali: The Failed Second Front." In *Warfare in Inner Asian History (500–1800)*. Edited by Nicola Di Cosmo, 295–334. Leiden: Brill, 2002.

———. "National Integration and Regional Hegemony: The Political and Cultural

Dynamics of Qing State Expansion, 1650–1750," Ph.D. dissertation, University of Washingtion, 1993.

Hevia, James. *Cherishing Men from Afar: Qing Guest Ritual and the Macartney Embassy of 1793*. Durham, N.C.: Duke University Press. 1995.

———. "Lamas, Emperors, and Rituals: Political Implications in Qing Imperial Ceremonies." *Journal of the International Association of Buddhist Studies* 16, no. 2 (1993): 243–78.

Ho Ping-ti. "Early-Ripening Rice in Chinese History," *Economic History Review*, new series 9, no. 2 (1956): 200–218.

———. *The Ladder of Success in Imperial China*. New York: Columbia University Press, 1962.

———. "NanSong zhijin tudi shuzi de kaoshi he pingjia" (An examination and evaluation on the statistics of arable land since the Southern Song dynasty). *Zhongguo shehui kexue* (Social sciences in China) 3 (1985): 133–60.

———. *Studies on the Population of China, 1368–1953*. Cambridge: Harvard University Press; 1959.

Hostetler, Laura. *Qing Colonial Enterprise: Ethnography and Cartography in Early Modern China*. Chicago: University of Chicago Press, 2001.

Huang Fensheng. *Zangzu shilüe* (A short history of the Tibetans). Beijing: Minzu Chubanshe, 1985.

Huang Pei. *Autocracy at Work: A Study of the Yung-cheng Period, 1723–1735*. Bloomington: Indiana University Press, 1974.

———. "Qing Shizong yu Nian Gengyao zhi guanxi" (The relationship between the Yongzheng emperor and Nian Gengyao). In *Qingshi ji jindaishi yanjiu lunji* (Collected studies on Qing history and modern history). Edited by Dalu Zazhishe, 63–72. Taipei: Dalu Zazhishe, 1960.

Huang, Ray. *Broadening the Horizons of Chinese History*. Armonk, N.Y.: M.E. Sharpe, 1999.

———. "Military Expenditures in Sixteenth-Century Ming China." *Oriens Extremus* 17 (1970): 39–62.

———. *Taxation and Governmental Finance in Sixteenth-Century Ming China*. New York: Cambridge University Press, 1974.

Huang Yanpei. *Shudao* (A voyage to Sichuan). Shanghai: Kaiming Shudian, 1936.

Hucker, Charles O. *A Dictionary of Official Titles in Imperial China*. Stanford, Calif.: Stanford University Press, 1985.

Hummel, Arthur W. *Eminent Chinese of the Ch'ing Period*. Washington, D.C.: U.S. Government Printing Office, 1944.

Hu Zhaoxi. *Zhang Xianzhong tu Shu kaobian—jianxi Huguang tian Sichuan* (A study of Zhang Xianzhong's alleged massacres in Sichuan, with an analysis of immigration from Huguang to Sichuan). Chengdu: Sichuan Renmin Chubanshe, 1980.

Hu Zhaoxi, Huo Datong, and Yang Guang. "'Guolu' kaoxi" (An examination of 'guolu'). In *Bashu lishi wenhua lunji* (Collected articles on the history and culture of Sichuan). Edited by Hu Zhaoxi, 202–18. Chengdu: Bashu Shushe, 2002.

Im, Kaye Soon (Ren Guichun). *Qingchao baqi zhufang xingshuai shi* (A history of Banner garrisons during the Qing dynasty). Beijing: Sanlian Shudian, 1993.

Isett, C. "State, Peasant, and Merchant in Qing Manchuria." *Late Imperial China* 25, no. 1 (2004): 124–86.

Isett, Christopher M. *State, Peasant, and Merchant in Qing Manchuria, 1644–1862*. Stanford, Calif.: Stanford University Press, 2006.

Jones, Susan Mann, and Philip A. Kuhn. "Dynastic Decline and the Roots of Rebellion." In *The Cambridge History of China*. Volume 10, *Late Ch'ing, 1800–1911*, part 1. Edited by John K. Fairbank, 107–62. Cambridge: Cambridge University Press, 1978.

Kahn, Harold L. *Monarchy in the Emperor's Eyes: Image and Reality in the Ch'ien-lung Reign*. Taipei: Rainbow-Bridge Book Company, 1971.

Kapstein, Matthew T. *The Tibetan Assimilation of Buddhism: Conversion, Contestation, and Memory*. Oxford: Oxford University Press, 2000.

Kessler, Lawrence D. *K'ang-hsi and the Consolidation of Ch'ing Rule: 1661–1684*. Chicago: University of Chicago Press, 1976.

Khodarkovsky, Michael. *Russia's Steppe Frontier: The Making of a Colonial Empire, 1500–1800*. Bloomington: Indiana University Press, 2002.

Kolås, Åshild, and Monika P. Thowsen. *On the Margins of Tibet: Cultural Survival on the Sino-Tibetan Frontier*. Seattle: University of Washington Press, 2005.

Kolmas, Josef. *Tibet and Imperial China: A Survey of Sino-Tibetan Relations up to the End of the Manchu Dynasty in 1912*. Canberra: Center of Oriental Studies, Australian National University, 1967.

Kuhn, Philip A. *Rebellion and Its Enemies in Late Imperial China: Militarization and Social Structure, 1796–1864*. Cambridge: Harvard University Press, 1970.

———. *Soulstealers: The Chinese Sorcery Scare of 1768*. Cambridge: Harvard University Press, 1990.

Lai Fushun. *Qianlong zhongyao zhanzheng zhi junxu janjiu* (A study of the logistics of the important campaigns of the Qianlong period). Taipei: National Palace Museum, 1984.

Lai Hui-min. "Qing Qianlongchao de shuiguan yu huangshi caizheng" (Customs houses and imperial income under the Qianlong emperor). *Zhongyang Yanjiuyuan Jindaishi Yanjiusuo jikan* (Bulletin of the Institute of Modern History Academia Sinica) 46 (December 2004): 53–103.

Lamb, Alastair. *Britain and Chinese Central Asia: The Road to Lhasa, 1767 to 1905*. London: Routledge and Kegan Paul, 1960.

Lattimore, Owen. *Inner Asian Frontiers of China*. Boston: Beacon Press, 1962.

———. *Studies in Frontier History: Collected Papers, 1928–1958*. London: Oxford University Press, 1962.

Launay, Adrien. *Histoire des missions de Chine: Mission du Se-tchoan* (History of the missions in China: Mission in Sichuan). Paris, 1920.

———. *Histoire générale de la Société des Missions-Étrangères* (A history of the Society of the Foreign Missions). 3 volumes. Paris, 1894.

Lee, James Z. "Migration and Expansion in Chinese History." In *Human Migration: Patterns and Policies*. Edited by William H. McNeill and Ruth S. Adams, 20–47. Bloomington: Indiana University Press, 1978.

———. "Ming Qing shiqi Zhongguo xi'nan de jingji fazhan he renkou zengzhang" (Economic development and population growth in southwest China during the Ming and the Qing). *Qingshi luncong* (Collected papers on Qing history) 5 (1984): 50–102, 287–88.

———. "State and Economy in Southwest China, 1250–1850." University of Michigan, 1987.

Lee, Robert H. *The Manchurian Frontier in Ch'ing History*. Cambridge: Harvard University Press, 1970.

Leonard, Jane Kate. *Wei Yuan and the Rediscovery of the Maritime World*. Cambridge: Harvard University Press, 1984.

Leonard, Jane Kate, and John R. Watt, eds. *To Achieve Security and Wealth: The Qing Imperial State and the Economy, 1644–1911*. Ithaca, N.Y.: East Asia Program of Cornell University, 1992.

Liang Fangzhong, ed. *Zhongguo lidai hukou, tiandi, tianfu tongji* (Statistics of households, land, and taxation in Chinese history). Shanghai: Shanghai Renmin Chubanshe, 1980.

Li Bozhong. *Agricultural Development in Jiangnan, 1620–1850*. New York: St. Martin's Press, 1998.

Li Chaozheng. *Qingdai Sichuan jinshi zhenglüe* (Brief biographies of those who held *jinshi* degrees from Sichuan during the Qing Dynasty). Chengdu: Sichuan Renmin Chubanshe, 1986.

Li Guangtao. *Ji Qianlong nian pingding Annan zhiyi* (A history of the Vietnamese campaign of the Qianlong era). Taipei: Institute of History and Philology, Academia Sinica, 1976.

Li Jieren. *Baofengyuqian* (On the eve of a storm). Beijing: Zuojia Chubanshe. 1956.

———. *Dabo* (Surges). 4 volumes. Beijing: Zuojia Chubanshe, 1958–1963.

———. *Ripples across Stagnant Water (Sishui weilan)*. Beijing: Chinese Literature Press, 1990.

Li, Lillian M. "Grain Prices in Zhili Province, 1736–1911: A Preliminary Study." In *Chinese History in Economic Perspective*. Edited by Thomas G. Rawski and Lillian M. Li, 70–100. Berkeley: University of California Press, 1992.

Lin Yongkuang. "Qingdai de chamamayi" (Tea-horse trade during the Qing dynasty). *Qingshi luncong* (Collected papers on Qing history) 3 (1982): 100–116.

Li Shiping. *Sichuan renkou shi* (A demographic history of Sichuan). Chengdu: Sichuan Daxue Chubanshe, 1987.

Liu Xianzhi. "Chengdu ManMengzu pianduanshi" (Some anecdotes of the Manchu and Mongol peoples in Chengdu)." In *Chengdu wenshi ziliao xuanji* (Selected collection of historical records of Chengdu), volume 4. Edited by Chengdu shi zhengxie, 156–63. Chengdu: Chengdu Wenshi Ziliao Weiyuanhui, 1983.

Lombard-Salmon, Claudine. *Un exemple d'acculturation chinoise: La province du Gui Zhou au XVIIIe siècle* (An example of Chinese acculturation: The province of Guizhou during the eighteenth century). Paris: École Française d'Extrême-Orient, 1972.

Luce, G. H. "Chinese Invasions of Burma in the Eighteenth Century." *Journal of the Burma Research Society* 15, no. 2 (1925): 115–28.

Luo Ergang. *Lüying bingzhi* (On the system of the Green Standard Army). Beijing: Zhonghua Shuju, 1984.

Luo Lida. "Mingmo Qingchu de Meng-Zang guanxi he GushiHan ruZang shijian" (Mongolian-Tibtan relations during the Ming-Qing transition and the incident of Gushri Khan's invasion of Tibet). *Qingshi yanjiuji* (Collection of studies on Qing history) 5 (1986): 40–65.

Luo Yudong. *Zhongguo lijin shi* (A history of the lijin system in China). Taipei: Wenhai Chubanshe, 1979.

Lü Zuoxie. "Ming Qing shiqi de huiguan bingfei gongshangye hanghui" ("Huiguan" of the Ming and Qing periods were not guilds). *Zhongguoshi yanjiu* (Studies on Chinese history) 2 (1982): 66–80.

Mancall, Mark. *Russia and China: Their Diplomatic Relations until 1728*. Cambridge: Harvard University Press, 1971.

Mansier, Patrick. "La guerre du Jinchuan (rGyal-rong): Son contexte politico-religieux" (Jinchuan war: Its political and religious context). In *Tibet, civilisation et société*. Edited by La Fondation Singer-Polignac. Paris: Éditions de la Maison des Sciences de l'Homme, 1990.

Maomao. *Wode fuqin Deng Xiaoping* (My father Deng Xiaoping). Hong Kong: Sanlian Shudian, 1993.

Marchal, Jean Joseph. *Vie de M. L'Abbé Moÿe de la Société des Missions-Étrangères: Fondateur de la Congrégation des soeurs de la providence en Lorraine, et des vierges chrétiennes directrices des écoles de filles au Su-tchuen, en Chine* (Biography of Father Moÿe of the Society of the Foreign Missions: Founder of the congregation of sisters of Providence in Lorraine, and virgin Christian principals of the girl schools in Sichuan, China). Paris: Bray et Retaux, 1872.

Ma Ruheng and Ma Dazheng. *Elute Menggu shi lunji* (Collected studies on the history of the Eleuth Mongols). Xining: Qinghai Renmin Chubanshe, 1984.

———. *Qingdai de bianjiang zhengce* (Frontier policy of the Qing dynasty). Beijing: Zhongguo Shehuikexue Chubanshe, 1994.

Ma Yao. *Yunnan jianshi* (A brief history of Yunnan). Kunming: Yunnan Renmin Chubanshe, 1991.

McCaffrey, Cecily M. "Living through Rebellion: A Local History of the White

Lotus Uprising in Hubei, China." Ph.D. dissertation, University of California, San Diego, 2003.

Mei Xinru. *Xikang* (Province of Xikang). Nanjing: Zhengzhong Shuju, 1934.

Meng Sen. *Qingdai shi* (A history of the Qing dynasty). Taipei: Zhengzhong Shuju, 1960.

Millward, James A. *Beyond the Pass: Economy, Ethnicity, and Empire in Qing Central Asia, 1759–1864*. Stanford, Calif.: Stanford University Press, 1998.

Miyawaki Junko. "The Qalqa Mongols and the Oyirad in the Seventeenth Century." *Journal of Asian History* 18, no. 2 (1984): 136–73.

Mori Kiko. "Shindai Sisen no imin keizai" (The migration economy in Sichuan during the Qing Dynasty). *Toyoshi kenkyu* (Journal of Oriental research) 45, no. 4 (March 1987): 141–68.

Mote, Frederick. "The T'u-mu Incident of 1449." In *Chinese Ways in Warfare*. Edited by Frank Kierman and John Fairbank, 243–72. Cambridge: Harvard University Press, 1974.

Mu Jihong, Chen Baoya, Li Xu, Xu Yongtao, Wang Xiaosong, and Li Lin. *Dian-Zang-Chuan dasanjiao wenhua tanmi* (An exploration of the cultures in the great delta of Yunnan, Tibet, and Sichuan). Kunming: Yunnan Daxue Chubanshe, 1992.

Myers, Ramon. *The Chinese Economy: Past and Present*. Belmont, Calif.: Wadsworth, 1980.

———. "The Usefulness of Local Gazetteers for the Study of Modern Chinese Economic History: Szechwan Province during the Ch'ing and Republican Period." *Tsing Hua Journal of Chinese Studies* 6 (December 1967): 72–104.

Naquin, Susan. *Millenarian Rebellion in China: The Eight Trigrams Uprising of 1813*. New Haven, Conn.: Yale University Press, 1976.

———. *Shantung Rebellion: The Wang Lun Uprising of 1774*. New Haven, Conn.: Yale University Press, 1981.

———. "The Transmission of White Lotus Sectarianism in Late Imperial China." In *Popular Culture in Late Imperial China*. Edited by David Johnson, Andrew J. Nathan, and Evelyn S. Rawski, 255–91. Berkeley: University of California Press, 1985.

Naquin, Susan, and Evelyn S. Rawski. *Chinese Society in the Eighteenth Century*. New Haven, Conn.: Yale University Press, 1987.

Overmyer, Daniel L. *Folk Buddhist Religion: Dissenting Sects in Late Traditional China*. Cambridge: Harvard University Press, 1976.

———. *Religions of China: The World as a Living System*. San Francisco: Harper & Row, Publishers, 1986.

Ownby, David. *Brotherhoods and Secret Societies in Early and Mid-Qing China: The Formation of a Tradition*. Stanford, Calif.: Stanford University Press, 1996.

Oxnam, Robert B. *Ruling from Horseback: Manchu Politics in the Oboi Regency, 1661–1669*. Chicago: University of Chicago Press, 1970.

Pan Xiangming. "Qingdai Yunnan de jiaotong kaifa" (Development in transportation in Yunnan during the Qing times). In *Qingdai bianjiang kaifa shi* (History of frontier exploration during the Qing dynasty). Edited by Ma Ruheng and Ma Dazheng, 364–93. Beijing: Zhongguo Shehuikexue Chubanshe, 1990.

Parsons, James Bunyan. *The Peasant Rebellions of the Late Ming Dynasty*. Tuscon: University of Arizona Press, 1970.

Pasquet, Sylvie. "Entre Chine et Birmanie: Un mineur-diplomate au royaume de Hulu, 1743–1752" (Between China and Burma: A minor-diplomat of the kingdom of Hulu, 1743–1752). *Etudes chinoises* (Chinese studies) 8, no. 1: 41–68, and 8, no. 2: 69–98.

———. "Image et réalité du systèm tributaire: L'exemple des confines sino-birmans au XVIIIe siècle" (Image and reality of the tribute system: The example of the Sino-Burmese borders in the eighteenth century). *Historiens-Géographes* (Historians-Geographers) 84, no. 340 (1993): 147–57.

———. *L'évolution du système postal: La province chinoise du Yunnan a l'époque Qing (1644–1911)* (Evolution of the postal system: The Chinese province of Yunnan during the Qing era [1644–1911]). Paris: Collège de France, Institut des Hautes Études Chinoises, 1986.

Peng Chaogui and Wang Yan. *Qingdai Sichuan nongcun shehui jingji shi* (A socioeconomic history of rural Sichuan in the Qing times). Chengdu: Tiandi Chubanshe, 2001.

Perdue, Peter C. *China Marches West: The Qing Conquest of Central Eurasia, 1600–1800*. Cambridge: Harvard University Press, 2005.

———. *Exhausting the Earth: State and Peasant in Hunan, 1500–1850*. Cambridge: Council on East Asian Studies, Harvard University, 1987.

———. "Fate and Fortune in Central Eurasian Warfare: Three Qing Emperors and Their Mongol Rivals." In *Warfare in Inner Asian History (500–1800)*. Edited by Nicola Di Cosmo, 369–404. Leiden: Brill, 2002.

———. "Military Mobilization in Seventeenth- and Eighteenth-Century China, Russia, and Mongolia." *Modern Asian Studies* 30, no. 4 (1996): 757–93

———. "The Qing State and the Gansu Grain Market, 1739–1864." In *Chinese History in Economic Perspective*. Edited by Thomas G. Rawski and Lillian M. Li, 100–25. Berkeley: University of California Press, 1992.

Perkins, Dwight. *Agricultural Development in China, 1368–1968*. Chicago: Aldine, 1969.

Perry, J. Elizabeth. *Rebels and Revolutionaries in North China, 1845–1945*. Stanford, Calif.: Stanford University Press, 1980.

Petech, Luciano. *Central Tibet and the Mongols: The Yüan-Sa-skya Period of Tibetan History*. Rome: Istituto italiano per il Medio ed Estremo Oriente, 1990.

———. *China and Tibet in the Early Eighteenth Century: History of the Establishment of Chinese Protectorate in Tibet*. Leiden: Brill, 1972.

———. "The Dalai-Lamas and Regents of Tibet: A Chronological Study." In *The History of Tibet*. Volume 2, *The Medieval Period, c. 850–1895: The Development of Bud-*

dhist *Paramountcy*. Edited by Alex McKay, 567–83. London: Routledge Curzon Press, 2003.

———. "Lajang Khan, the Last Qōśot Ruler of Tibet (1705–1717)." In *The History of Tibet. Volume 2, The Medieval Period, c. 850–1895: The Development of Buddhist Paramountcy*. Edited by Alex McKay, 584–601. London: Routledge Curzon Press, 2003.

Peterson, Willard J., ed. *The Cambridge History of China*. Volume 9, part 1, *The Ch'ing Dynasty to 1800*. Cambridge: Cambridge University Press, 2002.

———. "Introduction: New Order for the Old Order." In *The Cambridge History of China*, Volume 9, part 1, *The Ch'ing Dynasty to 1800*. Edited by Willard J. Peterson, 1–8. Cambridge: Cambridge University Press, 2002.

Pih, Irene. *Le Père Gabriel de Magalhães: Un Jésuite portugais en Chine au xviie siècle* (Father Gabriel de Magalhães: A Portuguese Jesuit in China during the seventeenth century). Paris: Centro Cultural Português, 1979.

Polachek, James M. "Gentry Hegemony: Soochow in the T'ung-chih Restoration." In *Conflict and Control in Late Imperial China*. Edited by Frederic Wakeman Jr. and Carolyn Grant, 211–56. Berkeley: University of California Press, 1975.

Pomeranz, Kenneth. *The Great Divergence: China, Europe, and the Making of the Modern World Economy*. Princeton, N.J.: Princeton University Press, 2000.

Pommaret, Françoise, ed. *Lhasa in the Seventeenth Century: The Capital of the Dalai Lamas*. Leiden: Brill, 2003.

Pu Wencheng. "Shilun Yongzheng guimaozhiluan de lishi yuanyuan" (On the origins of the 1723 rebellion). In *Zangzu xueshu taolunhui lunwenji* (Collected papers from the conference on Tibetan studies). Edited by Zhongguo Xinan Minzu Yanjiu Xuehui (Association for Studies on Southwest China's Ethnic Minorities), 148–70. Lhasa: Xizang Renmin Chubanshe, 1984.

Pu Xiaorong. *Sichuan zhengqu yan'ge yu zhidi jinshi* (A study of administrative areas and seats of local governments of Sichuan). Chengdu: Sichuan Renmin Chubanshe, 1986.

Rawski, Evelyn S. *The Last Emperors: A Social History of Qing Imperial Institutions*. Berkeley: University of California Press, 1998.

———. "Reenvisioning the Qing: The Significance of the Qing Period in Chinese History." *Journal of Asian Studies* 55, no. 4 (1996): 829–50.

Rawski, Thomas, and Lillian M. Li, eds. *Chinese History in Economic Perspective*. Berkeley: University of California Press, 1992.

Reardon-Anderson, James. *Reluctant Pioneers: China's Expansion Northward, 1644–1937*. Stanford, Calif: Stanford University Press, 2005.

Reed, Bradly W. *Talons and Teeth: County Clerks and Runners in the Qing Dynasty*. Stanford, Calif.: Stanford University Press, 2000.

Regmi, D. R. *Modern Nepal: Rise and Growth in the Eighteenth Century*, volume 1. Calcutta: K. L. Mukhopadhyay, 1975.

Ren Naiqiang. "Guanyu Zhang Xianzhong shiliao de jianbie" (An examination on the material relating to Zhang Xianzhong). In *Zhang Xianzhong zai Sichuan* (Zhang Xianzhong in Sichuan). Edited by Shehuikexue yanjiu congkan. Chengdu: Shehuikexue Yanjiu Congkan, 1981.

Richardson, Hugh E. "The Dalai Lamas." In *The History of Tibet*. Volume 2, *The Medieval Period, c. 850–1895: The Development of Buddhist Paramountcy*. Edited by Alex McKay, 554–66. London: Routledge Curzon Press, 2003.

———. *Tibet and Its History*. Boston: Shambhala Publications, 1984.

Rossabi, Morris. *China and Inner Asia: From 1368 to the Present Day*. New York: Pica Press, 1975.

Rowe, William T. *Hankow: Commerce and Society in a Chinese City, 1796–1889*. Stanford, Calif.: Stanford University Press, 1984.

———. *Hankow: Conflict and Community in a Chinese City, 1796–1895*. Stanford, Calif.: Stanford University Press, 1989.

———. *Saving the World: Chen Hongmou and Elite Consciousness in Eighteenth-Century China*. Stanford, Calif.: Stanford University Press, 2001.

Sage, Steven F. *Ancient Sichuan and the Unification of China*. Albany: State University of New York Press, 1992.

Sato Hisashi. "Daiichiji Guruka Senso ni tsuide" (On the first Gurkha war). In *Chusei Chibetto shi kenkyu* (Studies on the medieval history of Tibet). Edited by Sato Hisashi, 521–740. Kyoto: The Dohosha, 1986.

———. "Robuzandanjin no hanlan ni tsuide" (On Lobdzan Danzin's revolt). In *Chusei Chibetto shi kenkyu* (Studies on the medieval history of Tibet). Edited by Sato Hisashi, 383–423. Kyoto: The Dohosha, 1986.

———, ed. *Chusei Chibetto shi kenkyu* (Studies on the medieval history of Tibet). Kyoto: The Dohosha, 1986.

Shaha, Rishikesh. *Modern Nepal: A Political History, 1796–1955*. Volume 1, 1796–1885. 2 volumes. New Delhi: Manohar Publications, 1990.

Shakabpa, Tsepon W. D. *Tibet: A Political History*. New York: Potala Publications, 1984.

Shepherd, John Robert. *Statecraft and Political Economy on the Taiwan Frontier, 1600–1800*. Stanford, Calif.: Stanford University Press, 1993.

Shin, Leo K. *The Making of the Chinese State: Ethnicity and Expansion on the Ming Borderlands*. Cambridge: Cambridge University Press, 2006.

Skinner, G. William. 1987. "Cities and the Hierarchy of Local System." In *The City in Late Imperial China*. Edited by G. William Skinner, 275–351. Stanford, Calif.: Stanford University Press, 1977.

———, ed. *The City in Late Imperial China*. Stanford, Calif.: Stanford University Press, 1977.

———. "Marketing and Social Structure in Rural China." *Journal of Asian Studies* 24, no. 1 (1964): 3–34; 24, no. 2 (1965): 195–228; and 24, no. 3 (1965): 363–99.

———. "Mobility Strategies in Late Imperial China." In *Regional Analysis*. Volume 1, *Economic Systems*. Edited by Carol A. Smith. New York: Academic Press, 1976.

———. "Regional Urbanization in Nineteenth-Century China." In *The City in Late Imperial China*. Edited by G. William Skinner, 211–49. Stanford, Calif.: Stanford University Press, 1977.

———. "Sichuan's Population in the Nineteenth Century: Lessons from Disaggregated Data." *Late Imperial China* 7, no. 2 (1986): 1–79.

Smith, Kent Clarke. "Ch'ing Policy and the Development of Southwest China: Aspects of Ortai's Governor-Generalship, 1726–1731." Ph.D. dissertation, Yale University, 1970.

Smith, Paul J. "Commerce, Agriculture, and Core Formation in the Upper Yangzi, 2 A.D to 1948." *Late Imperial China* 9, no. 1 (June 1988): 1–78.

———. *Taxing Heaven's Storehouse: Horses, Bureaucrats, and the Destruction of the Sichuan Tea Industry, 1074–1224*. Cambridge: Harvard University Press, 1991.

Smith, Warren W., Jr. *Tibetan Nation: A History of Tibetan Nationalism and Sino-Tibetan Relations*. Boulder, Colo.: Westview Press, 1996.

Snellgrove, David, and Hugh Richardson. *A Cultural History of Tibet*. Boulder, Colo.: Prajñā Press, 1968.

Spence, Jonathan D. *Treason by the Book*. New York: Viking, 2001.

———. *Ts'ao Yin and the K'ang-hsi Emperor, Bondservant, and Master*. New Haven, Conn.: Yale University Press, 1966.

Spence, Jonathan D., and John E. Wills Jr., eds. *From Ming to Ch'ing: Conquest, Region, and Continuity in Seventeenth-Century China*. New Haven, Conn.: Yale University Press, 1979.

Stapleton, Kristin E. *Civilizing Chengdu: Chinese Urban Reforms, 1895–1937*. Cambridge: East Asia Center, Harvard University, 2000.

Stein, R. A. *Tibetan Civilization*. Stanford, Calif.: Stanford University Press, 1972.

Struve, Lynn A. *Voices from the Ming-Qing Cataclysm: China in Tigers' Jaws*. New Haven, Conn.: Yale University Press, 1993.

———. *The Southern Ming: 1644–1662*. New Haven, Conn.: Yale University Press, 1984.

Sun Xiaofen. *Qingdai qianqi de yimin tian Sichuan* (Migration to Sichuan during the early Qing period). Chengdu: Sichuan Daxue Chubanshe, 1997.

Sutton, Donald S. "Ethnicity and the Miao Frontier in the Eighteenth Century." In *Empire at the Margins: Culture, Ethnicity, and Frontier in Early Modern China*. Edited by Donald Sutton, Pamela K. Crossley, and Helen F. Siu, 469–508. Berkeley: University of California Press, 2006.

———. "Ethnic Revolt in the Qing Empire: The Miao Uprising of 1795–1796 Reexamined." *Asia Major* 3rd series, 17, no. 1 (2003): 105–51.

Suzuki Chusei. *Chibetto o meguro Chu-In kankeishi: Juhasseiki nakagoro kara jukyuseiki nakagoro made* (China, Tibet, and India: Their early international relations). Tokyo: Hitotsubashi Shobo, 1962.

———. "China's Relations with Inner Asia: The Hsiung-nu, Tibet." In *The Chinese*

World Order: Traditional China's Foreign Relations. Edited by John King Fairbank, 180–97. Cambridge: Harvard University Press, 1968.

———. *Chugoku shi ni okeru kakumei to shukyo* (Revolution and religion in Chinese history). Tokyo: Tokyo Daigaku Shuppankai, 1974.

———. *Sennen okoku-teki minshu undo no kenkyu: Chugoku, tonnan Ajia ni okeru* (A study of popular millenarian movements in China and Southeast Asia). Tokyo: Tokyo Daigaku Shuppankai, 1982.

Tan Qixiang. "Yuan Shaanxi Sichuan xingsheng yan'ge kao" (An examination of the evolution of Shaanxi province and Sichuan province during the Yuan dynasty). *Yugong* (Evolution of Chinese historical geography) 3, no. 6 (1935): 1–5.

Teng, Emma Jinhua. *Taiwan's Imagined Geography: Chinese Colonial Travel Writing and Pictures, 1683–1896*. Cambridge: Harvard University Asia Center and Harvard University Press, 2004.

Theiss, Janet M. *Disgraceful Matters: The Politics of Chastity in Eighteenth-Century China*. Berkeley: University of California Press, 2004.

Wakeman, Frederic, Jr. *The Great Enterprise: The Manchu Reconstruction of Imperial Order in Seventeenth-Century China*. 2 volumes. Berkeley: University of California Press, 1985.

Wakeman, Frederic, Jr., and Carolyn Grant, eds. *Conflicts and Control in Late Imperial China*. Berkeley: University of California Press, 1975.

Waley-Cohen, Joanna. *The Culture of War in China: Empire and the Military under the Qing Dynasty*. London: I. B. Tauris, 2006.

Wang Chen-main. *The Life and Career of Hung Ch'eng-ch'ou (1593–1665): Public Service in a Time of Dynastic Change*. Ann Arbor, Mich.: Association for Asian Studies, 1999.

Wang Di. *Kuachu fengbi de shijie—Changjiang shangyou quyu shehui yanjiu* (Striding out of a closed world: Social transformation of the upper Yangzi region, 1644–1911). Beijing: Zhonghua Shuju, 1993.

———. "Qingdai Sichuan renkou, gengdi ji liangshi wenti" (Problems of population, arable land, and grain in Sichuan during the Qing dynasty). *Sichuan daxue xuebao* (Journal of Sichuan University) 3 (1989): 90–105, and 4 (1989): 73–87.

———. *Street Culture in Chengdu: Public Space, Urban Commoners, and Local Politics, 1870–1930*. Stanford, Calif.: Stanford University Press, 2003.

Wang Furen and Suo Wenqing. *Zangzu shiyao* (Highlights of Tibetan history). Chengdu: Sichuan Renmin Chubanshe, 1982.

Wang Gang. *Qingdai Sichuan shi* (A history of Sichuan during the Qing dynasty). Chengdu: Chengdu Keji Daxue Chubanshe, 1991.

Wang Xiangyun. "The Qing Court's Tibet Connection: lCang skya Rol pa'i rdo rje and the Qianlong Emperor." *Harvard Journal of Asiatic Studies* 60, no. 1 (2000): 125–63.

———. "Tibetan Buddhism at the Court of Qing: The Life and Work of lCang-skya Rol-pa'i-rod-rje, 1717–86." Ph.D. dissertation, Harvard University, 1995.

Wang Yao. "Diba Sangjie Jiacuo zakao" (A study on *desi* Sangye Gyatso). *Qingshi yanjiuji* (Collection of studies on Qing history) 1 (1980): 183–99.

Wang Yeh-chien. *Land Taxation in Imperial China, 1750–1911*. Cambridge: Harvard University Press, 1973.

———. "Secular Trends of Rice Prices in the Yangzi Delta, 1638–1935." In *Chinese History in Economic Perspective*. Edited by Thomas G. Rawski and Lillian M. Li, 36–69. Berkeley: University of California Press, 1992.

Wang Zhonghan. *Qingshi zakao* (Collected articles on Qing history). Beijing: Renmin Chubanshe, 1957.

Wei Qingyuan. "Mingchu Jiangnan diqu jingji zhengce de ruogan wenti" (Some issues concerning the economic policy toward the Jiangnan area in the early Ming times). In *MingQingshi bianxi* (Analysis of Ming and Qing history). Edited by Wei Qingyuan, 1–33. Beijing: Zhongguo Shehuikexue Chubanshe, 1989.

Wei Qingyuan and Wu Qiyan. "Qingdai zhuming huangshang Fanshi de xingshuai" (The rise and fall of the Fan family, imperial merchants of the Qing dynasty). In *Dangfang lunshi wenbian* (Collected articles based on archival research). Edited by Wei Qingyuan, 42–69. Fuzhou: Fujian Renmin Chubanshe, 1983.

Wei Xiumei. *Qingdai zhi huibi zhidu* (The avoidance system of the Qing dynasty). Taipei: Institute of Modern History, Academia Sinica, 1992.

Wei Yingtao, Li Youming, Li Runcang, Zhang Li, Li Chuanying, and Zeng Shaomin. *Sichuan jindai shi* (A modern history of Sichuan). Chengdu: Sichuansheng Shehuikexueyuan Chubanshe, 1985.

Whitney, Joseph B. R. *China: Area, Administration, and Nation Building*. Chicago: Department of Geography, University of Chicago, 1969.

Widmer, Eric. *The Russian Ecclesiastical Mission in Peking during the Eighteenth Century*. Cambridge: Harvard University Press, 1976.

Wiens, Herold J. *Chian's March toward the Tropics: A Discussion of the Southward Penetration of China's Culture, People, and Political Control in Relation to the Non-Han-Chinese People of South China and in the Perspective of Historical and Cultural Geography*. New Haven, Conn.: Yale University Press, 1954.

Will, Pierre-Étienne. *Bureaucracy and Famine in Eighteenth-Century China*. Translated by Elborg Forster. Stanford, Calif.: Standord University Press, 1990.

——— and R. Bin Wong, with James Lee. *Nourish the People: The State Civilian Granary System in China, 1650–1850*. Ann Arbor: Center for Chinese Studies, University of Michigan, 1991.

Wong, R. Bin. *China Transformed: Historical Change and the Limits of European Experience*. Ithaca, N.Y.: Cornell University Press, 1997.

———, and Peter C. Perdue. "Grain Markets and Food Supplies in Eighteenth-Century Hunan." In *Chinese History in Economic Perspective*. Edited by Thomas G.

Rawski and Lillian M. Li, 127–45. Berkeley: University of California Press, 1992.

Woodside, Alexander. "The Ch'ien-lung Reign." In *The Cambridge History of China*. Volume 9, part 1, *The Ch'ing Dynasty to 1800*. Edited by Willard J. Peterson, 230–309. Cambridge: Cambridge University Press, 2002.

———. *Lost Modernities: China, Vietnam, Korea, and the Hazards of World History*. Cambridge: Harvard Unviersity Press, 2006.

———. *Vietnam and the Chinese Model: A Comparative Study of Nguyễn and Ch'ing Civil Government in the First Half of the Nineteenth Century*. Cambridge: Harvard University Press, 1971.

Wu Fengpei and Zeng Guoqing. *Qingchao zhuZangdacheng zhidu de jianli yu yan'ge* (Establishment and evolution of the Qing Amban system in Tibet). Beijing: Zhongguo Zangxue Chubanshe, 1989.

Wu Ren'an. "Mingdai ChuanShaan chamamaoyi qianshuo" (On the tea-horse trade in Sichuan and Shaanxi during the Ming dynasty). *Zhongguo shehuijingjishi yanjiu* (Studies on Chinese social and economic history) 2 (1984): 38–45.

Wu, Silas Hsiu-liang. *Communication and Imperial Control in China: Evolution of the Palace Memorial System, 1693–1753*. Cambridge: Harvard University Press, 1970.

Wu Xinfu and Long Boya. *Miaozu shi* (A history of the Miao nationality). Chengdu: Sichuan Minzu Chubanshe, 1992.

Xiao Yishan. *Qingdai tongshi* (A complete history of the Qing dynasty). 5 volumes. Taipei: Shangwu Yinshuguan, 1972.

Xie Guozhen. *NanMing shilüe* (A brief history of the Southern Ming regimes). Shanghai: Shanghai Renmin Chubanshe, 1957.

Xu Daling. *Qingdai juanna zhidu* (The system of purchasing offices by contributions during the Qing dynasty). Beijing: Harvard Yenching Institute, Yenching University, 1950.

Yang, C. K. *Religion in Chinese Society: A Study of Contemporary Social Functions of Religion and Some of Their Historical Factors*. Berkeley: University of California Press, 1961.

Yang Qiqiao. *Yongzhengdi jiqi mizhe zhidu yanjiu* (A study on the Yongzheng emperor and his secret memorial system). Hong Kong: Sanlian Shudian, 1981.

Yosei jidai no kenkyu (Studies on the Yongzheng era). Edited by Toyoshi kenkyukai. Kyoto: Dohosha, 1986.

Younghusband, Francis. *India and Tibet: A History of the Relations Which Have Subsisted between the Two Countries from the Time of Warren Hastings to 1910; with a Particular Account of the Mission to Lhasa of 1904*. Delhi: Oriental Publishers, 1971.

Yuan Sengpo. *Kang Yong Qian jingying yu kaifa beijiang* (The Qing governance and explorations of the northern frontiers during the Kangxi, Yongzheng, and Qianlong periods). Beijing: Zhongguo Shehuikexue Chubanshe, 1991.

Yuan Tingdong. *Zhang Xianzhong zhuanlun* (A commentary biography of Zhang Xianzhong). Chengdu: Sichuan Renmin Chubanshe. 1980.

Yu Li. "Social Change during the Ming-Qing Transition and the Decline of Sichuan

Classical Learning in the Early Qing." *Late Imperial China* 19, no. 1 (1998): 26–55.

Yu Songqing. *Ming Qing bailianjiao yanjiu* (A study of the White Lotus teachings during the Ming and Qing dynasties). Chengdu: Sichuan Renmin Chubanshe, 1987.

Zelin, Madeleine. *The Magistrates' Tael: Rationalizing Fiscal Reform in Eighteenth-Century Ch'ing China*. Berkeley: University of California Press, 1984.

———. *The Merchants of Zigong: Industial Entrepreneurship in Early Modern China*. New York: Columbia University Press, 2005.

———. "The Rights of Tenants in Mid-Qing Sichuan: A Study of Land-related Lawsuits in the Baxian Archives." *Journal of Asian Studies* 45, no. 3 (May 1986): 499–526.

———. "The Rise and Fall of the Fu-Rong Salt-Yard Elite: Merchant Dominance in Late Qing China." In *Chinese Local Elites and Patterns of Dominance*. Edited by Joseph Esherick and Mary Backus Rankin, 83–111. Berkeley: University of California Press. 1990.

Zhang Qiqin and Wu Fengpei. *Qingdai Zangshi jiyao* (Collected documents concerning Tibetan affairs during the Qing dynasty). Lhasa: Xizang Renmin Chubanshe, 1983.

Zhang Xiaotang. "Qianlong nianjian Qing zhengfu pingheng caizheng zhi yanjiu" (A study on the Qing state's management of its finance during the Qianlong period). *Qingshi yanjiuji* (Collection of studies on Qing history) 7 (1990): 26–60.

Zhang Xuejun and Ran Guangrong. *Ming Qing Sichuan jingyan shigao* (A draft history of salt industry in Sichuan during the Ming and Qing periods). Chengdu: Sichuan Renmin Chubanshe, 1984.

Zheng Tianting. *Qingshi jianshu* (A brief history of the Qing dynasty). Beijing: Zhonghua Shuju, 1980.

Zhuang Jifa. *Gugong dang'an shuyao* (An introduction to the archives in the National Palace Museum). Taipei: National Palace Museum, 1983.

———. "Qingdai Gelaohui yuanliu kao" (An examination of the origins of the Gelao society in the Qing dynasty). In *Qingshi lunji* (Collected essays on Qing history), volume 11. Edited by Zhuang Jifa, 19–35. Taipei: Wenshizhe Chubanshe, 2003.

———. *Qing Gaozong shiquan wugong yanjiu* (Studies on the Qianlong emperor's "ten military achievements"). Taipei: National Palace Museum, 1982.

Zhu Peilian. *Qingdai dingjia lu* (A list of the top people who held *jinshi* degrees during the Qing dynasty). Taipei: Zhonghua Shuju, 1968.

Zito, Angela. *Of Body and Brush: Grand Sacrifices as Text/Performance in Eighteenth-Century China*. Chicago: University of Chicago Press, 1997. Adshead, S. A. M., 247n18

INDEX

CPSIA information can be obtained
at www.ICGtesting.com
Printed in the USA
BVHW07s0459241018
530958BV00001B/3/P

9 780295 989525